Leipziger Altorientalistische Studien

Herausgegeben von
Michael P. Streck

Band 11

2019
Harrassowitz Verlag · Wiesbaden

Anna Perdibon

Mountains and Trees, Rivers and Springs

Animistic Beliefs and Practices in ancient Mesopotamian Religion

2019
Harrassowitz Verlag · Wiesbaden

Cover illustration: “Brunnen Relief”, Vorderasiatisches Museum, Berlin, © drawing by the author.

Bibliografische Information der Deutschen Nationalbibliothek
Die Deutsche Nationalbibliothek verzeichnet diese Publikation in der Deutschen Nationalbibliografie; detaillierte bibliografische Daten sind im Internet über http://dnb.dnb.de abrufbar.

Bibliographic information published by the Deutsche Nationalbibliothek
The Deutsche Nationalbibliothek lists this publication in the Deutsche Nationalbibliografie; detailed bibliographic data are available in the Internet at http://dnb.dnb.de.

For further information about our publishing program consult our website http://www.harrassowitz-verlag.de

Printed on permanent/durable paper.
Printing and binding: Hubert & Co., Göttingen
Printed in Germany

ISSN 2193-4436
ISBN 978-3-447-11321-2

To Paola, Vanna and Dario
& to my mountains

"I went to the woods because I wished to live deliberately, to front only the essential facts of life, and see if I could not learn what it had to teach, and not, when I came to die, discover that I had not lived." (H.D. Thoreau, *Walden*)

Contents

Table of Illustrations

Illustration 1: Akkadian Adda-seal, in Aruz/Benzel/Evans 2008, 281, fig. 177 (drawing by the author).

Illustration 2: Kassite seal, in Aruz/Wallenfels 2003, 213, fig. 139 (drawing by the author).

Illustration 3: Detail of the mold fragment attributed to Nāram Sîn, in Aruz/Wallenfels 2003, 207, fig. 133 (drawing by the author).

Illustration 4: "Brunnen Relief", Vorderasiatiches Museum, Berlin (drawing by the author).

Illustration 5: Seal of Rimutu, in Matthews 1992, fig. 148 (drawing by the author).

Illustration 6: View of the Jebel Bishri, SYGIS-Jebel Bishri: The Finnish Project in Syria (website). Courtesy: Prof. Minna Silver Lönnqvist.

Illustration 7: Mari shell seal, in Aruz/Wallenfels 2003, 221, fig. 151 (drawing by the author).

Illustration 8: "Investiture Fresco" of Zimri Lim, Mari palace, in Oates 1986, 62, fig. 42 (drawing by the author).

Illustration 9: Bronze door reliefs of Shalmaneser III, Tell Balawat (Imgur-Enlil), Relief Panel 10, detail (King 1915).

Illustration 10: Seal, in Collon 1987, 179, fig. 845 (drawing by the author).

Illustration 11: Modern copy of the "Garden scene" of Ashurbanipal. Courtesy: Prof. M.P. Streck, Altorientalisches Institut, University of Leipzig.

Illustration 12: Akkadian seal, in Orthmann 1985, 236, fig. 135i (drawing by the author).

List of Abbreviations

AfO	Archiv für Orientforschung, Berlin etc. 1923 ff.
AMD	Ancient Magic and Divination, Groningen 1999 ff.
AJSL	American Journal of Semitic Languages and Literatures, Chicago 1895-1941
AOAT	Alter Orient und Altes Testament, Neukirchen/Vluyn 1969 ff.
AOS	American Oriental Series, New Haven 1925 ff.
ARET	Archivi reali di Ebla. Testi, Rome 1985 ff.
ArOr	Archiv Orientalni. Quarterly Journal of African and Asian Studies, Prag 1929 ff.
ARM	Archives royales de Mari (TCL 22-31)
ASNSP	Annali della Scuola Normale Superiore di Pisa
BiOr	Bibliotheca Orientalis, Leiden 1943 ff.
BPOA	Biblioteca del Proximo Oriente Antiguo, Madrid 2006 ff.
BSA	Bulletin of Sumerian Agriculture, Cambridge 1984 ff.
CAD	The Assyrian Dictionary of the University of Chicago, Chicago 1956 ff.
CHANE	Culture and History of the Ancient Near East, Leiden/Boston 2000 ff.
CM	Cuneiform Monographs, Groningen/Leiden 1992 ff.)
CMAwR	Tz. Abusch/D. Schwemer, Corpus of Mesopotamian Anti-Witchcraft Rituals, Leiden/Boston 2011 ff.
CUSAS	Cornell University Studies in Assyriology and Sumerology, Bethesda 2007ff.
ePSD	electronic Pennsylvania Sumerian Dictionary Project http://psd.museum.upenn.edu/epsd/
ETCSL	Electronic Text Corpus of Sumerian Literature http://etcsl.orinst.ox.ac.uk/
HdOr	Handbuch der Orientalistik, Leiden 1948 ff.
JAOS	Journal of the American Oriental Society, New

	Haven etc. 1843 ff.
JCS	Journal of Cuneiform Studies (SS= Supplement Series), New Haven etc. 1947 ff.
JANER	Journal of ancient Near Eastern Religions, Leiden 2001 ff.
JNES	Journal of Near Eastern Studies, Chicago 1942 ff.
JSS	Journal of the Semitic Studies, Manchester 1956 ff.
KAR	E. Ebeling, Keilschrifttexte aus Assur religiösen Inhalts I/II (= WVDOG 28, 1919; WVDOG 34, 1923), Leipzig
LAPO	Littératures anciennes du Proche-Orient, Paris 1967 ff.
LKA	E. Ebeling, Literarische Keilschrifttexte aus Assur, Berlin 1953
MAOG	Mitteilungen der Altorientalischen Gesellschaft, Leipzig 1925 ff.
NABU	Nouvelles Assyriologiques Brèves et Utilitaires, Paris 1987 ff.
OBO	Orbis Biblicus et Orientalis, Friburg 1973 ff.
OECT	Oxford Editions of Cuneiform Texts, Oxford 1923 ff.
OIP	Oriental Institute Publications, Chicago 1924 ff.
OLP	Orientalia Lovaniensia periodica, Leuven 1970 ff.
RA	Revue d'Assyriologie et d'Archéologie Orientale, Paris 1886 ff.
RAI	Proceedings of the Rencontre assyriologique international
RIME	The Royal Inscriptions of Mesopotamia. Early periods, Toronto 1990ff.
RlA	Reallexikon der Assyriologie und vorderasiatischen Archäologie, Berlin 1928 ff.
SAA	State Archives of Assyria, Helsinki 1987 ff.
SAAB	State Archives of Assyria Bulletin, Padua 1987 ff.
SAALT	State Archives of Assyria Literary Texts, Helsinki 2001 ff.
SACT	Sumerian and Akkadian Cuneiform Texts in the Collection of the World Heritage Museum of the University of Illinois, Urbana 1972/1973
SANE	Sources of the Ancient Near East, Los Angeles/Malibu 1974 ff.
SEAL	Sources of Early Akkadian Literature, http://www.seal.uni-leipzig.de/
TAPS	Transactions of the American Philosophical Society

TCS	Texts from Cuneiform Sources, New York 1966 ff.
TSO	Texte und Studien zur Orientalistik, Hildesheim 1983 ff.
TUAT	Texte aus der Umwelt des Alten Testaments, Gütersloh 1982 ff.
UAVA	Untersuchungen zur Assyriologie und Vorderasiatischen Archäologie, Berlin etc. 1960 ff.
VAS	Vorderasiatische Schriftdenkmaler
WdO	Die Welt des Orients, Wuppertal/Göttingen 1947 ff.
WVDOG	Wissenschaftliche Veröffentlichungen der Deutschen Orient-Gesellschaft, Leipzig etc. 1900 ff.
YOS	Yale Oriental Series, New Haven 1915 ff.
ZA	Zeitschrift für Assyriologie und Vorderasiatische Archäologie, Berlin etc. 1886 ff.
ZDPV	Zeitschrift des Deutschen Palästina-Vereins, Wiesbaden 1953 ff.

Acknowledgments

This book is an adaptation of my PhD dissertation submitted in June 2018 and accepted in March 2019 (under the same title) at the Hebrew University of Jerusalem, under the supervision of Prof. Nathan Wasserman. I wish to express my deepest gratitude to my supervisor, without whom this work could not have been possible. Throughout this period, he has closely followed the flow of my ideas, carefully reading and editing the chapters, and offering his valuable suggestions and stimulating critiques, while providing me with essential practical and financial support. My deepest thanks to him for having supported this project from the very beginning.

I wish to thank my teachers at the Hebrew University: fruitful discussions with Prof. Wayne Horowitz, Prof. Uri Gabbay, and Prof. Tallay Ornan have inspired several parts of my research. I owe huge thanks to Prof. Nurit Stadler, who has been a great support for anthropological theory and beyond: her suggestions, critical feedback and constant encouragement have been a shining light on my path into the world of animism and anthropology of religions.

Special thanks are due to Prof. Tzvi Abusch, who has been a source of brilliant ideas and inspiring talks ever since our first meeting in Venice when I was a a young MA student, and later, during those precious occasions we had to discuss witchcraft, magic and ancient religions in Jerusalem.

During my doctoral years, I had the privilege of participating in the TEMEN, a joint project between the Georg-August Universität Göttingen and the Hebrew University of Jerusalem, to which I am extremely grateful for the cooperation between researchers and for the financial support. I wish to express my profound gratitude to Prof. Annette Zgoll: she offered me several occasions to share my findings and ideas in the welcoming context of the University of Göttingen, and provided me with rich insights into ancient mythology. A warm thank-you also to the members of the team: to Prof. Claus Ambos, to Dr. Giovanna Matini, and to Nadya Terechov.

During the last year of my doctorate, I had the good fortune to spend two semesters at the Altorientalisches Institut, at Leipzig University. I am indebted to Prof. Michael Streck for making me at home in the Institut, and for his constant help and advice throughout the final stages of the dissertation. Many thanks are also due to Dr. Johannes Hackl for the inspiring talks, as well as to the other students of the institute: to Maria Teresa Renzi-Sepe, Hannes Leonhardt, Antonia Pohl and Tommaso Scapelli for our friendship.

I wish to express my gratitude to Prof. Streck for welcoming my research to become a book in the series LAOS and for his precious help during the numerous revisions of the manuscript. I further wish to thank the English reviewers along the way: Dr. Leigh

Chipman for editing my PhD dissertation and Dr. Susan Martin for carefully checking the final manuscript.

Throughout the process of researching and writing my thesis, I was able to count on the assistance and support of many colleagues and friends. I would like to thank Massimo Maiocchi for the much-needed help with the Sumerian translations and for his patience in replying to my typographical doubts, Yasser Khanger for our inspiring talks about tablets and poetry, Yakir Paz for his positive feedback on the preliminary drafts of some chapters, and David Kertai for his insights into the world of iconography. Special thanks are due to Peter Zilberg for his steady support in the first phase of this doctoral path: I will be always grateful to his encouragement and closeness in such a delicate phase of my life.

Many more friends gifted me with their curiosity, patience and encouragement. My warmest gratitude to Francesca Gorgoni, whose friendship has been a shining light throughout these last years. I wish to thank Gabriele Campagna for inspiring me with his music, which gave me new energy to complete the thesis. My warmest thanks to Antonella and Luca Pojer for hosting me in their piece of paradise: their healing herbs and those convivial times spent together enriched and inspired me writing about nature on my beloved mountains. The constant and loving friendship of Ibrahim Abed Aldyem during the last dense years of writing have been for me a source of warmth, inspiration and energy, for which I will always be profoundly grateful.

This work could have never been accomplished without the never-ending support, patience and unconditional love of my family: to Paola, Dario and Vanna, Alfredo and Daniela, is due all my love and gratitude. I am immensely grateful to them, especially to my mother Paola, without whom I couldn't be the person I am.

Jerusalem/Leipzig/Venice, July 2019

Introduction

1 Introduction

This book explores how mountains, rivers, trees and plants were conceived of within the ancient Mesopotamian religious framework. At the heart of this book is the question: How was nature conceived of and engaged with by the ancient Mesopotamians? To answer this question, I base my analysis on reading the ancient myths, rituals, incantations, and other textual evidence dealing with religious life, through the lens of the current discourse on animism and anthropology of nature. The book sets out to shed new light onto some notions of divinity, personhood and nature in ancient Mesopotamian religion.

In ancient Mesopotamian myths and rituals, natural elements are referred to as living beings, acting in the world and partaking of the divine community. Mountains protect and heal, do not submit to deities and threaten them with their beauty, radiance and divinity. Rivers flow from the eyes of a dead watery god, establish verdicts and remove every evil, disease and impurity with their powerful waters. Sulphur, the daughter of the heavenly god Anu, and the tamarisk, the bone of the deity, are invoked for purifying and healing. The palm tree occurs as an emblem of the king and is referred to as a brother. This evidence speaks for different understandings of divinity, personhood and nature on the part of ancient Mesopotamians, as reflected by the literary and religious sources, and calls into question the various ways in which they related to, understood and conceptualized their natural surroundings and sacred landscape.

This study uncovers some modalities of the relationships between humans and non-humans by studying how mountains, rivers and trees were embedded within the ancient Mesopotamian religious framework. While exploring the ancient cuneiform-writing cultures, I use anthropological explanations to better understand the ancient myths and rituals, in order to investigate and further explain the connection between nature, the sacred and their materiality. I focus on the ongoing anthropological discussion over the term animism, with its innovative notion of personhood, which I apply as a conceptual tool in order to explore the ways in which the ancient Mesopotamians engaged with the major topographical entities and most attested vegetal and arboreal inhabitants of their landscape.

2 Scope of this study and the current state of research

This book explores a precise group of natural elements (i.e. mountains, rivers and trees), with their associated entities (i.e. anthropomorphic gods, *Mischwesen*,[1] animals and threatening agents), in the genres of myths and incantations belonging to ritual literature. These literary and religious sources can offer only one of several possible perspectives into the different and multifaceted ways in which the ancient Mesopotamians engaged with and conceptualized their natural surroundings. Mountains, rivers and trees have been chosen because they evince a synergic and entangled relationship throughout the literary sources. These natural elements are often recorded together in a dense network of symbolic and religious meanings: they are not only closely connected with one another but also with the great gods of the panthea, and with the divine and cosmic realms. In mythology, the mountain is portrayed as an organism inhabited by different entities: watercourses, trees and plants are the most prominent inhabitants of the mountainous landscape, together with stones, animals, legendary creatures and the gods. A particular entanglement between mountains, trees and rivers is on display in the cosmology of the eastern and western horizons: the divine River is closely associated with the mountains and their trees, and with the Sun in its daily journey over the horizon from east to west. In the incantations, these natural elements are invoked together: their agency and healing properties are called upon in the performance of ritual, displaying a complex religious connection between one another. Mountains, rivers and trees should thus be considered together, because they constitute a fertile repository of religious meanings in the eyes of the ancients, while participating in the physical and cosmic landscape of ancient Mesopotamia.

My book, *Mountains and Trees, Rivers and Springs,* explores these natural elements in order to describe the human-environmental relationships in Ancient Mesopotamian religion and literature in the light of the current debate about new animism and anthropology of religions. I claim that a general reassessment of the symbolic, literary and ritualistic roles of mountains, rivers and trees is necessary in order to shed new light onto the emic conceptualizations of nature, landscape, divinity, and personhood, while promoting the understanding and studying of the ancient Near Eastern religions as lived and material religions. This study revolves around the following intertwined questions:

1) **Personhood.** What is the evidence that the natural elements were considered as having agency and personality? Which roles are ascribed to them in the religious life of the ancient Mesopotamians? So far, in the Assyriological studies the matter of agency of different elements has been referred to as mere *materia magica* and *medica* within the magical and therapeutic performance. Indeed, the matter of magic has been constantly under discussion, pointing out the analogical thinking characterizing the ritual performance (e.g. Heßeel; Schwemer; Rochberg), but a more organic assessment of the so-called *materia magica* (i.e. plants, stones, animals, and man-made objects) that occur consistently in the rituals and myths is lacking.

2) **Divinity.** Were mountains, rivers and trees considered holy and/or regarded as deities? Were they conceived of as belonging to the divine world? How did they engage

1 The term *Mischwesen* refers to hybrid mythological creatures.

and relate with the great gods of the Mesopotamian panthea and with the cosmic realms? In order to explore the divinity and/or sacrality of mountains, rivers and trees, I consider whether they were worshipped, received offerings, and/or rites were held for them, both in the urban and temple context or immersed in nature. The traditional understanding of deity and divine (Bottéro 2001), Jacobsen's concepts of immanence and intransitiveness (Jacobsen 1946; Jacobsen 1976), Lambert's article about the non-anthropomorphic deities (1990), and the notions of "holistic embedded elements" within the "hegemonic and theistic cosmos" (Wiggermann and van Binsbergen 1999) are all essential steps that have paved the way to reconsider these natural elements within the ancient Mesopotamian lived and material religion. I base my methodology on Porter's article in the edited volume *What is a God?* (2009). This book deals specifically with the ancient emic notions of divine and divinity, pointing out that natural elements were part of the divine cosmos, and arguing for a necessary reassessment of the ancient Mesopotamian understandings of divinity and nature.

3) **Landscape and Cosmos.** The above-mentioned questions raise the consequent query about how the Sumerians, Babylonians and Assyrians perceived and conceptualized their environment, landscape and cosmos. Is it possible to reconstruct one or more sacred landscapes and religious topographies of ancient Mesopotamia? A renewed interest in the ancient Mesopotamian conceptualizations about nature, landscape and environment has been thriving in the last few decades. Horowitz's seminal study *Mesopotamian Cosmic Geography* (Horowitz 1998) has brought new insights into the ancient Mesopotamian conceptualizations of the earthly and cosmic realms. Specifically on the landscape of Sumerians, Black's article (Black 2002) considers the Sumerian mythical evidence with the different environmental settings of Southern Iraq, distinguishing the more familiar marshes of the fluvial plain and the coastal area from the steppe and the mountainous areas of the Zagros. More recently, Rendu-Loisel's book *Les Chants du monde* (2016) offers a unique portrayal of the auditory landscape of ancient Mesopotamia as mirrored by the literary evidence, bringing the dimension of sound into the studies of landscape and nature as an essential feature. However, a study entirely devoted to mountains, rivers and trees in the polytheisms of ancient Mesopotamia is a desideratum.

4) **Nature**. All these threads intertwine with the core question upon which this research revolves: How did the ancient Mesopotamians know, conceptualize, and engage with what we call nature? Did they have such a concept? And, did they distinguish a clear dichotomy between cultural and natural, natural and supernatural, subject and object, immanent and transcendent? In this direction, new research is flourishing in several disciplines, including those studying the ancient world and the broader field of history and anthropology of religions. Rochberg's groundbreaking book *Before Nature. Cuneiform Knowledge and the History of Science* (2016) explores some human-environmental relationships in the cuneiform world, aiming at assessing the *Sitz im Leben* of cuneiform knowledge within the history of science, while considering the emic concepts of nature before the notion of 'nature' existed as such. Pertaining to the Biblical World, Mari Jørstad's soon to be published dissertation, *The Life of the World: The Vitality and Personhood of Non-Animal Nature in the Hebrew Bible* (2016), argues that the biblical writers lived in a world populated with a wide variety of "persons," only some of whom are human. In consequence of such evidence, history should be understood as not merely a

human enterprise, but a cooperative venture between humans, their landscapes, and the monotheistic God.[2] In the literature about Indian religions, David Haberman's books, *River of Love in an Age of Pollution. The Yamuna River of Northern India* (2007), and *People Trees. Worship of Trees in Northern India* (2013), are essential steps forward not only for the history of the religions of India, but also for the broader discussion of ecological ethics in religious traditions past and present. Accordingly, the centuries-old devotion to the goddess Yamuna not only draws an intriguing picture of the diverse conceptions and theologies concerning the river deity, but also provides the conceptual and philosophical tools which could lead to necessary ecological action. Haberman's study of the sacred trees of India highlights the understanding and perception of trees as persons: this notion is widely shared by different cultures past and present, and is confirmed by contemporary biological and botanical studies.[3] These insights provide different modalities for relating to and engaging with our natural surroundings within the religious traditions, and represent some possible solutions for facing the environmental challenges of the contemporary world.

As part of this new wave of scholarly interest in the relationships of humans and the non-human, and human and nature, my research inserts and fills a consistent lacuna by readdressing how the ancient Mesopotamians conceptualized and related to their natural surroundings and their inhabitants, especially with reference to the mountains, rivers and vegetal beings which recur in Mesopotamian mythology and magic. These natural elements have been neglected for too long and considered as mere relics embedded into the anthropomorphic panthea, and the time is ripe for them to be reconsidered as a vital and essential part of the Mesopotamian religious experience. Considering mountains, rivers, trees and plants which are addressed as "other-than-human" persons, as deities and as cosmic entities participating in the divine and relational cosmos of the ancient Mesopotamians, is a step forward to readdressing and shedding light on their emic notions of divinity, nature and personhood, while contributing to reconsidering relevant aspects of the ancient Near Eastern history of religions. At the same time, it aims to contribute to the current discourse on animism, personhood and the anthropology of nature, the relevance of which is destined to increase exponentially due to the environmental crisis of our times.

3 Sources and methodology

In the attempt to draw a comprehensive picture of the Mesopotamian religious views of mountains, rivers and trees, my study is intentionally cross-generic and utilizes texts from different periods. I explore diverse types of sources written in Sumerian and Akkadian between the 3rd and 1st millennium B.C.E., with the focus on texts dealing with the religious sphere. The sources examined are all edited, and I utilize the most up-to-date transliterations available, for which I offer my new translations.

2 http://www.ancientjewreview.com/articles/2017/12/30/dissertation-spotlight-mari-jrstad.

3 Hall 2011; Hall 2013; Rival 1998. For some popular scientific works on the life and communication of trees see the books of Wohlleben 2015; Wohlleben 2017; Mancuso/Viola 2013; Mancuso 2018; Mancuso 2019.

My research centers on the textual genres of myths and incantations. Mythology represents the main core of the documentation that has been explored. The relevant Sumerian mythic and epic compositions *Inana and Ebiḫ*,[4] *Inana and Šukaletuda*,[5] *Lugale* or "Ninurta and the Stones",[6] *Enki and the World Order*,[7] *Enlil and Ninlil*,[8] and the epics *Lugalbanda in the Mountain Cave*,[9] *Lugalbanda and the Anzud Bird*,[10] and *Enmerkar and the Lord of Aratta*[11] are studied in the contexts of their multifaceted literary and religious worlds.[12] The epic of Gilgameš in its Sumerian[13] and Akkadian versions is considered.[14] Other significant Akkadian myths and epics are the *Enūma eliš*,[15] *Atraḫasīs*,[16] the myth of *Anzû*,[17] *Etana* and *Adapa*,[18] and further related texts (e.g. the *Song of Bazi*).[19] Incantations constitute the other major and complementary literary genre which is examined in this book. These literary sources are part of Mesopotamian ritual literature, and help shed light on magico-religious conceptions, beliefs and practices, both scholarly and popular. Sumerian and Akkadian incantations are studied, starting from the incantations of earlier periods (Ur III and Old Babylonian) and reaching the more complex ritual series and professional handbooks of the 1st millennium B.C.E. The older material is heterogeneous and consists mainly of single incantations addressing different demons and diseases (e.g. *utukkū lemnūtu*, Lamaštu), witchcraft, the evil eye and animals (e.g. dogs, scorpions).[20] The incantations are often bilingual and represent the complex world of magic in the 3rd and 2nd millennium B.C.E. As for the ritual compositions of the 1st millennium B.C., the study explores the main ritual series, especially *Maqlû*[21], *Šurpu*,[22] and *Mīs pî*,[23] together with their related texts. Also, the *Lipšur Litanies*, with their invocation of mountains and rivers, constitute essential evidence.[24] When relevant and complementary to the mythical and

4 See Attinger 1998; Attinger 2015a.
5 See Volk 1995.
6 See van Dijk1983; Seminara 2001.
7 See Kramer/Maier 1989; Mittermayer 2012.
8 See Steible 2015
9 See Wilcke 2015.
10 See Wilcke 2015.
11 See Mittermayer 2009.
12 For comprehensive studies on Sumerian literature see also the *Electronic Text Corpus of Sumerian Literature* (ETCSL); Bottéro/Kramer 1989; Kramer/Maier 1989; Black/Cunningham/Robson/Zólyomi 2004; Volk 2015.
13 *Gilgameš and Aga*, *Gilgameš and the Bull of Heaven*, *The Death of Gilgameš*, *Gilgameš, Enkidu and the Netherworld*, and *Gilgameš and Huwawa*.
14 George 2003.
15 Lambert 2013.
16 Lambert/Millard, 1969.
17 Vogelzang 1988.
18 Izre'el 2001.
19 George 2009, 1–15.
20 Geller 1985; Finkel/Geller 1997; Abusch/van der Toorn 1999. My main source for the Old Babylonian, Middle Babylonian and Middle Assyrian incantations is constituted by the online database SEAL (*Sources of the Early Akkadian Literature*).
21 Abusch/Schwemer 2011; Abusch 2015a.
22 Reiner 1958.
23 Walker/Dick 2001.
24 Reiner 1956, 129–149.

ritualistic material, the evidence offered by the repertoires of hymns, prayers, lexical lists (i.e. An=Anum), onomastic and offering lists, is considered and included in this study.

The literary sources are studied according to their contexts (literary, geographical and chronological), and across genres, time and space, in order to offer an organic picture of how mountains, rivers and trees were conceptualized over the course of time, according to literary genres and local traditions, aiming at detecting and following their essential and various features, along with the changes. Moreover, iconographical sources, such as seals, reliefs and statues, are taken into account as evidence complementary to the written material. In fact, some visual representations can better explain the ancient Mesopotamian conceptualizations of natural elements, especially of Mountain and River deities.

Methodologically, this study employs both the standard tools of Assyriological studies, combined with anthropological theory, in particular from the schools of structuralism, post-structuralism, and the new animism. The methodology pertinent to the philological approach to the ancient Mesopotamian literary sources consists of detecting and selecting the natural elements in the above-mentioned sources, of reading them carefully in the most up-to-date editions available, translating them, and studying them both contextually and diachronically in the light of the religious and anthropological theories.

Specifically, on the question of divinity ascribed to the natural elements in the cuneiform world, I utilize Porter (2009). Porter notices that certain natural phenomena and material objects are differently referred to as divine in the ancient cuneiform sources. Accordingly, the textual evidence is analyzed through an emic perspective, based on the three different ways non-anthropomorphic deities were identified in the sources:[25] 1) they are either explicitly said to be DINGIRs or *ilu*s or to behave in ways characteristic of DINGIRs and *ilu*s; 2) they are labeled as gods by the determinative DINGIR, the cuneiform sign which is placed before names referring to divinity; 3) and/or they are identified as DINGIRs by receiving a treatment reserved for gods, e.g. being recipients for food offerings or being utilized as theophoric elements in personal names.[26]

In exploring the ancient cuneiform cultures, I use a combination of anthropological theories applied to the ancient religious sources, in order to eplore and offer new interpretations about religion and nature. I utilize the term animism as argued for and promoted by the school of new animism (Bird-David 1999; Viveiros de Castro 1992; Viveiros de Castro 1998; Harvey 2006; Harvey 2013a, Harvey 2013b; Descola 1996; Descola 2005; Descola 2013), especially in its innovative notion of "other-than-human" person (Hallowell 1960; Harvey 2006; Harvey 2013a, Harvey 2013b; Hall 2011; Hall 2013). With the dismissal of the classic use of the term animism, a new usage of the term has come into being. According to the new animism, in some societies (or in some worldviews within a given society), the world is perceived and conceptualized as a relational and social one, as a "community of living beings" (Harvey 2013a; Harvey 2013b), populated by different persons, most of whom are non-human. The new animism highlights radically different understandings of divinity, person, and nature, calling into question the dualistic naturalistic worldview, with its oppositions of animate and inanimate, natural and cultural, natural and supernatural, immanent and transcendent (Latour 1993;

25 Porter 2009, 161.
26 Porter 2009, 161.

Descola 1996; Descola 2013). The predominant Western naturalistic mode of interaction with nature does not match the whole evidence attested in the cuneiform sources. Thus, animism represents a fertile conceptual tool to shed light upon relevant aspects of the relationship between humans and non-humans, which can illuminate various aspects of an ancient culture, distant from us in time and place, that has left us an unprecedented richness of written sources, while simultaneously bringing Assyriological studies into the broader current anthropological debate around religion, magic and nature.

Concerning the question of the applicability of anthropological methods and approaches to the study of such an ancient culture, I consider it a challenge and an opportunity to try to explore some aspects of how ancient human communities, far off in time and place, envisioned, knew and related to their world. In the field of Assyriology such approaches have been a matter of concern among the scholars ever since Landsberger asked a question destined to become famous: "To what extent is it possible to reconstruct vividly and faithfully an ancient, alien civilizations by philological means, without the help of a tradition continuing down to the present day?".[27] This question is at the very core of the problem of understanding the otherness by means of written records. As pointed out by Rochberg, this matter poses several challenges, but such an approach is required for anyone attempting to interpret and explore those societies, according to the different written sources.[28] Thanks to the advance of philological and linguistic understandings of the cuneiform sources, with the consequent flourishing of editions of different textual corpora, the ancient Mesopotamian documentation has become more easily available and awaits further studies on the *Sitz im Leben* of the ancient Mesopotamians. Hence, the anthropological methodology should not be assumed as establishing anachronistic and uncritical parallels between an ancient culture and a non-Western one, rather it should be utilized to explore different ways of interpreting the written sources while enhancing the dismantling of those Western dichotomies that influence us.[29] In the case of my study, the anthropological term animism offers one point of view through which to look at the multifaceted world of the ancient Mesopotamians, especially concerning the relationship between humans and nature, in the particular and circumscribed literary genres of myths and rituals.

4 Synopsis and findings

This book comprises five chapters, two methodological and theoretical, and three philological with some iconographical evidence when relevant. Chapter I contextualizes the *status quaestionis* of the current discourse revolving around the concept of animism, and of the place and consideration of mountains, rivers and trees within the ancient Mesopotamian

27 See Landsberger's inaugural lecture at Leipzig University in 1924, that was entitled "Die Eigenbegrifflichkeit der babylonischen Welt" (quoted in Rochberg 2016, 43).

28 Rochberg 2016.

29 Rochberg 2016.

religious experience. The history of the term animism (Tylor; Frazer; Durkheim; Lévi-Strauss), with its new notions proposed by the scholars dealing with new animism and anthropology of nature (Hallowell; Bird-David; Viveiros de Castro; Descola; Harvey), is traced, and it is followed by assessing the studies on natural elements in Assyriological studies (Bottéro; Jacobsen; Lambert; Wiggermann and van Binsbergen; Porter; Rochberg and Ornan).

Chapter II is a comprehensive survey of how mountains were considered and portrayed in myths, incantations and rituals, offerings, and personal names. The focus is on those testimonies where mountains are described as persons, as divine beings, and as topographical entities, in the attempt to draw a comprehensive picture of the different views of the ancient Mesopotamians of the majestic rocky entities which surrounded their alluvial plain, and of the cosmic and sacred landscape of ancient Mesopotamia. Both the unspecified and named mountains of the Mesopotamian landscape are considered in their cosmic, personal and divine features.

Chapter III deals with how rivers and springs were considered and addressed in the religious sources. The focus is on studying the evidence in which rivers are described as deities with proper agency and function in the religious framework. Especially relevant are the notions of the divine River conceptualized as a mother, as the great purifier of the world, and as the deity embodying and presiding over the divine River Ordeal. Specifically named rivers and sources will be included, to map some of the sacred and cosmic topography of ancient Mesopotamia. The river is a powerful and polyvalent entity that cannot be evaluated without considering its profusion of entangled meanings.

The most relevant evidence of cosmic trees and trees of life, of plants and trees conceived of as animated beings and as sacred entities in the rich repertoire of incantations, rituals and myths is presented in Chapter IV. Since trees and plants are copious in the literature, only those cases where these natural elements are referred to as sacred and cosmic beings, as mediators between worlds, as acting as "other-than-human" persons with definite agency (especially in the healing crafts), and as having kinship with humans, are taken into account.

A general assessment of the notions involved in animism within ancient cuneiform sources is found in Chapter V. This concluding chapter aims at merging the ancient religious sources with the notions borrowed from anthropology and history of religions, especially from the school of new animism, in order to offer some perspectives and possible new understandings of ancient Mesopotamian notions of divinity, personhood and nature. Analogism, metaphysical and relational animism, and the innovative notion of "other-than-human" personhood are all readdressed and considered in the light of the evidence about mountains, rivers and trees in the ancient polytheisms understood as a daily life experience and material religion(s).

The picture that emerges from myths and incantations, prayers and offerings, is that of a relational and sacred cosmos which was perceived and conceptualized as populated by several non-human persons, where deities and humans were part of a much more complex and multi-layered system. Rivers, trees and plants are major and omnipresent topographical and botanical entities in the landscape of the Mesopotamian plain, while mountains constitute a distant but bulky crown, which embraces the alluvial plain. The literary and iconographical motif of the cosmic mountain (or the Twin Peaks Mountain) points to the notion of the cosmic landscape on the eastern horizon, conceived as a holistic landscape inhabited by divine, fluvial and arboreal beings. The divine River is closely associated with the Sun god and with the cosmic Mountain of Sunrise, which was populated by evergreen trees –such as the cedar and the *ḫašurru*-tree. The rivers Baliḫ, Ḫabur and Ulāya are the main cosmic and netherworld rivers of Mesopotamian cosmology. The cosmic mountains – such as Aratta, Mt. Māšu, Mt. Ḫašur– were entangled both with the eastern and western horizons, thus with the Sun in its cyclical daily journey across the sky, and consequently corresponding to the netherworld. Moreover, mountains and trees are conceptualized as media between heaven and earth, and both assume the traits of *axis mundi*. All these elements partake of the cosmic and divine landscape of the ancient Mesopotamians. In the Mesopotamian literary and religious tradition, mountains and rivers are conceived of not only as cosmic topographical entities, but also as entities bearing a close and multifaceted relationship with deities and the other creatures inhabiting the Mesopotamian cosmos. Rivers are connected with the realm of Ea, the Apsû, and with the supreme judge of the Mesopotamian panthea, Šamaš. Mountains are related not only to the mountainous deities (i.e. Inana, Ninurta, Enlil, Amurru, Bazi and Šakkan) but also to some famous *Mischwesen*. Mt. Šaššar is entangled with the Anzû-bird in the Akkadian tradition, and the Cedar Mountain, with its evergreen trees, is intertwined with Ḫuwawa, its custodian.

Mountains, rivers, trees and plants recur consistently as "other-than-human" persons, while certain mountains and rivers feature the clearly divine status of deities. Mountains display protecting, purifying and motherly attributes, while rivers are conceptualized as mothers of all life, as great purifiers and healers, as impartial judges of mankind, and as guardians and protectors of gates and cities. Several rivers (e.g. the Tigris, the Euphrates, and their tributaries) feature a fully divine status within ancient Mesopotamian religious life, while the mountains conceived of with fully divine traits are fewer: the cases of Ebiḫ and of Aššur form the main evidence for mountain deities, but other mountains are evidenced as partaking of divinity (e.g. Aratta, Šaššar, the Cedar Mountain, Dipar and Saggar). Trees and plants were conceptualized as cosmic entities, as pillars of the world and media between dimensions, and as conscious, wise, protecting and healing beings, sacred to the anthropomorphic gods and to humans. Particular trees are clearly referred to as participating in divinity (e.g. the tamarisk), and as being kin to humans (e.g. the palm tree).

Chapter I

Animism and Mesopotamian Religion

1 What is animism? –History of the term in anthropological literature

Animism refers to a worldview where every natural being –humans, animals, stones, trees, seas, lakes, rivers, mountains, etc.– is living and has an inner spirit, energy, and personality. The animistic universe is permeated by personalities, forces and spirits, which are interconnected and related to one another. The term animism derives from the Latin word *anima*, "soul, spirit", and refers to the belief that a soul or spirit exists in every being, be it an animal, a plant, a river or an object. It has been considered one of the most ancient religious beliefs, and an essential part of any religious system, from the Paleolithic until modern times.

The classic use of the term animism has been progressively dismissed, due to its colonialist and evolutionist connotations.[1] Meanwhile, anthropologists have explored new ways for understanding the other as equal, and animistic beliefs are no longer regarded as mere relics of a savage mind. In the light of recent ethnographic, cognitive, literary, performative and material culture approaches, a new usage of the term has come into being. The new animism is relational, sees the world as a community and highlights radically different meanings of soul, person, and nature. Thus, animism calls into question the dualistic Cartesian worldview, with its oppositions of animate and inanimate, natural and cultural, natural and supernatural, immanent and transcendent.

The ongoing debate on animism involves and challenges modern Western worldviews, presenting other ways to live in and relate to the world. Moreover, animism can contribute to the discourse about ancient cultures and religions, thanks to its shifting perspectives. In fact, the dualistic worldview, which has been applied to ancient cultures for too long, is only one of the many different ways of knowing, perceiving and relating to the world, and it is locally and historically specific. The time is ripe for considering other possibilities of how ancient cultures may have perceived, experienced and conceptualized their immediate surroundings and sacred landscapes.

---

1 See the paragraphs below (§ 1) on the old animism, especially the discussion of Tylor.

1.1 Classical theories of animism

1.1.1 Tylor and the belief in spiritual beings

Animism refers to the belief that non-human beings and natural objects are infused with some spiritual essence.[2] Sir Edward Tylor, considered the father of anthropology, first used the term "animism" in his book *Primitive Cultures* (1871). In his anthropological and ethnographical research, he noted that "primitive people attribute life and personality to animal, vegetable and mineral alike":[3]

> First and foremost among the causes which transfigure into myth the facts of daily experience, is the belief in the animation of all nature, rising at its highest pitch to personification. This, no occasional or hypothetical action of the mind, is inextricably bound in with that primitive mental state where man recognizes in every detail of his world the operation of personal life and will. […] To the lower tribes of man, sun and stars, trees and rivers, winds and clouds, become personal animate creatures, leading lives conformed to human or animal analogies, and performing their special functions in the universe with the aid of limbs like beasts, or of artificial instruments like men; … [Such ideas] rest upon a broad philosophy of nature, early and crude indeed, but thoughtful, consistent, and quite really and seriously meant.[4]

According to his readings and understanding of the several ethnographical reports at hand in London, Tylor noticed that the belief in an animated and personified nature was a common feature. In many cultures and religious beliefs, nature is, indeed, considered animated and its different inhabitants have a personal life and will. Personality and animation are ascribed not only to animals, but also to plants, rivers, mountains, meteorological phenomena and artifacts. In the case of plants, Tylor argues for the notion of a "vegetable soul" of Aristotelian memory:[5]

> Plants, partaking with animals to phenomena of life and death, health and sickness, not unnaturally have some kind of soul ascribed to them. In fact the notion of a vegetable soul, common to plants and to the higher organisms possessing an animal soul in addition, was familiar in medieval philosophy, and is not yet forgotten by naturalists. But in lower ranges of cultures, at least within one wide district of the world, the souls of plants are much more fully identified with the souls of animals.[6]

Moreover, he stated that every man, in addition to his body, has a "ghost-soul", which is the "cause of life or thought in the individual it animates" and is capable "of leaving the

2 Howell 2013, 103
3 Quoted in Bird-David 1999, 69.
4 Tylor 1871, 258.
5 See, e.g. Hall 2011; Coccia 2016.
6 Tylor 1871, 474.

body far behind" and "continuing to exist and appear to men after the death of that body".[7] The belief in souls and the perception of nature as animated are the essential concepts on which Tylor based his theory of "animism". The term itself was chosen by Tylor because it derives from the Latin word for soul, "anima".[8] The concept of "soul" has, in fact, to be considered the most common "constant in human culture":[9]

> The conception of the human soul is, as to its most essential nature, continuous from the philosophy of the savage thinker to that of the modern professor of theology [...]. The theory of the soul is one principal part of a system of religious philosophy which unites, in an unbroken line of mental connection, the savage fetish-worshipper and the civilized Christian.[10]

Tylor makes the postulation of souls the essence of religion and considers the "belief in spiritual beings"[11] the basic definition of religion.[12] His aim was to find the simplest, most primitive and most archaic form of religion, which would eventually be replaced by science, according to the rationalistic and evolutionistic view of nineteenth-century Victorian England. Tylor considered animism a mere stage in the process toward the triumph of science. He suggested that this belief was a delusion, and he assumed that any traces of animism in the modern world were mere survivals, "relics of savage thought", stemming from an earlier and more "primitive" and childish perception of the world. He considered, in fact, that the belief in animated spiritual beings was still attested in children, English peasants (i.e. lower-class and uneducated people), and "savages", who represent some kind of earlier and simpler level of humanity.[13] In this view, any belief and practice which could not be considered part of rationalistic and scientific thought –such as dreams, funeral rites, ancestor worship, magic– was regarded as a fossil, a relic from earlier times.[14] For Tylor,

> The principles underlying astrology, witchcraft and divination and other "occult sciences" hail ultimately from the primitive "association of ideas", but that linkage of ideas is false wherever it is found, and the occult sciences are pseudo-scientific systems that belong to a period now beginning to pass away.[15]

7 Quoted in Bird-David 1999, 69.

8 Segal 2013, 58. His first choice would have been "spiritism", but since this was the name of a phenomenon in fashion at the time, he opted instead for animism.

9 Kippenberg 2002, 60 (quoted in Segal 2013, 58).

10 Tylor 1871, 1958 II 85-86 (quoted in Segal 2013, 58).

11 Tylor 1871, I, 383 (quoted in Stringer 2013, 64).

12 Segal 2013, 58; Stringer 2013, 64.

13 Segal 2013, 57.

14 Segal 2013, 55.

15 Segal 2013, 57. See Chapter V for the analogical thinking and the term of magic in ancient Mesopotamian scholarship.

Thus, these beliefs and practices were to be regarded as mere delusion and illusion.[16] In order to explain to the rational mind the reason for these relics of earlier stages of evolution still being rather lively in his time, he proposed the famous simile of dreams. While dreaming, people believe they are able to leave their physical body and conduct another life. This is the same situation as a trance and other ecstatic experiences, and also in those cases when a dead spirit appears. Because of this experience, it seems logical to assume that a physical body and a non-material essence (i.e. the soul) constitute the two parts of a person.[17]

In the scientific and positivistic horizon of his century, dominated by the Cartesian world view, there was no space for animism, because the dualistic axiom supposes science vs. animism, object vs. subject, natural vs. supernatural, culture vs. nature, and so on. Still, Tylor acknowledges that these animistic elements have been in conflict with the scientific progress for centuries: "The old and simple theory which explains the world at large as directly animated by a life like our own, or directly resulting from such life, has been for ages at war with an ever-accumulating and ever-encroaching scientific knowledge".[18]

The resistance of the theories of an animated world would suggest that these elements should be seen not as "relics and fossils", but rather as "fertile shoots", or rather as evergreen and constant coexisting features.[19] Accordingly, besides the notion of animism as the most primitive stage in the evolution of religion, Tylor refers to it as the essential religion, a "minimum of religion" which has gone through centuries and assumed different forms:[20] "animism characterizes tribes very low in the scale of humanity, and thence ascends, deeply modified in its transmission, but from first to last preserving an unbroken continuity, into the midst of high modern culture".[21]

This statement suggests that "elements of "animism" are retained in contexts where polytheism or monotheism are the dominant form of religion".[22] The continuation of Tylor's *Primitive Cultures* focuses on polytheism and monotheism and his discussion concludes by sketching the idea of animism as a philosophy of religion, "a way of being religious", such as monotheism or polytheism, rather than Hinduism or Christianity.[23] The implications of this tentative idea are interesting "food for thought" and represent "fertile shoots" for the discourse on Mesopotamian polytheism.[24]

16 Tylor was interested in and fascinated by the occult sciences, i.e. the phenomenon of Spiritism in fashion at his time. Still, he considered these phenomena mere relics of an ancient and primitive religious experience.

17 Stringer 2013, 65; Bird-David 1999, 59–60.

18 Tylor 1866, 72 (quoted in Segal 2013, 57).

19 Kippenberg 2002, 62 (quoted in Segal 2013, 56).

20 Tylor 1871, 385

21 Tylor 1871, 385

22 Stringer 2013, 66.

23 Stringer 2013, 66.

24 The implications of this assumption are clearly stated by Stringer: "Therefore, if we assume that animism is not a form of religion as such, in the way that Christianity or Islam is a form of religion, but rather a way of being religious, such as monotheism in general, it is clear from Tylor's own analysis that there are elements of animism in all societies, whether or not the dominant form of religion acknowledges them or not. It is not simply a developmental model, therefore, that Tylor is creating. If we take the diachronic and evolutionary element out of his analysis, then we could see the whole

Ethnographic fieldwork in many parts of the modern world confirms that the conception of an animated natural world, constituted by sentient non-human beings, exists among several peoples. Moreover, this brief overview has pointed out the fact that Tylor's work can still constitute a great repertoire of ethnographical evidence and of ideas and implications that are worth reconsideration. Nevertheless, anthropologists progressively distanced themselves from any notion of primitive, childlike and of mistaken knowledge, ending up dismissing the concept of animism altogether.[25]

1.1.2 Frazer and the worship of trees

Sir James Frazer, inspired by Tylor's book *Primitive Cultures*, and sharing the evolutionist worldview of Victorian England, is the author of what is considered another major classic work of anthropology, *The Golden Bough* (1890). His research focused on religious practices (and not on beliefs, as Tylor did) –such as rituals, worship and magic. In his two volumes Frazer examines the aspects of sacred kingship and of vegetation worship, and contributes in arranging Tylor's principles of association (i.e. analogism) in magic.[26]

Frazer assumes Tylor's concept of invisible other beings, and he regards religion as "a belief in powers higher than man and an attempt to propitiate or please them".[27] These superior powers are believed to control the course of nature and of human life. Thus, religious rites and magic are mere tools for controlling natural phenomena by primitive people.[28] Tylor's animistic beliefs are supported by Frazer in his understanding of the worship of cereals. In order to explain those propitious rites toward plants and trees, Frazer stresses the existence of a vital essence, a "soul" also inside a plant:

> They imagine that in the fibers of the plant, as in the body of a man, there is a certain vital element, which is so far independent of the plant that it may for a time be completely separated from it without fatal effects, though if its absence be prolonged beyond certain limits the plant will wither and die. This vital yet separable element is what, for the want of a better word, we must call the soul of a plant, just as a similar vital and separable element is commonly supposed to constitute the soul of a man; and so on this theory or myth of the plant-soul is built the whole worship of cereals.[29]

Moreover, Frazer contributed to assessing Tylor's thoughts about magic. He sorted the principles of association in magical thought into two basic types: the principle of similarity or resemblance (homeopathic) and the principle of contagion or contiguity.[30] Frazer

structure in synchronic terms and argue that all societies must express elements of fetishism, of polytheism, of monotheism and even of scientific rationalism. If this is the case, then, we need to ask what role animism plays within this schema as a whole" (Stringer 2013, 66).

25 Howell 2013, 104.

26 Cunningham 1999, 19–20.

27 Frazer 1990, 27 (quoted in Cunningham 1999, 19–20).

28 Cunningham 1999, 19–21; Tambiah 1990, 51–64.

29 Frazer [1890] 1922: 414 (quoted in Hall 2013, 386).

30 Tambiah 1990, 52.

subdivided magical systems into two sorts: "sympathetic magic" and "contagious magic" though he was aware that they overlapped in practice.[31] His discussion separates science, magic and religion with much stronger tones than in Tylor's animism. He argued that magic "was in some ways a precursor of science, but it was its bastard sister".[32]

Frazer did not support the idea that magic often dealt with spirits. In his view, when magic did so, it was actually treating the animated beings as "inanimistic agents", "that is, it coerced and constrained them instead of propitiating and conciliating them in a manner of religion".[33] As clearly pointed out by Tambiah in his discussion of Frazer's theories, it appears obvious that

> To coerce another person or being is not to make that entity "inanimate". Frazer resorts to this assertion precisely because he has decided that the magician and scientist share the same presuppositions concerning the "uniformity of nature" and impersonal causation. In making this equation Frazer, as well as Tylor in a less naïve way, have both introduced a distinction which was alien to medieval and Renaissance magic in Europe, that predicated on the mediation of angels and planetary spirits.[34]

1.1.3 Durkheim, and totemism as the most elementary form of religious life

Émile Durkheim follows the trend of finding and defining the simplest and most common form of religion. In his book *The Elementary Forms of Religious Life* (1912) Durkheim identifies the most basic religious phenomenon in totemism, after having discarded the previous theories of the origin of religion. His discussion starts with considering two religious phenomena which have been so far combined into animism, but which he distinguishes as *animism* and *naturism*. Durkheim states that "there is no religious system, ancient or recent, where one does not meet, under different forms, two religions, as it were, side by side, which, though being united closely and mutually penetrating each other, do not cease, nevertheless, to be distinct".[35] In his view, animism refers to the religion of the spirit *per se*, which "has spiritual being as its objects, spirits, souls, geniuses, demons, divinities properly so-called, animated and conscious agents like man, but distinguished from him, nevertheless, by the nature of their powers and especially by the peculiar characteristic that they do not affect the senses in the same way: ordinarily they are not visible to human eyes".[36] In contrast, naturism "addresses itself to the phenomena of nature, either the great cosmic forces, such as winds, rivers, stars or the sky, etc., or else the objects of various sorts which cover the surface of the earth, such as plants, animal, rocks, etc".[37] The intrinsic connection between naturism and animism is further stated by Durkheim:

31 Tambiah 1990, 52.
32 Tambiah 1990, 52.
33 Tambiah 1990, 52.
34 Tambiah 1990, 52–53.
35 Durkheim 1915, 64.
36 Durkheim 1915, 64–65. See also Descola 2013b (also below § 1.2.3); Abram 2013 on the ontologies of visible and invisible beings.
37 Durkheim 1915, 64–65.

> Religion really commences only at the moment when these natural forces are no longer represented in the mind in an abstract form. They must be transformed into personal agents, living and thinking beings, spiritual powers or gods; for it is to beings of this sort that the cult is generally addressed.[38]

This phenomenon has its origin in a "native incapacity of distinguishing the animate from the inanimate and an irresistible tendency to conceive the second under the form of the first".[39] Both religions have to be discarded since they do not represent the most elementary and shared religious element in mankind and because he considers the distinction of sacred and profane deriving from them impossible. In fact, the overwhelming feeling of man immersed in nature challenges and contradicts the dualistic axiom of sacred/profane, the foundation of religion according to Durkheim.[40]

The opposition of sacred/profane brings Durkheim to identify totemism as the most elementary form of religion. Totemism is defined as the worship of animals and plants associated with particular social groups.[41] Analyzing Australian religions, he noticed that "primitive people" regarded as kin and friends some entities that were considered animated (plants, animals, natural phenomena and elements) and they believed that the bonds between them and these natural entities were "like those which unite the members of a single family".[42] These natural entities are called totem, which serves to designate the clan collectively.[43] Furthermore, the totem is defined as a moral organization.[44]

Durkheim continues his argument, claiming that a totem represents not only a clan, but also what is religious to it. Accordingly, the clan worships itself: "The god of the clan, the totemic principle, can be nothing else than the clan itself, personified and represented to the imagination under the visible form of the animal or vegetable which serves as totem".[45] In this view, religion symbolizes a social structure, it serves as a classificatory system, and it functions to integrate society by reaffirming social identity. Social identity is reiterated and reinforced periodically through rites.[46]

Furthermore, Durkheim advances a definition of totemism as a religion of an impersonal and moral force:

> Totemism is the religion, not of such and such animals or men or images, but of an anonymous and impersonal force, found in each of these beings but not to be confounded with any of them. No one possesses it entirely and all participate in it. It is so completely independent of the particular subjects in whom it incarnates itself, that it precedes them and survives them. Individuals die, generations pass and are replaced

38 Durkheim 1915, 93.
39 Durkheim 1915, 93.
40 Durkheim 1915, 52.
41 Cunningham 1999, 44; Bird-David 1999, 70.
42 Durkheim, 1915, 139 (quoted in Bird-David 1999, 70).
43 Durkheim [1912] 1915, 123.
44 Durkheim [1912] 1915, 175.
45 Durkheim 1976, 206 (quoted in Cunningham 1999, 45).
46 Durkheim 1976, 387 (quoted in Cunningham 1999, 45).

> by others; but this force always remains actual, living and the same. It animates the generations of to-day as it animated those of yesterday and as it will animate those of to-morrow. Taking the words in a large sense, we may say that it is the god adored by each totemic cult, yet it is an impersonal god, without name or history, immanent in the world and diffused in an innumerable multitude of things.[47]

This impersonal force has both a physical and a moral aspect. The native peoples of Australia perform rites toward their totemic ancestors, who are considered sacred beings to be feared and respected. The totem should be understood as the source of the moral life of the clan, thus guaranteeing the respect of tradition.[48] Animism and totemism are to be seen as intertwined religious phenomena and categories. Along with animism, totemism has been recently and differently reassessed, and it is generally agreed by contemporary anthropologists that it should be referred to as a social aspect of animism.[49]

1.1.4 Lévi-Strauss and totemism

The most comprehensive and incisive discussion and critique of totemism in classical anthropology is offered by Lévi-Strauss, who discusses and explores the totemic world and other anthropologists' theories regarding it in his famous books *La pensée sauvage* (1962) and *Le Totémisme aujourd'hui* (1963). His most systematic theory and definition of totemism is found in *La pensée sauvage* where he actually dismantled the notion of totemism, and understood it as a mere classificatory system. As pointed out by Descola, the Lévy-Straussian theory of totemism is based on "the idea that discontinuities between species function as a mental model for organizing social segmentation among humans".[50]

As the main representative of modern structuralism, Lévi-Strauss built on the ideas of Radcliffe-Brown in an attempt to find the structures inherent to the totemic systems. Noticing difficulties in the study of totemism from a structuralist point of view, he drew a scheme to illustrate the abstract polarities that he observed in totemism as a phenomenon in human culture. He understands and defines totemism as a mere classificatory system, one among others, which works through a binary epistemology based on a dichotomous logic of resemblances. As argued by Lèvi-Strauss,

> Social structures previously simply juxtaposed in space are made to correspond at the same time as the animal and plant classifications of each tribe. According to their tribal origin, the informants conceived the dual scheme on the model of opposition of resemblance, and they formalized it in terms of kinship (father and son) or directions (east and west) or elements (land and sea, water and fire, air and land), or again in terms of the differences or resemblances between natural species.[51]

47 Durkheim 1915, 217.
48 Durkheim 1915, 218–219.
49 See below in this Chapter, § 1.2.3 and § 1.2.5.
50 Descola 2013a, 77.
51 Lévi-Strauss 1962, 158–159.

Lévi-Strauss claimed, in fact, to detect binary and antithetical thinking as a crucial structural principle in totemism, and believed that the similarity among totemic ideas in various cultures lay in similarities between systems of differences such as those documented in the natural sphere and those in the culturally defined social groups.[52] As he points out,

> The heterogeneous beliefs and customs arbitrarily collected together under the heading of totemism do not rest on the idea of a relationship of substance between one or more social groups and one or more natural domains. They are allied to other beliefs and practices, directly or indirectly linked to the classificatory schemes which allow the natural and social universe to be grasped and organized whole.[53]

Moreover, these associations and classificatory schemes can change and transform, featuring an inherent dynamism. Lévi-Strauss underlies this notion by stating that "the societies which we call primitive do not have a conception of a sharp division between the various levels of classification. They represent them as stages or moments in continuous transition".[54]

Lévi-Strauss concluded that the distinction between the classes of man and animal serves as the conceptual basis for social differences:[55]

> Totemism, or so-called totemism, confines itself to conceiving homology of structure between the two series, a perfectly legitimate hypothesis, for social segments are instituted, and it is in the power of each society to render the hypothesis plausible by shaping its rules and representations accordingly.[56]

As pointed out by Descola, while commenting on the Lévi-Straussian definition of totemism, "each totemic group has to be taken in itself", as "it tends to form a system, not any more with the other totemic groups, but with certain differential properties conceived as hereditary".[57] Accordingly, "instead of two images, one social one natural, […] a unique but fragmented socio-natural image" will be obtained.[58] This notion seems also to imply the overcoming of the dichotomy between nature and culture, which is a core issue of the current discourse around animism.[59]

For Lévi-Strauss, totemism should be considered an illusion, as a mere "logic that classifies", in which the structure of social relations is projected onto natural phenomena, not taken from them.[60] Thus, "the so-called totemism" is understood as "only a particular

---

52 Encyclopedia Britannica (online source).
53 Lévi-Strauss 1962, 135.
54 Lévi-Strauss 1962, 138.
55 Encyclopedia Britannica (online source).
56 Lévi-Strauss 1962, 227.
57 Lévi-Strauss 1962, 154–155 (quoted in Descola 2013a, 78).
58 Lévi-Strauss 1962, 154–155 (quoted in Descola 2013a, 78).
59 Descola 2013a, 78. See also Chapter VI.
60 Enciclopedia Britannica (online source)

case of the general problem of classification and one of many examples of the part which specific terms often play in the working out of a social classification".[61]

The relevance of Lévi-Strauss in classical anthropology does not end with his theories on totemism, since his analysis and theory about myths are also fundamental. According to structural theory, myths are to be understood as language: "myth is language: to be known, myth has to be told; it is part of human speech".[62] Structural analysis argues that any meaning underlying mythology "cannot reside in the isolated elements which enter into the composition of a myth, but only in the way those elements are combined". Moreover, the language which constitutes a myth has specific properties, which distinguish the mythical narration from language in general and exhibit complex and sophisticated features. Accordingly, these features comprise the constituent units that make up myths:[63] "the true constituent units of a myth are not the isolated relations but *bundles of such relations* and it is only as bundles that these relations can be put to use and combined so as to produce a meaning".[64]

Furthermore, the structuralist analysis of the relationship between myths and rituals should be mentioned. Lévi-Strauss argues that if "a myth always refers to events alleged to have taken place in time: before the world was created, or during the first stages, [...] what gives the myth an operative value is that the specific pattern described is everlasting: it explains the present and the past as well as the future".[65] Accordingly, "mythical history presents the paradox of being both disjoined from and conjoined with the present", but "thanks to ritual, the 'disjoined' past of myth is expressed, on one hand, through biological and seasonal periodicity, and, on the other, through the 'conjoined' past, which unites from generation to generation the living and the dead".[66]

The notions of animism, totemism, ritual and magic are all connected and have been fully readdressed by the recent wave of anthropological and religious studies on human-environmental relationships, especially within the so-called school of new animism.

1.2 The current debate over animism

1.2.1 Hallowell, the animate world of the Ojibwa and the "other-than-human" persons

Hallowell inaugurated the new path of animism, which is relational and has to do with treating the world as a community. In his article "Ojibwa Ontology, Behavior and World View" (1960), Hallowell reports his ethnographical fieldwork among the Ojibwa of Manitoba, Canada, and he introduces the notion of the "other-than-human" person.[67] Hallowell noticed that among the Ojibwa the term person is applied to "other-than-human" beings. The illustrative case for this evidence is the "manner in which the kinship term

61 Lévi-Strauss 1962, 62.
62 Lévi-Strauss 1955, 430.
63 Lévi-Strauss 1955, 431.
64 Lévi-Strauss 1955, 431.
65 Lévi-Strauss 1955, 430.
66 Lévi-Strauss 1962, 236.
67 Hallowell 1960, 19–52.

'grandfather' is used".[68] In fact, "it is not only applied to human persons but to spiritual beings who are persons of a category other than human".[69] The social and kinship characterization of the "other-than-human" persons required a more comprehensive understanding of the categories of "person" and of "animate/inanimate".[70]

Hallowell indicates that in Ojibwa and related Algonkian languages there is a pervasive grammatical distinction between animate and inanimate nouns and related parts of speech. In the Ojibwa language, "substantives for some, but not all –trees, sun-moon, thunder, stones, and objects of material culture like kettle and pipe– are classified as 'animate'".[71] A famous example is offered by Hallowell, who asked, while interviewing an elder, whether all stones are to be considered alive. The old man, he reports, after reflecting for a while, replied: "No! But some are".[72] This evidence suggests that "the allocation of stones to an animate grammatical category is part of a culturally constituted cognitive 'set'. It does not involve a consciously formulated theory about the nature of stones", but it indicates that "the Ojibwa recognize potentialities for animation in certain classes of objects under certain circumstances".[73]

Moreover, Ojibwa myths, tales and rituals reveal an animate universe. In these literary contexts the concepts of person and animate/inanimate are broader and acquire new meanings:

> In action and motivations the characters in the myths are indistinguishable from human persons. In this respect, human and other-than-human persons may be set apart in life as well as in myth, from animate beings such as ordinary animals and objects belonging to the inanimate grammatical category. But, at the same, it must be noted that "persons" of the other-than-human class do not always present a human appearance in the myths.[74]

Anthropomorphism is indeed not the feature that distinguishes a person from a non-person. In myths, thunder-persons are portrayed and referred to as birds. What makes the Thunderbirds persons is their behavior: Thunderbirds are "conceived to act like human beings" –i.e. they hunt, talk and dance– and their social organization is the same as the Ojibwa's.[75] The other attribute of personhood is represented by metamorphosis, a frequent occurrence in mythology. Thunderbirds can, in fact, change their external avian form into a human one.[76] Moreover, persons share the same internal structure: in fact, "all animate beings of the person class are unified conceptually in Ojibwa thinking because they have a

68 Hallowell 1960, 21.
69 Hallowell 1960, 21.
70 Hallowell 1960, 22–23.
71 Hallowell 1960, 21–23. See also Mithun 1999.
72 Hallowell 1960, 24.
73 Hallowell 1960, 25.
74 Hallowell 1960, 30.
75 Hallowell 1960, 33.
76 Hallowell 1960, 34–35.

similar structure –an inner vital part that is enduring and an outward form which can change".[77]

The picture of a personalistic world emerges from myths and from everyday stories. Hallowell points out that "the interaction of the Ojibwa with certain kinds of plants and animals in everyday life is so structured culturally that individuals act as if they were dealing with 'persons' who both understand what is being said to them and have volitional capacities as well".[78] The main practical implication of relating to "other-than-human" persons is a respectful behavior of humans toward the other members of the community. This respectful attitude to all the persons of the living community derives from the Ojibwa understanding that a good life cannot be "achieved without the cooperation of both human and "other-than-human" persons".[79]

The introduction of this notion has paved the way for a reassessment of the previously dismissed term animism. Being at the core of the school of new animism, it comprises also a fruitful conceptual tool for exploring and reading ancient sources and modern cultures with a different lens.

1.2.2 Bird-David and animism as relational epistemology

Bird-David follows up Hallowell's ideas, focusing on epistemology in the light of the modern environment and personhood theories. Her essay "'Animism' Revisited: Personhood, Environment, and Relational Epistemology" (1999)[80] deals with understanding the concept of the *Devaru*-person among the Nayaka people in India, and with reassessing the anthropological category of animism. *Devaru* can be seen as the "objectification of sharing relationships" according to the Nayaka notion of personhood. *Devaru* is believed to exist in the world and can be identified with "certain things-in-situations of whatever class, or better, certain situations".[81] *Devaru*s are all those "events involving mutual responsiveness and engagement between things, events, which prototypically involve the actor-perceiver".[82]

In the Nayaka's view, "the person is sensed as 'one whom we share with'. It is sensed as a relative and is normally objectified as kin, using kinship terms".[83] Accordingly, Bird-David argues that the central view of Nayaka social life has to be seen in the "idea that one shared space, things and actions with others".[84] Nayaka are, in fact, "attentive to, and work towards making, relatedness. As they move and generally act in the environment, they are

77 Hallowell 1960, 42.
78 Hallowell 1960, 36.
79 Hallowell 1960, 45.
80 Bird-David 1999.
81 Bird-David 1999, 75.
82 Bird-David 1999, 75.
83 Bird-David 1999, 73.
84 Bird-David 1999, 72.

attentive to mutual behaviors and events".[85] It is by engaging and maintaining relationships with other beings, making them "relatives", that the Nayaka understand them as persons.[86]

Bird-David continues her discussion by defining animism as a relational epistemology. What can be inferred from the understanding of *Devaru* is that "the object of this animistic knowledge is understanding relatedness from a related point of view within the shifting horizons of the related viewer".[87] Thus, the process of knowing is intended as "developing the skills of being in-the-world with other things, making one's awareness of one's environment and one's self finer, broader, richer, etc. Knowing grows from and is maintaining relatedness with neighboring others".[88]

1.2.3 Descola and the modes of interaction between humans and nature

The major part of Philippe Descola's work has been dedicated to the modes in which humans relate to the natural world, and on discussing the dichotomy of nature and culture. Throughout his discussion, Descola identifies four modes of interaction between humans and the natural world around them: animism, totemism, analogism and naturalism.

In his earlier essay "Constructing Natures: Symbolic Ecology and Social Practices" (1996), Descola reclaimed the notion of "animism", which he refers to as a system which "endows natural beings with human dispositions and social attributes".[89] Conversely, he understands totemic systems as those where "the differential relations between natural species confer a conceptual order on society".[90] According to these definitions, animic systems "use the elementary categories structuring social life to organize, in conceptual terms, the relations between human beings and natural species".[91] Descola further explains that while in "totemic systems non-humans are treated as signs, in animic systems they are treated as the term of a relation".[92] Naturalism is the third detected mode and it represents the typical Western worldview, based on an ontological duality of nature and culture. Nature is seen as the domain of necessity, while culture is the realm of spontaneity and freedom.[93]

The essay *Beyond Nature and Culture* (2013),[94] based on his major book that carries the same title (2005,) offers an updated and concise discussion on the previous three modes, with the addition of a fourth one: analogism. In this paper, Descola defines animism as "continuity of souls and discontinuity of bodies", which is found to be a common feature "in South and North America, in Siberia and in some parts of Southeast Asia where people endow plants, animals and other elements of their physical environment with a subjectivity

85 Bird-David 1999, 73.
86 Bird-David 1999, 73.
87 Bird-David 1999, 77–78.
88 Bird-David 1999, 77–78.
89 Descola 1996, 82–102.
90 Descola 1996, 87–88.
91 Descola 1996, 87–88.
92 Descola 1996, 87–88.
93 Descola 1996, 88. See also Viveiros de Castro 1998, 310.
94 Descola 2013a, 77–100.

and establish with these entities all sorts of personal relations, whether of friendship, exchange, seduction, or hostility".[95] Descola continues, arguing that "in these animic systems, humans and most non-humans are conceived as having the same type of interiority, and it is because of this common subjectivity that animals and spirits are said to possess social characteristics: they live in villages, abide by kinship rules and ethical codes, engage in ritual activity and barter goods". Thus, human and non-human persons share "a 'cultural' view" of life, and accordingly, even their physical differences have to be seen as behavioral and not substantial.[96]

The second type of identification is totemism, "where some beings in the world share sets of physical and moral attributes that seem to cut across the boundaries of species",[97] whose best example is constituted by Aboriginal Australia. In the Australian Aboriginal understanding of the world, "the main totem of a group of humans, most often an animal or a plant, and all the human and non-human beings that are affiliated to it, are said to share certain general attributes of physical conformation, substance, temperament and behavior by virtue of a common origin emplaced in the land".[98]

Naturalism "is predicated upon a discontinuity of interiorities and a material continuity" and "corresponds to the prevalent ontology of modernity".[99] Naturalism refers to the idea that nature exists in opposition to culture, and to the notion that "what distinguishes humans from non-humans is the mind, the soul, subjectivity, a moral conscience, language and so forth".[100] The naturalistic identification is the essence of the modern Western world, based on Cartesian dualism, which represents the main opposite to the animist worldviews.

Finally, analogism refers to "the idea that all the entities in the world are fragmented into a multiplicity of essences, forms and substances separated by minute intervals, often ordered along a graded scale, such as in the Great Chain of Being that served as the main cosmological model during the Middle Ages and the Renaissance".[101] This fourth mode of identification is a feature commonly found in China, Asia, West Africa, Mesoamerica and the Andes.[102] What is peculiar to analogism is the "recombination of the initial contrasts into a dense network of analogies linking the intrinsic properties of each autonomous entity in the world".[103] In such systems any resemblance between entities constitutes a method of deduction and explanation of the happenings of life, especially in the prevention and treatment of illness and adversity.[104]

It should be emphasized that these four modes of identification are not mutually exclusive and can be organically present within a single society, or "each human may

95 Descola 2013a, 79.
96 Descola 2013a, 79–80.
97 Descola 2013a, 82.
98 Descola 2013a, 82.
99 Descola 2013a, 84.
100 Descola 2013a, 84.
101 Descola 2013a, 83.
102 Descola 2013a, 84.
103 Descola 2013a, 83.
104 Descola 2013a, 83.

activate any of them according to circumstances".[105] Still, each one of them is dominant in a specific community, representing the leading framework through which reality is perceived and interpreted.[106] These four modes –and the combination of them– shall be considered also in the ancient Near East, because they represent good "food for thought" about the different ways humans relate to their surrounding world.

Entangled with the discussion about nature and culture is also the notion of natural/supernatural and immanence/transcendence. In his book *Beyond Nature* (2005), Descola cites Durkheim's insights about the supernatural:

> In order to call certain phenomena supernatural, one must already have a sense that there is a natural order of things, in other words that the phenomena of the universe are connected to one another according to certain necessary relationships called laws. Once this principle is established, anything that violates these laws necessarily appears to be beyond nature, and so beyond reason.[107]

Supporting Durkheim's argument, Descola stresses the fact that such a principle rose in a later phase of human history, which took shape with the progressive development of the positive sciences and with the full emergence of naturalism as the main mode of human-environmental relationship. Consequently, "the supernatural is an invention of naturalism, which casts a complacent glance at its mythical genesis, a sort of imaginary receptacle onto which once can dump all the excessive significations produced by minds said to be attentive to the regularities of the physical world but, without the help of exact sciences, not yet capable of forming an accurate idea of them".[108] Specifically dealing with the invisible inhabitants of the world according to several human cultures, Descola delves into the different ontologies of the 'incarnates' (i.e. spirits, deities and antecedents) in his article "Presence, Attachment, Origin: Ontologies of "Incarnates"" (2013b), where, talking about deities, he argues that deities are

> . . . generally firmly attached to places, where they are the object of genuine cults. They dwell in caves, in lakes, in springs, in mountains, in rocks, as well as in the various sorts of shrines that humans build for their accommodation. There they receive offerings and sacrifices; there prayers are addressed to them at particular times and it is expected of them that they will fulfill in exchange the wishes of their worshippers in the domain of expertise recognized as theirs. Although they are in no way transcendent to human existence, deities are thus less immanent than spirits: besides being located in a specific site –sometimes even embodied in an object (a stone, a piece of wood, a statue)– they are affiliated to a segment of the collective from which are eventually issued the ritual experts entrusted with their celebration, and specialized fields of intervention are assigned to them.[109]

105 Descola 2013a, 85.
106 Descola 2013a, 85.
107 Descola 2005, 82, note 45.
108 Descola 2005, 82, note 45. See also in Rochberg 2016, 162.
109 Descola 2013b, 41.

These insights about deities, with the discussion about the dichotomies natural/supernatural and immanent/transcendent, are particularly relevant to the discussion about the ancient Near Eastern polytheism, and, thus, represent fertile conceptual and theoretical tools in order to call into question the notions of divinity and nature in the ancient cuneiform cultures.

1.2.4 Viveiros de Castro and Amerindian perspectivism

Eduardo Viveiros de Castro adds to the discourse on animism the concepts of perspectivism and of multinaturalism, based on his study of the Amazonian community of the Araweté.[110] In his essay "Cosmological Deixis and Amerindian Perspectivism" (1996),[111] Viveiros de Castro presents Amerindian perspectivism, assessing it with respect to the literature on totemism, animism and myth.

His definition of perspectivism finds its roots in the Amerindian conception "according to which the world is inhabited by different sorts of subjects or persons, human and non-human, which apprehend reality from distinct points of view". [112] He argues that

> Typically, in normal conditions, humans see humans as humans, animals as animals and spirits (if they see them) as spirits; however animals (predators) and spirits see humans as animals (as prey) to the same extent that animals (as prey) see human as spirits or as animals (predators). By the same token, animals and spirits see themselves as humans: they perceive themselves as (or become) anthropomorphic beings when they are in their own houses or villages and they experience their own habits and characteristics in the form of culture.[113]

This idea of personhood is possible because of the notion that "the manifest form of each species is a mere envelope (a 'clothing') which conceals an internal human form, usually only visible to the eyes of the particular species or to certain trans-specific beings such as shamans".[114] Thus, animals and spirits are persons, because they possess a "soul or spirit" and share with humans the "capacities of conscious intentionality and agency which define the position of the subject", which enable them to have a point of view.[115]

The fact that animals and spirits see themselves as persons derives from the original state of non-differentiation between humans and animals, described in mythology. Myths and tales from the American continent are "filled with beings whose form, name and behavior inextricably mix human and animal attributes in a common context of intercommunicability".[116] In this respect, it should be pointed out that "the original

110 Viveiros de Castro 1992.
111 Viveiros de Castro 1998.
112 Viveiros de Castro 1998, 307.
113 Viveiros de Castro 1998, 308.
114 Viveiros de Castro 1998, 308.
115 Viveiros de Castro 1998, 314.
116 Viveiros de Castro 1998, 309.

common condition of both humans and animals is not animality but rather humanity", and, accordingly, "animals are ex-humans, not humans are ex-animals".[117]

This idea of perspectivism recalls Descola's concept of animism, which Viveiros de Castro refers to as "an ontology which postulates the social character of relations between humans and non-humans: the space between nature and society is itself social".[118] Descola's animism argues for a "continuity of souls and discontinuity of bodies",[119] which explains Amazonian perspectivism. Interestingly, in the Amazonian view a dichotomy between nature and culture exists, but it is culture and the soul that are the unifying elements, whereas physicality represents diversity. This notion leads to the concept of multinaturalism, which opposes Western multiculturalism.

Accordingly, the point of view is located in the body. The body is described as "a bundle of affects and capacities", the "origin of perspectives" and as the main locus for the creation of identity.[120] The body represents the place of "confrontation between humanity and animality": since the spiritual essence is the same and is not affected by changes, bodies are, instead, subjected to changes and metamorphosis.[121] Viveiros de Castro continues his argumentation stating that it is in "somatic perspectivism" that the Amerindian distinction of nature/culture lies, but also that this dichotomy is consequently dissolved into the "common animic human-animal sociality".[122]

The place where Amerindian perspectivism vanishes is myth. As already noted, in myth "every species of being appears to others as it appears to itself (as human), while acting as if already showing its distinctive and definitive nature (as animal, plant or spirit)".[123] In the mythical realm bodies, souls and names are intertwined, and the distinction between subjects and objects dissolves.

1.2.5 Harvey and the new animism

The scholar who has most contributed to the systematic reassessment of animism, with the plurality of its features, and who is considered to have launched the school of new animism is Graham Harvey. In his book *Animism. Respecting the Living World* (2006), Harvey focuses on the new animism, and offers a detailed panorama of the different aspects and issues that constitute animism in the contemporary world. After a preliminary survey on the history of the term, he presents some animist approaches to the world. The exemplary cases of Ojibwa grammar, myths and tales, Maori art and architecture, the land as conceived by the Australian Aborigines, and Neo-Pagan eco-activism, are all evidence for the different ways in which people and communities can be animist. His book continues focusing on the plethora of phenomena, beliefs and practices that are involved in animism: personhood,

117 Viveiros de Castro 1998, 309. This is a shared feature of many Indigenous American cosmologies and mythologies.
118 Viveiros de Castro 1998, 311.
119 See above on Descola, § 1.2.3.
120 Viveiros de Castro 1998, 316–317.
121 Viveiros de Castro 1998, 318.
122 Viveiros de Castro 1998, 318.
123 Viveiros de Castro 1998, 321.

ancestors and spirits, shamanism, totemism, ethics and elders, and environmentalism. The final part presents suggestions of what animism can offer to the contemporary world regarding ways to relate to and respect the Earth.

Pertinent to this study are Harvey's definitions and insights on animism, on personhood and on environmentalism. Harvey is the first scholar to argue explicitly that two types of animism exist, or, as he puts it, that "the word 'animism' is used in two ways".[124] The old usage of this term

> … refers to a putative concern with knowing what is alive and what makes a being alive. It alleges a belief in spirits or "non-empirical beings", and/or a confusion about life and death among some indigenous people, young children and all religious people. Sometimes it is party to the assertion of a confusion between persons and objects, or between humans and other-than-human beings. It may also be part of a theory about the origins of religions and/or the nature of religion itself.[125]

This metaphysical animism refers to the Tylorian notion with all its implications within the Western worldviews based on the Cartesian dichotomy, which considers "the myriad of multiplicity evident everywhere (internally, externally, physically, mentally, naturally, culturally, microscopically, macroscopically) to be problematic".[126]

Conversely, the new animism is relational and focuses on the celebration of plurality and multiplicity,[127] and on "knowing how to behave appropriately towards persons, not all of whom are human".[128] This new usage of the term refers to the understanding that "humans share this world with a wide range of persons, only some of whom are human".[129] Any phenomenon included in the new animism is diverse and unsystematic, and it can be seen in particular complexes of worldviews and communities or as elements within larger tradition, i.e. "not only are there animist cultures, but there are also cultures within which it is possible to act occasionally as an animist".[130] Hence, Harvey argues that animism comprises all those "theories, discourses and practices of relationship, of living well, of realizing more fully what it means to be a person, and a human person, in the company of other persons, not all of whom are human but all of whom are worthy of respect".[131]

At the heart of the matter lies the understanding of what a person is. Harvey embraces Hallowell's concept of "other-than-human" person and defines persons as any relational being, with whom you can "interact with varying degrees of reciprocity".[132] Thus, "persons may be spoken with. Objects, by contrast, are usually spoken about. Persons are volitional, relational, cultural and social beings. They demonstrate intentionality and agency with

---

124 Harvey 2006, xi.
125 Harvey 2006, xi
126 Harvey 2006, xiv.
127 Harvey 2006, xiv.
128 Harvey 2006, xii.
129 Harvey 2006, xii.
130 Harvey 2006, xv.
131 Harvey 2006, xvii.
132 Harvey 2006, xvii.

varying degrees of autonomy and freedom".[133] Accordingly, the prerogative to be or become an animist is to learn "how to recognize persons and, far more important, how to engage with them"[134] through respect and reciprocity.

Harvey points out that "Hallowell's term 'other-than-human person' celebrates two facts but does not confuse them: 1) it arises from animist engagement with a world that is full of persons, only some of whom are human; 2) while acknowledging that humans' most intimate relationships occur with other humans".[135] Notable, in the animistic discourse the "terms 'person' and 'other-than-human person' are not intended to replace words like 'spirit' or 'deity'". Personhood is, in fact, the essential feature, also when referring to the existence of deities or other discarnate persons.[136]

Especially relevant to this research are Harvey's remarks on plants, natural phenomena and places, all of which are considered "persons" in several contexts. Harvey explains that some "animists do 'speak with' and 'listen to' plants in what is both a respectful communing and a dialogue about information".[137] Not only communication, but also exchanges of gifts as an essential sign of respect and gratitude: while taking some part of the tree (e.g. leaf, sap, firewood, flower), other gifts are presented to the plant-person (e.g. a strand of wool, a drop of blood, tobacco, coffee, beer).[138] These behaviors represent the foundations for the established relationship.[139] Harvey continues, arguing that

> … plants are engaged with as powerful persons, some of whom, like animals, give their lives or part of themselves for the benefit of other persons (not only humans). Some, like tobacco, aid the rather feeble attempts of humans to communicate with the wider community of life, and especially with more powerful persons, by carrying prayers and invocations upwards and outwards.[140]

According to the animist notion of personhood, "all beings communicate intentionally and act toward each other relationally".[141] Thus, the concept of "other-than-human" person refers to the animate beings with whom humans share the world: being a "person" is "not defined by putatively human characteristics or behaviors. The term is a much larger umbrella than 'human'".[142]

Animists consider as relational persons not only plants, but also "particular places, waters, air, minerals, spaces, horizons, climates, seasons and weathers".[143] Places, in particular, "mould the diverse specificities that together are the community of life. Material, intellectual and spiritual cultures are rooted in all that surrounds and enfolds them. The

133 Harvey 2006, xvii.
134 Harvey 2006, xvii.
135 Harvey 2006, xviii. This argument leads to further considerations on anthropomorphism.
136 Harvey 2006, xviii. See also Descola 2013b.
137 Harvey 2006, 104
138 Harvey 2006, 105.
139 Harvey 2006, 105.
140 Harvey 2006, 105.
141 Harvey 2013b, 125.
142 Harvey 2013b, 125.
143 See Harvey 2006, 106–109.

ancestors dwell within the land".[144] The animistic worldview recalls the fact that humans live in environments as relating members of ecosystems. Moreover, it stresses the understanding of particular places as "persons, individuals, agents, active and relational beings, participants in the wider ecology of life" and not as mere environments.[145]

Consequently, the animist universe is permeated and inhabited by a multitude of persons, forces, spirits and deities, which are all interconnected and interrelated in a "heterarchy of related beings".[146] Such an ontology and epistemology implies the understanding and perception of a "pervasively relational cosmos".[147] All these notions call into question and dissolve categories such as nature, culture, and the supernatural.[148]

Together with personhood, the notion of totemism is also involved in the current discourse of the new animism. The word totem derives from the Ojibwa language, referring to clans that include humans, animals and plants. In his book *Food, Sex and Strangers* (2013b), Harvey points out that totemism "has been used by academics in theorizing about how people imagine and relate to (other) animals".[149] Harvey takes as a premise the observation of Knight, who describes totemism as "embedded in animism as an aspect of sociality".[150] Accordingly, for Harvey, totemism should be seen as "a more immediate and intimate mode of relating than the all-embracing relationality indicated by 'animism'. It does not refer, principally, to animals or plants but to associations or social assemblages of persons of different species who are treated as more intimate kin groups within the larger animate world. Animals and plants, in this context, are good as relatives".[151]

The new animism, with its consideration of personhood and of a relational world, radically challenges the dominant point of view of Western modernity.[152] Simultaneously, it offers an alternative to it. This alternative, according to Harvey, is "not an exercise in 'primitivism' because animism is far from primitive, nor is it about pre-modernity because animism does not serve as a precursor to modernity. Rather, animism is one of the many vitally present and contemporary other-than-modern ways of being human".[153]

Harvey gathers the plurality of souls of animism in the volume *The Handbook of Contemporary Animism* (2013a), which stands for its most comprehensive and updated discussion. Here animism is defined as "a label for a range of phenomena", but it is possible to distinguish two main, but different meanings: a metaphysical and a relational one. The metaphysical aspect refers to those religious practices, beliefs or experiences that involve encounters with tree-spirits, river-spirits or ancestor-spirits. "In such cases, the term resonates with its etymological predecessor, *anima*, to suggest some enlivening aspects

144 Harvey 2006, 109.
145 Harvey 2006, 109.
146 Hall 2011, 107.
147 Harvey 2013b, 102; Hall 2011, 105.
148 Harvey 2006, 185–186.
149 Harvey 2013b, 127. Harvey offers a short survey of the different utilizations of the concept of totem among the main scholars of classical anthropology: as magical source of sustenance and protection (Frazer 1910); as a food-selection methodology (Malinowski 1948); and as "good to think" (Lévi-Stauss 1969). See also Descola, § 1.2.3.
150 Knight 1996, 550 (quoted in Harvey 2013b, 127).
151 Harvey 2013b, 127.
152 Harvey 2006, xviii.
153 Harvey 2006, xxi.

(soul or spirit) within a person".[154] Alternatively, animism "can direct attention towards the continuous interrelation of all beings or of matter itself".[155] This aspect of animism stands for the effort "to re-imagine and redirect human participation in the larger-than-human, multi species community". In this sense, it is "relational, embodied, eco-activist and often naturalist rather than metaphysical".[156] Thus, animism describes performative acts in which people engage with other species or with material things. Possession, shamanism, trance and ecstatic practices, rituals engaging natural elements, animals and things, are all components of what can be labeled as animism.[157]

2 The state of research into Mesopotamian religion

The Mesopotamian cosmos is hierarchically structured, constituted by the great gods, minor deities, demons, *Mischwesen* and other entities organized in a pantheon. According to this framework, the divine realm is separated from humans, who try to approach gods and holiness through the cult. However, despite this predominant understanding of Mesopotamian divinity and polytheism, the evidence from Mesopotamian rituals, incantations, hymns, prayers, and myths, suggests much more differentiated and nuanced ideas on the concepts of divinity, personhood and nature. The following paragraphs present a short overview of how scholars have considered these concepts in Assyriological studies, especially focusing on non-anthropomorphic deities and natural elements.

2.1 Bottéro and the predominant view of an anthropomorphic divine

In his book *Religion in Ancient Mesopotamia* (2001), Jean Bottéro asserts that Mesopotamian religion was "resolutely polytheistic and anthropomorphist from the beginning".[158] In his understanding of Mesopotamian religion, gods were believed to be responsible "for certain natural phenomena and for certain human concepts", creating a "parallel universe of supernatural personalities whose names reflected their roles".[159] Despite the fact that his statements could imply a non-anthropomorphic notion of the divine alongside the anthropomorphic one, Bottéro dismissed this possibility, concluding that "the gods' image was basically anthropomorphic".[160] Referring to the non-anthropomorphic elements widely attested in the literature, he argued that heavenly bodies "were often more or less identified with the divinities who represented and ruled over them", nevertheless, "a true divination of the stars, making them equal to the gods, never seems to have been formally recognized". [161] Similarly, he suggests, "palpable realities superior to humans",

154 Harvey 2013a, 1–6.
155 Harvey 2013a, 6.
156 Harvey 2013a, 2
157 Harvey 2013a, 6.
158 Bottéro 2001, 44 (quoted in Porter 2009, 154).
159 Bottéro 2001, 44 (quoted in Porter 2009, 2).
160 Bottéro 2001, 64 (quoted in Porter 2009, 3 and 154).
161 Bottéro 2001, 63 (quoted in Porter 2009, 3).

such as mountains and bodies of water, were "endowed with a supernatural character" but remained "inferior to the gods themselves".[162] Even demons, whose divine character is often affirmed by the determinative used in cuneiform writing for divine beings, are to be regarded as "superior to humans and inferior to the gods" in Bottéro's understanding of Mesopotamian religion.[163] His assumptions preclude any possibility of challenging Western categories and/or of shedding light onto the emic ways in which the ancient Mesopotamians engaged with and conceptualized their natural surroundings.

2.2 Jacobsen and the concepts of immanence and intransitiveness

The first scholar to mention some concepts closely connected to animism within Mesopotamian religion was Thorkild Jacobsen. Despite the fact that he does not refer directly to the term animism or animistic in his writings, some phrases from his books seem to lead to this religious framework. In *The Intellectual Adventure of Ancient Man* (1946), he stated that

> Any phenomenon which the Mesopotamian met in the world around him was alive, had its own personality and will, its distinct self. But the self which revealed itself, for examples, in a particular lump of flint, was not limited by the particular lump, it was in it and yet behind it; it permeated it and gave it character as it did all lumps of flint. And as one such "self" could permeate many individual phenomena, so it might also permeate other selves and thereby give to them of its specific character to add to the qualities which they had in their own right.[164]

Later, in his influential book on Mesopotamian religion, *The Treasures of Darkness* (1976), Jacobsen introduced two interesting religious definitions: *immanence* and *intransitiveness*. By *immanence* he meant the attitude toward the religious experience as immanent rather than transcendent, while he understood *intransitiveness* as the phenomenon deriving from it. According to him, "the ancient Mesopotamian, it would seem, saw numinous power as a revelation of indwelling spirit, as power at the center of something that caused it to be and thrive and flourish".[165] *Intransitiveness* is defined as "the tendency to see numinous power as immanent" which "led the ancient Mesopotamian to name that power and attribute form to it in terms of the phenomenon, so it also determined and narrowed his ideas of that power's function".[166] This phenomenon stands against what he describes as the transitive, theistic approach, which is a predominant feature of Mesopotamian religion: "it is characteristic for all older figures and strata in the Mesopotamian pantheon and contrasts strikingly with the younger 'transitive' ruler gods,

162 Bottéro 2001, 63 (quoted in Porter 2009, 3).
163 Bottéro 2001, 63 (quoted in Porter 2009, 3).
164 Jacobsen 1946, 134.
165 Jacobsen 1976, 5-6.
166 Jacobsen 1976, 9.

who, though they too may be the power in a specific phenomenon, have interests, activity, and will beyond it".[167]

Jacobsen considers these "situationally determined, nonhuman, forms" as "survivals into a later stage", [168] and concludes that the alternative offered by the human form won them over at a very early time, so that "with the beginning of the third millennium, from Early Dynastic onward, the human form came to dominate almost completely, leaving to the older forms the somewhat ambiguous role of divine 'emblems' only".[169] Jacobsen's intellectual framework still relates to and partakes of the evolutionistic scheme of Tylorian memory, which aims at finding a chronological order from the most primitive to the most sophisticated (i.e. scientific and rational) for any apparently incongruous or unexplainable feature in a religious tradition.

2.3 Lambert and the non-anthropomorphic gods

Lambert, while arguing for "the prevailing anthropomorphic conception" of the gods in Mesopotamia,[170] acknowledges a larger role in Mesopotamian religion to non-anthropomorphic entities than previous scholars did. In his article "Ancient Mesopotamian Gods: Superstition, Philosophy, Theology",[171] he states that

> The official pantheon of Sumer and Babylon is easily seen as the outcome of reflection on the universe: these ancients were surrounded by forces of nature, real or imagined, which they identified as persons of superhuman power. There was always some ambiguity about the precise relationship of the deity to the aspect of nature, whether, for example, the sun god was in very fact the actual fiery ball moving across the sky, or whether he was not of human form, living in a palace and directing the actual solar body in its daily motions from a distance. Probably they were not so conscious of such problems as we are.[172]

According to Lambert, ancient Mesopotamians represented cosmic functions and processes through deities in the panthea: every aspect of the universe –such as storms, cereals, cattle and human crafts– had at least one patron deity.[173] Each deity was embodied in the cultic statue, which inhabited the temple and generally had an anthropomorphic form. The statue was indeed "conceived as a less than permanent abode of the divine essence", which had however to be activated and vivified every day by specific rites (e.g. the ritual *Mīs pî*).[174]

---

167 Jacobsen 1976, 9–10.
168 Jacobsen 1976, 9.
169 Jacobsen 1976, 9.
170 Lambert 1957, 544b.
171 Lambert 1990, 115–130.
172 Lambert 1990, 119–120.
173 Lambert 1990, 119–120.
174 Lambert 1990, 122–123.

Despite Lambert's assumption of the anthropomorphic representation of the gods, he continues taking into account the evidence for "forms of religion which seem to be survivals from a period before the extreme systematization which characterizes Sumerian and Babylonian religion".[175] This material is attested in two genres of textual sources: incantations and personal names.[176] In these sources, canals, temples, cities, winds, rivers, and mountains are all referred to as personal agents, often with divine features. This evidence indicates that "the concept of the gods as aspects of nature extends whereas it does not in the official Sumero-Babylonian religion".[177] Moreover, these elements point out that "the distinction we make between phenomena of nature, such as rivers, and human products, such as canals, was not part of their thinking".[178]

In his survey of non-anthropomorphic divine beings, Lambert dedicates more attention to three specific categories: rivers, mountains and temples. He points out that cults dedicated to the rivers (Tigris, Euphrates and Baliḫ) are evidenced in northern Mesopotamia in particular (i.e at Ebla and Mari). Moreover, rivers occur as theophorous elements in personal names, and in Lambert's view this data would suggest "that rivers were gods in prehistoric times, but gradually ceased to be in historical periods".[179] As for the case of mountains, Lambert argues that the god Aššur originated from the numinous hill carrying the same name, which subsequently became the state god.[180] In contrast, other mountains (i.e. Nimuš, Ebiḫ and Dipar) are attested as gods in personal names during the second millennium.[181]

Lambert continues his survey considering the evidence that temples, cities and objects were regarded as gods. He noted that most attestations are from southern Mesopotamia and are mainly recorded in the hymns. According to Lambert, this conception of divinity ascribed to architectural elements and man-made products stems from their contact with the deity. The god's aura would reach objects (e.g. swords, thrones), the temple and the city in which the god, in his earthly body in the temple, was dwelling, causing the man-made objects to share his divinity and to become recipients of offerings.[182]

The last category of divine creatures considered by Lambert is that comprising entities which are usually regarded as inferior to the gods but still part of the divine world: the *Mischwesen*. These beings are hybrid and composite creatures which were "involved with the major gods of the pantheon by having been defeated in time past. Others are servants of major gods, while some were respectable gods in their own right, but little worshipped for one reason or another".[183] He continues by stating that "all creatures of this kind were gods by the ancient Mesopotamian use of words".[184] In his concluding remarks, Lambert suggested that

175 Lambert 1990, 125.
176 Lambert 1990, 125.
177 Lambert 1990, 126.
178 Lambert 1990, 127.
179 Lambert 1990, 127.
180 Lambert 1990, 127. See also Lambert 1983, 84 and Chapter III, § 3.6.
181 Lambert 1990, 127–128. See Chapter III.
182 Lambert 1990, 129.
183 Lambert 1990, 129.
184 Lambert 1990, 129. See further, § 2.5.

> The basis for the Sumero-Babylonian pantheon was the deification of parts and aspects of nature as then perceived and understood. This raw material of a pantheon was then subjected to organization by the theologians, who wanted to spread the cults around the Sumerian towns so that each major deity was city patron elsewhere. These deities were also conceived as having personality of a very human kind, and over the millennia their relative statuses became a matter of great importance in ancient religion, usually due to the political power of their supporters. Gods not taken into this system, but aspects of nature and other categories, such as what would be called "demons" in some religions, also existed, and these were worked into the fringes of the official pantheon.[185]

This observation about the different levels of theological discourses –i.e. the scholarly and the popular– and the subsequent implication of the existence of a divinity which did not belong to the predominant system, is further elaborated by Lambert in "Gott: B. Nach Akkadischen Texten".[186] Here he argues that while uneducated ordinary people believed that the sun and the moon were actual gods, the scholars and the member of the élite, for whom the official theology was conceived, saw in the astral entities a mere manifestation of the anthropomorphic god.[187]

2.4 Wiggermann, van Binsbergen and the "embedded holistic elements"

A much-debated article about Mesopotamian magic is "Magic in History. A theoretical perspective, and its application to ancient Mesopotamia" (1999), where van Binsbergen and Wiggermann introduce the concept of holism in Mesopotamian magic.[188] Their discussion does not stop with magic, but covers different fields of Mesopotamian religious life, i.e. religious concepts, mythology, rituals. After defining magic as a way to control the world, two main domains of control are detected: one hegemonic and one domestic. While the hegemonic domain stands for the large-scale political institutions and is predominantly theistic, the domestic domain refers to the realm of production and processing of raw materials, of biological and cultural reproduction. According to the two scholars, this domain is very resistant to political and economic power, and has thus been "one of the main contexts in which the old holistic world-view and a variety of non-hegemonic cults have been preserved".[189]

185 Lambert 1990, 120–130.

186 Lambert 1957, 544b.

187 "Many deities seem to have been personifications of natural forces or aspects of the universe, whether real or mythical. The sun and moon, for example, were deified. However, the prevailing anthropomorphic conception created problems for intellectuals. The simple might be content to see the sun in the sky and to acknowledge it as Šamaš, but the theologians knew that Šamaš lived in the heavens in human form, like a king surrounded by family and court". Lambert, 1957, 544b. See also Porter 2009, 3.

188 van Binsbergen/Wiggermann 1999, 3–34.

189 van Binsbergen/Wiggermann 1999, 17.

Accordingly, the domestic domain should be regarded as the context, preponderantly feminine, of interpersonal care in the household, especially in times of hardship, illness, birth and death. Moreover, it has to be seen as the privileged locus of "magic, folklore and uncaptured 'paganism' throughout human history",[190] where supernatural beings –tutelary gods and ancestors– represent behavioral models for the elders of the community.[191] This domain features holistic and immanent characteristics which oppose the theistic and transcendental hegemonic framework. According to van Binsbergen and Wiggerman, "while the hegemonic idiom would emphasize distance, absolute difference and total submission between god and man, the domestic domain would tend toward far greater horizontality, complementarity if not interchangeability between man and nature, between body and consciousness, between person and object; such complementarity would stress the community between humans, but also between humans and the non-human aspects of nature".[192]

The two scholars point out that inside the scholarly collection of the Mesopotamian corpus, "elements can be detected that fit in only superficially, and implicitly challenge the hegemonic process that lends structure and direction to the royal and priestly extracting process governing Mesopotamian society. Viewed in isolation these embedded elements add up to a holistic world-view in which the boundaries between man and nature are far less strictly drawn than in the orthodox theistic repertoire".[193] In their understanding, magic should be defined as "a dislocated sediment of pre-hegemonic popular notions of control which have ended up in the hegemonic corpus".[194]

Examples of what the two scholars identify and describe as "holistic embedded elements" are the religious concepts of m e /*parṣu*, the Sumerian myths Anzû and *Lugale*, the system of divination, the animated *materia magica*, demons and witchcraft. These are all part of the evidence for "an empirical amoral world that precedes and underlies the cosmos structured in theistic terms, with its personal, moral, and transcendent leadership. It is through immanent concatenation of agency that man belongs to that world of the senses, and may interpret or re-direct it by using the powers that permeate it".[195]

2.5 Anthropomorphic and non-anthropomorphic deities in Mesopotamia

The most up-to-date work aiming at reassessing the emic concept of divinity in ancient Mesopotamia is the volume *What Is a God? Anthropomorphic and Non-Anthropomorphic Aspects of Deity in Ancient Mesopotamia* (Porter 2009). This book is the fruit of a symposium which aimed at assessing what was named "god", dingir/*ilu*, in the Mesopotamian textual and iconographical sources.[196] In addition to a methodological

190 van Binsbergen/Wiggermann 1999, 17.
191 van Binsbergen/Wiggermann 1999, 17.
192 van Binsbergen/Wiggermann 1999, 18.
193 van Binsbergen/Wiggermann 1999, 18.
194 van Binsbergen/Wiggermann 1999, 16.
195 van Binsbergen/Wiggermann 1999, 28. For a discussion and critique on the embedded holistic elements and its dichotomous implications see Chapter V, § 2.
196 Porter 2009.

introduction, the articles pertinent to my research are those by Ornan, Rochberg, and Porter. These contributions address the notions of anthropomorphic and non-anthropomorphic deities, projecting us into a much-required general reassessment of the notion of divinity through Mesopotamian eyes, and into notions which can dialogue with the contemporary studies of anthropology and history of religions.

Iconographical sources. In the article "In the Likeness of Man. Reflections on the Anthropocentric Perception of the Divine in Mesopotamian Art", Ornan explores the representations of gods in the iconographic sources, which are to be considered complementary to the textual evidence. Her discussion focuses on understanding the relationship between the anthropomorphic representation of the deities and all those non-anthropomorphic manifestations. The survey of reliefs, glyptics and statues reveals that "during the second half of the second millennium, and in the first half of the first, images of major gods and goddesses in human shape were outnumbered by non-anthropomorphic portrayals of deities".[197] Nevertheless, in her view, the Mesopotamian conception of the divine has to be seen as anthropocentric "since it centered on and was constructed after the human model in form and essence".[198] Ornan elaborates that the non-anthropomorphic representations of the divine represented various aspects "embedded in" and "related to" the image of the anthropomorphic god.[199] Accordingly, all those non-anthropomorphic agents –animals, hybrid creatures, natural phenomena, celestial bodies or inanimate objects– "relate to a personified deity in one way or another and thus are to be seen as emanating from this 'higher' personified divinity".[200]

Stars and heavenly bodies. Rochberg explores the various perspectives on gods and celestial bodies, and their composite relations to one another in "'The Stars their Likenesses': Perspectives on the Relation between Celestial Bodies and Gods in Ancient Mesopotamia". Pertinent to this discussion, Rochberg addresses the different concepts of divinity in celestial bodies: anthropomorphism, immanence, transcendence, symbolism and personality, which are all intertwined in the debate on animism and anthropology of religions.

Three perspectives are noticed: gods as celestial bodies, celestial bodies as manifestations of gods, and personifications of stars as gods. The first perspective focuses on the "astral nature of some deities" and understands the "divine to be visibly embodied by a plant or a star".[201] This is evident predominantly in mythical texts, where non-anthropomorphic and anthropomorphic features are mingled. As Rochberg explains, "the gods, being conceived of and imagined, not observed, may be differentiated from natural (perceptual) phenomena, yet the gods seem to have been viewed as immanent and active in the world of phenomena, as many instances of divine agency are preserved in Sumero-Akkadian mythology".[202]

197 Ornan 2009, 126. See also Ornan 2005.
198 Ornan 2009, 150.
199 Ornan 2009, 151.
200 Ornan 2009, 151.
201 Rochberg 2009, 46.
202 Rochberg 2009, 50.

The second perspective understands "celestial bodies as images of gods, i.e. as worldly objects that manifest divine agency and give perceptible form to certain deities". In this case, the principal sources for this evidence are omen texts and other astronomical treatments of stars, constellations and planets,[203] where celestial objects are to be considered emblems of the gods. This "idea that celestial bodies are visible indicators of the divine will derives from the principle of divination, i.e., that physical phenomena constitute signs (omens) that communicate divine will to humankind. As such, celestial objects, as in the case of all omens from natural signs, became physical mediators between human beings and gods".[204]

The third perspective focuses on personification and "on the divine nature of some of the heavenly bodies, e.g. on the sun as the sun-god, the moon as the moon-god, on Venus as Ištar, and on many other stars identified with other deities".[205] This perspective is adopted primarily in the prayers, although examples may be found in omen texts as well. In this genre, the key element is personification, "meaning that a celestial body is personified and so referred to as a god in anthropomorphic way".[206] The principal example of this perspective is offered in the Akkadian prayers to the "gods of the night" (*ilū mušīti*),[207], which invoke "the stars, constellations and planets to accept the speech of the supplicant, just as though the celestial objects were themselves divinities with the power to hear and act in response to human entreaty".[208] In this context, the heavenly bodies assume different shapes, most of them non-anthropomorphic, which are all personified "for the purpose of being asked to act upon various manipulations made by the diviner or magician".[209] Rochberg argues that the "essence of anthropomorphism" lies "more in the expectation of a response from them as gods".[210] Accordingly, the gods of the night are conceived of as divine persons: stars are recipients of offerings and invocations, because they are seen "as divine agents ready to hear the prayer and act favorably on behalf of human beings".[211] Moreover, "the invocations to personified celestial bodies suggest that in these instances the god and the celestial body are united in one divine nature".[212]

After this survey, Rochberg concludes her discussion by proposing a unification of these perspectives, which reflect the plurality of ways of understanding the divine in ancient Mesopotamia (i.e. anthropomorphic, non-anthropomorphic, transcendent, immanent, personification). Accordingly,

> … although the gods were sometimes described as being beyond the limits of perception, they were also thought capable of inhabiting the world, for example, in their temples or in ominous phenomena. Sîn, in this sense, was the moon and the

203 Rochberg 2009, 46–47.
204 Rochberg 2009, 65.
205 Rochberg 2009, 47.
206 Rochberg 2009, 47.
207 Rochberg 2009, 75. See also Reiner 1995.
208 Rochberg 2009, 76.
209 Rochberg 2009, 76.
210 Rochberg 2009, 76.
211 Rochberg 2009, 81.
212 Rochberg 2009, 81.

> moon-god. The transcendence of the god precludes any animistic interpretation of the divinity of the moon, yet the immanence of the god in the physical world mitigates any dualistic Platonic overtones. The moon cannot represent the totality of, but only a manifestation or image of, the god Sîn, who was conceived of as transcending the limits of the physical world, yet was manifested in lunar phenomena. Both notions, the transcendent and the immanent, were expressible.[213]

In this respect, Rochberg points to the inadequacy of the analytical categories used by modern scholars and stresses the necessity of identifying new modes of approaching Mesopotamian religion and culture.[214]

Mountains, rivers, crowns and drums. After stars and heavenly objects, the turn of natural elements and material objects arrives in Porter's article, "Blessings from a Crown, Offerings to a Drum: Were There Non-Anthropomorphic Deities in Ancient Mesopotamia?". Focusing on detecting non-anthropomorphic aspects of the anthropomorphic gods and non-anthropomorphic gods in the written sources, Porter surveys two major groups of non-anthropomorphic deities: natural elements and material objects.[215] Rivers, mountains and stones are examined along with boats, chariots, drums, harps, crowns and beds. All of them are considered living beings, acting in the world, and are identified as deities, implying a new outlook into Mesopotamian polytheism.

Porter starts her discussion pointing out that, despite the preponderant anthropomorphic vision of the divine supported by most scholars,

> … the ancient scribes' persistent use of the DINGIR determinative to label both the great gods and all the other entities suggests instead that the Mesopotamians themselves did not make such a distinction between gods envisioned in anthropomorphic form and gods envisioned as planets, demons, mountains or illnesses, instead including them all in the single category of DINGIR/*ilu*.[216]

The textual evidence is thus analyzed through an emic perspective, based on the three different ways gods were identified in the sources.[217] Porter notices that certain natural phenomena and material objects are: 1) either explicitly said to be DINGIRs or *ilu*s or to behave in ways characteristic of DINGIRs and *ilu*s; 2) labeled as gods by the determinative DINGIR, the cuneiform sign which is placed before the names referring to gods and

---

213 Rochberg 2009, 89.

214 "It may well be that our language of transcendence and immanence is inadequate to an analysis of Mesopotamian religion, not only because of unfortunate Christian theological overtones, but because the Mesopotamian conception of divinity seems to require greater differentiation than the simple duality of immanent vs. transcendent. Indeed it seems advisable to come away from such potentially misleading terminology to forge new analytic categories for the study of Mesopotamian religion. Meanwhile, however, I will reluctantly use these terms for convenience" (Rochberg 2009, 83, note 206). This argumentation is further explored and strongly affirmed in her newest book *Before Nature* (2016). See Chapter V.

215 For the variety of categories excluded from consideration in the article, see Porter 2009, 168, note 55.

216 Porter 2009, 159.

217 Porter 2009, 161.

divinities; 3) identified as DINGIRs by receiving treatment reserved for gods, i.e. being recipients of food offerings, which was "an honor and form of worship otherwise conferred only upon DINGIRs and *ilu*s typically represented in anthropomorphic form".[218] These three modes can occur simultaneously. After presenting the different entities considered deities in the texts, Porter suggests that

> The concept of deity in Mesopotamia was remarkably complex and varied. Not only did Mesopotamians in every period imagine DINGIRs in widely assorted forms, some anthropomorphic and some not, they also imagined even the DINGIRs in the non-anthropomorphic category as having a variety of different natures, functions and behavior as gods. To further complicate the picture, Mesopotamians in different cities or regions, and in different chronological periods clearly had different ideas about whether a particular non-anthropomorphic entity was a deity or not, and if it was, about its importance in comparison to other members of the pantheon.[219]

Porter argues that the anthropomorphic concept of divinity and the binary thinking that characterizes modern Western worldviews are "a preference that is not universally shared".[220] What emerges is a picture where Mesopotamian descriptions of some gods had "many forms or aspects" and this "suggests that the Mesopotamian model of god was not construed in binary terms", but "tended instead to envision a particular god as moving fluidly within a set of alternate forms".[221]

The evidence that non-anthropomorphic gods also received food offerings implies an understanding of these entities as "in some sense quite alive".[222] Indeed, "the elaborately ritualized presentation of food offerings even to gods that entirely lack personality suggests that all Mesopotamian gods were understood to be living beings endowed with awareness and feelings". Porter concludes that "the conviction of Mesopotamians that material objects such as thrones, harps and chariots could be living, cognizant divine beings may have its roots in a Mesopotamian understanding of the world in some ways fundamentally different from our own".[223]

Elaborating this statement, Porter refers explicitly to animism, by quoting Beatrice L. Goff. In her volume *Symbols of Prehistoric Mesopotamia* (1963), Goff proposes that prehistoric Mesopotamians "saw the world more than we do today as 'redundant with life'" and that in rituals they believed themselves to "handle living things".[224] Moreover, Goff argues that "everything was potentially charged with power, and recognizably potent objects were sought for every concern. […] The objects in antiquity were potent because

218 Porter 2009, 161.
219 Porter 2009, 187.
220 Porter 2009, 187–188. See also Saler 1993.
221 Porter 2009, 187–188.
222 Porter 2009, 188.
223 Porter 2009, 189.
224 Goff 1963, 169 (quoted in Porter 2009, 189).

they were animate",[225] thus presenting an "essentially animistic characterization of Mesopotamian ideas of the natural world".[226]

With a more nuanced assumption, Porter concludes that "the presentation of food offerings to certain selected material objects as well as to anthropomorphically conceived gods indicates that for Mesopotamians, objects were at least sometimes felt to be charged with life. By extension they were in some special circumstances recognized as living divinities".[227] Porter's evidence, methodology and anthropological insights constitute the main conceptual and methodological foundation for the present study from within the field of Assyriology.

225 Goff 1963, 169 (quoted in Porter 2009, 189).
226 Porter 2009, 189.
227 Porter 2009, 189.

Chapter II

Sacred Mountains and Mountain Deities

Is there a head for the upper *rma-rgyal* mountain?
If there is, is there any brain?
Is there a waist for the upper *rma-rgyal* mountain?
Is there a belly for the upper *rma-rgyal* mountain?
Is there is, are there any bowels?
(Old Tibetan song)

1 The mountain: an entangled sacred being in Mesopotamia and beyond

The relationship between humans and mountains is an ancient one, whose roots go deep into the mists of time. Mountains form innumerable prominent and majestic topographical entities, that have inhabited the Earth for millions of years, and which have shaped and marked the landscape with their encompassing physical presence of rocks, soil, snow, trees, grass, and animals. Together with rivers, deserts and seas, their inaccessible and impervious slopes have embodied the limits of human endeavors. With the multiplicity of their ecosystems and inhabitants (i.e. minerals, flora and fauna), they represent threatening and mysterious places.

Because of their rocky wombs extending into the bowels of the earth and their peaks reaching and mingling with the skies, mountains have represented a connector between worlds, assuming diverse and multifaceted meanings at each human encounter. The bodily, sensuous presence of rocks, valleys, slopes, forests, peaks, and watercourses has been perceived as imbued with a spiritual essence. Enshrouded by a mystical aura, mountains have been conceived of as repositories of wisdom and of memory. Thus, they have been approached with an attitude of reverential respect by many cultures. Mountains are also linked to spiritual elevation and immortality. For centuries, visionaries, ascetics, hermits, shamans and emperors have ascended sacred mountains, and some have made their solitary dwelling among their rocks and trees. Ascending to mountain peaks has also represented a spiritual journey, which would transform the human soul deeply through its getting closer or in touch with the divine and the mysterious.[1]

The names of Everest, Kilimanjaro, Fuji, Uluru, Aoraki, Machu Picchu, all evoke a sense of wonder and reverence, mixed with amazement at the width and depth of human engagement with mountains. In Asia, the traditions of China, Tibet, India and Korea each preserve rich repertoires of mythical and sacred mountains, and of mountain gods and goddesses. The five sacred mountains of ancient China were conceived of as being the cardinal points and pillars of the universe. These realms were guarded by monstrous beings, namely dragons and tigers, and their peaks were the temporary abode of the Immortals, not-fully divine persons who spent some centuries on the mountains pursuing the path of Tao. According to the Taoist view, these mountains are spiritual entities: climbing toward their peaks would have meant to aspire to grasping the mysterious essence of their spirit rather than the physical panorama beneath.[2]

In the heart of the Himalayan and Tibetan mountain ranges, the pre-Buddhist Tibetan religion considered mountain gods to be the most preeminent deities of their pantheon. Countless though they might be, each mountain was inhabited by a mountain god, whose anthropomorphic traits often mingled with a properly natural portrayal, and was often associated with an animal totem. Around each mountain deity a cornucopia of myths, legends, rites and sacrifices thrived.[3] Hindu and Buddhist cosmology places Mt. Meru as the *axis mundi* of the world, around whose five peaks the entirety of the universe, including the sun and the stars, revolves.[4]

Along the shores of the Mediterranean, until a few centuries ago, the Alps were considered to be inhabited by a crowded population of dragons. In Greece, Mt. Olympus was envisioned as the abode of the ancient Greek pantheon: on its peak, always enshrouded by dense clouds, the gods banqueted, immersed in secrecy. The volcanic Mt. Etna in Sicily was considered holy, home of the god Vulcan, the Latin god of fire and metals.

In the Near East, the religious traditions about mountains stretch for millennia. The mountainous landscapes of Anatolia and Iran have constituted the grounds for the development of several traditions concerning holy mountains and mountain gods. The most famous examples comprise Mt. Ararat, which is believed to be the mountain where Noah's ark ran ashore,[5] and Mt. Sinai, the place of the covenant for Judaism and where the monastery of Saint Catherine has stood since the early centuries of Christianity.

Mountains constitute a major topographical and geographical feature in the Near East and they represented a dialectic element with the flat urban setting where Mesopotamian civilizations flourished. The Mesopotamian core region consists of the alluvial plain between the rivers Tigris and Euphrates, and the watery environment of the Southern marshes alternates with the dry steppe far from the course of the rivers. Mountains are a crown that enfolds the Mesopotamian plain, from East through North to West, until the Mediterranean sea. From the East to the West, the main mountainous ranges of the ancient

1 Schama 1995, 411–423.
2 Schama 1995, 406–411.
3 Jisheng 2001, 343–363.
4 Eliade 1958, 375.
5 Book of Genesis 8:4.

Near East are the Zagros, the Taurus with its south-western extremity in the Amanus mountains, and the Lebanon mountain ranges. The Palmyrides mountains, which comprise Jebel Bishri, along with Jebel Abd el Aziz and Jebel Sinjar, are the arid mountains of Syria.

Throughout the millennia of Mesopotamian civilization, mountains have constituted a tangible border between the human and urban setting of the lowlands, and the wilderness. Thus, they have been obligatory gates to be crossed in order to connect to the world beyond. Enveloped in their mystery, they comprised a secret world inhabited by different forms of life and were thought of as partaking of the divine realm. Thanks to their distant but bulky presence, mountains have been a fertile ground for the flow of human imagination.

2 The mountain

In Mesopotamian literary and religious contexts, mountains play different roles. They have been perceived as cosmic and liminal entities, often threatening, considered equal or superior to the gods, and conceived of as pure places, the origin of essential materials for building, eating and healing, but also as threatening entities. Mountains represent a world inhabited by animals, plants, and rivers, along with their human and non-human dwellers. They comprise another type of reality, whose dwellers are not only the mountainous and nomadic peoples, but also different creatures (e.g. monsters, demons, witches), and gods. In some contexts, mountains recur portrayed with personalistic traits and connected with the divine sphere: they are considered cosmic and sacred entities strictly connected with the anthropomorphic deities, with an active role in the rituals, and fewer as deities *per se*.

The general term for mountain is k u r in Sumerian and *šadû* in Akkadian. The semantic use of the term k u r, generally used as a determinative for geographical places, comprises any reference to the land and the earth: it can be translated as "(single) mountain, mountain peak"; "land, country", "underworld", and even "east, east wind".[6] The Akkadian counterpart, *šadû*, is the word for "mountain, mountain region", "open country, steppe", and "east, east wind".[7] A further synonym is the Sumerian ḫ u r s a ĝ, "mountain, foothills; mountain range; steppe",[8] which corresponds to the Akkadian *ḫurš/sānu*.[9] The term *ḫuršānu*, frequently used in the plural, usually refers to the general, collective mountain and to mountain ranges. Interestingly, the same word refers also to the River Ordeal, or to the place of the ordeal.[10] Mountains are entangled with their arboreal populations, often being equated with their arboreal population. The main terms which refer to forest are *qištum*, "forest, grove",[11] *qīšum*, "thicket",[12] and *ḫalbum*, "forest, wood".[13]

6 Online Sumerian dictionary, ePSD; Horowitz 1998, 268–273; Attinger 2017.

7 CAD Š 49–61 (s.v. *šadû* A, B).

8 See the online Sumerian dictionary, ePSD. For the semantic distinction between k u r and ḫ u r s a ĝ see Steinkeller 2007, 223 ff.

9 CAD Ḫ, 253–254 s.v. *ḫuršānu* A and B.

10 CAD Ḫ, 254–255 s.v. *ḫuršānu* B. This probably refers to the fact that the River Ordeal was generally performed in the mountainous parts of the river, where the waters are precipitous. See also Chapter III, § 2.

11 CAD Q, 272–275, s.v. *qištu* A.

2.1 The cosmic mountain in mythical literature and iconography

The Mesopotamian cosmic mountain comprises several entangled and polyvalent meanings, in its being a cosmic entity, closely connected with the journey of the Sun across the sky and below the earth. It is also one of the main loci of pristine purity, and it was portrayed as the realm of otherness in the eyes of the flat Babylonian plain.

The cosmic mountain stands for an *axis mundi*, whose roots extend into the netherworld and whose peaks support the celestial vault.[14] Indeed, the Mesopotamian cosmic mountain represents the medium between cosmic and earthly dimensions, piercing the *šupuk šamê*, "the firmament", with its peaks, and reaching the *arallû,* "the netherworld". This cosmic representation of the mountain finds a parallel in the image of the cosmic tree or tree of life, which also stands as the medium between the earth and the sky.[15]

Several named mountains recur in the literature as cosmic mountains –such as Mt. Māšu, Mt. Ḫašur, Aratta and the Cedar Mountain.[16] Along with the named cosmic mountains of the eastern horizon,[17] an unnamed mythical place, source of all things, exists. This pristine place is Dukug, the Sacred Mound, which is the primeval location of the creation, original place of the gods and their dwelling, but also where sheep and grain were created, thus being the original place of civilization in the Sumerian tradition.[18] In some contexts, Dukug is identified with the cosmic Mountain of the Sunrise, being considered the "mountain of springs" and the place where fates are determined.[19] Contextually with the establishment of destinies, Dukug corresponds to the Mountain of Sunrise. The best evidence for this is to be found in the ritual *Bīt Rimki*:[20] "Šamaš, when you emerge from the great mountain, when you emerge from the great mountain, the mountain of springs, when you emerge from the Sacred Mound, where destinies are decreed".[21] In this purification ritual, the synergic relations between the Sun-god, the mountain and the holy mound, are all expressed and further bound with the establishing of fates. As we will see throughout the book, Sun, Mountain and River are deeply connected with the mythical place where destinies are fixed at every daybreak on the eastern horizon, as much as with the juridical roles that all three entities assume in Mesopotamian incantations and rituals.[22] Moreover,

12 CAD Q, 280–281, s.v. *qīšu.*

13 CAD Ḫ, 40–41, s.v. *ḫalbu.*

14 Eliade 1958, 374–379; Verderame 2013, 7.

15 See further Chapter IV.

16 In this book, those names which refer to cosmic and divine entities will be considered as proper nouns, written starting with capital letters.

17 See below § 3 on the specifically named mountains.

18 *Debate between Grain and Sheep* 26–27 (ETCSL 5.3.2). See also Woods 2009, 204.

19 Woods 2009, 203–204. See also Polonsky 1999, 89–100; Polonsky 2006, 297–311.

20 The ritual *Bīt Rimki*, "House-of-Bathing", is a Neo-Assyrian and Neo-Babylonian ritual performed for the king in order to dispel any impurity and evil from his person (see Læssøe 1955).

21 *Bīt Rimki* III 1–3, é n U t u k u r - g a l - t a u m - t a - è - n a - z u - š è : *Šamaš ultu šadî rabî ina aṣêka* k u r - g a l k u r - i d i m - t a u m - t a - è - n a - z u - š è : *ištu šadî rabî šad naqbi ina aṣêka* D u $_6$ - k u g k i - n a m - t a r - t a r - r e - e - d è u m - t a - è - n a - z u - š è : *ištu Duku ašar šimātum iššimma ina aṣêka* (Borger 1969, 2–3: 1–3). See also Woods 2009, 203.

22 See Chapter III, § 2 and § 3. On the cosmological conceptions of the Eastern horizon see Woods 2009.

the evidence for Dukug as the "mountain of springs" (k u r i d i m , *šad nagbī*) might refer to this cosmic hill as *pī narāti*, the mythical place where the cosmic river emerges from the Apsû.[23] Interestingly, the urban counterpart of the Holy Mound is the temple, which was conceived as a microcosm of the cosmos, and where a cultic installation displaying Dukug was placed, presumably consisting of a raised platform on which fates were decreed during the ritual performance.[24]

The conception of the cosmic mountain comprises different and opposite meanings, that refer to the cyclical journey of the Sun from the East to the West over the earthly sky, and from West to East through the netherworld at night. Mountains were, in fact, considered gates to the netherworld, or the netherworld itself, in both horizons.[25] On the western horizon, the Dark Mountain or Mountain of Sunset was believed to be the netherworld itself. In Sumerian literature, Mount Udug-ḫul corresponds to the Dark Mountain (h u r - s a ĝ / k u r g i$_6$ - g a), which is regarded as the remote birthplace of seven demons.[26] In another incantation for dispelling demons, a mention of the "mountain of the setting of the Sun" (h u r - s a ĝ ^{d}U t u - š ú - a - š è : *ana šadî ereb Šamši*) is found, whereas in the Akkadian tradition, a named mountain of sunset is Mt. Buduḫudug, which is referred to as the "entrance of Šamaš to Aya" (*nēreb Šamaš ana Aya*).[27] Interestingly, in the same ritual text, the seven demons of the Dark Mountain are said to surface on the Bright Mountain (h u r - s a ĝ / k u r b a b b a r - r a), the Mountain of Sunrise.[28]

This merging of opposite meanings indicates the cyclical characterization and intrinsic duality of the mountain, which is found throughout the literature and is also displayed in the iconographical evidence.[29] The glyptic offers several visual representations of the cosmic Mountain of Sunrise and/or Sunset, that can correspond both to Mt. Māšu or to Mt. Ḫašur of the literature.[30] In seals from the 3rd and 2nd millennium, it is generally delineated by a mountain with two peaks, where the Sun god is standing, and it is often accompanied by the image of a coniferous tree, and/or of the gate-keeper gods opening the gates of heaven.[31] The so-called Adda seal, from the Akkadian period, constitutes one of the earliest visual representations of the cosmic mountain with its two peaks (Illustration 1).[32]

23 Woods 2009, 204, and in particular note 84. See Chapter III.

24 Woods 2009, 203.

25 For the Sumerian term k u r designating the netherworld see Steinkeller 2007, 231. See also Diakonoff's interpretation of the ancient Mesopotamian netherworld conceptualized as an inverted mountain (Diakonoff 1995, 116).

26 SAACT 5, IV 1–12 (see below § 2.2). See also Woods 2009, 187.

27 *Utukkū Lemnūtu* IV 61 (Geller 2007, 112: 61); *Lipšur Litanies* 4 (Reiner 1956, 132–133) // URA = *ḫubullu* XXII 5 (Bloch/Horowitz 2015, 76). See also Woods 2009, 187; George 2003, 863–864.

28 SAACT 5, XIII–XV 1–5 (see below § 2.2). See also Woods 2009, 187; George 2003, 863–864.

29 The most eloquent example of the intrinsic duality displayed by the cosmic mountain is Mt. Māšu, which is the mountain of the Twin Peaks attested in the glyptic. I agree with the interpretation of Woods, who understands it as being simultaneously the Western and Eastern Mountain, according to the common symbolic and religious phenomenon of the *coincidentia oppositorum*. See below in the present chapter § 3.5.

30 See below § 3.5.

31 Woods 2009, 190. See in particular Figs. 5–12 (Woods 2009, 228–231).

32 Tsoparopoulou 2014, 41; Roaf 1990, 77; Orthmann 1985, 236.

Illustration 1: Akkadian Adda-seal displaying deities on the cosmic mountain with its twin peaks.

In this composition, the cosmic mountain is rendered by the motif of drill holes typical of the mountainous representations in the ancient Near Eastern art, and by its two peaks, among which the Sun-god is rising, carrying a saw. On the top of one of the mountain peaks, Ištar stands with her weapons, while the Anzû-bird, offspring of the mountains, is flying over the other peak. The water god Ea, stands on the slope of the mountain, and is depicted with two streams of water flowing from his shoulders, which is one of the most typical representation of the River gods and of water deities in the 2nd millennium.[33] Behind Ea, his vizier Usmu, with his typical Janus-head depiction, stands in a greeting posture.[34] A stylized tree, more resembling a bush, grows on the left peak of the cosmic mountain. On the left of the scene a warrior god (perhaps Ninurta) is depicted accompanied by a lion. This composition offers the most inclusive portrayal of the mountain motif, which is here represented together with all the natural elements, deities and *Mischwesesen*, that are connected with this cosmic entity in mythical and ritual contexts. A later representation of the Twin Mountains is found in a lapis lazuli Kassite cylinder seal, which bears the name of the Kassite King Burna-buriaš II and was found in a hoard at Thebes in Greece (Illustration 2).[35] The portrayed scene depicts two high mountains, where trees stand both at the bottom and on the top of the mount. A huge half-anthropomorphic figure (either interpreted as a divine entity connected with water or as Šamaš) emerges between the mountains, holding in both hands what seems to be a vase from which water pours and connects into two jars placed at the foot of the mountains.[36] The motif of water flowing between a deity and the

33 See Woods 2005, 15.

34 Orthmann 1985, 236.

35 Tsouparopoulou 2014, 44.

36 See also the interpretation of Orthmann, who understands the central figure as a genius with a lower body comprising a tree (Orthmann 1985, 249, fig. 269e).

vases is recurrent in the iconography, and appears to be a subject often associated with a mountainous setting and/or mountain and river deities. The mountains are flanked by two stars each, which might be a reference to the nocturnal journey of the sun through the Twin Mountains into the netherworld.

Illustration 2: Kassite seal portraying a figure rising between the Twin Mountains.

The symbolisms of the eastern Mountain of Sunrise and of the western Mountain of Sunset are complex and elaborate, because they have involved different visions and perspectives throughout the centuries. According to the cosmology of the eastern horizon in Sumerian literature, the cosmic Mountain of Sunrise is fully entwined with the East, and it comprises the mythical place where destinies are fixed every new day.[37] Several Sumerian mythical narratives take place in the mountainous lands in the East,[38] where geographical and cosmic features merge.

The Sumerian myth *Lugale* (or *Ninurta and the Stones*) gives an account of the origin of the eastern mountain and of the establishment of its destiny. After Ninurta's victory over the demon Asag and his army of rebellious stone-warriors, the god is told to create the mountain by piling up the bodies of the dead stones on the chaotic landscape, which displays scattered waters throughout the land. By piling up the stones, Ninurta built a wall, which barred the front of the land,[39] thus conveying the powerful waters into the Tigris and

37 As pointed out by Woods, "it is the identity of distance in space and distance in time that accounts for the Mesopotamian belief that fates were determined both at the beginning and, in mimicry of the event, each day at 'the place where the sun rises' (ki Utu è-a)" (Woods 2009, 207).

38 See, e.g., *Inana and Ebiḫ*, *Lugalbanda and the Anzud Bird*, *Lugalbanda in the Mountain Cave*, *Ninurta and the Stones* (*Lugale*), *Enmerkar and the Lord of Aratta*, and the tales of Gilgameš and Ḫumbaba.

39 *Lugale* 349–351, gu-ru-um na_4 kur-ra mi-ni-in-ak dungu dirig-ga-gin_7 á bí-in-sù-sù-ud bàd maḫ-gin_7 kalam-ma igi-ba bí-in-tab-[ba], "He (Ninurta) made a pile of stones in the mountain. Like a floating cloud he stretched out his arms over it. He blocked the land at its front side through a wall" (ETCSL 1.6.2: 349–351; van Dijk1983, 100–101: 349–351; Seminara 2001, 124: 349–351). For the most up-to-date translation in German of the myth *Lugale* see Heimpel/Salgues 2015, 33–67.

forming lakes in the mountains.[40] After piling up the dead stones, Ninurta establishes the destiny of the mountain.[41] By giving the name ḫ u r s a ĝ to the pile of dead-stones, Ninurta creates the mountain. Along with the creation of the mountain, the warrior god rewards the old lady who helped him during the battle over Asag by assigning to her dominion over the mountain. The woman's new name is Nin-ḫursaĝ, "Lady-of-the-Mountain" (or "Lady-Mountain"?). The mountain's destiny is that of bringing any kind of gift to its lady Nin-ḫursaĝ: aromatic herbs, wine, honey, thriving trees and ripe fruits shall grow in the mountain's meadows, slopes and hillsides, in a concert of divine perfume. Moreover, the mountain shall present to its lady precious metals (gold, silver, copper and tin) and enhance the proliferation of wild animals. The Lady-of-the-Mountain is thus exalted, being equal to Anu and wearing a terrifying splendor.[42]

In *Lugalbanda in the Mountain Cave*, the mountain is described from a human point of view and shows its twofold face, as a cosmic dimension and as a thriving natural entity. Upon falling sick during an expedition on the eastern mountains, Lugalbanda experiences the solitude of lying ill in a mountain cave. The harshness of the cave and of the mountainous setting enhances his state of distress, and the mountain is depicted as one of the most dreadful places on earth. Here the mountain's liminal and chthonic features are fully expressed. After some days of illness and of prayers to Utu, Inana and Suen, Lugalbanda recovers. As soon as he exits the darkness of the cave, the lonely hero finds himself in a luxuriant natural setting, where water and plants abound. The "life-saving plants" (ú n a m - t ì l - l a - k a) are said to be born from "the righteous one" (probably Utu), while the "life-saving water" (a n a m - t ì l - l a - k a) is brought by the Ḫalḫalla, the "Rolling River" (í d Ḫ a l - ḫ a l - l a).[43] This river is addressed as the "mother of the hills" (a m a h u r - s a ĝ - ĝ á - k e₄).[44] After having drunk water and eaten the life-saving plants, Lugalbanda gains new strength and bounds away like a wild donkey, running through the mountainous landscape at night.[45]

Through this adventure, Lugalbanda has a life-changing opportunity to engage with the reality of the cosmic mountain in the East, discovering an unexpected dimension, and also experiencing a spiritual transformation. The mountainous setting reveals to him a thriving world populated by water-courses, plants and animals. Lugalbanda observes wild bulls and wild goats resting, nibbling aromatic herbs, chewing cypress wood, sniffing the foliage, drinking the water of the rolling rivers and masticating *ilinnum*, the pure plant of the mountains.[46] The Sumerian portrayal of the mountainous setting intertwines the

40 *Lugale* 352–358 (ETCSL 1.6.2: 352–359; van Dijk1983, 101–102: 352–358; Seminara 2001, 352–358).

41 *Lugale* 390–410 (ETCSL 1.6.2: 390–410; van Dijk1983, 112–116: 390–410; Seminara 2001, 138–147: 390–410).

42 *Lugale* 406, z a - e n i n - m e - e n ì - d a - s á - s á - a A n - g i n₇ n í ḫ u š g ù r - r u , "You are the lady! You who has become equal to me, who wears the terrifying radiance like Anu" (ETCSL 1.6.2: 406; van Dijk1983, 116: 406; Seminara 2001, 144: 406).

43 *Lugalbanda in the Mountain Cave* 264–277 (ETCSL 1.8.2.1; Wilcke 2015, 239–240).

44 *Lugalbanda in the Mountain Cave* 266 (ETCSL 1.8.2.1). See more in Chapter III, § 4.1.2, about this river and the kinship between rivers and hills/mountains.

45 *Lugalbanda in the Mountain Cave* 277 (ETCSL 1.8.2.1; Wilcke 2015, 241).

46 *Lugalbanda and the Mountain Cave* 292–313 (ETCSL 1.8.2.1; Wilcke 2015, 241).

naturalistic description of the neighboring eastern mountains with the mythical features of the cosmic mountain, with its liminal and chthonic features. This representation portrays the mountain as both a living organism and an animated landscape.

The symbolism of the East involves also the conception of remote eastern lands as places where immortality and wisdom reign, along with a thriving pristine nature. For instance, Gilgameš' endeavor against Ḫumbaba consists of wandering through the "Mountain-where-the-one-lives" (k u r - l ú - t ì l - l a), which might allude to its custodian, Ḫumbaba, or to the dwelling place of Ziusudra, or which might refer to the wider and deeper belief that immortality is to be found on the eastern horizon.[47] It should be noted that, unlike the Akkadian tradition, Sumerian mythology envisions the Cedar Mountain of the Gilgameš Epic in the East. Another legendary land in the far East was Aratta, which was described as a mountainous domain imbued with numinous qualities.[48] Noticeably, the East inspired the imagination of the inhabitants of Mesopotamia, creating a proliferation of symbols and legendary mountains.[49]

Similarly, in Akkadian mythology mountains recur as a privileged setting for gods' and heroes' enterprises. Mythical and epic tales –such as *Anzû*, *Sargon in the Foreign Lands*, the *Song of Bazi* and some adventures of Gilgameš– take place in the mountains. However, from the Old Babylonian period onwards, the geographical and cosmic horizon of the mountains shifts to the West. The mountains and lands of the Amorites (the Anti-Taurus and Lebanon mountains) become the mountainous landscape *par excellence*. As an early example, in *Sargon to the Foreign Lands*, Mount Amanus and the Cedar Forest on Mt. Lebanon are stated as forming the boundary of Sargon's kingdom.[50] The Cedar Mountain constitutes the main example for this shift to the West in the mythical and cosmic landscape in the course of the 2nd and 1st millennia B.C.E.[51]

2.2 Liminal places and origin of pure and threatening entities in incantations

In the vast repertoire of incantations, the mountain occurs as a holy place, often considered as the place of origin of pure entities and beings, as the abode of the gods, and as a liminal place from where anti-social creatures come. As a place of origin of pure entities (plants, stones, etc.) and as the dwelling place of the gods, the mountain is charged with a pure and sacred status. Conversely, its liminal dimension and threatening characteristics are well expressed in those cases where the mountain is conceived as a defiling agent or as a place of origin of dangerous entities such as *Mischwesen*, demons, witches and diseases. The liminal nature of the mountain corresponds to its portrayal as the gate of the netherworld, or as the netherworld itself.

47 Woods 2009, 201. See below § 3.4.
48 See below § 3.2.
49 Another mythical land which inspired the Sumerians was Tilmun, modern Bahrain, in the deep South of the Persian Gulf, and the setting of a myth concerning the water god Enki. See Chapter III, § 3.
50 See TIM 9, 48: 11' –12', [*x Ḫa*]*manam uštētiq uštētiq* ⌜*um*⌝*mānšu Ḫama*[*nam*] *qišat erēnim ikšud*, "He lead across the Amanus, he lead his troops across the Amanus mountains. He reached the cedar forest" (Goodnick Westenholz 1997, 78–93).
51 See below in the present chapter, § 3.4. See also Horowitz 1998, 284.

In the ritual performance, the mountain recurs as a privileged place of origin of plants, trees and rivers, due to its pristine purity. The *kukru* plant recurs in several anti-witchcraft incantations, where it is called the "offspring of the mountain" (*kukra takūr šadî*),[52] *kukru* of the mountains (*kukru ša šadî*),[53] or "of/in the pure holy mountain" (*kukru ina šadânī ellūti quddušūti*).[54] The purity of this plant derives from the pure place where it grows, thus making it able to break the *kaššāptu*'s bond.[55] In *Šurpu*,[56] the "high mountains" (ḫ u r - s a g s u k u d - d a) are said to provide incense for purification, and the latter's purity derives from its mountainous origin.[57] Incense (Sum. n a - i z i, Akk. *qutrēnu*) is referred to as a mountainous inhabitant, being created in the mountains.[58] Another purifying element is syrup (Sum. l à l, Akk. *dišpu*), which was used in the mouth-washing ceremony of the divine statue. In this ritual, syrup is described as "abounding in the orchard, fruit born in the midst of the mountain",[59] and as having been brought down from the mountain by Utu.[60]

Mountains are the birth place of trees whose branches and leaves were used for purification and healing, and whose wood would comprise the earthly body of the deities. The cedar is attested as a purifier of the human and divine body in *Mīs pî*[61] and in *Šurpu*. In *Šurpu*, this tree is said to grow in the "high mountains", where its fate is determined, and the mountain (k u r) is addressed as the "pure place" (k i s i k i l).[62] Here the high mountains are the Ḫašur mountains, from which the cedar is described as stretching its branches and approaching heaven. This is interesting evidence for specific mountains mentioned in incantations. The mountain where the forest of cedar grows occurs also in the ritual of *Mīs pî*, where some incantations address the forest of cedar and of cedar-resin.[63] In

52 *Maqlû* V 49 (Abusch 2015, 330).

53 *Maqlû* VI 65–68 (Abusch 2015, 340).

54 *Maqlû* VI 24–25 // 34–35 (Abusch 2015, 338–339).

55 *Maqlû* VI 65–68. For a discussion of the *kukru*-plant, see Chapter IV, § 3.

56 The ritual *Šurpu*, "Burning", was performed when the patient ignored the reason he had offended the gods and disrupted the world-order by breaking a *māmītu*, "oath". The word *māmītu* is generally translated as "oath" or "taboo". This term refers to the fact that everything in Mesopotamian culture had a *māmītu*, which should be rather understood as the order and reason of being of any object, place and being. The *māmītu* could obviously be disrupted by humans consciously or accidentally. See Reiner 1958.

57 *Šurpu* IX 96–100 (Reiner 1958, 48).

58 *Šurpu* IX 96–100, é n n a - i z i k u r - t a r i - a k u r - r a - t a s i g$_7$ - g a n a - r i - g a - à m k u r - r a - t a è - a š i m - l i š i m - ĝ i š - e r e n n a - i z i k u r - t a r i - a á - g á l - e n a - i z i i m - m a - a n - š ú m ḫ u r (!) - s a ĝ s u k u d - d a n a - b a - š i - i n - r i, "Incantation: Incense, dwelling in the mountains, created in the mountains, you are pure, coming from the mountains! (Fragrance of) juniper, fragrance of cedar, incense dwelling in the mountains; the powerful incense has been granted, the high mountains provide it for purification(?)" (Reiner 1958, 48: 96–100).

59 *Mīs pî* I/II B 78–79, [é n l á l] x ŠÚ$^?$ UD$^?$ ^{ĝiš}k i r i$_6$ - t a d i r i - g a g u r u n š à ḫ u r - s a ĝ - ĝ à - t a t u - u d - d a (Walker/Dick 2001, 99–102).

60 *Mīs pî* 1/2, B 81, ^{d}U t u l u g a l - a n - k i - k e$_4$ k u r - t a i m - t a - è (Walker/Dick 2001, 99–102).

61 The ritual *Mīs pî*, "Mouth-washing", was performed on the cultic image of the deity in order to purify it from any contamination and to "vivify" the wooden statue. In fact, "the statue that has not had its mouth opened does not smell incense, does not eat food, and does not drink water" (Walker/Dick 2001, 18–19).

62 *Šurpu* IX 42–48 (Reiner 1970, 46: 42–48). See more in chapter V, § 2.4.

63 *Mīs pî* I/II C 51–52, [é] n ḫ u r - s a ĝ ĝ i š - t i r š i m - ĝ i š - e r e [n - n] a - k e$_4$, "Incantation: mountain, forest of the ce[dar-resin]" (Walker/Dick 2001, 107–111); *Mīs pî*, Nineveh tablet 45, é n

the *Mīs pî* the wood for the divine statue is addressed as the "wood of the pure forest", originating "from the pure mountain".[64] The ritual text for the Mouth-Washing of the god suggests that the wood of the tree from the pure mountain is not only pure and holy, but also alive and part of the living community of pure elements originating in the mountains.[65]

Water emerges from the womb of the mountains and constitutes the flowing body of the rivers, which descend to the plain, toward the sea. An incantation from the ritual *Šurpu* well expresses this flowing image: "Lordly waters, flowing straight from the high mountains. Waters, flowing out straight from the pure Euphrates".[66] Throughout the literature, rivers and mountains are deeply engaged and intertwined, in a complex relationship which will be further discussed later on.[67] So far, it should be highlighted that mountains are not only the places of origin of rivers and of water, but they also have a kin relationship. Evidence for this is found in an incantation addressing the statue of the god, which is born in heaven and in the mountain. This spell addresses the Tigris as the "mother of the mountain" (a m a ḫ u r - s a ĝ - ĝ á, *ummi šadî*), carrying pure waters (a k u g - g a, *mû ellūtum*).[68]

The offspring of the mountain's rocky womb are not only pure entities and *materia magica*, but also those malevolent and defiling agents that mountains and plants are called to counteract. In two Old Babylonian incantations concerning heart seizure, the mountains occur as the place of origin of a plant which affects gods, humans and animals.[69] In the first incantation,[70] we read that Šamaš tore off the plant-of-the-heart in the mountains (*Šamaš šammam ša libbi ina šadî issuḫam*), which seized the heart of Šamaš, of the bull in the stall, of the sheep in the sheepfold and of man. The dangerous plant is consequently conjured by the earth and the lakes in order to make it release the hearts from its seizure.[71] The second

ḫ u r - s a ĝ ĝ i š - t i r š i m - ĝ i š - e r e n - n a - k e₄ 3-*šú* ŠID-*nu*, "You recite the incantation, 'Mountain, forest of the cedar-resin', three times" (Walker/Dick 2001, 56).

64 *Mīs pî* I/II 13–15, [é n] ⌜è - a - z u - d è M I N g a l[?] - a⌝ ĝ i š - ⌜t i r⌝ - t a è - a - [z u - d è] [ĝ i š] - ⌜ĝ i š - t i r⌝ - k u g - g a ĝ i š - t i r - k u g - g a - t a è - ⌜a⌝ - [z u - d è] ĝ i š - ḫ u r - s a ĝ - k u g - g a [ĝ i š] ḫ u r - s a ĝ - k u g - g a - t a è - ⌜a⌝ - [z u - d è], "[Incantation:] As you come out, as you come out in greatness from the forest! Wood of the pure forest, as you come out from the pure forest! Wood of the pure mountain, [Wood], as you come out from the pure mountain!" (Walker/Dick 2001, 115 and 119–120).

65 See further in Chapter IV.

66 *Šurpu* IX 119–128, én a e n - e k u r - g a l - t a s i - n a m - m i - [š á] a [íd]U D - K I B - N U N[ki] k u g - g a - t a s i n a m - m i - [š á], "Incantation. High waters! Flowing straight from the high mountains. Waters, flowing out straight from the pure Euphrates" (Reiner 1958, 49: 119–128). For the whole text, see Chapter III, § 3.

67 See Chapter III.

68 *Mīs pî* IV A 23ab–26ab, é n a l a m a n - n a ⌜ù⌝ - [t u - u d - d a] *ṣalmu ša Anum ib*[*nû*] ḫ u r - s a ĝ k i - k u g - g a - t a [ ] *ina šadî ašar ellu* ⌜*ib*⌝- [x] í d Ḫ a l - ḫ a l - l a a m a ḫ u r - s a ĝ - g á - [k e₄] MIN *ummi šadî* a k u g - g a š à - b i m u - n i - i n - t ú m *mû ellūtum qerebšu ublū*, "Incantation: Statue born in heaven/created by Anu, from/in the mountain, a pure place ... The Ḫalḫalla (= Tigris), the Mother of the Mountain, carried within her the pure waters." (Walker/Dick 2001, 163–164 and 184). See also above, *Lugalbanda and the Mountain Cave* 266, where the rolling rivers are called the "mothers of the hills". See also Chapter III, § 4.1.2.

69 YOS 11, 12a: 1–8; YOS 11, 11: 1–17.

70 YOS 11, 12a: 1–8 (Veldhuis 1990, 28–29, 42–43).

71 YOS 11, 12a: 8, *uttammīka erṣetam u ḫammê*, "I conjure you by the earth and the lakes".

incantation reads that Šamaš brought over a plant from the mountain (*Šamaš šammam ištu šadîm ušebiram*), that is once more addressed as the cause of the disease which affects every creature (from the gods to animals and humans), and is explicitly called upon to release its victims.[72]

As previously seen regarding the mountains of sunset and of sunrise, demons are widely believed to be the offspring of the mountain, since it is a main passage between the infernal and the earthly realms. In an incantation of the canonical series *Utukkū Lemnūtu*, demons are said to be creatures of the netherworld and to emerge from the western gate.[73] This gate is considered a passage through the western Mountain of Sunset.[74] In a previously-mentioned incantation, the Seven Evil Demons are said to be born on the western mountains and to be raised on the eastern mountains.[75] These western and eastern mountains should be identified with the cosmic Twin Mountains of the mythical and iconographical evidence. The Twin Mountains are the gates of the netherworld, where the Sun enters every day for his nocturnal trip through the land of darkness and emerges every new day from the eastern Mountain of Sunrise.[76] The cosmic Holy Mound, Dukug, is also reported as the place of origin of demons. In a Sumerian incantation, the most dreadful demons (i.e. the evil Udug, the Ala, the evil ghost, and the Ĝulla-demons) are said to emerge from the mist of Dukug, the "mountain of the spring" (kur idim).[77] As we have seen, in Mesopotamian symbolism, the distant cosmic mountain, the holy mound, also represents a liminal dimension, a threshold between worlds, where demons, like other creatures of the wilderness, find their favorite dwelling place.[78]

Another threatening and anti-social agent that is believed to roam around the mountains is the *kaššāptu*, the Mesopotamian witch.[79] In *Maqlû*[80] the *kaššāptu* is said to

72 YOS 11, 11: 1–17 (Farber 1990, 308–309).

73 SAACT 5, IV 1–12.

74 See also Horowitz 1998, 332.

75 SAACT 5, XIII–XV 1–5, én imin-bi an-na ha-la ba-an-ne-eš gù du$_{11}$-ga-bi nu-sa$_6$ *sebettišunu šamê izuzzū ša rigimšunu l[ā damqu]* imin-bi ki-a ha-la ba-an-ne-eš múš-me-bi ì-kúr-ru-uš *sebettišun[u erṣet]i izuzzū ša zīmīšunu [ut]tak[karū]* ḫur-saĝ gi$_6$-gi$_6$-ga ba-tu-ud-dè-eš gù du$_{11}$-ga-bi nu-sa$_6$ *ina šadî e[r]eb Šamši i''aldu ša rigimšunu lā d[amqu]* ḫur-saĝ Utu-ra bulùg-gà-meš múš-me-bi ì-kúr-ru-uš *ina šadî ṣīt Šamši irbû ša zīmūšunu nakru* e-ne-ne-ne an-ki-a nu-un-zu-meš me-lám dul-la-meš *šunu ina šamê u erṣeti ul illammadū melammū katmū šunu*, "Its incantation: The Seven of them, whose clamor is unpleasant, shared out the heavens, the Seven of them, whose features changed, shared out the earth. They, whose clamor is unpleasant, were born on the dark slopes, and those whose features changed were raised in the mountain of the rising Sun. They are unknown both in heaven and earth, they are concealed by a radiance." (Geller 2007, 165 and 242: 1-5). According to Zgoll, the Seven Demons should be understood as two groups of seven demons for each horizon, West and East (personal communication).

76 Verderame 2013: 122–123; Horowitz 1998: 96–100. See below § 3.5.

77 Udug-ḫul VII 769// *Utukkū Lemnūtu* VII 70, Du$_6$-kug kur-idim-ta šà ì-im-ta-è, "from the holy Mound, the mountain of the spring, they emerged (from its midst)" (Geller 1985, 72–73: 769 // Geller 2007, 138 and 222: 70).

78 Verderame 2013, 122–123.

79 The *kaššāptu* was often believed to be a foreigner, a woman from the mountains in the collective image of the witch.

80 The ritual of *Maqlû*, "Conflagration", is the main anti-witchcraft ritual which was performed especially for the king during the 1st millennium. Its main targets were any sorcerer and sorceress, but other anti-

roam constantly over all lands and to cross over all mountains.[81] The incantation continues, referring to the counteractive measures against her approach to a man's house. The patient reports that he has installed a watch on his roof, a protective emblem at his gate, and, in a fragmentary passage, that he has poured out a "pure mountain" (*šadâ ella*).[82] The central importance of the mountain is here emblematic: in order to counteract the witch's roaming and to prevent any visit of this malevolent figure, the same mountain is used as a powerful tool to keep her far away. Here the ritual gesture of pouring a mountain probably refers to the placing of a stone embodying the mountain on the rooftop.

In another incantation, involving primarily the 'wood-of-release' and the river Ulāya, the *kaššāptu* is conjured and her witchcraft is called to "cross over the mountains".[83] Throughout the literature, mountains are attested as both a place of origin of threatening creatures and as the privileged place for dispelling any source of evil and defilement. This evidence confirms the conception of the mountain as an ambivalent figure and as a liminal dimension, emblem of otherness in the Mesopotamians' eyes.

2.3 The Mountain-person and the Mountain-god in incantations, rituals and iconography

The evidence for unspecified mountains considered as beings with an active role in the cultic performance and with divine features occurs mainly in Sumerian and Akkadian incantations and rituals. It is in this genre that the multifaceted nature of the mountain is expressed, since the mountain is featured as a purifying agent, described as acting as a person in the magical performance, and as a divine being, listed along major deities. The mountain is often considered to be a powerful being, so that in order to defeat sicknesses and evil forces, the afflicted person has to take recourse in its skills by calling upon its powers and of self-identifying with it. Needless to say, the traits of an "other-than-human" person, of a deity and of a place often overlap and mingle.

Together with being considered one of the privileged places of origin of the evil demons, mountains also recur as active agents on behalf of them. In a Sumerian incantation against the demons, those malevolent spirits are described as following the path from the gate of the netherworld through the horizon, and smashing and melting stones like liquids.[84] Then the demons are told to grasp the chosen victim, to arouse fear in the man and to place

social and hostile entities –such as demons and diseases– are also included and annihilated through it (Abusch 2015).

81 *Maqlû* VI 143''–145''// *Maqlû* VI 152''–157'' (Abusch 2015, 344–345).

82 *Maqlû* VI 152''–157'', [ÉN] *ē kaššāptiya elēnītiya* [*ša*] *tattanallakī kal mātāti tattanablakkatī kal šadâni anāku īdēma attakil takālu* [*ina ūriy*]*a maṣṣar*]*tu ina bābiya azzaqap kidinnu*[*y*]*a aštapak šad*[*â el*]*la*, "[Incantation]. Ha! my witch, my deceiver, You who (constantly) roam over all lands, Who cross to and fro over all mountains. I know and have gained full confidence (in my abilities to hold you off). I have installed a wa[tch on] m[y roof], a protective emblem at my gate. [At m]y [. . .] I have poured out a pur[e mo]untain." (Abusch 2015, 344–345: 152''–157'').

83 *CMAwR* 7.8.4: 77′, [*kišp*]*īšunu libbalkit*[*ū š*]*adî* (Abusch/Schwmer 2011, 190). For a detailed discussion of this incantation, see further in Chapter III, § 4.4.3, and Chapter IV, § 3.

84 Geller 1985, 34–35: 246–255.

him within a circle of mountains. The mountains, constituting a lethal net around the victim, "roar" at him "like wind in a porous pot".[85] In this case, the mountains are described acting on behalf of the evil demons, and appear both as a place of imprisonment of the victim, and as an entity capable of acting like a person.

In the Old Babylonian incantations, the unspecified mountain, *ḫuršānu*, occurs as a purifying divine entity. Despite the fact that it is written without the divine determinative, *ḫuršānu* is listed together with the River among the holy gods of the mountain (*ilū qašdūtum kalūšunu ša šadîm*) in an incantation against various diseases:

Adad Sumuqan Id Šamaš u Ḫuršānu	"May Adad, Sumukan, Id, Šamaš and Ḫuršānu,
ilū qašdūtum kalûšunu ša šadîm liššipūka	all the holy gods of the mountains, perform exorcisms for you,
ellūtum Igigū lillilūka	and may the pure Igigū purify you".[86]

Invoked as purifiers, *Ḫuršānu* and *Id*, the River, are recorded among the holy gods (*ilū qašdūtum*) in another incantation against various diseases.[87] In both contexts, the divine cosmic Mountain should be understood as the deity called upon together with the River and the other deities traditionally associated with the mountains.

In the world of anti-witchcraft rituals, mountains recur as agents called on behalf of the patient in order to destroy and dispel witchcraft.[88] The incantation *Maqlû* V 149–157 is the most eloquent example of the personalistic and animate features ascribed to the mountain in the magical setting:

85 Udug-ḫul, IV 246–255, én ⌜é⌝-nu-ru an An-né ri-a-meš dumu ki-in-du tu-da-meš um-me-da si-na ga ⌜è⌝-da-⌜a⌝-meš um-me-ga ⌜si-na ga⌝ s[ub$^{?}$-s]ub-a-meš a-ra-li-a gìri [mu]-⌜un-ne⌝-e-gar ⌜urugal-la⌝ ká mu-⌜un⌝-ne-⌜e⌝-gal abul ^{d}utu-šú-a-šè è-meš na$_4$^{na} di$_4$-di$_4$-lá in-[in]-ni-[zi]-re-dè na$_4$ gal-gal-lá a-gin$_7$ mu-un-dig-⌜dig-ge-dè⌝ ní mu-un-da-ri-eš su mu-un-na-gi$_4$-eš kalam-ma mu-un-da-ru-uš gam-kur-ra sa-pàr-[gi]n$_7$ mu-un-ne-gub-bu-uš ⌜kur⌝-re ^{dug}sahar-[gi]n$_7$ ⌜ara$_9$⌝ im-da-ab-⌜gi$_4$⌝-gi$_4$, "Enuru incantation. They are spawned by An, they are born (as) a child of earth. As for the nursemaid, they (the demons) draw milk from her fullness, they suck the milk of the wet-nurse in her fullness. In the netherworld, the path is laid out of them, in the underworld, the gate is open for them. (The demons) left the main gate (of the netherworld) toward sunset, they were smashing small stones, and they were softening large stones like liquids. They roused fear in him, they struck his body and shook the land. They placed him in the circle of mountains like a net, the mountains roared at him like (wind in) a porous pot." (Geller 1985, 34–35: 246–255). With some variants to the Sumerian precursor, in the canonical series the same portrayal of the mountains is attested, SAACT 5, IV 12, kur-ra ^{dug}sakar-gin$_7$$^{[s]a-kar-gin7}$ ara$_9$ mu-un-da-ab-gi$_4$-gi$_4$ [*šadâ k*]*īma karp*[*āti šaḫarrāti ušaš*]*gamū*, "they make the mountain roar like porous pots" (Geller 2007, 109–110 and 203: 12).

86 LB 1000: 8–10 (Geller/Wiggermann 2008, 153–156).

87 CT 42, 32: 12–13, *Adad Šakkan Nisaba Šamaš Id Ḫu*[*rsān*] *ilū qašdū*[*tum*] *šunu lillilūka*, "Adad, Sumukan, Nisaba, Šamaš, Id, and Huršānu, the holy gods, they may purify you" (Geller/Wiggermann 2008, 151). See also Chapter III, § 2.3.

88 The main ritual series is *Maqlû*, "Burning", which records the main anti-witchcraft ceremony (Abusch 2015). Together with this complex text, several texts deal with rituals performed to counteract any black magic (Abusch/Schwemer 2011).

ÉN *šadû liktumkunūši*	Incantation: "May the mountain cover you (pl.),
šadû liklākunūši	May the mountain hold you back,
šadû linēḫkunūši	May the mountain pacify you,
šadû liḫsīkunūši	May the mountain enshroud you,
šadû litēʾkunūši	May the mountain smother you,
šadû linēʾkunūši	May the mountain counteract you,
šadû likattinkunūši	May the mountain cover you over,
šadû dannu elikunu limqut	May a strong mountain fall upon you.
ina zumriya lū tapparrasāma TU_6 ÉN	From my body you shall indeed be separated!" Incantation Formula.[89]

Here the mountain is called upon to carry out a series of actions against the witches: to cover them (*katāmu*), to hold them back (*kalû*), to pacify, calm them (*naḫû*), to enshroud them (*ḫesû*), to cover up/smother (*têʾum*), to counteract (*nêʾum*) and to fall upon (*maqātu*) the malevolent agents, in order to annihilate the sorceresses by separating their spirit from the body. This series of actions portrays the mountain as a powerful animated agent, with a precise role in the ritual performance, i.e. counteracting witchcraft.[90]

In another anti-witchcraft incantation, the mountain is recorded in a list of natural elements counteracting the *qumqummatu-* and *naršindatu*-witches, and is called upon to "drive back the sorcerous devices" (*upīšī linēʾ šadâ eli kišpīki*).[91] The incantation has to be recited three times, while the *āšipu* burns the figurines of the witches and purifies the patient with a fumigation of *kukru*-plant. The text of the spell addresses the identity of the witches (*qumqummatu* and *naršindatu*), who took clay from the river in order to produce a figurine of the sick person, and asks the reason why they wish to bring the soul of the victim to the netherworld. For his part, the patient affected by witchcraft can rely on several natural elements (i.e. *maštakal*-soapwort, the 'heals-a-thousand' plant, the 'wood-of-release', the mountain, and the cone of the *qadištu*-votaries) and man-made objects (i.e. the bronze curved staff).[92] The panorama emerging from these incantations is that of an animated world, where every element is called upon in order to defeat any threat to a person's well-being, and consequently, that of the cosmos. Plants, mountains and objects are all portrayed as active agents in the magical performance.

89 *Maqlû* V 149–157 (Abusch 2015, 335).

90 This incantation is well attested in other anti-witchcraft texts by its incipit "May the mountain cover you", which occurs in several ritual contexts (*CMAwR* 7.6.3: 32–34; 8.7: 105‴–115‴; 9.2: 39–53; 9.3: 22′–23′). Often, this incantation is recorded associated with a ritual involving water, lupine, 'heals-twenty'-plant, and basalt as *materia magica* (*CMAwR* 7.5: 1–7; 7.8.7: 21′–23′; 8.5: 4′–8′; 9.2: 10–15; 9.3: 9–10). The basalt is called "the pure mountain", and this probably refers to the fact that a stone or an object of basalt was used in the magical performance to represent the mountain invoked in the incantation. It should be noted that the association of *dicenda* (the incantation) and *agenda* (the practical ritual action) is an essential and necessary feature of any magical performance (see Tambiah 1968, 175–208).

91 *CMAwR* 8.7: 106‴–115‴ (Abusch /Schwemer 2011, 347).

92 See further in Chapter IV, § 3.

In another anti-witchcraft incantation, the patient calls the entire realm of natural powers on his behalf, while self-identifying with them.[93] Along with the heaven, the earth/netherworld, a thorn-bush and the sting of the scorpion, the patient identifies himself with a high mountain. By embodying different powerful entities, the patient gains their abilities and characteristics. Heaven and the netherworld are impossible to reach and attack, the thorn-bush and the scorpion are not approachable because of their thorns and fatal sting, and the insurmountable mountain stands like a wall in its height.

The massive cosmic power of the mountains is well expressed in *Šurpu*, where the mountains, together with the rivers Tigris and Euphrates and the sea, are invoked to calm down together with the god of fire, Girra. This evidence stresses the conception of the mountain as a fierce power of nature along with the fire and the water entities of the cosmos:

ÉN *nūḫ Girru qurādu*	Incantation: "Calm down, oh fierce Girru
ittīka linūḫū šadâni nārāti	Let the mountains and the rivers calm down with you,
ittīka linūḫā Idiglat u Purattum	Let the Tigris and the Euphrates calm down with you,
ittīka linūḫ ayabba tâmātu rapaštim	Let the ocean, the wide sea, calm down with you".[94]

An entity capable of calming down the mountain is sulphur, as it is mentioned in an incantation of the ritual *Maqlû*: "like the mountain is made quiet by sulphur" (*kīma šadî ina kibrīti inuḫḫu*).[95]

The ritual *Šurpu* records a long list of *māmītu*s which the patient might have accidentally broken. Along with the entire realm of the cosmos, mountains also have their own *māmītu*.[96] Indeed, all the constitutive elements of the Mesopotamian world (gods, elements of nature, of the city and the temple, animals and human products) possess a *māmītu*, which can be seen as an eloquent insight into the understanding of the Mesopotamian cosmos and landscape as an animated and relational one. As further evidence for such an understanding is found in the ritual *Mīs pî*, where the mountains, together with the plain and the fields, the orchards and the marshes, are asked to bring offerings to the divine statue of the god.[97] The land and the sea, together with all the other

93 *Maqlû* III 147–153.

94 *Šurpu* V–VI 187–190 (Reiner 1970, 35).

95 *Maqlû* III 82 (Abusch 2015, 307: 82). For the agency and kinship of sulphur together with the River see Chapter III, § 2.1.

96 *Šurpu* III 65, *māmīt šadî u ḫurri*, "the oath of the mountain or of the cave" (Reiner 1958, 21); and *Šurpu* III 164, *māmīt šadî*, "the oath of the mountains" (Reiner 1958, 23).

97 *Mīs pî* IV 53ab, kur-ra gun gùr-ru gun ḫé-en-na-an-gu-ùr-ru: *šadû nāš bilti biltam liššīku*, "May the mountain, which carries tribute, bring you tribute!" (Walker/Dick 2001, 168 and 185); *Mīs pî* IV 57ab, [kur-ra ḫé-gá]l?-bi a-ab-ba ma-dam-bi gun gùr-ru gun ḫé-en-na-an-gùr-ru: *šadû ḫegallašu tâmtum ḫiṣibša nāš bilti* [MIN], "May the abundance of the mountain and the plenty of the sea, which carry tribute, bring you tribute!"

elements of the landscape, offer their gifts to the divine effigy, bringing to it their abundance and fertility.

An intriguing visual representation of mountain deities bringing offerings together with humans and a river deity is offered by a limestone mold fragment attributed to Narām-Sîn.[98] This mold fragment features the king and the goddess Ištar on a ziggurat, that is bordered by a female river goddess bringing offerings, together with human and divine prisoners kept captive by Ištar.[99] The divine prisoners are two half-anthopomorphic and half-mountain figures situated in a mountainous terrain (Illustration 3).[100] The montrosity of the landscape is rendered by a series of drill holes forming individual triangular shapes, which represent both a mountain range and the lower bodies of the prisoners. These prisoners are to be interpreted as mountain deities: their divinity is expressed by their hybrid half-anthropomorphic and half-mountainous appearance, by their hairstyle and by their horned crowns.[101] Each god carries in their hands an offering vessel as a tribute to the triumphant goddess.[102]

Illustration 3: Detail of the human and divine prisoners (Mountain deities) and of the River goddess on the mold fragment attributed to Narām-Sîn.

This motif of a half-anthropomorphic and half-mountainous body is a constant feature of the visual representation of mountain deities or divine mountains throughout the centuries. Most iconographical evidence comes from the 2nd millennium B.C.E., the most famous being the so-called *Brunnen Relief*, that was discovered within a holy well in the

(Walker/Dick 2001, 168 and 185).

98 Hansen 2002, 91-112; Aruz/Wallenfels 2003, 296–297; Woods 2005, 17–18.

99 For the River goddess see Chapter III, §2.1.

100 Hansen 2002, 95–96. See also Wiggermann 2013, 114–116.

101 Hansen 2002, 95–99. Hansen further argues that "such depictions of the mountain gods are a creation of the Akkadian period, even though only a few examples are known to us and none are preserved in this particular form. Such deities last into later periods, an excellent example being the mountain gods shown in a seal from Nippur of Lugal-engardu of the time of Amar-Sîn (Winter 1991, pl. 9, b,c, and pl. 10, a)" (Hansen 2002, 99).

102 Hansen 2002, 96.

temple of Aššur in Assur, and has been dated to the first half of the second millennium (Illustration 4).[103] This relief displays a central masculine figure, half-anthropomorphic and half-mountainous, which holds vegetation branches or sprouts in his hands, while another pair of sprouts emerges from his sides. The vegetation is being eaten by animals, probably to be identified as wild goats. At the sides of the central scene, two female half-anthropomorphic and half-fluvial figures with two streams flowing from each one's shoulders are represented. All the three half-anthropomorphic figures should be considered deities: the female entities are clearly the two River goddesses which recur consistenly in the iconographical evidence, while the bearded man with the mountainous lower body is a Mountain god. This god has been identified with the same god Aššur, because of its finding location within the temple area dedicated to this god, but due to the lack of any further evidence, this suggestion remains speculative.[104] The identity of this Mountain deity remains enveloped in mystery. However, it represents one of the few sculptural representations of the divine Mountain (or Mountain god) in ancient Mesopotamia. The composition of Mountain god, River goddesses, vegetation and animals expresses the synergic entanglement among these entities, which are all perceived as living and life-giving entities.

Illustration 4: Mountain god (Aššur?) carrying vegetation and accompanied by two River goddesses.

Kassite art offers intriguing examples of Mountain and River deities, with their traditional representation of anthropomorphic upper body and mountainous/fluvial lower body. Mountain gods and River goddesses are displayed as the main divine figures in the

103 Andrae 1931; Moortgat 1969; Orthmann 1985, 308; Roaf 1990, 148. This relief was probably thrown into the well of Aššur's sanctuary in order not to be seen nor captured during the destruction of the city in the 7th century B.C.E.

104 Roaf 1990, 148. See further in the present Chapter, § 3.6.

frieze of Inana's temple of Karaindraš at Uruk.[105] The reconstructed frieze features two rows of Mountains and Rivers deities that stand in wall niches. The Mountain deity is represented as a bearded man with a horned headdress: his upper body is anthropomorphic and his lower body is a mountain, represented with its typical scale pattern. Mountain deities or cosmic mountain persons are often represented in glyptics. The so-called seal of Rimutu displays an organic and holistic scene comprising a Mountain god, a small anthropomorphic kneeling figure with two water streams flowing from behind his shoulders (a River deity or the personification of a spring?), two griffins, two trees and a flock of birds flying in a starry sky (Illustration 5).[106] Interestingly, the Mountain god is portrayed with a Janus head and a tall headdress: can this evidence be understood as an alternative visual representation of the cosmic Mountain of Sunrise and Sunset, here conceptualized as a deity? It has to be highlighted that in the iconographical repertoire, as in the literature, Mountain and River deities often appear together, and they are often associated with vegetation and animals, by virtue of the profound and synergic relationship among all these living entities in the Mesopotamian worldview.

Illustration 5: Seal of Rimutu, displaying a Mountain god with a smaller River entity, vegetation and a host of animals.

In the Neo-Assyrian rituals, mountains occur as a collective entity and are referred to as entities able to grant life, to hear prayers and to bless the king and the land. In the Tākultu[107] ritual for Assurbanipal, the divine Mountain is recorded among the gods of the

105 Moortgat 1969, 94.
106 Matthews 1992, 114.
107 The term Tākultu (literally "meal") refers to the major Neo-Assyrian festival. As argued by Ermidoro, this rite was "stemming from an older tradition" connected to communal food consumption of the king with his officials and soldiers, but "gained an increasing popularity until it

house of the Seven Gods,[108] whereas in the same text the collective mountains are listed among deities belonging to the Assyrian pantheon. Here “mountains” (KUR.MEŠ) are called upon, along with the rivers, the Anunnaki gods, and various non-anthropomorphic entities –such as the brick and the palace– to grant life, hear prayers, bless the city of Aššur, the land of Aššur, and the king, and they are included among the “gods of the city of Tua”.[109] In the continuation of the same ritual, “mountains, springs, rivers and the four quarters (of the world)” (*šadâni nagbī nārāti kibrāt erbettim*)[110] are called upon to bless the king, together with the anthropomorphic gods, winds, parts of the temples and chapels. There are several attestations in the Neo-Assyrian rituals, in which mountains and rivers are listed together as collective deities venerated in the royal cult.[111] As pointed out by Porter, mountains “appear to have been a collective deity in Assyria, where mountains were a prominent feature of the landscape, although the evidence for this collective deity is somewhat ambiguous”.[112]

Furthermore, rituals devoted to the Lady-of-the-Mountain (^{d}GAŠAN KUR-*e*, *Bēlat-šadê*) are attested among the royal rituals in the Neo-Assyrian court. One ritual text preserves the royal instructions for performing a ritual in front of the god Aššur and the goddess Lady-of-the-Mountain. The king shall sacrifice a ram and present offerings of roasted meat,[113] while the *āšipu* of Aššur offers water from his hands to both the Lady-of-the-Mountain and the king.[114] To the Lady-of-the-Mountain (*Bēlat-šadê*) a more complex ritual is dedicated by the king Tukulti-Ninurta, who refers to this deity as his personal god (literally “gods”).[115] The setting of this ritual is on a river bank, where a tent has been set up, with a chair placed to one side and pointing toward the sunrise. Libations, fumigations, offerings of different types of bread and cakes, of wool and metals, and of incense and flour, and the sacrifices of a sheep and a ram are included together with several prayers and chants to the divine gathering of the great gods. This is a *nāṭu*-ritual, which aims at dispelling any impurity and sin from the person of the king, and it seems especially intended to restore his fertility. The mentioning of the semen of a sick man points to this

---

became one of the most important elements of State propaganda due to its universalistic and celebratory features that echoed the royal ideology” (Ermidoro in the *Introduction* of Parpola 2017, xxvi).

108 SAA 20, 40 iv 15: ^{d}KUR-*u* (*Šadû*) (Parpola 2017, 113).

109 SAA 20, 40 rev. ii 1–14, [*a-ši-bu*]-*ut* AN-*e* ^{d}*A-nun-*⸢*na*⸣-*ki* GAL.MEŠ *mu-kin-nu ma-ḫa-zi šadâni*(KUR.MEŠ) *nārī*(ÍD.MEŠ) URU BÀD$^{!}$ *še-lu-ru* SIG$_4$ É.GAL *u ḫi-ib-šú* É.URÌ.NA.KUG *šu*$^{!}$-*pal-síḫ*$^{!}$ *man-za-zu lim-ḫu-ru* TI.LA *liš-me-ú su-pe-e kur-ba a-na* URU–*Aš-šur a-na* KUR–*Aš-šur a-na* LUGAL EN-*ni* DINGIR.MEŠ *ša* URU–*Tu-a*, “[The gods dwel]ling in heaven (and) the great Anunnaki gods who established the holy places; the mountains, the rivers, the city, the city wall, the mortar, brick, palace and …, Eurinnaku, …, the place(s) – may they accept life and listen to prayers! Bless the city of Aššur, ditto the land of Aššur, ditto the king, our lord! The gods of Tua” (Parpola 2017, 116–117).

110 SAA 20, 40, rev. iii 40'–41', *šadâni n*[*agbī*] *nārāti kibrāt erbettim*” (Parpola 2017, 118). See also SAA 20, 42, rev. iii 17'–18', *šadâni n*[*agbī*] *Ḫalḫalla ana siḫ*[*irtiša*] (Parpola 2017, 123).

111 See SAA 20, 38 i 57, KUR.MEŠ ÍD.MEŠ (Parpola 2017, 104); SAA 20, 46 rev. ii 13', [KUR^{m}]^{eš} ÍD^{meš} (Parpola 2017, 127); SAA 20, 47 rev. 5, KUR^{meš} ÍD^{meš} (Parpola 2017, 127).

112 Porter 2009, 171.

113 SAA 20, 21: 3–17 and 21–25 (Parpola 2017, 55–56).

114 SAA 20, 21: 18–20 (Parpola 2017, 55–56).

115 SAA 20, 24 (Parpola 2017, 62–65).

interpretation, which is corroborated by the continuation of the ritual, where an "unwilling woman" is thrown into the pond.[116] Only then will the angry domestic god be reconciled with the man[117] and the man is allowed to enter his house and to kiss his wife's lips.[118] The colophon of the tablet preserves an interesting piece of information: the location of this ritual is to be in the middle of the mountain (*ina qereb šadê*), which provides one of the few cases of direct written evidence for a ritual performed in a mountainous setting.[119] The identity of this female deity is unknown: it might refer to those goddesses traditionally connected with the mountains –such as Ištar or Ninḫursaĝ, but it might also invoke an incarnation of the divine Mountain.

3 Specifically named mountains

3.1 Mountains in the *Lipšur Litanies* as healing "other-than-human" persons

An intriguing ritual text offers a repository of several specifically named mountains of the Mesopotamian geographic and cosmic landscape. The so-called *Lipšur Litanies* comprises a list of mountains, which are called upon "to absolve" (*lipšur*) the patient's sins and defilement.[120] The part addressed to the mountains is relevant to this study because it offers a glimpse into the sacred mountainous and animated landscape of Mesopotamia in the 1st millennium B.C.E.[121] While recording several names of mountains, with their epithets, the text refers to them as active agents and as "other-than-human persons" approached on behalf of the patient.[122]

The first four entries of the *Lipšur Litanies* invoke the mountains of the gods (Enlil, Bēlet-ilī, Adad and Šamaš). Enlil, Bēlet-ilī, Adad and Šamaš are the deities traditionally connected closely to mountains. Notably, the mountain of Bēlet-ilī is called Ḫursag, "mountain" in Sumerian, and it refers to the Sumerian mountain goddess Nin-ḫursag, which means "Lady-of-the-mountain", or even "Lady-Mountain". This evidence suggests a possible syncretism between Bēlet-ilī and Nin-ḫursag in the 1st millennium, as both goddesses are associated with the mountains. Mt. Budugḫudug bears the epithet *nēreb*

116 SAA 20, 24: 8–10 (Parpola 2017, 64).
117 SAA 20, 24: 10 (Parpola 2017, 64).
118 SAA 20, 24: 42'–43' (Parpola 2017, 65).
119 SAA 20, 24: 44' (Parpola 2017, 65).
120 See its main edition by Reiner 1956, 129–149. See in particular pp. 132–135: 1–47 for the section devoted to the mountains.
121 The following paragraph is dedicated to discussing those mountains, whose identification is possible but which do not have a further tradition as active animate agents and as holy places in incantations and myths. Those mountains mentioned in the *Lipšur Litanies* with a longer tradition in Mesopotamian religion and literature will be discussed separately in the pertinent paragraphs below.
122 The mountains are listed according to the epithets: from the gods, to trees, stones, and people, which characterize each mountain. Unfortunately, many of those mountains are not identifiable, and their names are lost in the mists of time. Some other epithets refer to mountains whose history covers the entire range of Mesopotamian civilization. It should be noted that in this 1st-millennium list, the older Sumerian mountains which we encounter in the Sumerian literature are not attested (except for the case of Mount Ebiḫ).

Šamaš ana Aya, "the entrance of Šamaš to Aya", and thus it is identified with the cosmic Mountain of Sunset. The connection with the western horizon and the nocturnal journey of the sun is evident from this epithet, since it is upon his return to the netherworld that the Sun-god is reunited with his spouse each night.[123]

The second section of the *Lipšur Litanies* comprises those mountains in association with their trees and forests. Their epithets feature the arboreal species traditionally ascribed to the respective mountains. Mounts Amanus, Ḫabur, Ḫašur and Sirara are called the mountains of cedar, while Mt. Lebanon is called the mountain of cypress. The latter is a curious occurrence, since Mt. Lebanon is traditionally considered a forest of cedar trees.[124] The ranges of Amanus, Ḫabur and Lebanon continue to have these names and refer to the same geographical entities in modern times, while Sirara is identified with the modern Anti-Lebanon mountain range. All these mountains stand out on the western horizon, with the exception of Mt. Ḫašur. This mountain, together with Mt. Lebanon, has a special place in the mythological and symbolical landscape of Mesopotamians.[125]

The 13th and 14th entries of the *Lipšur Litanies* record Mounts Dibar and Dabar, which should be considered the same mountain range.[126] This mountain is called the mount of "terebinths", and has been identified by Stol with Jebel 'Abd el 'Azīz, which is a mountain range extending between the Ḫabur and the Baliḫ.[127] This mountain occurs in the Old Akkadian personal names *Šu-Tibar*, "He-of-Tibar" and *Dān-Tibar*, "Tibar-is-Strong",[128] and in the Old Assyrian *Šu-Tí-bar*, "He-of-Tibar".[129] Moreover, Dibar is attested, together with Mt. Ebiḫ and the rivers Ulāya and Tigris, among the gods of the House of Aššur in Neo-Assyrian royal rituals.[130]

After trees, the third section of the text mentions mountains associated with metals and stones. Most of the names of the recorded mountains are not known in the literature, leaving their identity concealed. Only Meluḫḫa and Magan are better known parts of the Mesopotamian landscape: they refer to the Arabian peninsula, thus alluding to the southern horizon of the Persian Gulf.[131]

In the final part of the *Lipšur Litanies* some famous mountains of the Mesopotamian cultic and mythical landscape are called upon. Ebiḫ, Šaššar, Bašār and Nimuš have a special place in the mythical and ritual discourse.[132] The text specifies these mountains by the ethnic groups which have traditionally lived on their slopes –i.e. Amorites, Gutians, Subareans and Lullubeans. Only a few mountains are referred to without an ethnic characterization: Ebiḫ is here called the "bolt of the country" (*sikkūr māti*), while the unidentified Mt. Temenna is addressed as the "mountain of Elam" (*šad Elam*), and Mt.

123 See above in this Chapter, § 2.1.
124 See below in this Chapter, § 3.4 and Chapter IV, § 2.4 .
125 See below in this Chapter, § 3.4 and §3.5.
126 Stol 1979, 25–30.
127 Stol 1979, 25–30.
128 Roberts 1972, 53; Lambert 1983, 84.
129 Lambert 1983, 84.
130 SAA 20, 38 ii 1 (Parpola 2017, 104). See also Menzel 1981, T 113 ff.; Lambert 1983, 85.
131 See the Sumerian Dilmun myths (Kramer/Maier 1989).
132 See in the present chapter, § 3.2; § 3.3; § 3.5.

Ḫarsamna as the "mountain of horses" (*šad sišî*). Moreover, Mt. Saggar is the "mountain of millstones" (*šad erî*) and Mt. Kupin "the mountain of springs" (*šad kuppāni*).

The identification of Mt. Saggar with Jebel Sinjar has been proposed by Stol, based on the correspondence of Saggar with ᵈHAR in the cuneiform sources.[133] Accordingly, the equation ᵈHAR = Saggar stands for "the deified mountain range Jebel Sinjar".[134] This mountain range represents one of the major landmarks of Mesopotamia, separating the Jazira from Upper Mesopotamia, and it is generally referred to as a mountain where terebinths, almond trees and grapes grow.[135] Mt. Saggar occurs in theophoric personal names from Mari, indicating that some divine status was ascribed to this mountain at least in the region of Mari during the 2nd millennium B.C.E.[136]

3.2 Mount Ebiḫ, Aratta and the Zagros

The history of Mt. Ebiḫ in the literary and religious framework of Mesopotamian culture has a particular fortune and spans a considerable period of time. Ebiḫ (Sum. E n - t i , Akk. Ebeḫ or Abiḫ) appears in the Sumerian myth *Inana and Ebiḫ* as a powerful mountain deity, and his divine presence continues until Neo-Assyrian times. This mountain has been identified with Jebel Hamrin, which is an outlier in South-West Iraq, the western range of the great Zagros mountains.[137] The geo-morphological features of the Ebiḫ mountain range are reminiscent of Ninurta's creation of the Zagros mountain from the pile of dead stone-warriors.[138] As previously seen, the myth reports that the pile of rocky bodies arose like a great wall, barring the land of Sumer and Babylonia.[139]

The Sumerian myth *Inana and Ebiḫ* tells the battle that the goddess Inana initiates against the mountain Ebiḫ.[140] The mythical plot opens with a description of the goddess as deeply connected with the eastern mountains: Inana is told to wander around the mountains, to bring forth lapis lazuli, to bath in the mountain of carnelian and to give birth to the "multicolored mountain, the pure place" (k u r s ú b i k u r k i s i k i l ù - d ú - u d - d a - z a).[141] After having walked around the heavens and on earth, in Elam, Subir and on the Lulubi mountains, the goddess encounters outrageous behavior from Ebiḫ, the mountain that does not show any respect toward her divinity and supremacy:

i n - n i n $_9$ - m e - e n k u r - r e t e - a - m e - e n n í - b i n a - m a - r a - a k	"When I, the mistress, approached the mountain, it didn't show any fear to me,

133 Stol 1979, 75–80.
134 Stol 1979, 77.
135 Stol 1979, 77–78.
136 Durand 1991, 84–89.
137 Black 2002, 50.
138 Black 2002, 51.
139 See above on the *Lugale* 349–351 (§ 2.1).
140 For the main edition of the myth *Inana and Ebiḫ* see Attinger 1998, 164–195. See also Attinger 2015a, 37–45; Attinger 2015b, 353–363, for the most updated translations in German.
141 *Inana and Ebiḫ* 17 (Attinger 1998, 168).

^{d}Inana(-me-en) kur-re te-a-me-en ní-bi na-ma-ra-ak	when I, Inana, approached the mountain, it didn't show any fear to me,
ḫ[ur-saĝ] Ebiḫ^{ki}-ke$_{4}$ te-a-me-en ní-bi na-ma-ra-ak	when I approached the mountain range of Ebiḫ, it didn't show any fear of me.
ní-bi-ta na-ma-ra$_{7}$-da-ab-ak-gin$_{7}$	Since it showed me no respect,
giri$_{17}$-bi ki-šè na-ma(-ra)-ab-te-a-gin$_{7}$	since it did not approach its nose to the ground for me,
nundum saḫar-ra na-ma-ni-ib-ùr-ra-gin$_{7}$	since it did not rub (its) lips in the dust for me,
ḫur-saĝ zi šu-ĝu$_{10}$ ga-àm-mi-ib-si ní-ĝu$_{10}$ ga-mi-ib-⌜zu⌝	I shall fill my hand with the soaring mountain range, and it shall learn fear of me".[142]

In this meeting, the mountain is characterized in a personalistic and anthropomorphic fashion. Ebiḫ is described as behaving like a person, who shows no respect to the goddess and does not fear her divine status. By not bringing its nose to the ground and rubbing its lips in the dust, Ebiḫ refuses to act according the code of obedience and submission to the great gods. Upon the continuation of the narrative, Ebiḫ is not only described as a topographical entity, but also referred to as possessing a moral connotation. The mountain features a forest and an abundance of watercourses, and it is said to be wicked and inaccessible, while being part of the Aratta mountain range.[143] Inana turns to her father Anu, telling him of the mountain's arrogant conduct and her desire to destroy it/him. Ebiḫ is once more described both in anthropomorphic terms and in topographical ones: the mountain is characterized by its evil deeds of not putting its nose on the ground and its lips in the dust, but also by its majestic slopes, forest and watercourses.[144]

Anu's reply assumes a position in favor of Ebiḫ, that is referred to as a cosmic and divine mountain. Ebiḫ is the pure abode of the gods, whose fearful splendor is said to spread upon the land of Sumer and beyond. The *melammu* of the mountain is perceived as terrible and awe-inspiring, weighing upon all the lands, while reaching up to the heart of heaven with its height. The mountain emerges as a powerful entity, cloaked with a divine aura, that covers all the divine and human realms.[145] Anu continues with Ebiḫ's portrayal

142 *Inana and Ebiḫ* 29–35 (Attinger 1998, 170–171: 29–35; ETCSL 1.3.2: 30–36).

143 *Inana and Ebiḫ* 44–47 (Attinger 1998, 170: 44–47; ETCSL 1.3.2: 45–48).

144 *Inana and Ebiḫ* 89–106 (Attinger 1998, 170–174: 89–106; ETCSL 1.3.2: 89–107).

145 *Inana and Ebiḫ* 116–120, ki-gub diĝir-re-e-ne-ke$_{4}$ ní ḫuš im-da-ri-ri ki-tuš kug ^{d}A-nun-na-ke$_{4}$-ne su-zi im-du$_{8}$-du$_{8}$ ní-bi ḫuš-a kalam-ma mu-un-ri ḫur-saĝ(-ĝá)(ní) me-lim$_{x}$-bi ḫuš-a kur-kur-ra (ša-)-mu-ri sukud-rá-bi an-na šà-bi NIR mi-ni-i[b]-⌜è⌝, "The abode of the gods is covered by a fearful splendor, the pure dwelling of the Anuna (deities) is adorned with awe. Its furious splendor is spread over the land (of Sumer), the *melammu* of the mountain is terrible and is spread upon all the lands. With its height, is has formed an arch in the center of heaven" (Attinger 1998, 174–175: 116–120; ETCSL 1.3.2: 116–120).

focusing on the physical description of the mountain, which is depicted as a luxuriant forest, abundant with trees, fruits and wild animals, in a triumph of joy and exuberance.[146] Its thriving gardens and magnificent trees, which are called the "crown of heaven",[147] offer shelter and dwelling to lions, wild goats, red deer, and wild bulls. The mountainous forest emerges as a dimension abundant of life, radically different from the urban plain, and displays the features of the cosmic mountain. Anu's response stands for preservation and respect of the established cosmic order, which comprises the fearsomeness and the divinity of the mountain. Thus, Inana cannot enter in Ebiḫ's kingdom, nor oppose its supremacy.[148]

Despite Anu's denial, Inana, who cannot stand her pride to be hurt, prepares for battle against the mountain. The battle scene between Inana and Ebiḫ refers to the mountain with both anthropomorphic and natural features. Inana is said to kill the mountain in the same way a person is murdered: the goddess grasps its neck like alfalfa grass, presses the dagger in its interiors, and splits its big mouth like a thunderbolt. The stones, which form Ebiḫ's body, are said to be flesh themselves. Their collapse creates a dreadful noise, while Inana moves on in her fury cursing the forest, cutting the destinies of the trees short and making them die of thirst, scattering fire all over, until she spreads silence over the mountain.[149]

Affirming her victory over the mountain, Inana stands on the mountain range addressing it/him as a deity:

---

146 *Inana and Ebiḫ* 121–128 (Attinger 1998, 174–176: 121–128; ETCSL 1.3.2: 121–128).

147 *Inana and Ebiḫ* 122, ĝiš maḫ-bi TÙN(aga$_{x}$) an-na, "its majestic tree, crown of heaven" (Attinger 1998, 174: 122; ETCSL 1.3.2: 122).

148 *Inana and Ebiḫ* 121–128, ^{ĝiš}kiri$_{6}$ nisi-bi gurun im-lá giri$_{17}$-zal i[m-du$_{8}$-du$_{8}$] ĝiš mah-bi TÙN(aga$_{x}$) an-na ní di u$_{6}$ di-[dè ba-gub] Ebiḫ^{ki}-a ĝiš-an-dil$_{x}$ pa mul-mul-la-ba ug tab-ba mu-un-LU šeg$_{9}$ lu-lim-bi ní-ba mu-un-durun am-bi ú lu-a mu-un-DU duraḫ-bi ḫa-šu-úr ḫur-saĝ-ĝá-ka e-ne-sù-ud-bi im-me ní-bi ḫuš-a nu-mu-e-da(-an)-ku$_{4}$-ku$_{4}$ ḫur-saĝ-ĝá me-lim$_{x}$-bi ḫuš-a/àm ki-sikil ^{d}Inana saĝ nu-mu-e-dé-ĝá-ĝá, "In its flourishing gardens fruit hangs and joy spreads, Its magnificent trees, crown of heaven, (…) stand as a wonder to proffer. In Ebiḫ, lions are abundant under the protecting trees with their shining branches. Its lions are abundant companions, its stags stand on abundant grass, its wild goats of the Hašur-mountain are distant in playing(?). Its fearsomeness is terrible: you cannot enter! The *melammu* of the mountain range is terrible –Maiden Inana, you cannot oppose it!" (Attinger 1998, 174–177: 121–128; ETCSL 1.3.2: 121–128). See also in the present chapter, § 3.4.

149 *Inana and Ebiḫ* 141–150, Ebiḫ^{ki}-a/e gú-bi ^{ú}númun(-bur)-gin$_{7}$ šu ba-an-ši-in-ti šà-ba/bi gù miri-a ba-ni-in-ra ka gal kurku-gin$_{7}$ mu-un-si-il-(l)e Ebiḫ^{ki}-e na$_{4}$ su ní-ba-ke$_{4}$ bar-bi-a dub-dab$_{5}$ ḫé-em-mi-ib-za á-ta(-)ri-a-ta muš šà-tùr gal-gal-e uš$_{7/11}$ mu-un-gú-guru$_{5}$-gú $^{\text{(ĝiš)}}$ter-bi áš bí-in-du$_{11}$ ĝiš-bi nam ba-an-ku$_{5}$ ^{ĝiš}al-la-nu-um-bi su-ba mi-ni(-in)-ug$_{5}$ bar-bi-a izi mi-ni(-in)-ri ib(b)i$_{x}$-bi bí-in-mú in-nin$_{(9)}$-e kur-re me bí-in-tál, "She grasped the neck of Ebiḫ like alfalfa-grass. She pressed the dagger's blade in its heart. She split its big mouth like a thunder. On the flanks of Ebiḫ the stones, which are themselves flesh, crackled down in a rumbling noise. From its sides, she cut down the poisonous spittle of big horned vipers. She cursed the forest and decreed the fate of its trees. She made die its oaks with thirst, she set fire on the flanks and made grow smoke. The mistress .. spread silence over the mountain." (Attinger 1998, 176: 140–150; ETCSL 1.3.2: 141–150).

ḫur-saĝ $^{(d)}$Ebiḫ$^{(ki)}$-(a)-ke$_4$ im-ma-gub gù im-ma-dé-e	She went to the mountain range of Ebiḫ and called:
ḫur-saĝ íl-la-zu-šè sukud$_{(x)}$-rá/da-zu-šè	"Mountain range, because of your elevation, because of your height,
sa$_6$-ga-zu-šè si$_{12}$-ga-zu-šè	because of your goodness, because of your being green,
tu$_9$-ba$_{13}$ kù-ge mu$_4$-ra-zu-šè	because of your wearing a pure tuba-garment,
an-né šu si sá(-a)-zu-šè	because of your extending your hand straight to heaven,
giri$_{17}$ ki-šè nu-te-a-zu-šè	because you did not put your nose to the ground,
nundum saḫar-ra nu-ùr-ra-zu-šè	because you did not rub your lip in the dust,
mu-un-ug$_5$-ge-en ki-šè mu-un-sì-[ge-en(?)]	I have killed you and thrown you down into the earth".[150]

In this passage, the divine status of Ebiḫ is affirmed, with the reasons of Inana's anger. Ebiḫ's characteristics are elevation, height, goodness, beauty, and it is said to wear a holy garment typical of deities, and to reach heaven with its hand. Together with divinity and beauty, Ebiḫ shows a rebellious and powerful temperament: the mountain did not show any fear or respect to Inana, who could not stand to have such a majestic rival. The myth concludes with the establishment of a palace and a cultic area on Mt. Ebiḫ by Inana. Her triumph over the mountain was probably celebrated in the urban temple, during the rites for Inana or during a commemorative festival.[151]

Ebiḫ's divinity and agency continues until the 1st millennium, but appears in different genres. Onomastics highlight Ebiḫ's divinity. The mountain occurs as a theophorous element in personal names from late Early Dynastic to Old Babylonian times, especially in Semitic names from the Diyala region, until the Middle Assyrian period.[152] Names such as *Ir'e-Abiḫ* (written *Ir-e-*^{d}EN.TI), "Abiḫ-shepherded", *Ur-Abiḫ* (*Ur-*^{d}EN.TI), "Hero-of-Abiḫ", *Puzur-Ebiḫ*, "Shelter/Under-the-protection-of-Ebiḫ", and the Middle Assyrian *Ebeḫ-nāṣir*, "Ebiḫ is protector/protects", and *Ebeḫ-nērārī*, "Ebiḫ is my assistant", show Ebiḫ as a god actively involved with worshippers.[153] The theophoric name *Abiḫ-il* (written EN.TI-*il*), "Abiḫ-is-god", explicitly states the divine nature of the mountain.[154] This name is attested written at the back of an Early Dynastic statuette from Mari, which represents a man called *Abiḫ-il* and was found in the temple of Ištar.[155]

150 *Inana and Ebiḫ* 152–159 (Attinger 1998, 178: 152–159; ETCSL 1.3.2: 152–159).

151 *Inana and Ebiḫ* 171–173 (Attinger 1998, 178–179: 171–173; ETCSL 1.3.2: 171–173).

152 Lambert 1983, 84.

153 Roberts 1972, 12; Lambert 1983, 84; Porter 2009, 169.

154 Porter 2009, 169.

155 Orthmann 1985, 166; Hrouda 1991, 66.

Moreover, Ebiḫ recurs in the lists of deities and in rituals. Ebiḫ is recorded in an Old Babylonian god list from Nippur,[156] but it is in the rituals of the Assyrian kings of the 1st millennium that Ebiḫ emerges as a recurrent deity, invoked among the great gods and as a recipient of offerings.[157] In the Tākultu for Sennacherib in Nineveh, Ebiḫ is listed three times, among Mt. Dibar, and the rivers Tigris and Euphrates: it is recorded twice with the determinative for deity (^{d}*E-bi-iḫ*) while standing with the gods of the House of Anu and of those of the House of Sîn; while the third attestation refers to it in its topographical characterization (^{kur}*E-bi-iḫ*), but while including it in a list of deities.[158] In the Tākultu for Assurbanipal, the god Ebiḫ occurs four times, where it is invoked together among the great gods of the Assyrian pantheon and is the recipient of offerings in the various shrines in Assur. Ebiḫ stands among the great gods of the House of Anu and Adad of the Inner City together with the Ulāya river, in the House of Sîn and Šamaš, and among the gods whose name is to be invoked in the evening of Kurbail.[159] The divine Ebiḫ is recorded, once among the nine gods in the House of Anu and once among the five gods in the House of Sîn, in a text which displays the cultic topography of Assur.[160] In the royal coronation ritual, two stones are placed to represent this deity, while all the other gods are embodied by one stone each.[161] Finally, Ebiḫ, without the divine characterization, is invoked in the Tākultu ritual for Aššur-etel-ilāni together with the Tigris and the Upper and Lower Zab, all the villages and the divine boundaries.[162] All this evidence speak for the fact that this mountain was considered a deity of some importance within the Neo-Assyrian pantheon.[163]

Mt. Ebiḫ occurs in the 1st-millennium incantations as an active agent in ritual performance. As we have seen, Ebiḫ is invoked in the *Lipšur Litanies*, where it is called "the bolt of the country" (*sikkūr māti*).[164] This epithet reminds of the scene in the *Lugale* when Ninurta piled up the corpses of the stones, to bar the land with a wall. Ebiḫ is called upon, together with the temple E'ulmaš, in an incantation against the Lamaštu:

---

156 Lambert 1983, 85.

157 Menzel 1981; Lambert 1983, 84–85; Porter 2009, 169; Parpola 2017.

158 SAA 20, 38 ii 37, [^{d}*E-b*]*i-iḫ*; SAA 20, 38 ii 53, ^{d}*E-bi-iḫ*; SAA 20, 38 iv 3', ^{kur}*E*-[*bi*]-[*iḫ*] (Parpola 2017, 105–107).

159 SAA 20, 40 ii 15, ^{d}*E-be-eḫ*; SAA 20, 40 ii 28: ^{d}EN.TI; SAA 20, 40 rev. i 4, ^{d}*E-be-eḫ*; SAA XX, 40 rev. iv 34', ^{d}*E-bi-iḫ* (Parpola 2017, 112 ff.) See also duplicate SAA 20, 41 ii 1 ^{d}[*E-be-eḫ*] (Parpola 2017, 120); and a fragment of a Takultu text SAA 20, 46 rev. i 5', ^{kur}*E-b*[*i-iḫ*] (Parpola 2017, 126).

160 SAA 20, 49 57 and 64, ^{d}*E-be-eḫ* (Parpola 2017, 133–134).

161 SAA 20, 7 rev. iii 26, 2 ^{d}*E-be-eḫ* (Parpola 2017, 18). This evidence leads me to wonder whether it could be a reference to the fact that in this context Ebiḫ was equated to the cosmic mountain of sunrise with its twin peaks. This is a mere suggestion, that cannot be developed without further evidence.

162 SAA 20, 42 rev. iii 3', ^{kur}*E-b*[*i-iḫ*] (Parpola 123). See further in Chapter III.

163 Porter argues that "these references establish that Ebiḫ was viewed as a living and active divine entity. They do not refer however to the physical form in which Ebiḫ was represented in temples or how he (or it) was envisioned, although they seem to imply a non-anthropomorphic form by giving the deity the name of the well-known mountain range." (Porter 2009, 169).

164 *Lipšur Litanies* 37 (Reiner 1956, 134–135).

ÉN *anamdi šipta lazzu milikki*	Incantation: "I am casting a spell (against) your persistent counsel:
ul uššі qātēki Ebiḫ šadû dannu	Ebih, the strong mountain, was unable to remove your hands,
E'ulmaš qašdu šubat ilī rabûti	(nor) holy E'ulmaš, the residence of the great gods".[165]

In this incantation Ebiḫ is not characterized by the determinative for deity, but by that of mountain (kur), and its epithet is "strong mountain" (*šadû dannu*), referring to it as topographical entity. However, in this passage the two topographical entities, the mountain and the temple, are considered helpless with regard to the wicked actions of Lamaštu, since they are said to have been unable to remove her defiling hands from the chosen victim. Mountain and temple are seen as active and powerful entities, which would have normally been able to act on behalf of the patient against the demonic forces.

In the myth *Inana and Ebiḫ* other mountains are mentioned. Lulubi, Zubi and Aratta are all eastern mountain ranges. While Lulubi and Zubi recur in the literature with only topographical connotations, the mountain range of Aratta presents a more intriguing case. Aratta recurs in the literature addressed as the "mountain of the pure me" (Arata^{ki} kur me sikil-la),[166] it is portrayed as an eastern mountainous land, rebellious against the goddess Inana and the sovereignty of Uruk, and as a cosmic mountain that mingles its traits with a cosmic tree.

In *Enmerkar and the Lord of Aratta*, Inana's messenger is told to ascend to and descend from the Zubi mountains, to reach Susa and the land of Anšar, and to traverse seven mountains, until finally reaching Aratta.[167] According to its literary image, Aratta represents the counterpart to the land of Sumer, and its legendary existence speaks of a tension between the Mesopotamian world and the Iranian high lands, a relationship alternating between mutual respect and open rivalry.[168] The identification and location of Aratta has been subject to several interpretations, and it is generally agreed that the city and the land of Aratta should be considered a legendary land.[169] This understanding is supported by the fact that Aratta occurs only in literary sources, which describe it as a vague and mystical land in the far East.[170]

In *Enmerkar and the Lord of Aratta*, Aratta is also described as a cosmic mountain, whose portrayal mingles the image of a tree with the features of a bird. This great mountain range is referred to as a *mēsu*-tree, which grows high in the sky, while its roots form a snare and its branches are a snare. Moreover, the tree-mountain assumes the features of a bird (either an Anzû-bird or an eagle).[171] In the same myth, the goddess Inana is once more

165 *Lamaštu* II 1–3 (Farber 2014, 164–165).

166 See *Lugalbanda and the Mountain Cave* 22 (ETCSL 1.8.2.1: 22) and *Enmerkar and the Lord of Aratta* 223 (Mittermayer 2009, 126).

167 *Enmerkar and the Lord of Aratta* 163–171 (Mittermayer 2009, 124: 163–171).

168 See Mittermayer 2009, 38–39.

169 Potts 2004, 6.

170 Mittermayer 2009, 26–39; Potts 2004, 1–11; Woods 2009, 202.

171 *Enmerkar and the Lord of Aratta* 243–245, ḫur-s[a]ĝ gal ^{ĝiš}mèš an-da mú-a úr-

considered a deity closely connected to the mountains: she is addressed as "the great queen of heaven, who rides upon the awesome m e , who has taken place on the mountain range of the Bright Mountain, who has adorned the dais of the Bright mountain".[172]

3.3 Mounts Šaššar and Bašār

Mounts Šaššar and Bašār are often associated with each other in the literary texts. In an Old Babylonian inscription of Narām-Sîn, Mount Bašār is said to lie across the Euphrates for those coming from the Tigris,[173] and it has been identified with Jebel Bishri, "a ridge of high land that stretches west-southwest from the middle Euphrates to Palmyra" (Illustration 6).[174] Jebel Bishri is part of the Great Southwest Asian Arid Zone, and forms a border region between pastoral nomadic groups and sedentary agriculturalists.[175] As pointed out by George, "by virtue of its elevation and springs, the ridge has afforded good grazing and watering to pastoralists throughout history, and has also often been put to defensive use."[176] Following Lambert, the distribution of Šaššar and Bašār indicates that they both refer to the same mountain, "with Bašār the name found in 'more prosaic texts'", and with Šaššar occurring "only in the literary and scholastic tradition".[177]

Illustration 6: View of Jebel Bishri.

Šaššar and Bašār appear to be closely connected with the West Semitic cultural milieu. These two mountains are paired in the *Lipšur Litanies* 38–39, and in the lexical text URA = *ḫubullu* XXII 38–39, where both mountains are referred to as "the mountain of the Amorites" (*šad Amurrī*).[178] This expression, referring to Mt. Bašār as the mountain of the Amorites, is already attested in the 3rd millennium B.C.E., and signifies its north-western

---

bi-šè sa-par$_4$-àm pa-bi ĝiš-búr-àm⌜x(x)⌝ umbin-bi ⌜Anzu⌝^{mušen} ḫu-rí-in-na (Mittermayer 2009, 128: 243–245). See also Chapter IV, § 2.2.

172 *Enmerkar and the Lord of Aratta* 229–231, nin gal an-na me ḫuš-a u$_5$-a ḫur-saĝ kur-súbi-ka dúr ĝar-ra para$_{10}$ kur-súbi-ka še-er-ka-an du$_{11}$-ga (Mittermayer 2009, 126: 229–231).

173 RIME 2 ii 14–19: *Purattam ībirma ana Bašār šadû Amurrī*, "Narām-Sîn crossed the Euphrates until Bašār, the mountain of the Amorites" (Frayne 1993, 90–94).

174 George 2009, 12; Lönnqvist *et alii* 2011.

175 Beaulieu 2002, 39; George 2009, 12; SYGIS-Jebel Bishri: The Finnish Project in Syria (with the edited volume, Lönnqvist et alii (eds.), 2011, *Jebel Bishri in Focus*).

176 George 2009, 12.

177 Lambert 1989, 17; George 2009, 12.

178 Reiner 1956, 134–135; Bloch/Horowitz 2015, 81.

horizon.[179] The Amorites were wandering in this mountainous area, and their god Amurru was intertwined with the image of a mountainous deity.[180] Much evidence from iconography and religious literature associates the god Amurru with the mountains:[181] Amurru is addressed as the one "who resides in the pure mountain" (kur-sikil-la tuš; kur-sikil-la ti-la; tuš ḫur-saĝ-ĝá-sikil-a-ke$_4$),[182] "who dwells in the mountains" (*wāšib ḫuršānim*),[183] and "who occupies a holy dais in the mountains, the pure place" (ḫur-saĝ ki-sikil-la bára-kù-ge si-a).[184] The mountain in this context is described as a sacred location, the dwelling of gods. Amurru is also evoked as a hero, who controls the distant mountains and their borders, thus acquiring the status of a warrior god.[185] Later, Amurru gains the epithets "lord of the mountain" (^{d}mu-lu-ḫur-saĝ = ^{d}lú ḫur-saĝ = ^{d}Mar-tu) in Emesal, and "the great mountain" (^{d}KUR.GAL) in Kassite Babylonia.[186] Thus, the god appears to have been viewed firstly "as a mountain dweller, later as a warrior who subdues the mountains, and finally a deity who embodies the cosmic mountain".[187]

The conception of this mountain as a cosmic mountain with divine traits is underlined by the evidence of offerings to the mountain from a very early era. An Ur III administrative tablet records offerings to the god Amurru, and to Mt. Bašār during the reign of Dungi.[188] At Mari Mt. Bisir (Jebel Bishri) occurs, together with Saggar and Ebiḫ, in theophoric personal names of the pattern Mut-DN, "Man-of-DN".[189] Furthermore, in the pantheon of Mari, a goddess was associated with Mt. Bašār, whose name is Ištar-of-Bišra (^{d}U-DAR *bi-iš-ra*).[190]

The numinous nature of Šaššar and Bašār is evident through their presence in myths, where these two mountains are intertwined with gods (Bazi and Enki/Ea) and *Mischwesen*s

179 Narām-Sîn mentioned *Ba-sa-ar sa-dú-i Mar-dú*^{ki} (Sommerfeld 2000, 423–424) and Gudea referred to Ba$_{11}$-sal-la ḫur-saĝ Mar-dú (Stat. B vi 5–6, Edzard 1997, 34). See George 2009, 12; Buccellati 1966.

180 For the Sumerian god Martu in the literature, see Klein 1997, 99–116.

181 Beaulieu 2002, 38. It is worth pointing out Beaulieu's remark that "the references to 'mountains' could also be understood as allusions to the steppe, since the word *šadû* (= kur) conveys the two meanings". These are, in fact, to be understood not as two meanings, but as representing a single entity: the steppe, seen from the Euphrates valley, lies high like a mountain (Streck personal communication). For a comprehensive portrayal of Amurru, see Kupper 1961.

182 For the references of cylinder seals, see Beaulieu 2002, 38: note 38.

183 OECT 11, 1; Beaulieu 2002, 38.

184 Hymn SRT 8: 3–4 (see Beaulieu 2002, 38).

185 Beaulieu 2002, 38.

186 Beaulieu 2002, 38. The epithet "great mountain" typically denotes the god Enlil.

187 Beaulieu 2002, 39. It should be noted that the god Amurru and the Amorites are not only associated with Mt. Bašar. In fact, other mountains are referred to as the mountain of Amurru (e.g. Ditana and the region of Lullubû), suggesting that the Amorites were not "the inhabitants of one specific mountain range", but they should rather be seen "as a powerful migrating people that moved from northwest to east and brought under its control the various mountain areas from Lebanon in the West to the border of Elam in the East. In other words, they were the mountaineers *par excellence*" (Beaulieu 2002, 40).

188 Dhorme 1912, 57, pl. I, SA 3, 1 and 3: "1 sila$_4$ ^{d}Mar-tu [...] 1 sila$_4$ ḫur-saĝ ba-ša-ar". See also Beaulieu 2002, 39.

189 George 2009, 14; Durand 1991, 84–89.

190 George 2009, 14; Lambert 1985, 527.

(Anzû). Šaššar and Bašār occur in the *Song of Bazi*,[191] where a god named Bazi establishes his dwelling on Mt. Šaššar. On this mountain a sanctuary is said to rise from the womb of the earth.[192] This text offers a unique description of a god's house in a natural context. The rocky, mountainous and watery setting is rich in symbolic meanings concerning gods and nature:

imḫaṣ šadâm erṣetam ušpelki	He (Bazi) smote the mountain, opened wide the earth.
bītum [b]ani mû ubāʾūnim	A house was built –waters used to flow forth from it.
ina qereb mêšu bani bīssu	In the midst of its waters his house was built.
libnātum uqnû dalātum ebbum	The bricks were lapis lazuli, the doors were shining;
askuppātum ša ḫurāšim bašmū šukû ša daltim	The thresholds were of gold, dragons were the door poles.
ḫār ṣippassu qê dibbā⸢šu⸣	*Palm shoots*(?)*(were) its cones*(?), copper its twin panels.
ilum mītum ukkal sikkūram atû mūtum	A dead god used to oversee the bolt. The door-keepers were death.
ina qereb bītīšu ibbalakkatu mû mišlum balāṭu mišlum mūt[um]	In the midst of the house waters used to cross, half were life, half were death.
bītum mali tašēlātim	The house was full of celebration.
ina papāḫim Šamaš ina bītim Šakkan	In the cella was Šamaš, in the house was Šakkan:
nērma ^{d}*Šakkan ša rušê*	Slay, o Šakkan, the one of witchcraft,
Šamaš ša dāmi Id rabû ša kišpi {ras.}	O Šamaš, the one of blood, o great River, the one of sorcery![193]

Bazi's dwelling is in a hole, or in a cave on the mountain, its slopes reaching deep into the earth and high into the sky, and the most striking feature is the profusion of water. The walls of the dais are made of precious stones, offspring of the womb of the mountain, and its gates are protected by dragons and dead gods. References to gates and mountains as thresholds of the netherworld are abundant in ancient Mesopotamia. Traditionally, the gate-

191 George 2009, 1–15; Zgoll 2015, 68–73. Zgoll's translation into German offers an innovative interpretation of this composition as a cultic song to be performed by several actors (Zgoll 2015).

192 *Song of Bazi* 16, [*ad*]*dikkum Šaššar u Bašār šadâmma*", "I hereby give you the mountain Šaššār and Bašār", and line 18, "*ana* [*Š*]*aššar ūṣi parakku ana* [*šubtika*] ", "At Šaššār a cult-dais rose forth for [your abode(?)]" (George 2009, 7–8: 16 and 18). See also Zgoll 2015, 70–71.

193 *Song of Bazi* 23–33 (George 2009, 7–8: 23–33; Zgoll 2015, 71–72, SEAL 1.1.12.1). It should be noted that George solves the Sumerograms ^{d}ÍD GAL as *Nāru rabītu*, but it also possible to read them as *Id rabû*. According to the context of judgment and because of the association with Šamaš, I would opt for the reading *Id rabû*. See further in Chapter III, § 2 and § 3.

keepers of the divine realm are Dumuzi and Gizzida, who are dead gods and stand at Anu's gate in heaven in the myth of *Adapa*.[194]

The house is filled with flowing waters, half are death and half are life (*ina qereb bītīšu ibbalakkatu mû mišlum balāṭu mišlum mūtu*). This watery setting refers to the River Ordeal, a notion that is supported by the identity of the three gods invoked in the text. Šakkan and Šamas, together with Id, the divine River, are called upon to judge, slay and purify those convicted of witchcraft (*ša rušê*), of murder ("the one of blood", "*ša dāmī*") and of sorcery (*ša kišpi*).[195] Šamaš and Id are the supreme judges presiding over the legal practice of the River Ordeal, while Šakkan, being Šamaš' son and god of wild animals and herds, matches the mountainous setting perfectly.

Mt. Šaššar (Jebel Bishri) has been noted for its springs since antiquity, some of which still provide water, and deep wells.[196] In one Babylonian version of the Gilgameš epic, "wells of the hill-flanks" are said to be excavated by the hero on his way to the Cedar Forest.[197] The watery setting of Mt. Šaššar is closely related to the god Bazi. This god appears to have been a legendary ruler of Mari, who became deified with time and was conceived as a divine herder due to his connection with the high lands of the west.[198] Interestingly, Bazi is referred to as a king, ruling over the sacred people, and as a ram, presumably being represented with animal features.[199] His presence in the southern Mesopotamian panthea does not occur, but in this text Bazi is called son of Enki/Ea. This evidence indicates that the divine herder of the mountains was assimilated into the southern pantheon as the son of the god of spring water.

The evidence from the lexical lists shows that a (at least scholarly) connection between the god Amurru and the Apsû, realm of Enki/Ea did exist, indicating that the West with its mountains was considered part of Enki's domain. In the lexical list An = *Anum* II Amurru is recorded as the "great e n s i of the Apsû,[200] and the divine Mt. Šaššar occurs as the twenty-eighth name of Ea (^{d}*Šár*$^{\textit{šá-ar}\text{-MIN}}$-*šár*).[201] The divine Šaššar, along with the gods

194 *Adapa*, fr. B 20 and 39. Edition by Izre'el 2001, 16–21.

195 See Zgoll's translation and interpretation of this passage (Zgoll 2015, 72). For a comprehensive discussion of the River Ordeal and the relationship between rivers, mountains and deities, see Chapter III.

196 For a possible location of the cult-dais of Bazi on Mt. Šaššar/Bašār, see George's suggestion of the basin of Al-Qawm, which lies at the west of Jebel Bishri. "The basin is the site of many prominent tells of strange formation, partly natural and partly man-made, that lie over springs, so that some are equipped with deep wells. Water from this oasis was still plentiful enough in the early Islamic period to be channelled to the Umayyad fortified settlement at Qasr al-Hair ash-Sharqi, more than thirty kilometers away. The combination of high places and deep water in a single location has been a strategic resource for local pastoralists and long-distance travelers since the Paleolithic era" (George 2009, 13). Instead, according to the Finnish Expedition in Jebel Bishri, the plenitude of water may refer to "the water sources in the eastern central areas such as Nadra which has large springs. Other water sources are at Qebaqeb to the south, and as previously mentioned, there are artesian springs at El Kowm on the western piedmont" (Lönnqvist 2011, 200).

197 George 2009, 13; George 2003, 98.

198 George 2009, 11–12.

199 George 2009, 7–8: 34–35, *ellētim nišī ibêl kazzum etellum ša ālišu*, "He (Bazi) rules the sacred people, the ram, monarch of his city." See also Lönnqvist 2011, 200.

200 An = *Anu* II 292–293 (George 2009, 13).

201 An = *Anu* II 163 (George 2009, 13).

Amurru, Šakkan and the Great Mountain (^{d}KUR.GAL), is attested in another lexical list (An = *Anu ša amēli*: 100-105).[202] Accordingly, Mt. Šaššar appears to have been considered not only a holy place, but a divine, numinous mountain.[203] Its cosmic features are clearly expressed in a passage of the *Song of Bazi*, where Mt. Šaššar is said to pierce the netherworld and to touch the heavens.[204]

This western mountain and the shepherd-god Bazi refer explicitly to a "mythical journey of a divine ram to raise flocks in his new home on Mts. Šaššar and Basār",[205] perfectly matching the transhumance that did occur seasonally in Babylonia. The *Song of Bazi* should thus be understood as a composition intended to be performed at an annual festival for the herding season, and it offers a glimpse into a more "popular" Babylonian religion.

The *Song of Bazi* introduces the dialectic between mountains and temples. As holy places, mountains represent a natural mirror of the urban temple, whose parts are built and named according to the natural cosmic geography.[206] Conversely, mountains (i.e. Ebiḫ, Šaššar) comprise cosmic entities and embody the temple in the wildness, beyond the boundaries of civilization, where a reality run by another type of order and of divinity exists. Furthermore, the evidence offered by the *Song of Bazi* might be a hint of a real presence of temples and shrines in the mountainous context, as much as of seasonal festivals and/or processions *in loco*.

The divine Mt. Šaššar is closely connected to another famous character in Babylonian mythology and religion, the Anzû-bird. A fragmentary passage of the Babylonian Thunderbird's myth[207] seems to suggest that the birthplace and dwelling place of Anzû is Šaššar, which is called the "lap of the Anunnaki" (*ina utliša Anunnaki*).[208] Anzû is the

202 An = *Anu ša amēli* 100–105 (CT 24 42 89–94), ^{d}GÌR = ^{d}GÌR *šá bir-qi* : ^{d}KUR.GAL = MIN *šá te-lil-te* : ^{d}MAR.DÙ = MIN *šá Su-ti-i* : ^{d}MAR.DÙ = MIN *šá Su-ti-i* : ^{d}*Šár.šár* = MIN *šá Su-ti-i* : ^{d}GÌR = MIN *šá šadî*, "Šakkan is Šakkan of lightning : Great Mountain is Šakkan of purification : Mardu is Šakkan of the Suteans : Amurru is Šakkan of the Suteans : Šaššar is Šakkan of the Suteans : Sumuqan is Šakkan of the mountains" (George 2009, 13). As pointed out by George: "Through their shared association with ^{d}*Šár-šár*, Ea and Šakkan even came to be equated, so that in the section of the god-list AN = *Anum* treating the court of Šamaš, where Šakkan finds a place as the son of Šamaš, the following entry occurs (An III, 198): ^{d}MIN (*Su-mu-qa-an*) *É-a* = MIN (^{d}GÌR DUMU ^{d}UTU.KE$_4$), thus Ea can be read as Sumuqan, who is Šakkan, son of Šamaš. All this speaks for a local, Syrian image of Ea as a herdsmen's god, quite distinct from his role in conventional Babylonian folklore" (George 2009, 14).

203 George 2009, 12-13. George argues that "the god ^{d}*Šár-šár*, identified in Babylonian theology with Ea and Šakkan of the herds and hailing from the land of the Suteans, can be none other than the deified Mt. Šaššar. The deification of mountains is a religious phenomenon much attested in ancient north Mesopotamia. Examples are Aššur, Kawkab, Dibar (Jebel al-Aziz), Saggar (Jebel Sinjar) and Ebiḫ (Jebel Makhul), and it is no surprise that also Jebel Bishri could be held in such honor (George 2009, 14).

204 George 2009, 8–9: 42, *ušapliš erṣetam u šamê īmid*, "It pierced the netherworld and leaned on the heavens".

205 George 2009, 14–15.

206 Horowitz 1998.

207 See Vogelzang 1988; Annus 2001.

208 *Anzû* I 25–27, *ina Šaršar šadî eli* [*xx*] *ina utliša Anun*[*naki xx*] *ittalad Anz*[*â x x*], "On Šaššar, a mountain over/of ... In the lap of (?) the Anunnaki ... has given birth to Anzu" (Annus 2001, 19: 25–27).

offspring of this mountain, having been conceived by the earth and born from the rocks of the mountains, in a watery setting:

ellūti mê ilāni šūt A[psî x x]	Pure water of the gods of Apsû.
īrišuma erṣetum šu[ddultum]	The wide earth conceived him,
ina kāpī šadî šū[ma iwwalid]	from the rocks of the mountain he [*was born*(?)].[209]

The whole context expresses the cosmic and divine features ascribed to the mountainous birth place of Anzû: the pure underground water pouring from the Apsû and the wide earth that is womb to the Thunderbird reveal also the netherworld nature of the mountain.

Anzû's presence in the mountains is noticed by the gods, who suggest to Enlil to appoint this creature of rocks and waters as guardian of the shrine of the king of gods. In this shrine, the Tablet of Destinies is preserved, where the entire order of the world, divine and human, is written, and without it, the gods themselves have no power. For a while Anzû is the perfect gate-keeper, but, while observing everything that happens in the temple, he starts plotting. Finally, one day, while Enlil is taking a bath, he steals the Tablet of Destinies, depriving the world of the Enlil-ship, and flies to "his mountain"(*šadûššu*).[210]

The Thunderbird's mountain is referred to as the "inaccessible mountain" (*šad lā a'āri*), where the divine bird flies with the stolen Tablet of Destinies.[211] Ninurta is then chosen as the champion of the gods for the mission of destroying the *Mischwesen* and the mountains, in order to bring back the still-forming rites and to build the cult places.[212] The meeting of the two divine characters occurs on the slope of the mountain. The Thunderbird's anger is portrayed with a visual image comparing his grinding teeth to a storm, while covering the mountain with his *melammu*:[213]

ina šaḫāt šadî Anzû u Ninurta ittanmarū	On the flank of the mountain Anzû and Ninurta looked at each other.
īmuršuma Anzû irūbaššu	Anzû saw him and became furious with him.
ikṣuṣ kīma ūmu melammašu šadê iktum	He ground his teeth like a storm demon and he covered the mountain with his *melammu*.[214]

209 *Anzû* I 51–53 (Annus 2001, 19).

210 *Anzû* I 81–83, *tuppī šīmāti ikšudā qātuš[šu] Enlilūta ilteqe nadû [parṣī] Anzû ipparišma šadâssu [igguš]*, "He (Anzû) grasped the Tablet of Destinies in his hands: he took away the Enlil-ship, the rites were abandoned. Anzû flew away and went to his mountain" (Annus 2001, 20).

211 *Anzû* I 106 and 127 (Annus 2001, 20).

212 *Anzû* II 20–27 (Annus 2001, 23).

213 The word *melammu* can be translated as "aura". It refers to something physical and powerful which protects and give power at the same time, like a protecting luminous shield. It is typically possessed by gods and other divine beings. For further mentions of *melammu*, see the "cloaks of radiance" of Ḫuwawa (see below in the present chapter, § 3.4).

214 *Anzû* II 35–37 (Annus 2001, 23).

After a furious battle and upon the advice of the wise Ea, Ninurta is able to send Anzû's feathers on the wind as good tidings. This sign establishes Ninurta's victory over Anzû and the mountains. Once back from the mountains to the city temple, the Ekur, the god is welcomed as a hero, because "he killed the mountains, he disturbed and flooded their environs" (*Ninurta īnar ḫursānī qerbīssunu udalliḫ irḫiṣ*).[215] The mountains, together with the *Mischwesen*, are said to have been slain and killed, an expression generally used of persons. Ninurta's return is praised among the gods for his bringing back the Enlil-ship and the rites, and he is addressed as the god for whom the "rites of the mountain" (*paraṣ šadî*) were created.[216]

Interestingly, the Sumerian myth of the Anzû-bird tells a different story. In the 3rd-millennium tale of *Lugalbanda and the Anzû-bird*, the encounter of the human hero and the Thunderbird occurs in the Zabu and Lullubu mountains, which are eastern mountain ranges. In this mythical context, Anzû is described as having a lion's face and the body of an eagle, but his behavior is entirely human, acting in the myth as a divine person. Moreover, his role in the mythical narrative is positive, establishing fate according Enlil's rules. Anzû has been appointed by Enlil as the prince who decides the destiny of the rolling rivers, as the one who helps humans to follow the righteous path of Enlil and as the guardian of the entrance to the mountains.[217]

The constant connection of the mountains, with their creatures, to the eastern horizon in Sumerian mythology is once more affirmed. In the Sumerian myth of Anzû, the Thunderbird is considered the inhabitant and guardian of the cosmic Mountain of Sunrise. Its cosmic features are expressed by the fact that it is addressed as the locus where the destinies are fixed. This understanding is supported by an early Semitic literary text where a clear connection between Anzû, Mt. Šaššar (ḫ u r - s a g *Sa-sa-ru*$_{12}$) and the Sun rising from the netherworld is expressed.[218] The establishing of the destinies, or rather, the "cutting of destinies" by Šamaš, might explain a correspondence with the name Šaššar and the *šaššaru*-saw of the iconographical sources.[219] As suggested by Woods, this "saw is symbolic of the cutting of judgments, d i - k u d , that Šamaš executes, and the cutting of fates, n a m - t a r , that Šamaš facilitates, on the eastern horizon".[220] Accordingly, all these associations speak for the designation of Mt. Šaššar as one of the cosmic mountains of Sunrise in Sumerian symbolism and cosmology. The fact that in the later Akkadian tradition, the literary Mt. Šaššar is equated with Mt. Bašār, i.e. the Jebel Bishri of cuneiform sources, and thus with

215 *Anzû* III 17–21 (Annus 2001, 27).

216 *Anzû* III 122–126, *Ninurta aššu taqtarduma šadê tanarru kullat nakirī tušakniša ana šēpē abka Enlil bēlūta tagdamar kullat gimrī parṣī mannu ša kīma kâta ibbanû paraṣ šadî narbû šarkūka parak ilāni šīmati*, "O Ninurta, because you became brave and killed the mountains, you made all enemies kneel at the feet of your father Enlil. You have assembled lordship, each and every rite. For whom but you were the rites of the mountain created? Greatness is given to you at the dais of the gods of destinies" (Annus 2001, 28).

217 *Lugalbanda and the Anzû bird* 99–110 (ETCSL 1.8.2.2). For the animistic features of Anzû, see Chapter V.

218 ARET V, Nr.6, col. VI 1–6 (Edzard,1984, 28–30). See also Woods 2009, 218–219.

219 See, e.g., above in this chapter, § 2.1, Illustration 1.

220 Woods 2009, 218. In addition, Woods proposes translating Mt. Šaššar as Mt. Saw, establishing a connection with the name Sierra (Woods 2009, 218–219).

the north-western horizon, should be considered a "late toponymic transfer".[221] The existence of two traditions inherent to Mt. Šaššar is evident also in the myth of Erra, where despite the clear location of this mountain in the North-West, the presence of *hašurru*-trees evokes the Mountain of Sunrise.[222]

3.4 Mount Labnanu and the Cedar Forest, mountain of Ḫuwawa

Mt. Labnanu corresponds to the Lebanon mountain range, one of the main mountain ranges in the west, close to the Mediterranean Sea. It has been traditionally referred to as the mountain of cedar trees, because of the prevalence of this arboreal species, and has thus been considered the Cedar Forest of the Gilgameš Epic. Interestingly, Mt. Lebnanu is invoked in the *Lipšur Litanies*, where it is addressed as the "mountain of cypress" (*šadû šurmēni*).[223] This reference to Mt. Lebanon is one of the few occurrences of this mountain described as an active entity in the ritual performance.

The other occurrence is found in the standard Babylonian version of the Gilgameš Epic, and attests Mt. Lebanon as a powerful entity which has to be worshipped for incubation rites. When the heroes Gilgameš and Enkidu head to the Forest of Ḫuwawa and wander through remote mountain ranges, they get closer to Mount Lebanon, where they stop and spend the night.[224] Before the night, Gilgameš pours an offering of *maṣḫatu*-flour on the top of the mountain in order to attain a dream that would tell him about the encounter with Ḫuwawa and the outcome of the expedition.[225] The mountain is here addressed as an entity capable of bringing a dream to Gilgameš as a sign of good fortune. The narration continues with the setting up of Gilgameš' sleeping place by his comrade Enkidu, who makes a *zaqīqu*-house and lets Gilgameš lie on a circular structure. Natural settings –such as mountains, hills, rivers and springs– have traditionally been believed to be ideal places for incubation and visions.[226]

In one Old Babylonian version of the epic, Gilgameš reports the details of his dreams to Enkidu.[227] What Gilgameš saw in his dream is a mountain collapsing on him. After surviving the avalanche, a man appears surrounded by a shining brightness. This man is wrapped in a (presumably) bright and royal cloak and his radiance spreads all over the land. Then, the man helps Gilgameš, pulling the hero forth from under the mountain.[228] The

221 Woods 2009, 218. See also Lambert 1989, 17.

222 Cagni 1977, 56.

223 *Lipšur Litanies* 9 (Reiner 1956, 132–133) // ḪAR = *ḫubullu* XXII 10 (Bloch/Horowitz 2015, 77). See above § 3.1.

224 *Gilg.* IV 1–5 (George 2003, 588–589).

225 *Gilg.* IV 7–9 // *Gilg.* IV 85–87 // *Gilg.* IV 127// *Gilg.* IV 168–170, *īlima Gišgimmaš ina muḫḫi šadî maṣḫassu utteqqa ana ḫursāni šadû bila šutta amat damiqtī*[?] *lūmur*, "Gilgameš went up on to the top of the mountain, he made his offerings of *maṣḫatu* flour to the hill: 'O mountain, bring me a dream, let me see a message of *good fortune*!'" (George 2003: 588–589 ff.).

226 See Zgoll 2006. See also Chapter III, § 5.

227 *Gilg.* OB Schoeyen 2: 5–16 (George 2003: 232–235).

228 *Gilg.* V 5–12, *ina būdiya ēmidam šadâm šadûm iqūpamma īsiḫan*[*ni*] *birkīya* ⌜*ilta*⌝*wi lūtum ahīya šalummatum uddannin ištēn eṭlum lāb*⌜*iš*⌝ [*pal*]*âm ina mātim nawirma d*[*u*]*mqamma d*[*amiq*[?]] *iṣbatma kubur em*[*ūqi*]*ya šaplānu šadîmma ištalpanni*, "With my shoulder I propped up a mountain;

meaning of his dream is revealed by Enkidu. This man is nothing less than Ḫuwawa himself:

inanna ibrī ša nillaku⸢šum⸣	"Now, my friend, the one to whom we go,
ul šadûmma nukkur mi⸢mma⸣	is he not the mountain, is he not very strange?
inanna Ḫuwawa ša nillakušu[m u]l šadûmma nukkur m[im]ma	Now, Ḫuwawa to whom we go, is he not the mountain, is he not very strange?"

Enkidu refers to him as the mountain itself (*šadûmma*), and as a strange person, different in every possible way (*nukkur mimma*). The radiance refers to Ḫuwawa's seven auras (*melammu*) or seven cloaks of radiance (7 *naḫlapāti ša namrī*), which protect him and make him unapproachable and invincible.[229] When Ḫuwawa loses his *melammu*s, he finds himself vulnerable and can be defeated by Gilgameš. An expressive scene is described before Ḫuwawa's defeat, when his shining *melammus* are said to be escaping in the wood, and his "awe-inspiring radiances" (*namrīrū*) to be fading into the mist.[230]

Ḫuwawa's mystical auras are traded by the same Ḫuwawa in the Sumerian account of Gilgameš's enterprise against the Cedar Mountain. Huwawa bargains his "terrors" (n i - t e) with what Gilgameš offers him: wives, flour, a waterskin, shoes and semiprecious stones. These trading gifts appear to be products of the urban society of Sumer, and they were presumably unknown to Ḫuwawa.[231]

In both Sumerian and Akkadian mythical narratives Ḫuwawa is described as a person (*awīlu*), despite his monstrous features. According to both textual and iconographical sources, Ḫuwawa is portrayed as a *Mischwesen*: anthropomorphic and non-anthropomorphic features were intertwined and produced several visual combinations throughout the centuries. The characteristic features of his face are attested in several omens, where faces resembling Huwawa are observed in humans and lambs.[232] His face is

---

the mountain collapsed on me and girt me around. Feebleness surrounded my knees, (but) a radiant brightness gave strength to my arms. There was a man, clad in a *royal* [*mantle*,] he was shining brightest in the land and was most [comely] in beauty. He took hold of my upper arm, from under the mountain itself he pulled me forth" (George 2003: 232–235).

229 *Gilg.* V 97–99, *ē taplaḫ izizzassu lā* [*irrub ana šubtiš*] *lā urrad ana ḫalbimma* [*lā* ...] *lām iḫḫalpu* 7 *naḫlapātišu ša namrīri* [1-*et*] *ḫalip* 6 *šaḫit*, "Fear not, stand against him! He must nor [enter his dwelling]; he must not go into the grove, he must not [...]! Before he has wrapped himself in his seven cloaks [of radiance]: one he is wrapped in, six he has divested." (George/Al-Rawi 2014, 69–90).

230 *Gilg.* OB Ischali 12' –13', ⸢*melemmū*⸣ *iḫalliqū ina qīši melemmū* [*iḫ*]*alliqūma namrīrū* ⸢*i*⸣*rrupū ana er*[*pi*](?), "The auras are escaping in the wood, the auras are fugitive and the radiant sheens are darkening into the *mist*." (George 2003, 262–263).

231 According to Woods, in fact, Ḫuwawa is portrayed as a "provincial bumpkin", who has no knowledge of civilization because of his living in the remote far East. (Woods 2009, 208)

232 See, e.g., the Neo-Babylonian baked clay model of animal entrails in the shape of the face of the demon Ḫuwawa, used in divination (Green 1999, 152, fig. 3).

generally referred to as having a bulbous nose and wide eyes.[233] As seen, he is referred to as a person, but with strange features, and he is also considered the mountain itself.

The connection between Ḫuwawa and the mountain of cedar trees is complicated. Ḫuwawa is the offspring of the mountain,[234] and somehow the Cedar Mountain itself. Ḫuwawa was not only born in the mountains, but he is the offspring of the rocky womb of the Cedar Mountain itself, as we can read in the Sumerian version *Gilgameš and Ḫuwawa* B. In this text Ḫuwawa explains that his mother was a cave in the mountains, and his father was a cave in the hills, but eventually he was left there alone by Utu.[235] Moreover, in *Gilgameš and Ḫuwawa* A, the Cedar Forest is referred to as the "Living One's Mountain" (kur lú tìl-la), a name that evokes both the divine nature of Ḫuwawa, and his deep entanglement with the living mountain.[236]

In the Sumerian tradition, the mountain in question is the cosmic Mountain of Sunrise, which stands out on the eastern horizon and is deeply implicated with the Sun. The close connection between Ḫuwawa, the Sun and the Mountain of Sunrise is expressed by the fact that Ḫuwawa is said to be raised in the mountain by Utu and that the Cedar Mountain is explicitly referred to as Utu's domain. In fact, *Gilgameš and Ḫuwawa* A reports that every decision concerning the Cedar Mountain is Utu's business, thus the Sun-god must be informed.[237] This evidence supports the interpretation that in the Sumerian tradition the Cedar Mountain, the realm of Ḫuwawa, was conceived of as being in the far East, beyond the Zagros, pertaining to and partaking of the cosmic realm.

The mountainous abode of Ḫuwawa is enveloped in a dense mist of mystery. From the Sumerian to the Akkadian tradition, the Cedar mountain is imbued in secrecy, belonging to the divine realm. In the Sumerian account, the king of Uruk expresses his yearning to learn about the dwelling of Ḫuwawa, which is explicitly referred to as a place which cannot be known.[238] The very act of discovering the secret abode of the Anunnaki is cited in an Old Babylonian manuscript, which describes the impious actions of Gilgameš and Enkidu in walking into the forest and cutting its sacred trees:

---

233 George 2003, 144–147.

234 See the Sumerian *Gilgameš and Ḫuwawa* A 155–157: ^{d}Utu ama tud-da-ĝu$_{10}$ nu-um-zu a-a bulùĝ-ĝá-ĝu$_{10}$ nu-um-zu kur-ra mu-un-tud-dè-en za-e mu-un- bulùĝ-e ^{d}Gilgameš zi an-na ma-an-pàd zi ki-a ma-an pàd zi kur-ra ma-an-pàd; "Utu, I never knew a mother who bore me, nor a father who brought me up! I was born in the mountains, you brought me up! Yet Gilgameš swore to me by heaven, by earth, and by the mountains" (ETCSL 1.8.1.5: 115–157). See also the most up-to-date translation by Edzard (2015, 293). The close connection between Ḫuwawa, Utu/Šamaš and the mountains is stated in *Gilgameš and Ḫuwawa* B 164–166 (ETCSL 1.8.1.5.1: 164–166).

235 *Gilgameš and Ḫuwawa* B 164–166, ama tud-da-ĝu$_{10}$ hur-ru-um kur-ra a-a tud-da-ĝu$_{10}$ hur-ru-um hur-saĝ-ĝú ^{d}Utu dili-ĝu$_{10}$-ne kur-ra mu-un-dè-en-tuš-en, "The mother who bore me was a cave in the mountains. The father who engendered me was a cave in the hills. Utu left me to live all alone in the mountains!" (ETCSL 1.8.1.5.1: 164–166).

236 George 1999, 149 ff.; George 2003, 144–147; Edzard 1990, 165–203; Edzard 2015, 283–295.

237 ETCSL 1.8.1.5: 9–12.

238 *Gilgameš and Ḫuwawa* A 138: kur-ra tuš-a-zu ba-ra-az kur-ra tuš-a-zu he-zu-am, "The mountain where you sit cannot be known! The mountain where you dwell I want to know!" (ETCSL 1.8.1.5: 138).

ūridma irtahiṣ qištam	He went down and flooded the forest.
mūšab Enunakī puzzuram ipte	He disclosed the secret abode of the Anunnaki:
Gilgameš iṣī ubattaq Enkidu uharra urbazilli	Gilgameš felling the trees, Enkidu choosing the *best timber*(?)" [239]

In the Akkadian tradition, the Cedar Mountain is conceived of as located in the West, being equated with the Lebanon or Amanus range, by virtue of its thriving cedar population. Still, the Cedar Forest in the western horizon is envisaged as part of the cosmic and divine realm. The Mountain of Ḫuwawa is a liminal place, belonging to the gods, where a different type of power and divine exists. The forest is called the "secret abode of the Anunnaki" (*mušab Enunaki puzuram*), and the "dwelling of the gods, throne-dais of goddesses" (*mušab ilī parak Irninī*).[240] Ḫuwawa's kingdom is wonderfully described in a recently found and published tablet which completes the previous lacuna in the portrayal of the Cedar Mountain through the incredulous eyes of Gilgameš and Enkidu:[241]

izzīzūma inappatū qiš[ta]	They stood *marvelling* at the forest,
ša erēni ittanaplasū mīlašu	observing the height of the cedars,
ša qišti ittanaplasū nērebšu	observing the way into the forest.
ašar Ḫumbaba ittallaku šakin kibsu	Where Ḫumbaba came and went there was a track,
ḫarrānātu šutēšurāma ṭubbat gerru	the paths were in good order and the way was well trodden.
[ē]marū šadû erēni mūšab ilī parak Irnini	They were gazing at the Cedar Mountain, the dwelling of the gods, the throne-dais of the goddesses,
[ina p]ān šadîmma erēni naši ḫiṣibšu	[on the] very face of the mountain the cedar was proffering its abundance,
[ṭ]ābu ṣillašu mali rišāti	sweet was its shade, full of delight.
[šutēl]up giṣṣu ḫitlupat [qi]štu	[All] tangled was the thorny undergrowth, the forest was a thick canopy,
[x x-p]u erēnu ballukkumma	[...] cedar, *ballukku-tree* ... [...][242]

The view that is disclosed in front of the adventurers is stunning in its beauty: a thriving forest abounding with life and joy. Wherever Ḫuwawa walks he leaves a track in the forest, and these paths are tidy and well kept. The lofty cedar trees are entangled with *bullukku*-trees and cypresses, in a luxuriant arboreal dome. Crickets, birds and monkeys are singing through the canopy of trees, delighting Ḫuwawa with their music at daytime.

239 *Gilg.* OB Iščhali 37'b–40' (George 2003, 264–265)
240 *Gilg.*V 7 (George/Al-Rawi 2014, 76–77).
241 George/Al-Rawi 2014, 76–77: 1–26.
242 *Gilg.*V 1–10 (George/Al-Rawi 2014, 76–77: 1–10).

This thriving world will be soon destroyed by the fury of Gilgameš and Enkidu, who slay the lofty cedar tree, together with the seven sons of Ḫuwawa. After the destruction of the Cedar Forest a glare of awareness and fear hits the two young heroes:[243]

[*ibrī ana*] *tūšar ništakan qišta*	"My friend, we have reduced the forest [to] a wasteland,
[*min*]*â ina Nippuri nippal Enlil*	[how] shall we answer Enlil in Nippur?
[*ina du*]*nnikunuma maṣṣara tanārā*	(Enlil will ask:), '[In] your (pl.) might you slew the guardian,
[*mī*]*nû uzzakunuma taraḫḫiṣā qišta*	what was this wrath of yours that you have washed away the forest?'"[244]

Indeed, the ventures of Gilgameš and Enkidu against the Cedar Forest and its guardian constitute a sacrilegious act. The two adventurers are aware of the taboo that they are breaking, and they are hurrying to slay Ḫuwawa, "before Enlil the foremost has learned about it" (*lām išmû asarēdu Enlil*), fearing the anger of the great gods.[245] Ḫuwawa was, in fact, appointed by Enlil as a deterrent to anyone searching for valuable timber in the ancient forest, which was part of the divine realm.[246] By killing the guardian, the two heroes also kill the numinous mountain and its living trees. The expedition concludes with the dead cedar trees carried by the waters of the Euphrates to Nippur to be used for building, and a desolated mountain left behind.[247]

3.5 The cosmic mountains Māšu, Ḫašur and Nimuš

Mt. Māšu, which is probably to be translated "Twin Mountain", is the cosmic mountain traditionally referred to as the access of the "Path of the Sun" (*ḫarrān* ^{d}*Šamši*) into the region of darkness that extends to the shores of the cosmic sea.[248] This mountain is mentioned once in the written sources, while we find several iconographical correspondences in the glyptic.[249] In the Gilgameš Epic, after Enkidu's death, a despairing Gilgameš initiates a journey beyond the borders of the world until he reaches Utnapištim's

243 *Gilg.*V 303–308 (George/Al-Rawi 2014, 82–83).
244 *Gilg.*V 303–306 (George Al-Rawi 2014, 82–83)
245 *Gilg.* V 185–186 (George 2003, 610–611).
246 George 2003, 144–147.
247 *Gilg.* V 303–308 (George/Al-Rawi 2014, 82–83).
248 Horowitz 1998, 96–98. Moreover, Horowitz equates this mountain with the cosmic Mountain of Sunset, arguing that "the dark mountain of sunset may be compared with Mt. Māšu in *Gilg.* IX, where Gilgamesh encounters a region of darkness. Mt. Māsu, of course, is located on the central continent. Gilgamesh only reaches the sea coast in *Gilg.* X after crossing Mt. Māšu and the region of darkness. Sargon of Akkad encounters a similar region of darkness in the mountains east of Mesopotamia. On the World Map, however, a region 'where the sun is not seen' is located across the northern portion of the cosmic ocean *marratu* from the mountain on the continent" (Horowitz 1998, 332).
249 See above in this chapter § 2.1.

dwelling "in the Mouth-of-the-Rivers" (*ina pī nārāti*).[250] He wanders alone through the steppes, until he approaches a mountain, whose gate separates the human world from the realm of gods:

ša šadî šemušu Māš[*umma*]	Of the mountain its name was Māšu.
ana šad Māši ina kaš[*ādišu*]	Upon his reaching Mount Māšu,
ša ūmišamma inaṣṣaru aṣ[*ê šamši*]	Which daily guards the rising [of the sun],
elûšunu šupuk šamê e[*ndū*?]	Their peaks [*abut*] the foundation of the skies,
šaplis arallê irassunu ⸢*kašdat*⸣	Below, their breast reaches into the netherworld.
girtablulū inaṣṣarū bābšu	Scorpion-men were guarding its gate,
ša rašbat pulḫassunuma imrassunu mūtu	Whose fearsomeness was terrifying and whose glance was death,
galtū milammūšunu saḫip ḫuršānī	Whose radiance was fearful, enshrouding the mountains:
ana aṣê šamši u ereb šamši inaṣṣarū šamšima	At sunrise and sunset they guard the sun.[251]

The cosmic nature of this mountain is here fully expressed. The mountain guards the rising and the setting of the Sun/Šamaš, in its/his cyclical trip, and its roots reach the netherworld (*arallû*) while its peaks pierce and mingle with the firmament (*šupuk šamê*). Its entrance is guarded by the Scorpion-men and Scorpion-women, who also guard Šamaš at sunrise and sunset. Mt. Māšu's dwellers are described as dreadful creatures, whose eyes are death, and their fearsome aura (*melammu*) encompasses the mountain.[252] Its intrinsic duality is not only apparent from its name "Twin Mountain", but is also expressed by its being simultaneously the mountain of sunrise and of sunset, and by the presence of Scorpion-men as its guardians. Scorpions comprise polyvalent and opposite meanings in Mesopotamian symbolism, being both symbol of death and night, and of life and rebirth.[253]

Another cosmic mountain of the rising sun is Mt. Hašur, which is traditionally described as a mountain standing out on the eastern horizon in the literature. This legendary mountain, whose name stems from the evergreen *ḫašurru*-trees, is found only in literary contexts. The close connection of this mountain with the Sun and its daily rising over the horizon in the East is evident in the passage "Utu, as you emerge from the pure heavens, in your crossing over Mt. Hašur" (^{d}U t u an-š à k u g - g a - t a e - d ì - a - z u - n e k u r Ḫ a - š u r - r a - t a b [a] l a - d a - z u - n e: ^{d}*Šamaš ultu šamê ellūti ina aṣêka šadû Ḫašur*

250 See below, Chapter III, § 3.

251 *Gilg.* IX 37–45 (George 2003, 668–669).

252 See Anzû's and Ḫuwawa's *melammūs* encompassing their mountains.

253 Woods 2009, 192–193. Woods moves further, arguing for the existence of the phenomenon of *coincidentia oppositorum*, which is "a cross-culturally observed mythological theme in which the paradox of divine and mythical reality is conceptualized as a union, and thereby transcendence of contraries" (Woods 2009, 197). For the symbolic meanings of scorpions see also Zernecke 2008, 107–127.

ina nabalkuttika).[254] Utu is explicitly called lord of the mountain of ḫ a š u r -trees (^{d}U t u e n k u r ^{ĝiš}ḫ a - š u - ú r - r a),[255] and is often portrayed as a bull rising from this mountain and dwelling on it. In a Sumerian hymn to Utu, the Sun-god is described as a "bull which drinks among the dewy e r e n -trees, which grow on Mt. Ḫašur" (g u d ^{ĝiš}e r e n d u r u$_5$ n a ĝ - a Ḫ a - [š u] - ú r - ⸢r a p e š⸣ - a).[256]

The traditional fauna of the Ḫašur mountain are the bison and the bezoar-goat, whereas its main arboreal species is the *ḫašurru*-tree.[257] The name of this mountain probably derives from this tree, which is often equated with the cedar (e r e n). As previously shown, Mt. Ḫašur is regarded as the pure place of origin of the tall cedar, and the locus where the destiny of the tree is established in *Šurpu*,[258] a conception that is found also in the *Lipšur Litanies*.[259] These two arboreal species are intertwined, and often merged together in the literary tradition, as the evergreen trees entangled with the cosmic Mountain of Sunrise.[260] Mt. Ḫašur as the Mountain of Sunrise perfectly matches its cosmic connotation of the location where destinies are fixed at every daybreak. In *Lugalbanda in the Mountain Cave*, Utu is described as "the bright bull" which "rose from the horizon, bull of Mt. Ḫašur, which determines fates" (g u d b a b b a r a n - ú r - t a è - a g u d Ḫ a - š u - ú r - r a n a m - e - a a k - e).[261] Furthermore, some traditions refers to Mt. Ḫašur as the mountain of the sources of the Tigris and of the Euphrates, as we read in an Assyrian incantation: "Pure waters of the Tigris and the Euphrates, which come forth from (their) springs to Mt. Hašur" (*mû Idiqlat mû Puratti ellūti ša ištu kuppi ana Ḫašur aṣûni*).[262]

The cosmic nature of this mountain is further expressed in its connotation of secrecy and boundary of the known world. Ḫašur is referred to as the unknowable and/or unapproachable mountain. In *Lugalbanda and the Anzû bird*, the setting of the mythical venture and nest of the Thunderbird is "Mt. Hašur, the unknowable mountain, where no snake slithers, no scorpion scurries" (Ḫ a - š u - u r n u - z u k a r - r a - k a m u š n u - u n - s u l - s u l g i r i n u - s a - s a),[263] an epithet which recurs frequently in the narration.[264] The mystery which surrounds this cosmic mountain is attested also in *Lugalbanda and the*

254 K 3052+5982: 11–14 (Meek 1913, 66–68: 11–14). Further evidence for the connection between Mt. Ḫašur and the sun can be found in *Enki and the World Order*, where Utu is referred to as a bull rising from the Ḫašur-mountain (ETCSL 1.1.3: 373, g u d Ḫ a - š u - ú r - t a è) and in a Sumerian hymn to Ninurta, where Utu is said to emerge from Mt. Ḫašur (TCL 15, 7: 13, ^{d}U t u Ḫ a - š u - ú r - [t] a è - [a] (ETCSL 4.27.01: 13)). See George 2003, 864; Woods 2009, 190.

255 VAS 2, 73 12.

256 Utu Hymn B 10 (ETCSL 4.32.2: 10).

257 Woods 2009, 189–191.

258 *Šurpu* IX 42–48 (Reiner 1958, 46). See above in this chapter, § 2.2.

259 *Lipšur Litanies* 7, KUR *Ḫa-šur* MIN KUR *e-re-ni* (Reiner 1956, 132–133) // URA = *ḫubullu* XXII 8 (Bloch/Horowitz, 77). See also above, § 3.1.

260 For a comprehensive discussion of the cedar tree and *ḫašurru*-tree, see Chapter IV, § 2.4.

261 ETCLS 1.8.2.1: 228–229. On the symbolism of the Eastern horizon and the fixing of destinies see Woods 2009, and on the cosmological aspects of birth see Polonsky 2006, 297–311.

262 KAR 34 14–15 (Ebeling 1919). See Woods 2009, 202–203.

263 ETCSL 1.8.2.2: 36–37. See Woods 2009, 207.

264 See *Lugalbanda and the Anzû bird* 36, 62, 129 (ETCSL 1.8.2.2: 36, 62, 129).

Mountain Cave, where the hero begs Inana to spare him from dying in the midst of the "secret place of Mt. Hašur" (á-úr kur ha-su-úr-ra-ke$_4$).[265]

The Mountain of Sunrise belongs to the divine and cosmic realm, and comprises the mystical place where destinies are fixed and where the future unfolds after its fluid gestation during the night. Destinies are beyond human knowledge and they are thus projected in the midst of the cosmic mountain on the eastern horizon, where the sun's rays first touch the earth. Thus, the secrets of this Mountain shall be preserved from human eyes and understanding. Accordingly, as seen for Cedar Mountain, the very fact of Gilgameš wandering in the mists of the cosmic mountain and getting to know the "secret abode of the Anunnaki" represents a sacrilegious act.

The legendary mountain where Utnapištim's boat ran aground after the Flood is Mount Nimuš:

ana šadî Nimuš ītemid eleppu	On Mount Nimuš the boat ran aground,
sadû Nimuš eleppa iṣbatma ana nâši ul iddin	Mount Nimuš held the boat fast and did not let it rock.
išten ūma šanâ ūma sadû Nimuš KIMIN	One day, a second day, Mount Nimuš held the boat fast and did not let it rock,
šalša ūma rebâ ūma sadû Nimuš KIMIN	A third day, a fourth day, Mount Nimuš held the boat fast and did not let it rock,
ḫamša šešša sadû Nimuš KIMIN	A fifth, a sixth, Mount Nimuš held the boat fast and did not let it rock.[266]

The mountain is said to hold the boat fast (*sadû Nimuš eleppa iṣbat*) and to not let it rock (*nâši ul iddin*), in a poetic personalistic description of the mountain as an embracing mother who does not let the boat shift down from its slopes. The second attestation of this mountain in the literary sources is in the *Lipšur Litanies*, where it is summoned on behalf of the patient, to release him from his unknown sins. In this ritual composition and in its parallel lexical list, Mt. Nimuš is addressed as the "mountain of the Gutians" (*šadû Gutî*), projecting its possible localization on the north-eastern horizon.[267] Notably, the specific name of the legendary mountain where Utnapištim's ark ran aground is found only in these 1st-millennium literary sources, with the Old Babylonian version of the Flood not mentioning any specific mountain. This might suggest that a named legendary mountain entered the literary and mythical realm only in later traditions.

265 ETCSL 1.8.2.1: 196. See also Woods 2009, 211.

266 *Gilg.* XI 142–147 (George 2003, 712–713).

267 *Lipšur Litanies* 41 (Reiner 1956, 145–135) // URA = *ḫubullu* XXII 44 (Bloch/Horowitz 2015, 81).

3.6 Aššur: divine mound and god

Last but not least, one of the most eloquent cases of how a mountain became a fully personified god is Aššur. The topographical features of the site of Assur consists of a natural hill, a spur of Jebel Makhul, which is a continuation of the Jebel Hamrin range on the west side of the Tigris, and its rocky slopes as seen from the river tower impressively over the plain.[268] This hill was presumably conceived of by its inhabitants as a holy spot in prehistoric times, being imbued with a divine nature, or believed to be a *numen loci*.[269]

This argumentation has been proposed by Lambert (1983) and it has been assumed valid by the scholarship ever since. The correspondence of the name Aššur –being the name of the location of the town of Aššur, of the city Aššur itself and of the local city god– constituted the first step in advancing this hypothesis of Aššur being the deified city or mountain.[270] The Old Assyrian evidence from the trading colonies in Kaneš features a lack of distinction between the city and the god when the name Aššur is used.[271] Moreover, the god's non-canonical identity further supports this conclusion. Aššur lacks the traditional identity and family connections which characterize the major deities of the Mesopotamian panthea: his divine family was borrowed from the Babylonian tradition at a late stage, and he is generally referred to as the "Assyrian Enlil",[272] whereas in personal names the god is generally referred to as *ilum/ilī* "the god/my god".[273]

Lambert argues the god Aššur lacks the typical epithets generally attributed to the Mesopotamian deities and does not seem to have been conceived of and worshipped as "a manifestation of any of the great powers of nature".[274] After this contradictory statement, his argumentation moves forward, taking into account those mountains and rivers which have been considered divine entities belonging to city panthea throughout Mesopotamian history –such as the mountains Ebiḫ and Dipar, and the rivers Ulāya and Baliḫ.[275] Most occurrences come from the North and from Anatolia, a feature that is unsurprising given the flat landscape which characterizes southern Mesopotamia. In this evidence it is not possible to discern a god of the mountain or of the river and to separate it from the geographical feature, a notion that leads to the fusion of topographical entity and deity.[276]

According to my understanding, the argumentation regarding the lack of relation to any natural manifestation of Aššur, in opposition to the other great gods, needs to be

268 Lambert 1983, 85.
269 Lambert 1983; Livingstone 1997, 165; Frame 1997, 55, note 2.
270 Lambert 1983, 85.
271 Lambert 1983, 83.
272 Lambert 1983, 83.
273 Lambert 1983, 83.
274 Lambert 1983, 82–83, esp. note 7.
275 See *passim* throughout the book.
276 "In all these cases there is no patron god of the mountain or river who can be distinguished from the geographical feature. In one sense the mountain or river is the god. This kind of deity is distinct from those of the traditional Sumero-Babylonian pantheon probably in ideology, but almost certainly in cult. No temples of these deities are known to have existed. One is reminded of numinous mountains to the west: Ṣaphon, Sinai and Olympus, but they were the seats of gods, at least in historical times, and not gods themselves. But perhaps the passage of time made the difference. Personal names of the type we have cited seem to die out over the second millennium" (Lambert 1983, 84).

reconsidered. While evaluating further evidence on divine mountains and rivers whose topographical and divine features merge, Lambert seems to keep those notions apart, bearing in mind only the anthropomorphic conception of deity. This conception should be overturned, since Aššur is a natural feature itself, a rocky hill, which was conceived of as being imbued with divine or numinous qualities, and regarded as a god *per se*. Even its commonest epithet, KUR.GAL, "Great Mountain" (if it is the case of a borrowing from the traditional epithet of Enlil), calls attention to the image of a god equated with that of a mountain.

In his iconographical representations, the god Aššur is portrayed with anthropomorphic features, such as a bearded man whose upper body is human and who is inserted within a winged solar disk.[277] His lower body is never fully represented, and, it could be hypothesized that his lower body would have been portrayed with the common motif of the stylized mountain.[278] This interpretation is still speculative, but further support for this understanding is offered by the so-called *Brunnenrelief*, whose central figure portraying a mountain god has been related to the visual representation of the god Aššur.[279] In both literary and iconographical representations of the mountain deities, anthropomorphic and topographical features coexist and specify these divine natural elements. As seen regarding Ebiḫ, this double characterization does not contradict the religious understanding and perception of a mountain god, rather it actually displays the entangled meanings proper to such natural deities.

Lambert's discussion represents fruitful progress in the much-needed assessment of natural elements as an integral part of the religious life and of the symbolic and sacred landscape of Mesopotamians. However, his argumentation runs aground when he presents this evidence as mere relics, destined to die out during the second millennium. The consideration of those elements as the survivals of Tylorian memory impedes an organic reconsideration of those natural and geographical features whose traits are not merely pure and holy places, but fully divine entities in the Mesopotamian panthea (e.g. the enduring cult of Ebiḫ). The Neo-Assyrian evidence of mountains and rivers included in royal rituals offer the clearest indication that their cult was thriving during the 1st millennium among the Assyrian kings, presumably in accordance with the same mountainous tradition that lead to installing and worshipping Mt. Aššur as the chief god of their pantheon.

---

277 See, e.g., Parpola 1993, 166.
278 See above § 2.1 and § 2.3.
279 See above, § 2.3, Illustration 4.

Chapter III

River Deities, Cosmic Rivers and Sacred Springs

Πάντα ρέι (Eraclitus)

"The river is everywhere at the same time, at the source and at the mouth, at the waterfall, at the ferry, at the current, in the ocean and in the mountains." (H. Hesse, *Siddharta*)

1 Bodies of flowing water: places, persons and gods

Rivers are bodies of flowing water, which wind across the land from their sources to their delta, shaping the landscape and comprising a border for human endeavors. Their waters have been used for drinking, cleaning, and for creating the energy necessary for human activities, thus enabling the flourishing of major urban centers along their banks from past to present. Rivers have been regarded as sacred places, as cosmic elements, as purifying and cleansing entities, often conceived of as deities. Throughout history, they have been worshipped as natural forms of divinity in the religious traditions of many parts of the world. Watercourses have been envisioned with both masculine and feminine traits. However, rivers have tended to be conceived of as maternal beings, due to their role of generating and nurturing life, and providing fertility with their body of flowing water. The notion of water as the source of life has informed the symbolism inherent to water in the mythologies, beliefs and cults of a great number of cultures.[1] Water "symbolizes the primal substance from which all forms come and to which they will return",[2] and has, thus, been worshipped in a profusion of ways as the Universal Mother.[3]

Hinduism's religious tradition displays an elaborated and complex conception of the holiness and divinity of rivers.[4] As stated in the *Skanda Purana*, "there are hundreds of

1 Haberman 2011, 39. As pointed out by Haberman, "in many parts of the world rivers are referred to as 'mothers': Narmadai, 'Mother Narmada'; the Volga is Mat Rodnaya, 'Mother of the Land'. The Thai word for river, *mae nan*, translates literally as 'water mother'" (Haberman 2011, 39).

2 Eliade 1958, 188 ff.

3 Eliade 1958, 188 ff.; Haberman 2011, 39.

4 von Behr 2007, 1964–1965; Haberman 2011.

rivers. All of them remove sins. All of them are bestowers of merit. Of all the rivers, those that fall into the sea are the most excellent. Of all those rivers, Ganga, Yamuna, Narmada and Sarasvati are the most excellent rivers" of India.[5] In his recent work on the Yamuna River, Haberman offers a comprehensive historical, religious and ecological picture of this river. The Yamuna is conceptualized as a prominent goddess, daughter of the Sun and sister of Yama, the lord of Death, mother of all beings with particular life-protecting and life-purifying features, who saves from death and grants a good life.[6] The theologies regarding the Yamuna and the Ganges are similar, but with the major difference that the Ganges exists to provide liberation at death, whereas the Yamuna gives salvation to the living, by developing the spirituality of her devotees.[7]

In antiquity, the River Boyne was sacred to the ancient Celts and was believed to be the offspring of the goddess Boann in Ireland.[8] The River Tiber has been associated with the very existence of Rome since its foundation, and festivals in its honor, the Tibernalia, were celebrated throughout the year. The traits of this fluvial entity mingled with those of the demi-god Tiberinus (*Pater Tiberinus*), who was the son of Janus, the god of the sun, transformations and landscapes, and of the nymph Juturna, sister of Saturn and lady of waters. After his drowning in the river, the watercourse was given his name, and the two, river and demi-god, became one entity.

The worship of rivers and especially of their sources is a widespread phenomenon in the ancient Mediterranean and beyond. In France, the archaeological evidence attests to the existence of a temple at the source of the River Seine, which was sacred to the goddess Sequana, and where rites were performed in her honor.[9] In ancient Anatolia, due to the karstic geological features of the mountains, springs were conceived of as sacred places, gates and channels leading into the netherworld, but also channels of communication between gods and humans, and deities *per se*.[10]

Together with mountains, rivers, canals, springs and underground waters are prominent topographic features and powerful natural elements in the Mesopotamian landscape. The Tigris and the Euphrates constitute and flow through the flat Mesopotamian alluvial plain, together with a myriad of tributaries, canals and irrigation channels, and the maze of the Southern marshes. This fluvial landscape has represented entangled meanings in the eyes of Mesopotamians. Rivers are sources of both fertility and destruction, of life and death, of healing and polluting, thus embodying the intrinsic ambivalence of existence with their body of flowing waters.

In literary and religious contexts, rivers and bodies of water play different roles in the eyes of ancient Mesopotamians. These major topographical entities are referred to as flowing places, which carry pure waters, sources of life and nourishment for the land and its inhabitants, but they are also characterized by destructive powers, such as the occasional floods, and as the origin places of threatening beings. Rivers are cosmic entities, which

5 *Skanda Purana*, pt. II, translated by Deshpande 1990, 2110 (quoted in Haberman 2011, 41).
6 Haberman 2011, 43–64.
7 Haberman 2011, 45.
8 McCully 2001, 10 (quoted in Haberman 2011, 39).
9 Bord and Bord 1985, 111 (quoted in Haberman 2011, 39).
10 Erbil/Mouton 2012, 53–74; Steitler 2019, 1–29. See also further in this chapter § 4.1.4.

feature complex entanglements with the cosmic mountain, with the sun and its journey, and with the Apsû; and they are conceived as active agents, often characterized by divine status. Rivers are portrayed with motherly attributes, because of their self-renewing and life-giving features, and are called upon for their calming and purifying powers. Moreover, rivers display a judicial aspect, when they are involved with the practice of the River Ordeal. In their topographical characterization, they constitute a border and connector between civilization and the wilderness beyond it, and between the world of the living and that of the dead. Being a main mean of connection between worlds, rivers are an ideal place for contacting the gods and the ancestors.

2 The divine River: mother, healer and judge

The river recurs in the religious sources, described as a place, as person and as a deity, comprising a body of flowing waters. In the rituals, the river is often mentioned without a divine determinative, but in light of its description and its role in the ritual setting, it should be considered as an animate agent with cosmic features. Some contexts indicate the fully divine personality of the river.[11] The general term for river is íd (or $i_7(d)$) in Sumerian and *nāru* in Akkadian. Another word which refers to a watercourse is *na'ilu*.[12] The Sumerian logogram íd is widely used in Akkadian literature, and it often occurs with the divine determinative (^{d}ÍD). The Sumerian logogram ^{d}ÍD refers mainly to the masculine River god, and it is generally translated as *Id*. This logogram has been considered a loanword in Akkadian, that would have replaced the Semitic name for this deity.[13] However, syllabic evidence of a ^{d}*Nārum* exists in Northern Mesopotamia sources, raising the possibility of reading *Nāru* for the logogram ^{d}ÍD in certain contexts, and vice versa.[14]

2.1 Duality and gender fluidity of the River

The river features a gender fluidity and alternation, which is mirrored in Akkadian grammar. The term *nāru* is grammatically feminine, but features also a masculine gender.[15] In both written and iconographical sources, rivers are alternatively represented as female and male entities.[16] In the realm of the incantations, the River is referred to as a life-generating entity, often clearly defined as a goddess, and as a judge of mankind together with the Sun god. Thus, both terms *Nāru* and *Id* can refer to the divine River, preventing a clear differentiation between female and male River based solely on grammar. Throughout the literature, it is noticeable that whenever the life-giving River is referred to, it is generally seen as a goddess or a dyad of female deities, while, when the River god in its

11 Throughout this book, the term "River" will indicate those understandings of the river as a cosmic and divine being, whereas the common name "river" refers to the topographic entity alone.
12 CAD N/1, 150 s.v. *na'ilu*.
13 Roberts 1972, 46; Lambert 1965, 11; Woods 2005, 20–21, note 51.
14 Woods 2005, 19–20.
15 Streck 2000, 298; Woods 2005, 19–20; Lambert 2013, 430.
16 Woods 2005, 19–20; Lambert 2013, 430.

role of supreme judge of the River Ordeal is meant, it is mainly portrayed with masculine traits.[17] This is a general observation regarding the gender alternation of the river, which appears to be fluid and with numerous exceptions.

The gender fluidity of the river reflects its intrinsically dual nature. As is well expressed in the iconographical representations, the river is often portrayed as female or male, half-anthropomorphic and half-water dyad. As seen on the 3rd millennium mold fragment attributed to Narām-Sîn, silhouetted against the mountain range, a River goddess is represented.[18] This fluvial deity is portrayed as a female figure, who wears a horned crown similar to those of the Mountain gods. Her upper body is anthropomorphic and wears only a belt, while the lower part of her body is represented by water, which is rendered by a series of undulating parallel lines which flow beneath the ziggurrat.[19] Similarly to the Mountain gods, the River goddess also carries an offering in both hands.[20] Her watery body passes beneath the temple terrace and the river is flanked by a row of drill holes demarcating the river bank.[21] Since only the right part of the mold is preserved, the entire scene would probably be restored with another female half body on the left side, according to the traditional iconographical representation of River deities as a dyad in Mesopotamian art from the 3rd millennium onward.[22]

One of the oldest visual representations of the River goddess as a dyad comes from a unique (Pre-)Sargonic seal from Mari.[23] This shell seal portrays a central male deity (Enlil?) sitting on a mountain and flanked by two female half-anthropomorphic and half-fluvial figures (Illustration 7).[24] The mountain on which the deity sits features two birds' heads emerging from it, each expelling a stream of water from its beak.[25] These two rivers merge into twin goddesses with tree branches sprouting from their upper anthropomorphic body.[26] Like the Mountain god, these female fluvial entities also wear horned headdresses, which is a typical characteristic of the visual representation of deities.[27] The two goddesses present offerings to the mountainous god. The offerings of a vessel by one deity and of a stand or plant by the other suggest that these deities depend on the mountain god for their plenty and fertility.[28] These twin goddesses are variously identified as vegetation

17 See passim in the present chapter.
18 See Chapter III, § 2.3, Illustration 3.
19 Hansen 2002, 96.
20 Hansen 2002, 97. According to Hansen, this River goddess might refer to the mountainous region "ruled over by the mountain gods, for just like them, she presents an offering to the enthroned divinities on top of the terrace. Yet, at the same time, her body underlies this very temple terrace indicating, perhaps, that she belongs in Agade and that she is the Euphrates or the Tigris, the river beside which Agade was built" (Hansen 2002, 102).
21 Hansen 2002, 102. This way of displaying the river stems from at least the Uruk period, and is later rendered in a more developed form in the seal of the scribe of Shar-kali-sharri (see Amiet, 1980, fig. 603; Amiet 1976, 113, pl. 73).
22 Hansen 2002, 102.
23 Aruz/Wallenfels 2003, 220–221; Woods 2005, 17–18.
24 A different interpretation is offered by Wiggermann, who understands the two deities as Mountain goddesses bringing tribute to Enlil seated on his mountain (Wiggermann 2013, 114).
25 Woods 2005, 18.
26 Woods 2005, 18.
27 Woods 2005, 18.
28 Aruz/Wallenfels 2003, 220–221.

goddesses,[29] and as embodiments of the divine Euphrates.[30] However, a third interpretation which combines textual and iconographical sources is possible. These two female fluvial deities could also be understood as the cosmic divine rivers which emerge from the *pī nārāti* (which can also be the Tigris and the Euphrates). This seal could, in fact, offer one of the rare iconographical renderings of the *pī nārāti*, the "Mouth-of-the-Rivers" of the literary sources. Moreover, the two mouths of the rivers, here envisioned as two birds from whose beaks the streams pour out, can be related to the names of *pī nārāti*, which are attested in the incantation of the *kiškanû*-tree: Kaḫegal, "Mouth-of-Plenty", and Igiḫegal, "Eye-of-Plenty".[31]

Illustration 7: Mari shell seal displaying a Mountain god sitting on a mountain from which two rivers merge into a couple of River goddesses with sprouting branches.

This motif of representing the fluvial deity as a dyad is recurrent throughout the 2nd millennium. Glyptics from the Old Babylonian period offer several examples of the visual conceptualization of the River deity as a dyad, often associated with Enki.[32] The female gender of the divine River is found once more in Old Babylonian Mari. The divine Euphrates is represented as a couple of fluvial goddesses in the so-called "Investitute Fresco" of Zimri-Lim, that was displayed in the royal palace at Mari.[33] The *Brunnen Relief* and the Kassite frieze of Inana's temple are further examples of the ancient Mesopotamian conceptualization of the river deity as a female dyad. As previously seen, the frieze of Inana's temple of Karaindraš at Uruk displays River goddesses, whose bodies are represented as half anthropomorphic and half aquatic, the lower part being waves. The deities hold a vase from which streams of water flow, connecting the entire frieze with an

29 Aruz/Wallenfels 2003, 220–221.
30 Woods 2005, 18.
31 See below in this chapter, § 3. See also Woods 2005, 17.
32 Woods 2005, 14–16 (see in particular Figs. 1–6).
33 See below in this chapter § 2.4, illustration 8.

undulating motif. At the bottom of the flowing waters, pairs of mountains (or twin-peaked mountains) are represented by a motif of semicircles.[34]

Occurrences of a divine fluvial couple, comprising a male and a female deity, are recorded in the Mesopotamian written sources. Cases such as the Assyrian divine couple Ḫabur and Ḫaburtum, and the Baliḫ expressed in the dual form, speak to the dual nature of the river.[35] A comparison with a neighboring river is provided by the Nile, which was represented as a hermaphroditic being, depicted with beard and breasts, but without genitalia. The divine Nile was also represented as a pair, which symbolizes its role unifying Upper and Lower Egypt.[36]

This intrinsic duality can be ascribed to physical and symbolic attributes. It can refer to the terminal points of a watercourse (i.e. source and delta), to its upper and lower traits, to an alternation of underground and over-ground traits, and also to its opposing banks. The last interpretation appears to be supported by the visual representations of the River deity as a dyad.[37] Its essential duality is to be found also in the religious and symbolic domain. The river is a twofold and contradictory entity, which brings life and death at the same time: its waters bring bounty to the land, but can also carry everything away. Moreover, rivers are liminal and cosmic entities, connected to the light and to the darkness of the earth's interior, emerging from the mountains and pouring into the sea, in a constant cycle of opposing and merging symbolic values. What can be inferred is that gender alternation and duality are peculiar traits of the River deity in the Mesopotamian worldviews, which are subject to local variations.

2.2 Life giving and purifying attributes of the River

The intrinsic gender duality of the River is well expressed in its life-giving and purifying attributes. A common action of the River is to self-impregnate.[38] In an Old Babylonian incantation for potency, the river is said to impregnate "itself" (*irḫû ramānša*),[39] while in an Old Babylonian incantation against a scorpion, the river is told to "impregnate its own banks" (*kīma nāru irḫû kibrīša*).[40] Along with self-impregnation, another characteristic action of the River is to renew itself (m ú - m ú - d a - b i), and this attribute is often utilized

34 Moortgat 1969, 94. See also Chapter II, § 2.3.

35 Mander 2008, 64; Gordon 1992, 127; Woods 2005, 21; Meinhold 2009, 160.

36 Woods 2005, 21; Butzer 2001, 550; Helck/Otto 1982, 486–487.

37 Woods argues that the essence of the river is "defined by its two opposing banks, a notion that meshes well with the binary character of the male-female pair Ḫabur and Ḫaburtum and perhaps with the indeterminate sex of the river dyads in general" (Woods 2005, 21).

38 For a literary and poetic discussion of the expressions "self-impregnating" and "impregnating its own banks" see Cooper 1996, 47–55.

39 TIM 9, 73b: 4–7, [*uš*]*šapka ramāni a*[*ra*]*ḫḫīka pagrī kīma* [id]LU.UḪ.DA.X [x] *irḫû ramā*[*nša*], "I will enchant you, myself! I will inseminate you, my body! As the river LU.UḪ.DA.X [x] has inseminated itself" (Cavigneaux 1999, 264–265: 4–7).

40 YOS 11, 2: 1–2, *araḫḫi ramāni araḫḫi pagarī kīma nārum irḫû kibrīša*, "I impregnate myself, I impregnate my body, just as the river has impregnated its own banks" (Cavigneaux 1999, 265–266: 1–2).

in ritual purifications of an affected person.[41] The expressions of self-impregnating and of impregnating its own banks offer valid support from the written records about interpreting the River as a hermaphrodite being. Indeed, water is once fecundating and fecundated.

Watercourses and other bodies of waters are invoked as entities and places capable of establishing an oath against evil agents. In an Old Babylonian incantation, the patient conjures the heart seizure by the earth and the lakes (*uttamīka erṣetam u ḫammê*),[42] while in an Old Assyrian spell against the evil eye we read that the evil action is conjured by the oath of Anu and Antum, Laḫmum and Dūrum, the netherworld and its watercourses[43] (*tamuāti Anam u Antam Laḫmam u Dūram erṣatam u na'ilīša*).[44]

The so-called River Incantation addresses the fully divine River goddess. This incantation is attested in several different Neo-Babylonian texts where the river plays a major role,[45] and it comprises a mythical narrative, usually preceding ritual instructions.[46] In this literary composition the River, *Nāru*, is called upon as the "creatress" of everything (*banât kalāma*):[47]

ÉN *attī Nāru bānât kalāma/mimma šumšu*	Incantation: "You, River! Creatress of everything!
enūma iḫrûki ilū rabûtu	When the great gods dug you,
ina aḫiki iškunū dumqa	They placed favor at your side.
ina libbiki Ea šar Apsî ibnâ šubassu	Within you Ea, king of the Apsû, built his dwelling.
išrukkimma uzza namurrata puluḫtam	He gave you fierceness, radiance and dread,
abūb lā maḫār šumki imbi	The "irresistible flood" he called your name,
nēmeqi Ea u Asalluḫi išrukū[ki]mma	The wisdom of Ea and Asalluḫi they gave you.

41 See, e.g., *Šurpu* I, obv. 6, [é n] í d - l ú - r u - g ú - g i n₇ m ú - m ú - d a - b i ŠID-*ma* LÚ.GIG *tú-ḫap*, "the incantation 'Like the River who renews himself constantly' you recite, then purify the patient" (Reiner 1958, 11: 6).

42 YOS 11, 12a: 8 (Veldhuis 1990, 28–29: 42–43).

43 According to Streck, the word meant here is either *nā'ilu*, "the one making wet", or *na'īlu*, "the one made wet" (personal communication).

44 Barjamovic/Larsen 2008, 145–146: 20–24, *tamuāti Anam u Antam Laḫmam u Dūram erṣatam u na'ilīša lā tatūrīma lā taṣbitīšini*, "You are held by the oath of Anum and Antum, Laḫmum and Dūrum, the netherworld and its watercourses: 'You shall not return! You shall not snatch her!'".

45 This incantation is known from several sources, and is often found in n a m b u r b i rituals, along with incantations to Šamaš. See Kunstmann 1930, 99; Bottéro 1985, 44–45 and 288–291; Bottéro/Kramer 1989, 486–487; Maul 2004, 43–54; Lambert 2013, 396–398. Interestingly, "all the known copies are of first-millennium date. So far, no Middle or Old Babylonian copy has turned up, nor any Sumerian antecedent" (Lambert 2013, 397).

46 Bottéro 1985, 44–45 and 288–291; Bottéro/Kramer 1989, 486–487; Maul 2004, 43–54; Lambert 2013, 396–398.

47 For the different manuscripts see Lambert 2013, 396. The present translation and transliteration are based on Lambert's simplified form reconstructed from the different sources (Lambert 2013, 397–398: 1–10). For the variants, see Lambert 2013, 397–398, and Maul 2004, 43–54.

dīn tenēšētum tadinnī	You judge the judgment of mankind.[48]
nār rabâti nār ṣīrāti	River, you are great! River, you are lofty!
nār ešrēti šūšurū mûki	River, you are upright, your water keeps things in order".

In this incantation, all the features characterizing the River are expressed. *Nāru* emerges fully in her divine garb of cosmic River goddess, as the deity presiding over the River Ordeal, and as a cosmic place connected with the Apsû. The divine River is described both as the creatress of everything and as being created by the great gods. The latter notion implies the existence of the great gods before their watery progenitor. Ea is said to assign her fierceness, radiance and terror, along with the name "irresistible flood", which refers to the practice of the River Ordeal. The legal context is affirmed further in the text, where the River is referred to as judging mankind and keeping things in order through carrying away any sin and defilement. Accordingly, the two main aspects of the River are here expressed: its life-giving nature is intertwined with its judicial attribute.

Simultaneously, *nāru* is also expressed in its topographical aspect. The river is the place where the god Ea builds his dwelling, which is the Apsû, the subterranean cosmic water.[49] However, the ritual functions of the river –such as the River Ordeal and the purifying rituals– took place on earth.[50] The River deity should thus be considered not only as a major cosmic power below, but also as a physical and geographical presence above.[51] With its flowing and powerful waters, the River bring those defiling elements down to the Apsû in a continuous dialectic and exchange between above and below, upstream and downstream.

A mythical context similar to the River incantation is found in the incipit of a *Šurpu* incantation, where the River is addressed as the "river of the gods, who has borne everything" (íd dingir-re-e-ne níg-nam-ma tu-ud-da).[52] Once more, the characterization of Id/*Nāru* as a creating goddess while being created by the great gods (i.e. Enki, Anu and Enlil) recurs, entangled in the mythical narrative of the 1st-millennium incantations for purification rituals.[53] The River's maternal nature is displayed in a zi-pà formula, where the River is referred to as the "mother of the Apsû" (^{d}Íd ama-En-gu-ra-ke$_4$).[54] This epithet aims at emphasizing and reinforcing the River's purifying and healing powers in a dialectic relationship with the Apsû, which is traditionally considered the first generating principle of sweet pristine waters.

48 Cf. the variant **n** (Lambert 2013, 397–398: 7–8).

49 Bottéro/Kramer 1989, 288–291; Beaulieu 1992/1993, 58–60. Throughout the selected literature it is striking how much water, rivers, sweet water bodies, the Apsû, and the god Enki/Ea are deeply intertwined. Being aware of the breadth of this subject, it seems nevertheless necessary to mention these relations in the light of the connections between natural elements and the great gods. (see below §3).

50 Lambert 2013, 397.

51 Lambert 2013, 397.

52 *Šurpu* IX 70–87 (Reiner 1958, 47–48: 70–87).

53 Reiner 1958, 47–48: 71.

54 PBS 1/2 112 30 (ArOr 21, 395: 30). See also below § 3.

All these elements reinforce the polyvalent and dual nature of the divine River. There is no doubt that the River was considered a generating cosmic principle in the Mesopotamian tradition. Embodying the force of water, which is healing and purifying, the River was considered a proper non-anthropomorphic (or half-anthropomorphic) deity (either female or male according to the context).[55] The divine River may have been seen as the primeval mother-goddess in some vernacular or earlier traditions, and subsequently became embedded in the pantheon of the great gods.

Another evidence for the generating female River is found in the mythical composition *The Theogony of Dunnu*.[56] In this mythical text, the divine generating River is named Id and it is considered the third female cosmic principle, after the first two feminine entities, Earth and Sea. These female creator deities are paired and married to shepherd-gods.[57] The myth recounts a series of incestuous marriages and parent killings: the son of Laḫar, whose name is not preserved, marries "River, his own sister" (*Idda aḫāt ramānišu*).[58] This occurrence of *Idda*, read syllabically, supports the understanding that the names Id and *Nāru* were interchangeable. Moreover, this evidence speaks for the notion that the femininity of the River, here clearly stated to be a sister, is displayed when its cosmogonic features are expressed.

2.3 Id, Nāru and the divine River Ordeal

Id, marked with the determinative for deities, and predominantly featuring masculine traits, recurs consistently in the incantations, where it is regarded as a divine being with its own features, personality and actions. Id is a healing and purifying deity, and a righteous judge together with Šamaš. The divine River's judicial role has to be considered in connection to the ritual and legal practice of the River Ordeal (Sum. í d - l ú - r u - g ú , Akk. (logographic) ḪUR.SAG, *ḫurš/sānu*). In the Old Babylonian incantations, Id is invoked to purify and dispel various diseases along with Mountain (*ḫuršānu*) and the other holy gods,[59] while in a fragmentary incantation the divine River Ordeal, ᵈ*Ḫursag*, is listed with Nuska, Nissaba and Šamaš.[60] The two names, Id and Ḫursag refer both to the divine River and to the divine River Ordeal, which lead me to wonder whether they should be considered as referring to

55 Bottéro/Kramer 1989, 290–291.

56 Lambert 2013, 387–395. See also The *Theogony of Dunnu* in Stol, *The Melammu Project* (http://melammu-project.eu/database/gen_html/a0001475.html).

57 As pointed out by Lambert, "Earth is the commonest first principle. Sea is less common, but it may be noted that the early form of Anu's theogony begins with water and then puts earth, the opposite of what our text has. River is closely related to Sea, like Anu and Anšar, so they had to come together, if distinguished. The first three in the female line are thus in the main stream of cosmological thought. A second category is represented by Šakkan, Laḫar, and Gaʾum, all shepherd-gods in other texts. There are traces of a creation myth in which the deities presiding over the basic human crafts are brought into being. [...] Properly, these deities belong to a story not on the origins of the universe but on the origins of civilization" (Lambert 2013, 389–390).

58 Lambert 2013, 392–393.

59 LB 1000, 8–10 (Geller/Wiggermann 2008, 153–156); CT 42, 32: 12–13 (Geller/Wiggermann 2008, 151). See Chapter II, § 2.3).

60 MS 3105/1 (No. 22a): 10', ᵈ*Ḫur-sa-ag*, "River Ordeal" (George 2016).

two separate deities or rather they were conceived of as different aspects of the same fluvial deity.

In the 1st-millennium ritual *Šurpu*, Id is listed among the great gods.[61] In this ritual context, the divine River consistently appears connected with the oath, the *māmītu*. The *māmītu* is compared to the continually renewing features of the River (dÍ d - l ú - r u - g ú - g e n₇, *Id eddēšû*).[62] Moreover, the *māmītu* of the River is recorded along with several entities, natural elements, places and objects, all of which possess a *māmītu* in the Mesopotamian worldview.[63]

The divine River plays a major role, in the context of the anti-witchcraft incantations and rituals, recurring consistently besides other gods traditionally connected with dispelling witchcraft, and with its supporting judicial role along with the supreme judge Šamaš. In *Maqlû* III 61–76,[64] pure River (*Id ellu)* and holy Sun (*namru quddušu*) are invoked by the patient, who self-identifies with these two natural and pure entities. After detecting the agents of witchcraft against his person (the Sages of the Apsû and the heavenly Daughters of Anu),[65] the patient affirms his victory over the evil agent thanks to the powers of River and Sun. After the defeat of his magical enemies, he proclaims his purity and brightness. River and Sun are called upon to establish their retreat (*Id u namru nabalkattašunu liškunūma*), and the patient/magician gives praise in his intent to become pure, like River, in his mountain (*anāku kīma Id ina šadîya lū ellēku*). As noted by Abusch, the context is one of divine judgment, where the supreme judge Šamaš together with the divine River Ordeal are establishing their verdict on the evil actions of *kaššāptu*. The legal context of the divine River Ordeal re-enacts the cosmic setting of the Mountain of Sunrise, where the destinies of the world and of its inhabitants are decreed at every daybreak.[66]

In another incantation, the witch is said to be a Sutean and an Elamite, and her craft produces waves and current which cover the victim of witchcraft (or she transforms herself into wave and current).[67] Against her craft, Girra, companion of Šamaš, is called to stand by the patient "like the mountain is made quiet by sulphur" (*kīma šadî ina kibrīti inuḫḫu*).[68] The incantation follows addressing the divine River:

Id ellu libbaša liḫpe	"May pure River smash her heart,
mû nāri ellūtu lipšurū kišpīša	May the pure waters of the river release

61 *Šurpu* VIII 18–20, ÉN *Anum Antum [Enlil] Ninlil Ea Sîn Šamaš Adad Marduk ilī qardūti Id Kiša Nammu u Nanše Tispak Ninazu Ningirim [x] Tiranna Manzât* [KIMIN], "Incantation. Anu, Antu, [Enlil], Ninlil, Ea, Sin, Šamaš, Adad, Marduk, the valiant gods, Id (and) Kisa, Nammu and Nanše, Tispak, Ninazu, Ningirim, [...], Tiranna, Manzat [may release you, may absolve you]" (Reiner 1970, 40).

62 *Šurpu*, Appendix, obv. 22–29 and rev. 1–4. In particular see the beginning of the incantation, lines 22–23, é n dí d - l ú - r u - g ú - g i n₇ m ú - m ú - d a - b i : dÍD *ed-de-šu-ú*, "Incantation. Its ever-renewing is like (that of) the River, River who renews himself constantly" (Reiner 1970, 52-53). The incipit of this incantation is recorded in the first tablet of *Šurpu* I rev. i 13'.

63 *Šurpu* III 47, [*mām*]*īt* GIŠ.MÁ *u* dÍD, "[the 'oa]th' of boat or River" (Reiner 1970, 20).

64 Abusch 2015, 306–307.

65 Abusch 2002, 202–203.

66 Abusch 2002, 197–216. See passim in the present chapter, and Chapter II.

67 *Maqlû* III 77–87 (Abusch 2015, 307).

68 See further in the present chapter, § 2.5.

	her witchcraft.
u anāku kīma Id ina šadîya lū ellēku ÉN	And may I, like River, become pure in my mountain. Incantation."[69]

The divine River is called upon in order to act personally against the *kaššāptu*, by smashing her heart, so that its waters may release the patient from her evil craft. It should be noted that when referring to the waters of the river in its topographical aspect, the word river lacks the divine determinative. The alternation between the divine River and the physical river is affirmed by the last line of the incantation, where the patient hopes to become pure in his mountain, like the divine River.

Id is praised as the tutelary god of the bewitched person in *Maqlû* VI 106–111. The patient affected by witchcraft calls upon the River, thanking this god for regaining his normal life: he resumed eating, drinking, dressing and feeling safe at his house. This incantation is recorded in a sequence of spells for dispelling witchcraft through the river and other related mineral and herbal entities.[70] Another mention of the River as a god is found in the incipit of an obscure anti-witchcraft incantation, which records the River along with the gods Šakkan and Sîn, and with the *illammê*, "pure in divine powers", or "pure in me".[71]

In another incantation, both the divine and the topographical feature of the river occur. In *Maqlû* VIII 35–52, the *kaššāptu* is told to cross the river (*nāru*), haunting the quay and the ferry. In doing so, the *kaššāptu* traverses a border and breaks a taboo, a fact that captures the attention of the river and its inhabitants. The reactions of the divine entities inhabiting the physical river are described: the sages of the Apsû see her, Ea overwhelms her with *bennu*-epilepsy, confusion and trembling, and Id casts her own fear upon her (*Id puluḫtaša iddâ elīša*).[72]

The divine River occurs as one of the several natural and divine entities with which the bewitched person identifies himself in order to gain their power. In another spell in *Maqlû* VI 98–104, we read:

ÉN *Id qaqqadī kibrītu padattī*	Incantation: "River is my head, Sulphur my physique.
šēpāya nāru ša mamma lā īdû qerebš[a]	My feet are the river whose interior no one knows.

69 *Maqlû* III 85–87 (Abusch 2015, 307).

70 *Maqlû* VI 106–111, ÉN *Id ākul alti app[aši]š aḫḫ[alip(?)] ātapir(i) Id allab[iš* …] *Id akalī u mê apṭur*(?) *Id dal[ta*(?) …] ⸢*sippa arkus*(?)⸣ *Id* x […] *Id paršik[ku* …], "Incantation. O River, I have eaten, I have drunk, I have salved my[self], I have cl[othed myself], I have donned a headdress, River, I have dressed my[self, I have . . .], River, food and water I have cleared away(?), River, [I have . . .] the do[or(?)], I have put the doorjamb into place(?), River, . . . [. . .] River, turba[n! [. . .]" (Abusch 2015, 342: 106–111).

71 *CMAwR* 7.8.8: 15′–17′, *[k]aššāptam Id ruḫut Šakkan bēlet rēmînni iršâmšum īmuršima Sîn* (var.: *Ellil*) *ireddīši [i]llammê illaka arkīša*, "The witch, the River god, the … of Šakkan –'Lady, have mercy on me'. Sîn (var.: Enlil) beheld her and was pursuing her, 'Pure-Powers' was going after her." (Abusch/Schwemer 2013, 194: 15′–17′).

72 Abusch 2015, 360: 35'–52'.

anḫullû pīya ayyabba tâmtu rapaštu rittāy[*a*]	The *Anhullû*-plant is my mouth, Ocean, the vast sea, is my hands.
kīma Id qaqqadī kīma kibrīti elleti qimm[*atī*]	Like River my head (is pure), like pure Sulphur my hair (is pure),
kīma anḫullî imḫur-līm šam[*mū*] *pišerte*	Like *Anhullû*$^{!}$-plant and *Imḫur-līmu*, the plants that release,
⌜*mešrētū'a*⌝ *ebbā x x x* [*š*]*a*(?) *kibrīti*	My limbs are pure, ... Sulp[hur]".[73]

The natural elements invoked here are all purifying entities: divine River, Sulphur, the *anḫullû*-plant, the *imḫurlīmu*-plant and the Ocean, all corresponding to parts of the bewitched body. Interestingly, the feet of the patient affected by witchcraft are identified with the river, which is followed by the epithet "whose interior no one knows" (*ša mamma la īdû qerebša*). This expression is found often associated with the river, and it refers to the mysterious body of flowing water which emerges from the earth's womb and flows on the earth's surface with its mass of pure waters and stunning power.

The divine personality ascribed to the River is demonstrated in much non-literary evidence from Northern Mesopotamia. Attestations of ^{d}*Nāru*(*m*) exist in Old Babylonian Mari,[74] Old Babylonian Sippar[75] and from the Neo-Assyrian period.[76] Moreover, from Old Babylonian Mari there is evidence of a temple or shrine dedicated to the divine River,[77] while an Old-Assyrian document attests to the existence of a priest specifically devoted to the cult of *Nāru*.[78] The conception of the divine River is found also in epistolary correspondence and in personal names. Šulgi made a dedication "to the River, his lord" (*ana* ^{d}*Id bēlišu*)[79], and Zimri-Lim wrote a letter "to the River, my lord" (*ana* ^{d}*Id bēliya*).[80] In the latter epistolary evidence, the full divinity of Id is expressed: the River is not only called the lord of the king, but it is also a recipient of offerings and is characterized by those actions typically ascribed to a god. A golden vessel is offered by the Mari king, who has received a (favorable) sign from his Lord, the River. The River is called upon by the supplicant king not to forget to protect his person, not to turn his attention away from him, nor to give his favor to anyone else but him.[81]

---

73 *Maqlû* VI 98–103 (Abusch 2015, 342: 98–103).

74 KA-^{d}*Na-r*[*u*$^{?}$] (ARM 7, 346).

75 *Na-ru-um* DINGIR (CT 4, 50b 8).

76 ^{d}*Na-rum* (K 4271 2).

77 KA-^{d}*Na-r*[*u*$^{?}$] (ARM 7, 346); É *Na-ri-im* (ARM 7, 163 5). See also a É *Na-'à-ri-im* at Tell Bīʿa/Tuttul (WVDOG 100, 25, 7.27 1), where offerings were given to the River.

78 *ku-um-ri-im ša Na-ri-im* "priest of the river(-god)" (AfO Beiheft 12, 82 and 26; see Hirsch, AfO 22, 1968–1969, 38).

79 RIME III/2 137 (Lambert 2013, 430).

80 ARM 26, 191 (Durand 1988, 413). See also Lambert 2013, 430; Sasson 2015, 238.

81 ARM 26, 191: 5–16, *anūmma kāsam ellam ana bēliya uštābilam ina pānītim ṭēmī ana bēliya ašpuram bēlī ittam*$^{!}$ *ukallimanni bēlī ittam ša ukallimanni lišaklilam u ana naṣār napištiya bēlī ay īgi ašar šanî bēlī pānēšu ay usaḫḫir ullânūya bēlī šanêm ay iḫšeḫ*, "I am herewith dispatching a gold vessel to my Lord. When in the past I sent tidings to my Lord, my Lord showed me a sign. May my Lord accomplish the sign he showed me. In protecting my life, may my Lord not be negligent! May my Lord not turn his attentions elsewhere! May my Lord not favor anyone else but me!" (Durand 1988, 413; Sasson 2015, 238).

In Pre-Sargonic and Sargonic personal names, the divine River stands for either a source of protection (*Puzur-Nāri*, "Protection of the River") or in its motherly attribute (*Iddin-Nāru*, "the River gave an heir"),[82] while in Old Babylonian personal names the River is invoked in its judicial aspect, together with its fatherly and divine features: ^{d}*Id-dayyān* ("River is judge")[83], *Nārum-ilu* ("the River is god"),[84] ^{d}*Id*$^{?}$*a-bi*$^{?}$ ("River is my father"),[85] and ^{d}Íd-lú-ru-gú-*na-id* ("River Ordeal is attentive").[86]

In the god lists, Id is recorded associated with other deities. In the Old Babylonian forerunner of An = *Anum*, ^{d}Íd-dalla, "resplendent River", is attested as the last name of Ea,[87] and in the god list An = *Anum* II, Id is identified with Namma:

^{d}Íd = Šu	River = Namma
^{d}Íd-gal = Šu	Great River = Namma
^{d}Íd-silim = Šu	Peaceful River = Namma
^{d}Íd-lú-ru-gú = Šu	River that receives a man = Namma
^{d}Ki-ša$_{6}$ = dam-bi-munus	Kiša = his wife
^{d}Šà-zi = dumu ^{d}Íd-ke$_{4}$	Šazi = son of River
^{d}*Nēr-ē-tagmil* = sukkal ^{d}Íd-ke$_{4}$	"Strike! Do not have mercy!" = vizier of River[88]

Here the intrinsic gender fluidity of the divine River is displayed. In its being equated with Namma, the River should be understood as a feminine divine entity. Namma is, in fact, a water goddess, who is generally regarded as the mother of the god Enki/Ea. However, the River is referred to as a masculine deity because of the reference to his wife Kiša. According to this lexical evidence, the River was conceived of as both feminine and masculine also when concerned with the River Ordeal. Indeed, his fourth name, Id-lurugu, "River that receives a man", the function of his son Šazi as a god presiding the River Ordeal in Old Babylonian Elam, and the name of his vizier, *Nēr-ē-tagmil*, "Strike! Do not have mercy!", all point to Id coinciding with the divine River Ordeal.[89]

In the Neo-Assyrian rituals, which record the offerings presented to the gods throughout the country's temples, rivers recur as a collective entity and are referred to as deities. In the Tākultu-rituals for Sennacherib and for Assurbanipal, rivers are included among the gods of the House of Aššur.[90] In the Tākultu for Assurbanipal, rivers recur consistently, where they are not only listed among the great gods of the land of Assyria, but

82 Roberts 1972, 46; Porter 2009, 161–162.

83 SO I 261 (Lambert 2013, 430).

84 CT 4, 50, Bu 88–5–12, 731: 8 (Lambert 2013, 430).

85 CT 6, 38, Bu 91–5–9, 733: 23 (Lambert 2013, 430).

86 UET 5, 491: 1 (Lambert 2013, 430). See also Durand 2008, 291–292.

87 TCL 15, pl. xxvi 83 (Lambert 2013, 430).

88 An = *Anum* II 276–282 = CT 24 ,16: 23–29 (Lambert 2013, 430).

89 Lambert 2013, 430. See also note on *Enūma Eliš* VII 35–55.

90 SAA 20, 38 i 32 and 41, ÍD.MEŠ (Parpola 2017, 103–104); SAA 20, 40 i 27, ÍD.MEŠ (Parpola 2017, 111). See also two fragments of Tākultu texts, where rivers are invoked together with the mountains: SAA 20, 46 rev. ii 13', [KUR.M]EŠ ÍD.MEŠ (Parpola 2017, 127) ; and SAA 20, 47 rev. 5, KUR.MEŠ ÍD.MEŠ (Parpola 2017, 127).

they are described as acting as gods. Along with the mountains and other parts of the cities, the rivers are called upon to accept life and listen to prayers (an action traditionally ascribed to the gods), and are included among the gods of Tua.[91] Further in the same ritual text, "mountains, springs and rivers of the four corners (of the world)" (*šadâni nagbī nārāti kibrāt erbetti*), are called upon to bless the city and the land of Aššur and to grant long life to the Assyrian king.[92] Furthermore, one text displays the collective rivers recorded with the determinative for gods. Here the divine rivers are listed together with the divine Tigris, among the great gods of Aššur.[93] From this ritual context it is evident that rivers were fully featured as gods, affecting the lives of humans like their anthropomorphic counterparts, and, as in the case of mountains, both collective and specifically named rivers should be recognized as an organic part of the Assyrian cult during the 1st millennium.[94]

Among the royal rituals during the Neo-Assyrian empire, there is evidence for a ritual held for the Lady-of-the-River and one for the Daughter-of-the-River. The *nāṭu*-ritual for the Lady-of-the-River (GAŠAN-ÍD, *Bēlet-Nāri*) is part of the cult instituted by Tukulti-Ninurta I, who was devoted to this goddess as his personal god (*ilišu*).[95] The ritual seems to be performed in a healing context similar to the rite for the Lady-of-the-Mountain, due to the occurrence of fertility problems of the king.[96] The ritual setting is a tent on the river bank, which has to be placed facing the sun, with a chair at its side. Libations, fumigations and offerings of different joints of meat, of bread and cakes, of precious metals and wood, of flour and incense, are presented to the great gods, along with chanting. After these purifying rites, the seed of the king is expected to "solidify" and the evil affecting him to dissolve. The fertility context is confirmed by the presence of a mysterious female figure, whom the king should kiss and let dwell in his house.[97] Because of the fluvial setting and of the reverent address to Bēlet-ilī, I would suggest that the identity of the Lady-of-the-River is that of the River goddess in her creating and healing aspects. Bēlet-ilī is, indeed, praised as the great mother of heaven and earth, as the queen of the Apsû, the wife of Ea, who descends into the netherworld.[98] This evidence leads to the understanding that the Lady-of-the-River is addressed as the generating Lady-of-the-Gods, who is closely connected to the realm of the Apsû and is told to descend into the underworld. The River goddess is perceived as a body of flowing waters, which can carry away, down into the underworld, the impurities and diseases of the affected king.

An intriguing *nāṭu*-ritual for the Daughter-of-the-River is performed by a suffering person.[99] In this ritual, the sufferer and the cultic performers go to the river, where they

---

91 SAA 20, 40 rev. ii 4', ÍD.MEŠ (Parpola 2017, 116). See Chapter II.

92 SAA 20, 40 rev. iii 40'–41' (Parpola 2017, 118).

93 SAA 20, 40 vi 19, dÍD.MEŠd+id M[AŠ.GÚ.QAR] (Parpola 2017, 115).

94 As pointed out by Porter, "rivers, clearly thought of as bodies of water and parts of the landscape, nevertheless emerge in these texts as divine beings, being that are in this case as active in the lives of their Mesopotamian worshippers as the DINGIRs and *ilu*s imagined in anthropomorphic form" (Porter 2009, 162). See also Chapter II.

95 SAA 20, 25 (Parpola 2017, 65–69).

96 See Chapter II, § 2.3.

97 SAA 20, 25: 43'–46' (Parpola 2017, 68–69).

98 SAA 20, 25 rev. i 5–6 and 13–4 (Parpola 2017, 67–68).

99 SAA 20, 32 (Parpola 2017, 85–87).

pitch a tent facing the desert. After collecting seeds, which are subsequently thrown into the river, a bed is set up inside the tent, where jars filled with grain and bound with multicolored wool are placed. A table and a reed table are prepared at the head of the bed, where a virgin ewe is bound with a multicolored cloth and dressed in a white wool dress. The ritual proceeds with the setting up of the seven divine judges on a linen cloth, with a multicolored cloth fastened to their heads and a food bowl in front of them. The sufferer pours a cup of water and a cup of first quality beer into the river, and he sings several prayers to the divine judges (i.e. Ištar, Enlil, Aššur, and Ea) while offering libations to them. While praying to the last divine judge, the sufferer confesses that his goddess has become hostile to him, while the singer recites "You are god, you are queen, O Daughter-of-the-River" (*ilāki šarrāki Mārat-Nāri*).[100] A combination of prayers and purifying rites (i.e. cleansing with water, incense burning, libations and offering of cakes) continues to be performed in front of Šamaš and the other divine judges. After that, the cultic performer is instructed to wash the feet of the sinful person, who must subsequently descend into the river. The ewe is probably slaughtered and all the *materia magica* utilized during the ritual is thrown into the river, in order to remove and dispel any sin and impurity from the body of the sufferer once and for all. At the end, the person wears a new garment, calling upon the divine judges in the hope they have been satisfied and he has been cleansed of any curse by his personal god. According to the context of the assembly of the divine judges and the legal setting, the Daughter-of-the-River should be probably be understood as the River in its judicial aspect, i.e. the River Ordeal. This evidence speaks for the fact that the divine River, even in its judicial garb of the River Ordeal, could be conceived of both as a female and a male being, in a fluidity and interchangeability which is a constant feature of the representation of the fluvial person.

The divinity of the River and its specific role as a judge together with Šamaš finds its clearest expression in the practice of the River Ordeal (Sum. ^{d}í d - l ú - r u - g u, Akk. *ḫurš/sānu*).[101] The practice of throwing the accused person into the waters of a river, so that the River covers the person under trial, establishing his innocence or guilt, is attested from the early 2nd millennium B.C.E. onwards in Babylon and Mari.[102] The legal cases which required the River Ordeal generally concerned accusations of witchcraft, adultery, betrayal and quarrels about property and material goods (e.g. fields and/or herds).[103] Apparently, there was a favorite place for performing the River Ordeal, in Hit, a locality on the Euphrates, famous for its thermal and bitumen springs.[104]

100 SAA 20, 32 rev. 2, DINGIR-*a-ki šar-ra-ki* DUMU.MÍ-ÍD (Parpola 2017, 86).

101 The Sumerian word for the River Ordeal, ^{d}Í d - l ú - r u - g u , means literally "River that receives a man". In contrast, the Akkadian term, *ḫurš/sānu*, means both River Ordeal and mountain according to the context (see also Chapter II, § 2). Moreover, as we have seen, the divine River, Id, refers both to the River-god and the River Ordeal.

102 For the Divine Ordeal see Bottéro/Kramer 1989, 288–291; Bottéro 1981, 1005–67; Beaulieu 1992/1993, 58–60; Durand 1988, 507–539; Heimpel 1996, 7–13; Durand 2000, 150–160; van Soldt 2003–2005, 124 ff.; Sasson 2015, 289–293.

103 Durand 1988, 507–539; Durand 200, 150–160.

104 As argued by Heimpel, "the new material published by Durand demonstrates that Hit was the preferred location for the river ordeal in the orbit of Mari. Single ordalists and plunging parties came from Mari, Karkemish, Aleppo, the Ḫabur triangle, and Elam. Hit is of course best known from its bitumen springs. There is a cluster of such springs close to the modern town and on the bank of the

In this legal practice, the divine nature of the River is explicit. This notion is clear in the Code of Ḫammurapi, where the River Ordeal is referred to by the name Id,[105] and in some letters from Mari. The epistolary evidence attests that the person under trial "plunges into the god" (*ana libbi ilim imqutma*),[106] and that "the god poured out the third woman" (*šinništam šaluštam Id irḫû*) under ordeal.[107] As pointed out by Porter, the divine River is described "quite literally as being a body of water into which the accused person 'plunges' or which 'submerges' him", thus attesting the non-anthropomorphic form of the fluvial deity.[108]

Another literary text which refers to the divine River and to the practice of the Ordeal is the *Song of Bazi*, where the minor god Bazi establishes his temple in the mountainous setting of mount Šaššar. As previously seen,[109] the house is filled with flowing waters, and these waters are half death and half life (*ina qereb bītišu ibbalakatū mû mišlum balāṭu mišlum mūtu*), reflecting the intrinsically dual nature of the river, and perfectly matching the judicial context of the River Ordeal. With its flowing waters, the river can grant both life and death, fecundity and destruction, healing and defilement. Thus, the River becomes a major god which can establish verdicts and proclaim the purity and innocence of an accused person or his guilt, then carrying away his body together with his defilement and sin. Further on in the text, Id, Šakkan and Šamaš are called upon to judge, slay and purify those convicted of witchcraft (*ša rušê*), of murder (lit. "the one of blood", *ša dāmi*) and of sorcery (*ša kišpi*).[110]

The interrelation between the healing waters of the River, its being able to establish destinies and its Eastern origin, has informed conceptions of the River since the 3rd millennium. In the Sumerian hymn of Ibbi-Sîn, the cosmic River, whose lords are Lugalerra and Meslamtaea, is addressed as a powerful river, which establishes destinies, and as the Great River pouring out from where the sun rises.[111] The connection between river and

---

Euphrates, some springs are on the opposite side of the river, and a string of springs stretches for some 20 miles south from Hit to Abu-Ǧīr, "Father of Bitumen". The springs are circular ponds. [...] Naphtha, a volatile variety of petroleum now called benzene, and a whole range of noxious gases bubble up with warm saline water in these springs, creating strong turbulence and rendering them highly toxic." (Heimpel 1996, 8).

105 See the Code of Ḫammurapi, § 2: *šumma awīlum kišpī eli awīlim iddīma lā uktīnšu ša elīšu kišpū nadû ana Id illak Id išalliamma šumma Id iktašassu mubbiršu bīssu itabbal šumma awīlam šuāti Id ūtebbibaššuma ištalmam ša elīšu kišpī iddû iddâk ša Id išliam bīt mubbirišu itabbal*, "If a man charges another man with practicing witchcraft but cannot bring proof against him, he who is charged with witchcraft shall go to the divine River Ordeal, he shall indeed submit to the divine River Ordeal; if the divine River Ordeal should overwhelm him, his accuser shall take full legal possession of his estate; if the divine River Ordeal should clear that man and should he survive, he who made the charge of witchcraft against him shall be killed; he who submitted to the divine River Ordeal shall take full legal possession of his accuser's estate". (Roth 1997, 81).

106 ARM 26, 253: 12'–13' (Durand 1988, 532–533). See also Durand 2000, 154–157.

107 ARM 26, 249: 12–13 (Durand 1988, 527–529); Durand 2000, 157–160.

108 Porter 2009, 162.

109 See Chapter II, § 3.3.

110 See George 2009, 7–8: 31–33; Zgoll 2015, 68–69. For the whole text and its commentary see Chapter II, § 3.3.

111 Ibbi-Sîn B, Segment A 23–24, í d - z u í d k a l a g - g a - à m í d n a m - t a r - r a - à m í d - m a ḫ k i u d è i g i n u - b a r - r e - d a m, "Your (Lugalerra's) river is mighty, the river which

sunrise might explain the network of meanings around the conception of the River as supreme judge of mankind together with Utu/Šamaš. During the divine River Ordeal, the River is told to pour out of the Apsû and to return to it, bringing the verdicts with it, in a dynamic cycle of continuous exchange between above and below, light and darkness, life and death, east and west.[112]

2.4 The divine River and its cult

Both *Nāru* and Id probably refer to the cosmic divine unspecified River but also to a particular river in each case, especially to the two main Mesopotamian rivers, the Tigris and the Euphrates.[113] Since the practice of the River Ordeal was prevalently performed along the banks of the Euphrates, it might be inferred that in most cases where Id is addressed, the implicit physical river is the Euphrates in its divine garb. This suggestion is based on the distribution of the concept and worship of the divine River along its course. The cult of the divine River appears in cities like Tuttul, Mari, Hit and Sippar, where veneration of the deified Euphrates occurred.[114]

Emblematic is the case of Mari, where the worship of Id is attested from the 3rd millennium up until the Old-Babylonian period. A stone vessel dedicated to Id and Ištarat on behalf of Ikūn-Šamagan is evidence for royal patronage of the River god already in the Early Dynastic period.[115] Contemporaneous personal names attest the divine River as a theophoric element (e.g. *I-dì-*ᵈÍD). A votive inscription from the *šakkanakkum*-period found in Sippar claims the erection of a royal effigy in front of his lord, ᵈÍD, MAŠ.TAB.BA and Ištaran, by Itlal-Erra, king of Mari.[116] Referring to Id as the lord of the king of Mari is a practice that continued for some centuries, and it is still attested in the epistolary correspondence of Zimri-Lim. By setting the roots of his kingship in the waters of the Euphrates, a particular devotion to the divine River is shown by this king of Mari in the pictorial representations of his palace.

---

establishes destinies, the Great River where the Sun rises, no one can look at it" (ETCSL 2.4.5.2: 23–24). See also Woods 2009, 220. For the pair of netherworld gods Lugalerra and Meslamtaea, see Black/Green 1992, 123–124.

112 See Ibbi-Sîn B, Segment B 2–3, 2-na-ne-ne lugal íd-da-me-eš ᵈíd-lú-ru-gí lú zid dadag-ga-[àm], "They (Lugalerra and Meslamtaea) are the lords of the divine River Ordeal, which clears the right person" (ETCSL 2.4.5.2: Segment B 2–3). Woods 2009, 220, note 155.

113 According to Porter, this entity "called simply 'River'" probably referred to "a particular unspecified river in each case" (Porter 2009, 161–162). However, it can refer to the cosmic River, which can be identified or not in the ritual context.

114 Woods 2005, 33–34.

115 Cooper 1986, 87; Woods 2005, 34.

116 Woods 2005, 34–35.

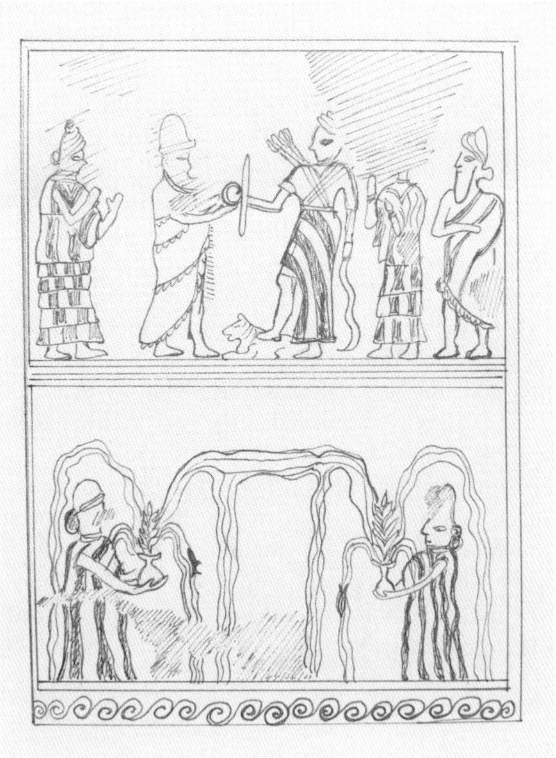

Illustration 8: Detail of the "Investiture Fresco" of Zimri-Lim, Mari palace.

In the so-called "Investiture Fresco", the divine Euphrates is portrayed as a feminine dyad. (Illustration 8).[117] While the upper register preserves a scene where Zimri-Lim stands in front of a martial Ištar in a gesture of adoration, the lower register presents two female River goddesses in a scene full of water.[118] Each goddess holds an overflowing vase, from which streams of water and sprouts of vegetation emerge. The streams are flanked by fish swimming up and down and between the two River goddesses, giving the scene a sense of fluidity and movement. This sense of flowing water is emphazised by the dresses of the goddesses, which are drawn using parallel undulating vertical lines, and by the spirals in the lower register, which recall the movement of waves. As pointed out by Woods, the placing of the divine Euphrates in the lower register of a scene which aims at establishing the king's legitimacy probably refers to the deeply rooted belief in water as the basis of everything, including kingship.[119] Accordingly, also the motherly nature of the Euphrates is fully expressed.

117 Woods 2005, 18–19. See above in this chapter, § 2.1.

118 Woods 2005, 18–19.

119 Woods 2005, 19.

Another relevant case is that of Sippar, whose logographic name (UD.KIB.NUN^{ki}) and location on the site closest to the Euphrates, places this city as the Euphrates' city *par excellence*. Sippar was traversed by a network of tributaries and channels –such as the Zubi, Irnina, Araḫtum and Abgal– and canals joining the Tigris. This confluence between Euphrates and Tigris, in a myriad of watercourses and streams, created the perfect natural setting for the worship of the fluvial deity.[120] Sippar should be considered an early holy site associated with the river.[121] The city was the religious center of the Sun-god as the supreme judge of mankind, at least from the 3rd millennium. It can be assumed that a synergic relationship between these two gods took place in the city of Sippar, where the association of Šamaš and Id resulted in enhancing the judicial roles of both deities.[122] This special relationship emerges from the anti-witchcraft and purification rituals throughout the 2nd and 1st millennium. In the anti-witchcraft incantations that we have encountered, Id occurs often together with the Sun god. In these contexts, the divine River is called upon in both its aspects of purifying and life-giving deity, and as the god presiding the River Ordeal.

The veneration of the divine River was bound to the topography and it must be seen as a predominantly northern religious phenomenon.[123] In the upper courses of the Euphrates and of the Tigris much evidence of a cult of the divine River exists in the 3rd and 2nd millennium B.C.E, while the Southern Sumer exhibits scarcer evidence of fluvial worship.[124] Both in the Sumerian context and in the later tradition from the South, the presence of the River-god is "almost entirely tied to the River Ordeal, and the River god does not appear to be topographically bound, nor does he enjoy the royal patronage and

---

120 Woods 2005, 39.

121 Woods argues that "Sippar's relationship with the river manifested itself in the worship of the Euphrates, evidence of which can be found in the Itlal-Erra and Šulgi inscriptions, and in the very writing of Sippar with a graphic composition, KIB.NUN, borrowed from the spelling of the Euphrates. Finally, the bond between the city and the river may find expression in what appears to be a relatively high proportion of watercourse personal names at Sippar, particularly those referring to the Euphrates and the Arahtum, e.g., *Abdi*-^{d}ÍD; ^{d}ÍD-*abī*; ^{d}ÍD-DI.KUD; ^{d}ÍD-*rabi*; *Ipiq-Idiglat*; *Ipqu-Araḫtum*; *Mār-Araḫtum*; *Mārat-Araḫtum*; *Mār*-^{íd}*Purattim*; *Nārum-ilī*; *Ummī-Araḫtum*; ^{íd}*Sikalum-ummī*" (Woods 2005, 37–39).

122 Woods 2005, 42.

123 Woods 2005, 43. About the function of topography as a relevant and essential feature of the worship of rivers and natural elements in general, Woods argues that: "the promotion of rivers to gods is but one facet of the broader phenomenon of the *numen loci* that encompasses the deification of mountains and cities; it is the more tangible counterpart to the deification of heavenly bodies and natural phenomena, familiar aspects of Mesopotamian religious thought. As the geographical and temporal distribution of our evidence suggests, the raising of topographical features of the Mesopotamian landscape to divine status may belong to the earliest discernable strata of the Semitic religious conception. In essence, topographical features that were considered to be of inherent significance, inspiring awe and reverence, were held to be imbued with a numinous quality and so were incorporated into the pantheon, if only in name. But the fact that the Euphrates and the Baliḫ both received offerings shows that at certain northern locations, such as Mari and Ebla, rivers could assume a personified form, as the evidence from the glyptic confirms, and thus stand on par with other gods" (Woods 2005, 23–24).

124 According to Woods, the River-god presumably represents an early syncretism between Sumerian and Semitic gods, but its cult seems to "gravitate more toward the Semitic than to the Sumerian religious sphere" (Woods 2005, 43). See also below in this chapter, §4.1.

divine status which are attested in offering texts known from the Northern sources".[125] The Sumerian and Southern conceptions focus on the divine River in the mythical discourse, where it is entangled with the Eastern mountains, the legendary place of pristine purity and of the cosmic mountain where the destinies are decreed at every sunrise. The divine River ceases to be worshipped after the second millennium, but it emerges as a divine power in the rituals and incantations throughout the first millennium, especially in the Assyrian context.

2.5 Sulphur, offspring of the River

The divine River not only generates life, but also other entities, including an interesting mineral, sulphur. In Mesopotamian rituals, sulphur (Sum. KI.A.^{d}ÍD or PIŠ.^{d}ÍD, Akk. *kibrītu*) recurs as an important calming and purifying agent.[126] Moreover, in the anti-witchcraft rituals, sulphur features a kinship with the River, being the offspring of Id. In the incantation *Maqlû* VI 78–84, Sulphur is invoked and called the "daughter of the River" (*mārat Id*) and the "daughter-in-law of the River" (*kallāt Id*):

ÉN *kibrītu kibrītu kibrītu mārat Id kibrītu kallat Id*	Incantation: "Sulphur, Sulphur, Sulphur, daughter of River, Sulphur, daughter-in-law of the River,
ša sebe u sebe kaššāpātūša [*ša*] *sebe u sebe ayyābūša*	Whose witches are seven and seven, whose enemies are seven and seven.
ēpušāniššim[*ma*] *ul inneppuš*	They performed sorcery against her, but she is not ensorcelled,
ukaššipāniššima ul ikkaššip	They bewit[ched her], but she is not bewitched.
mannu ša ana kibrīti ippuša kišpī	Who is it that can perform witchcraft against Sulphur?
kibrītu ša sebe u sebe īpušāni lipšur	May Sulphur rele[ase] the sorcery that the seven and seven have performed against me.
KIMIN [x (x)] *lipšurma anāku lubluṭ* TU$_6$ É[N]	*Ditto* may release, so that I may live". Incantation formula.[127]

Sulphur is here described as a female entity, related to the divine River, Id, and as an extremely powerful agent against sorcery. Sulphur is portrayed as the arch-enemy of the seven and seven witches: it is called upon to release their sorcery, since no one can perform witchcraft against her.[128] Moreover, sulphur is believed having a powerful calming effect.

125 Woods 2005, 43.

126 See *Maqlû* VI 85–97 (Abusch 2015, 341). See also Abusch 2002, 207–208, over the connections between Id, sulphur (*kibrītu*), bitumen (*iṭṭû*), and the *atā'išu*-plant.

127 Abusch 2015, 79: 78–84.

128 See also *CMAwR* 7.8.3: 2'–11'. Here Sulphur occurs together with colocynth as purifiers and helpers

As previously seen, sulphur has the ability to calm down the mountain: "like the mountain is made quiet by sulphur" (*kīma šadî ina kibrīti inuḫḫu*).[129] Whether this calming property derives from the inhalation of the gas (can it inhibit the nervous system?), or because of its association with a fluvial setting and its sensorial experience (i.e. hearing of the flowing waters), is a matter of speculation.

In the anti-witchcraft rituals, another type of sulphur is attested as the main purifier in conjunction with the Day of the New Moon.[130] An anti-witchcraft spell opens with the statement that the bewitched person has equipped himself with *ru'ītu*-sulphur (ÚḪ.^{d}ÍD).[131] This mineral, presumably a greenish type of sulphur, is called "the daughter of the great gods" (*mārat ilī rabûti*) and invoked due to its properties of undoing "witchcraft on the day of the New Moon"(*ša ina bibli kišpī*), and dissolving the curses (*māmâti*) "on the vigil of the 7th day" (*ina nubatti sebî ūmi*).[132] According to the context of the spell, the *ru'ītu*-sulphur is closely connected with the undoing of the *māmītu*.

As for both types of sulphur, it has to be highlighted that their name includes the logogram ^{d}ÍD.[133] The connection with the divine River and Sulphur appears to be obvious in the light of the setting of the River Ordeal. In fact, the ideal locations for this legal practice, like the thermal springs of Hit, were sulphurous springs, where sulphur and bitumen bubbled forth from the waters.[134] This fact not only connects the sulphur with the River as active agent in the rituals, but it links it to the divine realm. The connection of this mineral entity to the realm of the gods is further affirmed by the epithet "Daughter of Id" and "Daughter of the Great Gods", establishing an intriguing kinship between Sulphur, the River and the great gods.

3 Waters, springs and the Apsû

Water has a polyvalent symbolism: it is considered the source of life, of abundance, of divine radiance, of purification and salvation, but also of death, diseases and punishment.[135]

---

of the Day of the New Moon, which is called the "purifier of heaven and of the subterranean ocean" (*mullil šamê Apsî*), and the one "who undoes witchcraft (and) magic" (*mupaššer kišpī ruḫê*). See in particular line 9′: *mannu ša ana kibrīti īpušu* [*kišpī*], "Who is it that can perform [witchcraft] against sulphur?" (Abusch/Schwemer 2011, 187).

129 *Maqlû* III 82 (Abusch 2015, 307: 82). See Chapter II, § 2.3.

130 See above in the present section, note 107, for the conjunction of sulphur and the New Moon.

131 *CMAwR* 7.8.3: 46′–55′ (Abusch/Schwemer 2011, 188: 46′–55′).

132 Abusch/Schwemer 2011, 188: 46′–48′.

133 Abusch argues for a verbal connection "between ^{d}ÍD, the deified river, and *kibrītu*, sulphur, for the latter is often written logographically KI.A.^{d}ÍD (and interpreted as if it meant) 'the bank of the river', *kibir* ^{d}ÍD" (Abusch 2002, 208).

134 Abusch 2002, 208. See Ainsworth 1888, 440–442: "Sulphur is also precipitated, but not in sufficient quantities to be of any commercial value. The historian Xiphilinus describes the chief fountain as a lake of sulphur, and Dion Cassius asserts that the exhalation from the springs was so strong that no animal or bird could breathe it without dying" (quoted in Heimpel 1996, 14). See also Abusch 2002, 208.

135 See Eliade 1958, 188–215; von Behr 2007, 1963–1968. See also the *Song of Bazi* 29a, "In the midst of the house waters used to cross, half were life, half were death" (George 2009, 7–8: 29a; see Chapter II, § 3.3 for the whole text).

References to the purity of water are copious throughout the literature, and the complex relationship between waters, springs, rivers and the Apsû exceeds the limits and purposes of this study.[136] However, contextually to the interest of this book, the intrinsic connection between water, the river with its sources, and the Apsû should be mentioned, being a recurrent motif in Mesopotamian mythology and incantations.

Rivers are conceived of as pouring out from the Apsû, which is traditionally referred to as the abode of the god Enki/Ea. The connection between the Apsû and the god Ea is a continuous and widespread tradition throughout the literature and religious practices. In Old Babylonian, Atraḫasīs, the wise man of the Flood Story, praises Ea while standing on the banks of a river, with the intention that his prayer and dream will reach the god in the Apsû.[137] The Apsû is the male cosmic principle in the 1st-millennium creation story, *Enūma Eliš*, alongside his female counterpart, Tiamat. The male principle is traditionally understood as the sweet waters of the underground, which is paired with the salt sea waters of the female cosmogonic entity. After being slaughtered, the Apsû becomes the abode of the god Ea and his wife Damkina, turning into the cosmic place of pristine water.

In the realm of incantations, the evidence associating the Apsû with rivers is copious and multifaceted. The River is addressed as the chosen dwelling-place of Ea, king of the Apsû, in the River Incantation,[138] while in another version of the same incantation, the river is called upon in order to carry evil away to the Apsû.[139] Contextually, the Apsû should be regarded as the depths of the river.[140] A related zi-pà formula refers to the divine River as the mother of Apsû: "Be exorcised by the River, mother of the Apsû" (zi ^{d}Íd ama-En-gu-ra-ke$_4$ [ḫ]é).[141] In this incantation formula, the healing and purifying power of the divine River is expressed, while establishing a kinship with the Apsû itself, while in an Old Babylonian incantation, it is the Tigris that is addressed as the "blood of the Apsû"

136 See Horowitz 1998, 334–347 on the geography of the Apsû: "The various aspects of Apsû share a number of common elements. The Apsû is always filled with waters, the Apsû is always lower than the earth's surface, and waters identified with Apsû are found below the surface of rivers, seas, and other bodies of water. For example, ground waters in the Apsû are located beneath the earth's surface, and Apsû waters in marshes, swamps, seas, and rivers are lower than the banks of these bodies of water. These common elements suggest that the Apsû can be thought of as a cosmic subterranean lake that maintains a constant surface level. If so, it would be logical for the Apsû to form ground waters below the earth's crust, where the earth's surface is higher than the Apsû, but also possible for Apsû waters to seep into marshes, swamps, rivers, and the ocean, when the earth's crust dips below the level of the Apsû. Other deeper portions of the Apsû, of course, could be located beneath the hard floors of these bodies of water, just as ground waters flow below the courses of rivers and canals. Nonetheless, it is clear that there were many different conflicting views of the Apsû in antiquity, and a few authors apparently ignore the existence of the Apsû altogether" (Horowitz 1998, 344).

137 See below in the present chapter, § 5.

138 Lambert 2013, 396: 4. See above in the present chapter, § 2.

139 Caplice 1971, 135: 24, *[ešrēt]a Id šūridī Apsûki Id lemnu šâšu yâši u bītiya lā iqarrubu,* "[You are strai]ght, O River! Take it down to your Apsû, O River! May that evil not approach me or my house". See Horowitz 1998, 338.

140 Horowitz 1998, 338.

141 PBS I/2 112 30 (ArOr 21, 395: 30). See Horowitz 1998, 338–339. See above in the present chapter, § 2.2.

(^{íd}Idigna ù-mu-un Abzu), thus embodying the very vital essence of the cosmic entity.[142]

An incantation which offers a holistic portrayal of water, mountains, trees, rivers, heaven, Apsû, Enki and humans is to be found in the 1st-millennium invocation for purifying the body of a sick person:

én a en-e kur-gal-ta si-nam-mi-[sá]	Incantation: "Lordly waters, flowing straight from the great mountains,
a ^{íd}Buranun^{ki} kug-ga-ta si-nam-mi-[sá]	Waters, flowing straight from the pure Euphrates,
sig$_7$-ga Abzu-ta nam-me ba-rig$_7$-[ga]	Born out of the Apsû, granting the me-ship,
sig$_7$-ga Eridu-ga-ke$_4$ RU bí-in-[tag]	Born in Eridu, you have touched the ...,
^{giš}erin bí-in-tag ^{giš}ḫa-šur-ra bí-in-[tag]	You have touched the cedar, you have [touched] the *ḫašurru*-tree,
An-na an-na mu-un-tag ^{d}Ki ki(-a) mu-un-tag	You have touched Anu in the heaven, you have touched the divine Earth on the earth,
^{d}En-ki lugal-Abzu-ka sikil-la mu-un-tag	You have touched Enki, the king of the Apsû, the pure one,
lú-u$_{18}$-lu dumu-dingir-ra-na su-na mu-un-tag	You have touched the body of (this) man, son of his god,
mu-un-sikil-la mu-un-dadag-g[a]	You have made him pure, you have made him clean,
eme-ḫul-gál bar-šè ḫé-[im-ta-gub]	May the evil tongue [stand] aside!"[143]

The pure waters, pouring from the high mountains, purify and heal everything with their flowing touch, while simultaneously connecting the river, the Euphrates, the Apsû, the city of Eridu, heaven and earth, and trees.[144] In this context, the mention of the cedar and of the ḫašur-tree is a further indication that the purity of the waters flowing from the mountains are connected to the eastern horizon, where these evergreen cosmic trees grow, and where the cosmic Mountain of Sunrise houses the source of the rivers.[145]

The name for a water source is Sum. idim, Akk. *nagbu*, whose main meaning is "spring, fountain", but it might also refer to "underground water".[146] Another term which refers to an opening in the ground from which water pours out is *kuppu*.[147] It designates either a natural pond or source, or a human-constructed well: according to the CAD, *kuppu*

142 Kramer 1985, 115–135 (see Blaschke 2018, 128).
143 *Šurpu* IX 119–128 (Reiner 1970, 49).
144 See also, e.g. the Incantation of the *kiškanû*-tree in Chapter IV, § 2.5.
145 See further in Chapter IV, § 2.4.
146 CAD N/1, 108–110 s.v. *nagbu* A.
147 CAD K, 550–551 s.v. *kuppu*.

means "any catchwater or pond constructed at a spring in order to increase its yield".[148] With the expression *pî nāri/nārāti*, lit. "mouth of the river(s)", several meanings are involved, creating a blurring of significances. This expression can refer alternately to the delta of a river,[149] to the place where tributaries merge into a main course,[150] or to a water hole.[151] The latter understanding refers to any place where waters emerge from an underground tract, and thus it might be understood as another synonym for the source of a watercourse.[152] Furthermore, the evidence for a town called Pî-nārātim, whose location was probably situated along the course of the Euphrates in central or northern Babylonia, speaks of a place of confluence of watercourses into the Euphrates.[153] Thus, the expression *pî nārāti* should be considered referring to any "opening" that a watercourse encounters in its path: either the opening where the water from the underground pours and initiates a river (i.e. the source), or the place where a watercourse pours into another watercourse, or into the sea (i.e. the delta).

In the Sumerian tradition, the sources of the rivers are located in the "mountain of the spring" (k u r i d i m). This mountain is Dukug, the Holy Mound, which is the mythical remote place where the subterranean water emerges from the ground and gives birth to the cosmic, life-generating rivers. A reference to the "distant sources of the Ḫalḫalla (the 'Rolling River')" (í d Ḫ a l - ḫ a l - l a a - k i - t a s ù - u d - b i - š è), is found in a Sumerian hymn to Utu.[154] This evidence suggests the connection between the river Ḫalḫalla, the Sun and the east. In both Sumerian and Akkadian traditions, Mt. Ḫašur is considered the place where the Tigris and the Euphrates have their origin. This mountain stood out on the eastern horizon, and was envisioned as the cosmic Mountain of Sunrise.[155] The waters flowing from the cosmic Mountain of Sunrise are imbued with miraculous healing properties, together with the ability to determine destiny.[156]

The cosmic source of all rivers is the *pī nārāti*, the "Mouth-of-the-Rivers", of the literary account. Its name evokes the opening of the earth with its outpouring of fresh pure water from the darkness, coming directly from the Apsû. The *pī nārāti* was conceived of as the source of the cosmic rivers, and was traditionally localized in the eastern mountainous lands.[157] References to the *pī nārāti* are found in the traditions of the Flood Story and of the

148 CAD K, 550–551 s.v. *kuppu*.

149 CAD P, 470 s.v. *pû*, 9d. For the terms expressing the delta of the river, see Blaschke 2018, 380–384, according to whom the term *pû* never refers to the delta, but rather to any branching of a watercourse.

150 See Streck, *RlA* 10, 566–567. See also George on the name *zibbatum*, lit. "tail" of a river, which is understood as the technical term for the mouth of a river or canal (George 2009, 139, note 1, with reference to Vallat 1987).

151 CAD P, 470 s.v. *pû*, 11.

152 A similar conceptualization of the source of a river is displayed in India, where the sources of the sacred rivers are referred to as the "mouth" of the river (e.g. Gangotri, "Mouth-of-Gange"; Yamunotri, "Mouth-of-Yamuna"). (Haberman 2011, 44–47).

153 Streck 2005, 566–567; George 2009, 46–47, note to lines 14–15. As pointed out by Streck, "Der Name von Pî-nārātim, ‚Mündung der Flüsse/Kanäle', selber legt eine Stelle am Euphrat nahe, an der mehrere Kanäle oder Seitenzweige in den Fluß mündeten" (Streck 2005, 567).

154 ETCSL 4.32.f: 30. See below § 4.1.2.

155 See Chapter II.

156 Woods 2009, 220–221.

157 Albright 1919, 176–177; George 2003, 864; Woods 2009, 202–203.

Gilgameš Epic. The Sumerian Flood Story transmits that Ziusudra was allocated by the gods to guard mankind at great distance from Uruk, "in an oversea country, in the land Tilmun, where the sun rises" (kur-bal kur Dilmun-na ki ^{d}Utu è-šè mu-un-tìl-eš).[158] This tradition survives until the 1st-millennium Gilgameš Epic, where the wise Utnapišti is said to live beyond the cosmic ocean (*marratu*) of the Waters-of-Death (*mê mūti*), in a distant land at the Mouth-of-the Rivers, the *pī nārāti*:

lū ašimma Ūta-napišti ina rūqi ina pī nārāti	Utnapišti shall dwell far away, at the Mouth-of-the-Rivers
ilqûnnima ina rūqi ina pī nārāti uštēšibūni	They took me and settled me far away, at the Mouth-of-the-Rivers[159]

This passage mentions *pī nārāti* as a remote land belonging to the cosmic realm, but any reference to its location is lacking. Traditionally, according to the western horizon in which Gilgameš is said to wander in the Akkadian account, the location of the *pī nārāti* is envisioned as being in the far west, beyond Mt. Māšu and the cosmic ocean, *marratu*. However, in the prologue of the Epic, Gilgameš is praised as the one who "crossed the ocean, the vast sea, as far as the sunrise" (*ēbir ayyabba tâmati rapašti adi ṣīt šamši*).[160] This evidence, together with the Sumerian tradition, speaks for the existence of a tradition which considered the abode of the sage of the Flood in the distant east, possibly in Tilmun.[161] Tilmun, deep in the south-east of the Persian Gulf and identified with modern Bahrain, was a land between legend and reality in the eyes of the Mesopotamians. Due to the profusion of water sources and its eastern location, Tilmun was identified with the cosmic *pī nārāti*. This understanding is supported by the later classical and Arabic sources, which refer to it as the place where the Tigris and the Euphrates re-emerged in the deep South-East after sinking into the marshes.[162]

The number of the cosmic rivers flowing out from the *pī nārāti* is reported in some mythical narratives. In *Lugalbanda and the Anzû-bird*, the cosmic tree, abode of the Thunderbird, is said to stand on a cosmic mountain and to sink its roots deep "in the midst of Utu's River of the Seven Mouths" (íd ka 7 ^{d}Utu-ka $šag_4$-ba).[163] In this case, the reference to Utu affirms that the location of this river should be understood as the cosmic Mountain of Sunrise. Instead, according to the Incantation for the *kiškanû*-tree two are the mouths of the two rivers. This tree is said to be rising from the Apsû, in the midst of the Mouth-of-the-Two-Rivers (dal-ba-na íd-da ka-min-kám-ma: *ina bīrit pī nārāti killalān*), where Šamaš and Dumuzi stand.[164] The text offers a unique attestation of the names of the two mouths of the rivers: Kaḫegal, "Mouth-of-Plenty" and Igiḫegal, "Eye-of-Plenty", whose possible iconographical representation as two birds' heads is found on a

158 ETCSL 1.7 4. See also Horowitz 1998, 194.
159 *Gilg.* XI 205–206 (George 2003, 716–717).
160 *Gilg.* I 40 (George 2003, 540–541). See Horowitz 1998, 332–333.
161 Horowitz 1998, 104–105 and 332–333.
162 George 2003, 864; Woods 2009, 202.
163 ETCSL 1.8.2.2: 35.
164 Geller 2007, 169–171: 99–100. See Chapter IV, § 2.5.

seal from Mari.[165] Interestingly, both bodily parts (i.e. mouth and eye) allude to an opening in the ground from which water pours out. Indeed, in the literary sources the term "eye" (Sum. igi, Akk. *īnum*) is cited as a synonym for the source of a river.[166] This image recalls the creation of the rivers Tigris and Euphrates from the body (i.e. the eyes) of Tiamat as reported in the *Enūma Eliš*.[167] In this incantation, the implied rivers can be the Tigris and the Euphrates, but also the cosmic river(s) can be inferred. This evidence could also be seen as a further insight into the Mesopotamian conception of the river as a dual entity.

Springs were also cultic places, where shrines were built and rites were held.[168] Evidence for this understanding is found in the *Song of Bazi*, which refers to a sanctuary placed among the springs of mounts Šaššar and Bašār. The temple is located in an aquatic setting, where the underground waters emerging from the Apsû merge into the divine River, Id, and engage with Ea. The specific reference that half the waters are death and half the waters are life alludes to the practice of the River Ordeal.[169]

4 Specifically named rivers

4.1 The Tigris and the Euphrates

The major rivers from which Mesopotamia derives its name, the Tigris (Sum. Idigna, Akk. *Idiglat*) and the Euphrates (Sum. Buranuna, Akk. *Purattu*), are omnipresent entities in the religious sources.[170] Since these two rivers occur in all contexts of Mesopotamian life, here only the relevant evidence for rivers portrayed as personal agents and as deities is considered and highlighted. It should be emphasized that both names are feminine.

4.1.1 The divine creation of the Tigris and of the Euphrates in myths

In the mythical evidence, the two rivers recur as offspring of the gods. In the Sumerian myth *Enki and the World Order*, the Euphrates and the Tigris come into being as a result of the god Enki ejaculating into the river beds, filling them with his semen:

ki-bi-ta igi-ni ĝar-ra-[ta]	After he had moved his gaze from that place,
a-a ^{d}En-ki ^{id}Buranun-na nam-mi-in-⌜íl⌝-a-ta	After father Enki raised the waters of the Euphrates,
gud du$_7$-du$_7$-gin$_7$ ù-na mu-	He stood like an impetuous lusty

165 See above § 2.1, Illustration 7.
166 Blaschke 2018, 234–239.
167 *Enūma Eliš* V 55 (Lambert 2013, 100–101).
168 See, e.g., below in the present chapter, § 4.1.4.
169 See in the present chapter, § 2.3, and Chapter II, § 3.3.
170 A recent and comprehensive study of the two rivers is Blaschke 2018.

un-na-gub	bull for her,
ĝìš im-zi-zi dùb im-nir-⸢re⸣	Lifted his penis, ejaculated,
^{íd}Idigna a zal-le im-ma-⸢an⸣-[si]	Filled the Tigris with shining flowing water.
šilam ^{ú}numun-na amaš ĝirí-tab-ba amar-bi gù di-⸢dam⸣	He was like a cow mooing in the alfalfa grass –the scorpion-infested stall(?).
^{íd}⸢Idigna⸣ gud du$_7$-gin$_7$ á-na mu-na-⸢ab⸣-[...]	He [leant] over the Tigris, like a rampant bull,
ĝìš im-zìg níĝ-mussa nam-de$_6$	He lifted his penis, he brought the wedding gift:
^{íd}Idigna am gal-gin$_7$ šag$_4$ im-ḫúl ù-tud-ba mu-⸢ni⸣-[...]	The Tigris rejoiced in its heart like a great wild bull, when it was given birth (. . .).[171]

In this narrative, the river Tigris is said to be rejoicing in its heart due to its being filled by the waters of Enki, the god of the pristine waters generated in the Apsû. The image of the god, portrayed as a rampant bull, expresses the powerful fecundity of these two rivers.

In the 1st-millennium Babylonian creation myth *Enūma Eliš*, it is from the dismembered body of the primeval cosmic divinity Tiamat that the two rivers come into existence. After Tiamat's defeat by the hero-god Marduk, the king of the gods creates the world from the body of his grandmother. From her eyes the water of the Tigris and Euphrates poured into the world:

iškun qaqqassa x (x) [x (x)] x išpuk	He put her head in position and poured out .. [..]
nagbu uptettâ ⸢mû⸣ ittešbi	He opened the abyss and it was sated with water.
iptēma ina īnīša Puratta Idiglat	From her two eyes he let the Euphrates and Tigris flow,
nāḫirīša upt[e]ḫḫâ x x (x) ētezba	He blocked her nostrils, but left …
išpuk ina ṣirtīša [šad]ê birûti	He heaped up the distant [mountains] on her breasts,
nambāʾī uptalliša ana babāli kuppu	He bored wells to channel the springs.[172]

The body of the ancestral grandmother is transformed into the different constitutive elements of the cosmos: along with the two main Mesopotamian rivers, mountains are heaped on her breasts, and springs are opened in their midst. Accordingly, the two rivers exhibit a divine origin and nature, being the direct offspring of the female divine ancestor of all gods. In a 1st-millennium learned commentary on the *Enūma Eliš*, additional details

171 *Enki and the World Order* 250–258 (Kramer/Maier 1989, 47–48; Mittermayer 2012, 243–258; ETCSL 1.1.3: 250–258).

172 *Enūma Eliš* V 53–58 (Lambert 2013, 100–101: 53–55).

of the origin of the two rivers are preserved. In this commentary, the Tigris is said to be Tiamat's right eye, while the Euphrates her left one.[173] This image recalls the tears flowing from the eyes of the defeated ancestral mother, suggesting the transformation of the salty tears flowing from the saltwater deity of the sea into the sweet water which fills and forms the Tigris and the Euphrates. The association between bodily parts and natural elements should be emphasized: the sources of the rivers are conceptualized as the eyes of the divine body of the Mother-of-the-Gods.[174]

The cosmic and divine nature of the Tigris and of the Euphrates is a recurrent and intertwined feature throughout the literature. The two rivers are often mentioned together as twins among other mythical pairs of geographical and natural elements,[175] while in a 1st millennium ritual text, they occur together with other natural elements, cosmic entities and natural phenomena.[176] In this ritual text, the four winds, the rivers, the mountain and the seas are presented before the great gods, in a net of correspondences between the gods and the cosmic divine entities. This text refers to a ritual to be held on the top of a temple, where the image of the South Wind is placed in front of Ea, that of the East Wind before Enlil, that of the North Wind in front of Adad and Ninurta, while that of the West Wind is displayed with Anu. The images embodying the mountain and the Tigris are placed in front of Enlil, the representations of the Upper Sea and that of the Euphrates are located in front of Šamaš, the image of the Lower Sea in front of Ea, and that comprising the desert and the steppe is placed in front of Ištar. The encompassing world is here displayed, and every cosmic domain is associated with an anthropomorphic deity.

4.1.2 Life-generating beings: the Euphrates, the Tigris, and the Ḫalḫalla, mother of the mountains

In the Gilgameš Epic, we encounter the river Tigris invoked together with another holy river, the Ulāya.[177] Here these two rivers are called upon to participate in Gilgameš's mourning for Enkidu's death and are addressed as pure entities acting as persons.[178] In this literary passage, the Euphrates bears the epithet *elletu* "holy, pure", and is invoked in order

---

173 SAA 3, 39 rev. 3, ^{id}ḪAL.ḪAL IGI^{II} ZAG-*šá* ^{id}UD.KIB.NUN^{ki} IGI^{II} 150$^{!}$-*šá*, "The Tigris is her right eye, the Euphrates is her left eye" (Livingstone 1989, 101: 3).

174 For an interesting discussion of the metaphors and concepts of the body in gynaecological texts, where the body parts are associated with watercourses, see Steinert 2013, 1–23.

175 See e.g. the zi-pà-Incantation I 250–254, a-ab-ba sig a-ab-ba nim-ma a-dé a-si-ga a ^{íd}Idigna ^{íd}Buranuna^{ki} ḫur-saĝ ĝi$_{6}$-ga ḫur-saĝ babbar-ra, "The Lower Sea and the Upper Sea, the Flood and Low Tide, Water of the Tigris and of the Euphrates; the Black Mountain and the White Mountain" (Borger 1969, 1-22). See also Blaschke 2018, 340.

176 Nougayrol 1966, 72–74: 7–10.

177 *Gilg.* VIII 19 (George 2003, 650–651).

178 See below § 4.4.3. See also Edzard 2003/2005, 434, on the personification of rivers and other natural elements. Moreover, concerning the personification of the rivers, see also a Sumerian proverb where the two rivers are said to assume the form of animals: ^{íd}Idigna uz^{mušen}-àm ^{íd}Buranunana kur-gi$_{4}$^{mušen}-àm, "The Tigris is an uz-bird, the Euphrates is a kur-gi$_{4}$-bird" (SumProv. 15 Sec. C 15 23).

to mourn Gilgameš' best friend (*libkiku elletu Purattu*, "May the holy Euphrates mourn you").[179]

In incantations and rituals, the two rivers recur consistently as active agents, summoned on behalf of the patient during the magical performance, often invoked together. The Euphrates and the Tigris are called upon as personified agents in order to calm, to purify and absolve sins and defilement with their pure waters. The Tigris and the Euphrates are mentioned together with gods, cardinal points, times of the day, objects and other rivers (the Diyala and the Zab) in order to release the patient affected by a curse.[180] In the ritual *Šurpu*, the *māmītu* of the Euphrates is recorded: *māmīt bēl ṣarbatim u Purattim*, "the 'oath' of the Lord of the poplar and of the Euphrates".[181] In the same ritual, the two rivers are invoked to be calmed down along with the god of fire, Girra, the collective mountains and the ocean.[182]

The Tigris and Euphrates are mentioned often as the origins and carriers of the pure water which flows in them, coming down from the mountains and pouring into the sea. The pure water of the Tigris and the Euphrates recurs in purifying incantations and in rituals for dispelling diseases, sins and pollution. The purity of the water of the two rivers derives from the close and deep connection between water, rivers and the Apsû, as we can read in an Old Babylonian namburbi-incantation:

íd kug-ga-à[m]	"The River is pure,
a ^{íd}Idigna sikil-à[m]	The water of the Tigris is clear,
a ^{íd}Buranuna dadag-ge	The water of the Euphrates is shining:
téš-ba lú Abzu-ke$_4$	In their unity, the one of the Abzu,
Ḫal-ḫal-la ama ḫur-saĝ-ĝá-[ke$_4$]	Ḫalḫalla, the mother of the mountains,
^{d}En-ki lugal Abzu-ke$_4$	Enki, king of the Abzu,
^{d}Asar-lú-ḫi	Asarluḫi,
dumu Eridu^{ki}-ga-ke$_4$	The son of Eridu:
šu-ĝu$_{10}$ ḫé-em-kug-ga	May they make my hand pure!
ka-ĝu$_{10}$ ḫé-em-sikil-e	May they clear my mouth!
ĝíri-ĝu$_{10}$ ḫu-mu-un-dadag-ge	May they let my foot shine!
eme-ḫul-ĝal bar-šè ḫé-em-ta-gub	May the evil tongue stand aside!"
inim-inim-ma-a-gúb-ba-kam	Incantation formula for the pure water.[183]

179 George 2003, 650–651: 19.

180 Geller 1998, 131 and ff.: iii 29–30, KI ^{id}IDIGNA *u* ^{id}BURANUN [MIN] KI ^{id}*Túr-an u* ^{id}*Zab-ban* [MIN].

181 *Šurpu* III 146 (Reiner 1958, 23: 146). From the context, I suggest that the "Lord of the poplar" is the river Euphrates itself.

182 *Šurpu* V–VI 189: *ittīka linūḫā Idiglat u Purattu*, "Let the Tigris and the Euphrates calm down with you" (Reiner 1958, 35: 189). For the whole text, see Chapter II, § 2.3.

183 YOS 11, 48: 1–9 (Conti 1988, 124). See also the almost identical Neo-Assyrian namburbi-incantation incantation, Caplice 1971, 141 34′–39′, [én-é-nu-ru íd-da kug-ga íd-da

The theme of the pristine and purifying waters of the Tigris and Euphrates is a constant feature throughout incantations from the 2nd millennium onward.[184] In the 1st-millennium rituals, as previously described, the pure water of the Tigris and Euphrates is mentioned often for its purifying power. In the ritual *Mīs pî* the "pure water which runs in the Tigris" (é n a k u g - g a a ^{íd}I d i g n a g u b - b a) is called upon to purify the wooden statue of the god,[185] whereas another incantation concerns the purification of the waters themselves through different cleansing plants, which is a necessary condition for performing a *bīt rimki*.[186] Here the water is addressed as the "water of the Apsû, brought from the midst of Eridu, water of the Tigris, water of the Euphrates, brought from a pure place".[187] At the end of a purification ritual, the patient is finally released from any *māmītu* and defilement, as we can read in *Šurpu*: "he is purified, cleansed, bathed, washed, cleaned with the water of the pure Tigris and Euphrates, the water of the sea (and) [vast] ocean" (*ūtallil ūtabbib urtammik umtessi uzzakki ina mê Idiglat Purattim ellūti mê ayabbim tâmati* [*rapašti*]).[188]

The rivers are not the original places of their flowing waters alone, but also of other entities. The Tigris, especially, is thought to generate animals (i.e. reptiles) and mountains. An Old Babylonian incantation reads that the Tigris gave birth to a reptile (*Idiglat ulissu*), while the river Ulāya raised it.[189] This description affirms the creating and life-bringing aspect of the rivers, which are addressed as female entities. The creator and feminine characterization of the Tigris finds its clearest expression when associated with the mountains, where its motherly features emerge fully through its recurring epithet "mother of the mountains" (a m a ḫ u r - s a ĝ - ĝ á - k e$_4$).[190] In an Old Babylonian incantation

---

s i k i l - l a a ^{íd}I d i g n a k u g - g a ^{íd}B u [r a n u n a ! ?] t é š - b i l á - l á A b z u - k e$_4$ ^{íd}Ḫ a l - ḫ a l - l a a m a ḫ u r - s a ĝ - ĝ á - k e$_4$ a n - g i n$_7$ ḫ é - e m - k u g - g a k i - g i n$_7$ ḫ é - e m - s i k i l - l a š à a n - g i n$_7$ ḫ é - e m - d a d a g - g e, "Enuru-incantantion. The river is pure, the river is clear, water of the pure Tigris, (water of) the Euphrates, in its unity with the Apsû; the Ḫalḫalla, mother of the mountains, may they make [me] pure like the sky, may they make [me] clean like the earth, may they make [me] bright like in the midst of heaven!". In both incantations, it appears that the river Ḫalḫalla should be considered differently from the Tigris. In fact, while this river is often identified as corresponding to the Tigris, in this context it should be understood as a cosmic entity *per se*, being called upon in ergative together with the Apsû and its related deities and dwellers (see below in this section).

184 See also the Old Babylonian incantations VS 17, 15: 1–7 (Conti 1988, 116–117), and CUSAS 32, II.A.8 (Nr. 6i) iv 30–32 (George 2016, 67–68).

185 *Mīs pî*, Nineveh Ritual Tablet 52 (Walker/Dick 2001, 56: 52).

186 *Mīs pî*, Incantation Tablet 3: 76ab–82ab (Walker/Dick 2001, 141–142: 76ab–82ab).

187 *Mīs pî*, Incantation Tablet 3: 76ab–82ab: "Water of the Apsû, brought from the midst of Eridu, water of the Tigris, water of the Euphrates, brought from a pure place: tamarisk, soapwort, heart of palm, *šalālu*-reed, multi-colored marsh reed, seven small palms, juniper, (and) white cedar throw into it; in the garden of the canal of the pure orchard build a *bīt rimki*. Bring him out to the canal of the pure orchard, to the *bīt rimki*. Bring out this statue before Shamash" (Walker/Dick 2001, 141–142: 76ab–82ab).

188 *Šurpu* VIII 83–84 (Reiner 1958, 43–44: 83–84).

189 Sb 12630: 1–2, *Idiglat ūlissu Ulāya urabbīšu*, "The river Tigris bore it, the river Ulāya raised it" (Cavignaux 2003, 61–62). In another spell, the scorpion is said to be dwelling between the Tigris and the Lagaš-canal (YOS 11, 4b: 23).

190 See *Mīs pî* 4 A 25ab, ^{íd}Ḫ a l - ḫ a l - l a a m a ḫ u r - s a ĝ - ĝ á - k e$_4$ (Walker/Dick 2001, 163: 25ab). For the whole excerpt, see Chapter III, note 60.

which addresses the pure water of the Euphrates and of the Ḫalḫalla, the name Ḫalḫalla should be understood as a synonym for the Tigris, that is here referred to as the "mother of the mountain".[191]

The river Ḫalḫalla is traditionally another name of the Tigris in the 1st-millennium literary texts. However, in the Sumerian and Old Babylonian literature it seems to refer to a mythical river flowing through the Eastern mountains.[192] The Ḫalḫalla, translated as the "Rolling River", recurs in the myth of *Lugalbanda in the Mountain Cave* as the luxuriant river on the mountains. In this text, this river is called the "mother of the mountains", which "brings the water of life" (a m a ḫ u r - s a ĝ - ĝ á - k e$_4$ a n a m - t i l - l a i m - t ù m),[193] whereas in *Lugalbanda and the Anzû-bird* it is the Anzû which establishes the destiny of this river.[194]

The deep bond between the river Ḫalḫalla and the Eastern mountains is found in the mythical narrative of *How Grain came to Sumer*. In this text, the two brothers Ninazu and Ninmada go up to the mountains where barley and flax grow, and where the river Ḫalḫalla has its origin. In fact, the source of the Rolling River is found on these mountains.[195] Moreover, in a Sumerian hymn to Utu, Inana exhorts her brother Utu to go together to the mountains, which are called the "distant source of the Rolling River" (í d Ḫ a l - ḫ a l - l a a - k i - t a s ù - u d - b i - š è).[196]

It should be noted that the epithet "mother of the mountains" always occurs with the term ^(íd)ḪAL.ḪAL, even when it clearly refers to the Tigris.[197] The interrelation between the Ḫalḫalla, the Tigris and the mountains continues throughout the first millennium and clear evidence is to be found in a bilingual Neo-Babylonian incantation, where not only the logogram Ḫalḫalla stands for the Tigris, but it is clearly stated that it is the "river of the mountain" (í d ḫ u r - s a ĝ *nāri šadî*).[198] In a Neo-Assyrian *Explanatory God List* from Niniveh, the divine Ḫalḫalla is recorded.[199] In this list, the god ^(d)ḪAL.ḪAL.LA is equated with the god Ninurta, who is called the "protector of the decisions of father Enlil" (ù r u e š - b a r *abi Enlil*).[200] This entry recalls the connection between Ninurta and the Sumerian

---

191 CUSAS 32, II.A.8 (Nr. 6i) iv 30–32, a ^(íd)B u r a n u n a s i k i l - e - d è a Ḫ a l - ḫ a l - l a a m a ḫ u r - s a ĝ - ĝ á - k e$_4$ a n a m - t a r - r a ^(d)E n - k i - g a - [k e$_4$], "Pure Water of the Euphrates, Water of Ḫalḫalla, the mother of the Mountains, water whose destiny is established by Enki" (George 2016, 67–68). See also CUSAS 32, II.A.4 (Nr. 5i) col. v, 21' (George 2016, 60).

192 Blaschke 2018, 120–128.

193 ETCSL 1.8.2.1: 266; Wilcke 2015, 239: 260. See also Chapter II, § 2.1.

194 ETCSL 1.8.2.2: 98–99; Wilcke 1969, 100–101: 98–99; Wilcke 2015, 258: 99. See Chapter II, § 3.3.

195 ETCSL 1.7.6: 17, [í d] Ḫ a l - ḫ a l a k i - t a D U - D U , "The Ḫalḫalla river, (which wells up) from the earth". See also Bottéro/Kramer 1989, 515–517.

196 ETCSL 4.32.f 30; Kramer 1985b, 122: 132.

197 See the Old Babylonian incantations YOS 11, 48: 1–9 (Conti 1988, 124) and CUSAS 32, II.A.8 (Nr. 6i) iv 30–32 (George 2016, 67–68), and NA incantation BaF 18, VIII.10 34′–37′. See the discussion above in the present section.

198 ADFU 10, 5: 6, í d ḫ u r - s a ĝ *nāri šadî Idiglat* ^(íd)Ḫ a l - ḫ a l - l a .

199 See Blaschke 2018, 120–128. Further occurrences of the divine Ḫalḫalla are found in the so-called *Götteradressbuch* from Assur (Text d iii 2 und Text e ii 17′.). See also the argument in favor of the correspondence of the Hurrian name **Ḫalla*(*š*), **Ḫaḫalla*(*š*) or **Ḫalḫalla*(*š*) with the source of the Tigris (note 535, p. 126).

200 Annus 2002, 26–27.

Anzû, confirming the intertwinement between rivers, mountains, gods and other divine and mythical creatures.

The relationship between rivers and mountains is entangled and deeply rooted in the Mesopotamian worldview. This interconnection finds its clearest expression in the kinship between mountains and rivers: rivers are the "mothers" of the mountains, thanks to the life-creating power of the feminine River.[201] Conversely, rivers find their birthplace in mountain springs and wells,[202] and then grow during their flowing path toward the sea.

4.1.3 The divine Tigris and Euphrates

The rivers Tigris and Euphrates recur as deities *per se* in several contexts throughout the different periods and sources. They are sometimes explicitly referred to as gods through the divine determinative, [203] but more often their divinity is manifested by being recorded among other gods in myths, incantations and rituals, god lists, offering lists and personal names.

In an Early Dynastic hymn the Euphrates and Tigris are mentioned together with the god Zababa.[204] While in the Old Babylonian incantations we have encountered, there is no specific evidence of the divine Tigris and Euphrates for this period, the Tigris occurs as a fully divine entity in Assyria from the second millennium onward. In the Middle Assyrian incantations and rituals, the Tigris is written with the determinative for deity (^{d}IDIGNA) and listed among other gods.[205] In the Neo-Assyrian royal rituals, the Tigris is recorded together with the great gods of the pantheon and recurs often with the divine determinative. The divine Tigris is represented by a stone and mentioned together with Sîn-of-Heaven, Adad-of-Heaven, Šamaš-of-Heaven, Ištar-of-Heaven, the Twins and Narudi, in a ritual held for the gods of Kār-Tukultī-Ninurta in Aššur.[206] Together with the divine collective rivers, the divine Tigris is listed among the gods of Aššur in the Tākultu of Assurbanipal,[207] while it is recorded among the nineteen gods of the House of Gula in a text comprising all the

201 See above in the present chapter, § 2.

202 See e.g. the incantation *Utukkū lemnūtu* I 47′–48′, *mê Ḫalḫalla mê Puratti ellūtu ša ištu kuppi ana Ḫašur aṣûni*, "the water of the Tigris, pure water of the Euphrates, which go out from the well to Mount Hašur"(Geller 2016, 50). Here the term *kuppu* occurs for "spring, source". See *AHw*. 509, "starke Quelle" and CAD K, 550–551, "man-made enlargement of a spring for the purpose of ensuring water supply". See below, § 4.1.4, on the source of the Tigris.

203 In several non-literary sources, the Tigris is written with the determinative for deity (^{d}Idigna). See e.g.: ^{d}IDIGNA in RIMA 1.0.78.22 Tukultī-Ninurta I 49 (MA, Kār-Tukultī-Ninurta); ^{d}IDIGNA in KAV 78 20 and KAR 137 iii 34 (MA, Assur); ká ^{d}IDIGNA in RIMA 1.0.76.8 Adad-nārārī I ex. 1: 26, ex. 2 28 and RIMA 2.0.87.3 Tiglath-pileser I 39 (MA, Assur). Moreover, the name Tigris occurs specified with both divine and river determinative (e.g. *Rochester* 22: 2 (Ur III, Puzriš-Dagan) $^{d+id}$IDIGNA; TCL 15, 10 83 (OB) $^{d+id}$IDIGNA; *Götteradressbuch* Text d iii 2 und Text e ii 17′ (NA, Assur) $^{d+id}$ḪAL.ḪAL; *Tintir* Taf. 2 Text j 33 (NB) $^{d+id}$IDIGNA; CUSAS 17, 68 (Tiglatpileser I.) 45, $^{d+id}$IDIGNA (see Blaschke 2018, 555–579).

204 IAS 142 xiv 9–11, ^{d}(U D)[Z a - b a$_4$] - [b a$_4$] [I d i g n a] B u r a n u n a[$^{k i}$] g u d u d u e r í n [m u (N U N)] - t ú m (L A G A B) (Biggs 1974).

205 Alster 1999, 870; Saporetti 1970, 310–311; Woods 2005, 22.

206 SAA 20, 7 rev. iii 34, 1 ^{d}MAŠ.GÚ.QAR (Parpola 2017, 18).

207 SAA 20, 40 vi 19, ^{d}MAŠ.GÚ.QAR (Parpola 2017, 115)

gods, shrines and holy places of Aššur.[208] It should be noted that all the gods mentioned have some roles in the healing and therapeutic crafts.

Referred to in its fluvial connotation, the Tigris is invoked as an animate and divine topographical entity in the Tākultu-ritual for Sennacherib, where it is invoked with other natural and topographical elements, such as Ebiḫ, the land of Uraš and of Zabban, the Upper and Lower Zab, the city, the city wall, the mortar and the brick.[209] In the Tākultu-ritual of Aššur-etel-ilāni, the Tigris recurs twice: once together with Ebiḫ, the Upper and Lower Zab, the villages and the borders among the gods who dwell in the land, and once among all the constitutive parts of the Assyrian empire, which include mountains, springs, the Tigris, the seas, the corners of the world, the stars, the entirety of the earth and of the sky.[210] The Tigris occurs named in two ways: with the Sumerograms MAŠ.GÚ.QAR and ḪAL.ḪAL, which are both translated in the Akkadian as *Diglat*. Moreover, in a rations list of cedar balm for the sanctuaries of Aššur, the divine Tigris is recorded among other gods as recipient of offerings.[211] Furthermore, in a Neo-Assyrian incantation the Euphrates and the Tigris are mentioned together with the gods Anu, Enlil and Ea: "Incantation: By the life of Sirius, by the life of …, by the life of Anu, Enlil and Ea, (by the life of) Tigris and Euphrates, may you be conjured!".[212]

The Tigris is recorded in lexical lists from the 2nd and the 1st millennium, along with other gods. The Old Babylonian "Genouillac List" registers the divine Tigris between the gods Lugal-abzu and Nin-ildu,[213] while another Old Babylonian god list mentions this river as a member of Enki's court.[214] In the Neo-Assyrian *Götteradressbuch*, the divine Tigris (d+ídḪAL.ḪAL) is recorded with the deities Gula, Uraš, Gunura, Šuriḫa, Ištar, Mārat-bīti, and Bēlet-Eanna, who all belong to the temple dedicated to Gula.[215]

Both rivers are recorded as the recipient of offerings only during the 3rd millennium. The oldest list of offerings which attests the divine Euphrates is a text from Pre-Sargonic Mari, where the divine Euphrates is offered wheat.[216] The list mentions other deities (i.e. Enki and Rašap), showing a combination of Mesopotamian and Syrian gods, and it refers to the *gi-ti-um* ritual. Interestingly, the name of the Euphrates is recorded twice. This evidence speaks of the dual nature of the river, which was portrayed as a dyad. The divine Tigris is recorded as a recipient of offerings in an Ur III text, which mentions the offering of a goat to the River deity (1 m á š d+ídI d i g n a).[217]

In personal names, both rivers recur consistently according to the geographical and temporal contexts. The Euphrates appears in the Old Babylonian names *Mār-Purattim*

---

208 SAA 20, 49: 101, dḪAL.ḪAL (Parpola 2017, 134).

209 SAA 20, 38 iv 4', ídMAŠ.GÚ.QAR (Parpola 2017, 107).

210 SAA 20, 42 rev. iii 4' and 18', ídḪAL.ḪAL (Parpola 2017, 123).

211 KAV 78: 20, [2?] [s ì l a x x] [x] dIDIGNA, "2 liters for … and the divine Tigris" (Meinhold 2009, 480).

212 KAR 76 rev. 25–28, ÉN *nīš Šiltāhi nīš* MU[L …] [*nī*]*š Anim Enlil u Ea n*[*īš*…] [*nīš*] *Idiglat u Purat*[*ti*] [*lū*] *tamâtin*[*a* …] (Ebeling 1953).

213 TCL 15, 10 83.

214 RA 20 (1923), 100 ii 34.

215 *Götteraddressbuch* 100–103 (Meinhold 2009, 427–444 (Text Nr. 15)).

216 Charpin 1987, no. 7 ii 3–6: šeZÍZ *gi-ti-um* AN.KIB.NUN.A AN.KIB.NUN.A.

217 Ur III text for/from Puzriš-Dagan (?), Rochester 22 (Šulgi 48) 1–2.

"Son-of-the-Euphrates," and *Purattum-ummī* "My-Mother-is-the-Euphrates". The Tigris appears in Old Babylonian personal names (e.g. *Idiglat-ummī*, "My-Mother-is-the-Tigris"; *Mār-Idiglat*, "Son-of-the-Tigris", *Ummī-Idiglat*, "The-Tigris-is-my-Mother"), but it is in Assyria that the Tigris was very popular during the 2nd millennium.[218] Several Middle Assyrian names display the Tigris as a recurrent theophoric element: *Idiglat-rēmīnni* "Tigris-have-mercy-on-me", *Tašme-Idiqlat* "Tigris hears", *Urad-Idiqlat* "Tigris descends", *Idiqlat-erriš* "Tigris demands (offerings)"; *Kidin-Idiqlat* "(The-One-Under-)the-Protection-of-the-Tigris", *Sīqe-idiqlat*, "Lap-of-the-Tigris", *Ṣillī-Idiqlat*, "The-Tigris-is-my-Protection", *Šēp-Idiqlat*, "Foot-of-the-Tigris".[219] In these names the Tigris is clearly referred to as a god, both because of the presence of the divine determinative and because of the actions that are ascribed to the river: having mercy, hearing and demanding an offering are, in fact, actions typically ascribed to the gods.[220]

Further evidence of the divine Euphrates comes from a Kassite letter from Nippur, where "the gods of the Euphrates" (*ilāni Puratti*) are mentioned.[221] In this case, the plural form of the gods of the Euphrates refers to the fact that the divine Euphrates was conceived of as a dual or plural deity, a notion that is affirmed by Kassite glyptic and architectural decoration.[222] This attestation, which invokes the gods of the Euphrates in order to grant protection, has been interpreted as a Kassite religious belief, according to the assumption that Mesopotamians did not have any belief in the River gods.[223] Instead, in light of the several testimonies speaking for a cult of the Euphrates, this evidence should rather be understood as a later reference of the Euphrates as a god *per se* during the 2nd millennium,[224] while it affirms the conception of this river as a dual or plural deity.

As this textual overview has shown, the two major rivers of Mesopotamia were considered gods especially in the 3rd-millennium Sumerian panthea, in the Old Babylonian Syrian context and in Assyrian religious frameworks during the 1st millennium B.C.E. Moreover, the interaction and intersection between Syrian and Mesopotamian religious views constituted a fertile ground for the cult of rivers also in the Southern Mesopotamian panthea. What emerges from this picture is that the cultic practices and religious beliefs regarding the divine River is not only subject to temporal parameters, but is also bound to geographical and topographical features.[225]

The Tigris recurs more frequently as a deity especially in the Assyrian context, where it is prevalently described having maternal attributes, and with a complex interaction with other rivers (i.e. Ḫalḫalla) in the religious narratives. The fact that the Tigris is sometimes labeled with both the determinative for god and for river is an indication that, when the

218 Woods 2005, 22; Durand 2008, 293; Blaschke 2018, 562–569.

219 Alster 1992, 870; Saporetti 1970, 310–311; Woods 2005, 22; Porter 2009, 161–162; Blaschke 2018, 562–569.

220 Porter 2009, 161–162.

221 BE A 17/1: 87, *ilāni Puratti napšātika liṣṣurū*, "May the gods of the Euphrates protect your life".

222 Woods 2005, 22; Blaschke 2018, 569–576. See above in this chapter § 2.1.

223 Waschow 1936, 16.

224 Woods 2005, 22.

225 Woods 2005, 22. Woods understands it as a "primarily an early phenomenon and one with an unmistakably northern flavor" (Woods 2005, 22).

river was conceived of as a deity, it was represented in a fluvial form.[226] This notion is valid also for the Euphrates and the other divine rivers. With the support of the iconographical sources, it can be argued that the River deity was portrayed as both half-anthropomorphic and half-non-anthropomorphic, another fact that might explain the double determinative.

The relative paucity of evidence for the divine Euphrates is a further indication of the fact that this river was implied in the majority of cases when the unspecific divine River, Id, was mentioned. As previously seen, the cult of the divine River was prevalent along the course of the Euphrates, in the cities of Tuttul, Mari, Hit and Sippar during the 3rd and 2nd millennium B.C.E.[227] In these locations, not only was the practice of the River Ordeal particularly used for solving legal matters, but the divine River was regarded as a deity *per se*, subjected to royal patronage and recipient of offerings.

4.1.4 The Source of the Tigris

The Source of the Tigris, or Tigris Tunnel, has been a cultic place visited by ancient and modern locals, travelers, conquerors and political actors since antiquity. The place traditionally referred to as the Source of the Tigris is characterized by multiple caves, rock outcrops, and gorges, known as the Birkleyn cave system. This geological formation is located at the north of the Diyarbakır Plain, in southeastern Turkey, where the Dibni Su, one of the tributaries of the Tigris, emerges at the end of a 1018 meter-long natural tunnel under the Korha Mountain, and flows southwest through an incised valley. Its paleovalley is surrounded by four other resurgence caves.[228]

In the first part of the 1st millennium B.C.E., the Tigris Source was at the heart of the Hurrian kingdom of Šubria, a conflicting neighbor of the Assyrian empire.[229] As pointed out by Harmanşah, in this liminal and contested territory, the Assyrian kings "performed sacrificial rituals, held sumptuous feasts, received tribute and gifts from the submissive local rulers, and had their craftsmen carve commemorative inscriptions and 'images of kingship' on the bedrock at the mouth of multiple caves".[230] These commemorative and ritual events are attested in several sources, among which are the royal image inscribed on the rocky wall of the cave *in situ*, and the iconographical representations inscribed on the bronze registers of the Balawat Gate.

The Balawat Gate, with its bronze registers, comprises a narrativized map of the king Shalmaneser's travels along the empire's frontiers. The seventh year of the king's campaign is narrated on the relief Band X, whose culminating episode is the ceremonial scene of Shalmaneser visiting the Source of the Tigris (Illustration 9).[231] The upper register of this episode portrays a scene of sacrifice and offerings while, within a large cave-like space, the image of the king is carved. In the lower register, sacrificial animals are led toward the

226 Porter 2009, 161–162
227 See above in this chapter §2.3 and § 2.4.
228 Harmanşah 2007, 185; Harmanşah 2014, 147–148; Harmanşah 2015, 127.
229 Radner 2014, 1–4.
230 Harmanşah 2015, 130.
231 Harmanşah 2007, 194.

source and the carving of the royal effigy on the rocky surface are displayed. The visual representation of the topography of the Birkleyn caves is realistic and accurate in regard to the natural caves and the streams emerging from the earth.[232]

Illustration 9: Bronze door reliefs of Shalmaneser III, Tell Balawat (Imgur-Enlil), relief panel X (detail).

In addition, the bronze band carries a summary inscription above the scene. This insription refers to the rituals performed at the Source of the Tigris: "I entered the opening of the river, made offering to the gods (and) set up my royal image".[233] According to Harmanşah, the Assyrian king "directly communicates with the cults of the place or the cave", but it should not be assumed that "the Assyrian deities are being referred to here, but more appropriately the cults of the locale".[234] In fact, while the act of carving rock monuments promoted the idea of uninhabited lands in the wilderness which were conquered by the Assyrian rulers, the reality underlying these testimonies tells another story.[235]

What is presumable according to Harmanşah is that the Assyrian king engaged with the local gods of the rivers and of the springs, which in the Anatolian/Hurrite tradition were deities of the underworld and referred to as the DINGIR.KASKAL.KUR, the "Divine Road of the Earth". Due to the karstic geology which characterizes Anatolia –rich in springs, natural tunnels and caves– the Hittites' sacred sites were at prominent rocky landscapes and sacred springs. The Hittite expression DINGIR.KASKAL.KUR refers to those divine paths

232 Harmanşah 2007, 194–195.

233 Harmanşah 2007, 185; Harmanşah 2015, 135; Yamada 2000, 281.

234 Harmanşah 2014, 151; Harmanşah 2015, 135.

235 "Starting with the Early Iron Age, Assyrian rock monuments appear especially in borderland and frontier contexts, as Ann Shafer has meticulously argued (Shafer 1998, 2007). These rock reliefs that are usually composed of both images and inscriptions are most often located in rural landscapes at strategic, symbolically charged places such as mountain passes, stone quarries, springs or river sources" (Harmanşah 2015, 135). For a more detailed discussion of the wide spread of rock inscriptions, see Harmanşah 2007, 196.

of the underground water and to those sites where water emerged above the ground. These places were considered liminal territories, entrances to the underworld.[236] Springs, river sources and potholes constituted the main communication path with the ancestors and the underworld, being a "symbolically charged and mythologically potent liminal place".[237] Moreover, these cultic areas signified the thresholds of political territories.[238]

Accordingly, the Source of the Tigris must have been one of these DINGIR.KASKAL.KUR, "Divine Road of the Earth", which puts the world of the ancestors of the locals into contact with this world. In addition, as a political threshold, Assyrian kings were "possibly appropriating the Anatolian practice of the DINGIR.KASKAL.KUR in ritualizing sacred topographies and settling their political disputes with the Hurrians of Šubria".[239] By doing so, the Assyrian king was not only assuming "an already symbolically charged powerful landscape, but also that cultural landscape's cult practices and political gestures".[240]

The site of the Source of the Tigris has been repeatedly visited at least from the early eleventh to the late ninth century B.C.E. It became a rock sanctuary, where ancestors were venerated, inscriptions were carved and religio-political encounters took place.[241] Consequently, the Source of the Tigris, functioned as an "*environment of memory*" referring to a local cultic practice associated with the 'Divine Road of the Earth',[242] but was also "transformed by the sponsorship of the Assyrian kings to a site of memory through multiple commemorative ceremonies and inscription of the place, historically linking themselves to the deep history of Assyrian kingly presence at the site".[243]

The Source of the Tigris is a relevant case of a cultic place in a natural context, which has been subject to veneration and worship for millennia. It is one of the few well documented examples of a spring cult in Mesopotamia, where the several symbolic and religious meanings of a spring are entangled. This source comprises Anatolian and Mesopotamian conceptions of the spring *per se* as a liminal entity, as

236 Erbil/Mouton 2012, 53–74.
237 Harmanşah 2007, 196.
238 Harmanşah 2007, 196.
239 Harmanşah 2007, 196.
240 Harmanşah 2007, 196-197. As pointed out by Harmanşah: "Given the fact that Early Iron Age Šubria was still a heavily Hurrian cultural domain, the local cultural imagination of the Source of the Tigris site as a Divine Road of the Earth is more than likely. […] In the absence of the representation of any deities, it may be possible to suggest that the Assyrian king is himself interacting here with the underground world of divinities at the site. In this way it is possible to establish that the representation of the Assyrian king's image is not solely distributing the agency of kingship to the site through his *ṣalmu*, but that his *ṣalmu* is indeed performatively engaging with the place as a sacred, god-filled landscape. Through the transportation of the Source of the Tigris performative event into the public realm by means of pictorial representations and display inscriptions, the Assyrians are presented with a state spectacle, curiously located in a remote and exotic mytho-poetical landscape charged with associations of the world's edge. On the other hand the king's own body and its efficacious powers were distributed to the imperial frontiers through such commemorative, spatializing acts, which were re-presented in the narrative programs of the state" (Harmanşah 2007, 196–197).
241 Harmanşah 2015, 132.
242 Harmanşah 2015, 132. See also Nora 1989.
243 Harmanşah 2015, 132.

DINGIR.KASKAL.KUR, and as the source of the holy Tigris, representing not only a religious and cosmic place, but also a political threshold.

4.2 The rivers Id-sala and Id-kura in Sumerian myths

Along with the omnipresent Tigris and Euphrates, and together with the Ḫalhalla, other watercourses are mentioned in the Sumerian mythical narrative. Some of these rivers are explicitly considered holy entities, closely connected with the deities, and clearly referring to the River Ordeal.

In the myth *Enlil and Ninlil*,[244] the river Id-sala is called the holy, pure river (Íd-sal-la íd kug-bi).[245] Bathing in its waters is forbidden, because Id-sala is the river of Enlil, who would attempt to seduce and impregnate whoever would enter its waters.[246] Ninlil is warned by her mother of the prohibition on entering the holy river:

íd kug-ga-àm nu-nus-e íd kug-ga-àm a nam-mi-tu$_5$-tu$_5$	"The river is pure, woman! The river is sacred: don't bathe in it!
^{d}Nin-líl-le gú Íd-nun-bi-ir-túm-ka nam-mi-in-du-dè	Ninlil, don't walk along the bank of the Id-nunbir-tum!"[247]

But Ninlil, attracted by the fresh waters of the river, bathes in it.[248] In doing so, she breaks a taboo and her mother's warning becomes reality: Enlil looks at her and seduces her, pouring his semen into her womb and then abandoning her.

In the same myth, Enlil approaches the man of the Id-kura, who is referred to as the "Man-Eating-River" (Íd lú gu$_7$-gu$_7$-e).[249] Both the name of the river, Id-kura, and its epithet, connect this fluvial entity to the netherworld. In fact, the name itself can be translated both as the "River of the Mountain", but also as the River of the netherworld, since the term kur refers to both. As we have seen, mountains are closely connected to the

244 See Behrens 1978 for the *editio princeps*. I refer here to the more updated transliteration offered in ETCSL 1.2.1.

245 *Enlil and Ninlil* 4–8, Íd-sal-la íd kug-bi na-nam Kar-ĝeštin-na kar-bi na-nam Kar-a-sar kar ^{ĝiš}má ús-bi na-nam Pú-làl pú a dùg-ga-bi na-nam Íd-nun-bi-ir-túm pa$_5$ mul-bi na-nam, "Id-sala is its holy river, Kar-ĝeština is its quay. Kar-asar is its quay where boats make fast. Pu-lal is its freshwater well. Id-nunbir-tum is its branching canal" (ETCSL 1.2.1: 4–8). See also the German translation by Steible 2015, 24.

246 *Enlil and Ninlil*, ETCSL 1.2.1: 15–21. See also Steible 2015, 25.

247 *Enlil and Ninlil*, ETCSL 1.2.1: 15–16.

248 *Enlil and Ninlil* 23, íd kug-ga-àm munus-e íd kug-ga-àm a im-ma-ni-tu$_5$-tu$_5$, "The river is holy; the woman bathed in the holy river"(ETCSL 1.2.1: 23). See also Steible 2015, 25.

249 *Enlil and Ninlil* 93–94, [lú Íd-kur-ra] Íd lú gu$_7$-gu$_7$-e [^{d}En]-líl im-ma-te [lú] [Íd-kur]-ra Íd lú gu$_7$-gu$_7$-ĝu$_{10}$$^{!}$, "Enlil approached the man of the Id-kura, the man-eating river: 'My man of the Id-kura, the Man-Eating River!'" (ETCSL 1.2.1: 93–94). See also Steible 2015, 28.

realm of the dead, and the sources of the rivers from the rocky womb were portrayed as privileged accesses to the netherworld.[250] Moreover, the connection of this river with death is affirmed by its epithet of "Man-Eating River". This epithet refers not only to the netherworld, but also to the River Ordeal, when the River basically "ate" the guilty person.[251]

4.3 Rivers and channels as life-giving and healing persons and deities in the *Lipšur Litanies* and beyond

In the *Lispšur Litanies* several rivers and channels, along with mountains, are called upon to release and purify an afflicted patient. The text refers to these fluvial entities as animated agents, capable of protecting and acting against evil forces. The names of the watercourses are accompanied by epithets whose motifs are life, abundance, and order, while some are related to animals and to gods.[252]

Among the fifteen watercourses called upon on behalf of the patient against his/her own diseases and sins, the Tigris and the Euphrates are recorded as the first two entries. The Tigris is invoked as "the one that brings abundance" (*bābilat nuḫši*) and the Euphrates as "the life-bringing of the land" (*napišti māti*). The invocation continues by calling upon a series of watercourse: Araḫtum, "the one that brings life to Babylon" (*ana Babili ubbalu napišta*); Mê-Enlil-canal, "whose canal inspector is Marduk" (*ša gugallaša Marduk*); Duran, "mother of the rivers" (*umme nārāti*); Daban, "whose canal inspector is Tišpak" (*ša gugallaša Tišpak*); and Me-kalkal, "healer of (every) living being" (*muballiṭat šiknāt napišti*).

Some of these watercourses are tributaries or canals of the rivers Tigris and Euphrates, and they occur in personal names as divine beings. The Araḫtum is an affluent of the Euphrates and is attested in Old Babylonian personal names (e.g. *Mārat-Araḫtim*, "Daughter-of-the-Araḫtum", *Mār-Araḫtim*, "Son-of-the-Araḫtum", *Ummī-Araḫtum*, "My-Mother-is-Araḫtum", and *Ipiq-Araḫtim* "Grace-of-Araḫtum).[253] Despite the lack of a graphic indication for the divinity of the Araḫtum, this canal was addressed with the reverence and the consideration typically ascribed to a divine mother. The same divine nature is ascribed to Daban (also Taban, Ṭaban), a river or canal flowing east of the Tigris and whose exact location is uncertain.[254] This river is attested as a theophoric element in personal names from Pre-Sargonic Dilbat (e.g. Ur - ^{d}Dab$_4$ - a n), and from Sargonic Ešnunna (e.g. ka-*Ta-ba-an*, [*Ki*]$^{?}$-*nam-Ta-ba-an*).[255] This evidence reveals that this tributary of the Tigris was referred to as a deity over an area stretching from western Akkad through

250 See Chapter II, and above in the present chapter, § 4.1.4.

251 See above § 2. According to Zgoll, this myth should be understood as an aetiology of channels and their associated gods: Enlil and Ninlil, together with the mentioned infernal deities (e.g. Id-kura), bring forth the gods of water channels (e.g. Enbilulu) (Zgoll 2011, 287–299; Zgoll 2013, 79–107).

252 Reiner 1956, 134–135.

253 Groneberg 1980, 274–275.

254 Blaschke 2018, 584.

255 Woods 2005, 23.

the Diyala region in the 3rd millennium.[256] Moreover, Daban was worshipped as a god *per se* in Tutub, displaying the divine status of this river in a specific city.[257] It is notable that the name Taban features a dual suffix: this evidence speaks to the dual nature of the rivers, and supports the understanding that watercourses were conceptualized as dyads. Another interesting river which recurs in the incantations as a personal agent and as a flowing creatress is the river Ulāya. This river is called the one "who brings her plenty to the sea" (*ana tiāmtim ubbalu ḫiṣibša*).[258]

The following mentioned rivers carry names that refer to animals. The 56th, 57th and 58th entries of the *Lipšur Litanies* record respectively the River of Fish (*nāru nūnī*), the River of Birds (*nāru iṣṣūrī*) and the River of Snakes (*nāru ṣerrī*). The last four rivers are linked to the great gods and to the prosperity which accompanies the fluvial courses. Ninissinna, the river of Gula; Tutu, the river of Marduk; Ḫegal-canal, the canal of abundance (*ḫegallu*); and the Šamaš-canal, the river of Šamaš, are called upon. It should be noted that the gods they are connected to are all deities of healing and magical-medical practices –such as Gula, Marduk and Šamaš. Whether all these names refer to real watercourses or whether some of them are literary creations, what is relevant to this research is the fact that these watercourses were considered active agents in ritual performances. They act as "other-than-human" persons invoked by the patient and are associated with epithets referring to prosperity and healing.

Besides the fluvial entities recorded in the *Lipšur Litanies*, other rivers and channels recur as deities. During the 3rd millennium the Diyala (Sum. Dur-ùl) occurs in the Sargonic personal names Ì-me-Dur-ùl and *Šu-Dur-ùl/al*, while it is mentioned once in the Old Babylonian period, written ^{d}Dur-ùl.[259] Moreover, the Pre-Sargonic and Sargonic evidence attests several branches and channels referred to as deities (e.g. ^{d}Ìd-Akšak^{ki}, ^{d}Id-Am-si-HAR, Ka-^{d}Íd-Énsi, ^{d}Íd-Kiš^{ki}, ^{d}Íd-Má-gur$_{8}$), but already by the Ur III period many of these watercourses were deprived of their divine status.[260]

In a 1st-millennium namerimburruda-incantation, the Diyala occurs together with the Tigris, the Euphrates and the Zab. The four main rivers of Mesopotamia are summoned, with the gods and all the animated powerful elements of the world, in order to dispel any evil.[261] The Upper and Lower Zab appear among the gods of the land of Aššur in two Neo-Assyrian Tākultu-rituals. The two Zabs are recorded with Ebiḫ, the Tigris, the lands of Uraš and Zabban, the city, the wall, the mortar and the brick in the Tākultu for Sennacherib,[262] while they are invoked together with Ebiḫ, the Tigris, the villages and the divine borders of the land, and the gods who dwell in the land in the Tākultu for Aššur-etel-ilāni.[263]

256 Woods 2005, 23.
257 Blaschke 2018, 584.
258 See below in the present chapter, § 4.4.3.
259 Roberts 1972, 58; Woods 2005, 23.
260 Woods 2005, 23.
261 BM 50658: 29-30 (Geller 1998, 131 and 134). See above in the present chapter, § 4.1.2.
262 SAA 20, 38 iv 6'-7', ^{id}*Za-ban* AN.[TA] ^{id}*Za-ban* KI.[TA] (Parpola 2017, 107).
263 SAA 20, 42 rev. iii 5', ^{id}*Za-ba* A[N.TA *u* KI.TA] (Parpola 2017, 123). For the cosmic characterization of the city Zabban and its fluvial location, see Abusch 2002, 249–269.

4.4 The cosmic and netherworld rivers Baliḫ, Ḫubur and Ulāya

The rivers Baliḫ, Ḫubur and Ulāya are watercourses traditionally portrayed with cosmic and infernal features in the Mesopotamian and Syrian worldviews. The Baliḫ and the Ḫubur refer to rivers that are main tributaries of the Euphrates and whose origins are in the Taurus mountains, thus belonging to the Western horizon. In contrast, the Ulāya is an Eastern river, which flowed through Susa and its region, from the Zagros to the Persian Gulf. The infernal nature of the rivers is not only connected with the location of the setting of the sun, but also with their role of connectors between the above and below, with their waters emerging from the womb of the earth and returning to the Apsû.[264] The Mesopotamian infernal rivers were understood as flowing both in the west and in the east, all leading to the region of darkness.[265]

4.4.1 The Baliḫ

The Baliḫ River is a watercourse that originates in the karstic spring of 'Ayn al-'Arus in Syria and, after the Ḫabur River, is the largest tributary of the Euphrates on Syrian soil. This river has been regarded as a deity from the 3rd millennium onward. The god Baliḫ is attested in an Early Dynastic god list from Abū Salabiḫ,[266] while in Ebla the name recurs sporadically in administrative documents and more frequently in incantations. Five Eblaite incantations mention this divine River,[267] one of which addresses the god Baliḫ (^{d}*Ba-li-ha-a*) directly.[268] In another Eblaite incantation, addressing the sea and the dragon of the sea, the Baliḫ in the dual form (2 *Baliḫâ watiya*) is mentioned.[269] This very notion of the dual nature of the river has raised other interpretations besides the one suggested by Woods, as referring to its opposing banks. According to Gordon, the dual form utilized for the Baliḫ is meant to address this river as "two deified rivers", referring to a northwestern tradition of the supreme god dwelling at the source of the "Two Rivers",[270] whereas Archi understands it as due to its karstic geomorphology. The watercourse disappears under the ground for a

264 The netherworld is considered a region of darkness, which is sometimes identified with the same Apsû, but is generally regarded as a separate region, while dust and earth are its constitutive elements (Horowitz 1998, 334–362).

265 According to Woods, "these are the primordial waters of the eastern edge of the world, waters that assume a variety of mythical manifestations that draw upon either their connection with the netherworld or the Sun-god's mastery over this domain" (Woods 2009, 220–221).

266 Woods 2005, 22–23.

267 ARET 5, 4; ARET 5, 5; ARET 5, 16; ARET 5, 18a; Krebernik 1996, 21–27.

268 ARET 5, 16, ÉN.É-*nu-ru ki* ÉN.É-*nu-ru* ^{d}*Ba-li-ha-a* (Krebernik 1984, 130).

269 ARET 5, 4 II 5–6, 2 ^{d}*Ba-li-ḫa* PI-*ti-a* (Edzard 1984, 24: 5–6)

270 Mander 2008, 64; Gordon 1992, 127. Gordon argues that "the invocation of the two holy rivers reflects a northwest Mesopotamian variant of a widespread theme that the supreme god dwells at the source of 'the Two Rivers'. One may think of the Twin Rivers of Mesopotamia as inspiring the motif; and of the representation of the Mesopotamian goddess with the flowing vase, whence emerge the two streams. But the clearest formulation of this theme does not come from Mesopotamia, but from Ugarit on the shores of the Mediterranean. Ugaritic mythology describes El's abode as at the sources of the two rivers or two deeps (UT 19.1623)" (Gordon 1992, 127).

while and re-emerges in a valley. This geomorphic alternation could have lead to referring to this river in the dual form for expressing the underground and over-ground traits of the river.[271] Moreover, this karstic feature of the Baliḫ connected it with the netherworld: the Baliḫ was, in fact, conceived of as one of the cosmic rivers leading to the netherworld, and was thus suitable for purification rites dispelling any impurity and evil.[272] The Sumerogram for Baliḫ, KASKAL.KUR, refers explicitly to the journey into the womb of the earth which characterizes this river and reaffirms its intrinsic infernal nature. In the Syrian milieu, the netherworld was located in the western mountains of the Taurus.[273]

In the Old Babylonian period, the Baliḫ recurs in the pantheon of Mari as a proper god.[274] In the region of Mari, a spring in the temple of the god Ba'iḫ (*Bâḫ*) is attested, which appears to be a dialectal form for the river Baliḫ.[275] In this case, the source must refer to a way of collecting and storing water for the temple.[276] The god Ba'iḫ was the recipient of animal offerings, as attested in an Old Babylonian offering list from Mari.[277] The divine characterization of this river is reaffirmed in the personal name *Kurub-Balīḫ*, "pray to Baliḫ".[278]

The divinity of the Baliḫ continues up to the 1st millennium, especially in the incantations. In an anti-witchcraft incantation, the divine Baliḫ (dBALIḪ) is mentioned.[279] In this *Maqlû* spell, the bewitched person identifies himself with pure sulphur (*kibrītu elletu*) and *atā'išu*, the holy plant, while the Sages of the Apsû and the heavenly Daughters of Anu correspond to the sorcerers and sorceresses. A passage follows where the bewitched person states his ability to overpower his magical enemies: he rises like a fish from the water, like a pig from the mud, like soapwort from the flood plain, like grass from the canal bank, and like seed of ebony from the seashore. The watery environment is evident, as becomes clearer in the last part of the incantation, where the divine Baliḫ and its inhabitant are mentioned in an enigmatic passage:

ē ša Balīḫi ē ša Balīḫi	"Hey! You of the Baliḫ, Hey! You of the Baliḫ,
narqâni ana qaqqari	Hide yourselves here in the ground,
ša tunassisāni qimmatkunu yâši	You who shook your crest out at me".[280]

271 This interpretation is also suggested by prof. Zgoll (personal communication).
272 Archi *Fs Alp*, 8; Mander 2008, 64.
273 Durand 2008, 289. See also above about the Source of the Tigris and the Anatolian/Hurrite DINGIR.KASKAL.KUR, § 4.1.4.
274 Durand 2008, 291; Sasson 2015, 237.
275 Durand 2008, 291.
276 Durand 2008, 291.
277 Nakata 1991, 256–257.
278 Roberts 1972, 17. Porter argues that "its role as an appropriate recipient of prayers is a further indication of its divinity" (Porter, 2009, 162).
279 *Maqlû* VI 85–97 (Abusch 2015, 79).
280 *Maqlû* VI 95–97 (Abusch 2015, 79). See also Abusch 2002, 207 ff.

The identity of the "one of the Baliḫ" (*ša Balīḫi*) is mysterious. There is no evidence as to whom it might refer, whether to the sorcerer or sorceress who conjured against the patient and lives on the banks of this river, or a plant of the Baliḫ, whose "hair" was shaken toward the victim. If the meaning of this passage remains obscure, it still confirms that the Baliḫ was considered a divine fluvial entity, clearly expressed by the divine determinative. Furthermore, a specific *māmītu* for the Baliḫ is recorded in the ritual *Šurpu*: "together with the *māmītu* of the Baliḫ, source, brook and reservoir" (*itti māmīt Balīḫi quppu naḫlu u māḫāzi*).[281] It should be noted that in this context, the Baliḫ is written without divine determinative, but by possessing a *māmītu* its agency is expressed.

4.4.2 The Ḫubur and the divine Ḫabur

The Ḫabur, whose name is identical to the modern Ḫabur river, is the main tributary of the Euphrates in Syrian territory and originates in Turkey. The karstic springs around Ra's al-'Ayn are the river's greatest source of water. In addition, several permanent wadis, joining the Ḫabur in its northern part, create the so called Ḫabur Triangle. The Ḫubur (Sum. i g i - k u r) is the name traditionally ascribed to the cosmic river of the Akkadian netherworld. Sharing the same karstic features of the Baliḫ, with its mass of water flowing from the Taurus mountains and alternating constituent parts of its course underground, it was entangled with the netherworld in Akkadian eyes. Its Sumerian name, i g i - k u r, suggests two possible understandings of this river: on one hand it can be translated as the "Eye-of-the-mountain/netherworld", an attribute that finds other equivalents for the sources of the rivers,[282] or as "In-front-of-the-mountain/netherworld".

While both Sumerian and Akkadian texts mention a river flowing at the entrance of the underworld, only Akkadian sources from the 1st millennium refer to this particular river.[283] In the *Babylonian Theodicy*, the destiny of all mankind is established and part of it consists of following a road to the infernal river Ḫubur,[284] while in an evil-dispelling incantation Dumuzi is told to wander along a path leading to the Ḫubur river.[285] According to these testimonies, the river seems to be located at the end of the road to the underworld. This notion could be supported by one of the two possible readings of the Sumerogram, IGI.KUR, "in front of the mountain/netherworld", as evidence for envisioning this river as

281 *Šurpu* VIII 54 (Reiner 1958, 42: 54). Another river which has its own *māmītu* is the Saliḫu river, *Šurpu* III 64. This river is mentioned together the *māmītu*s of rivers, canals, mountains, sources and torrents.

282 See the origin of the Tigris and of the Euphrates from the eyes of Tiamat, but also on the terminology concerning the sources of the rivers: "eye" and "mouth" are typical names associated with the birthplace of a watercourse (see above in the present chapter § 3 and § 4.1.1).

283 Horowitz 1998, 355.

284 BWL 70: 16–17, *na[d]nūma abbūnu illakū uruh mūt[u] nāri Ḫubur ibbir qabû ultu ulla* , "Our fathers are given away, they are travelling the road of death: 'He crosses the river Hubur' as the old saying goes.'" (Horowitz 1998, 354).

285 *Ištar and Dumuzi* 137, *enūma tallaku uruḫka lemnu suḫhirsuma pānuška lillik enūma tebberu Ḫubur tummišuma Eama ay iturra*, "When you go on your road, turn the evil away, let it go before you. When you cross the Ḫubur, exorcise it by Ea so that it will not come back" (Farber 1977, 179–182: 137). See also Horowitz 1998, 354.

flowing at the gate of the netherworld.[286] This conception suggests that the dead would have to cross the infernal river in order to access the gate of the netherworld, recalling the image of Charon transporting the dead over the Styx to Hades in Greek mythology.[287] The idea of crossing the Ḫubur is found in an anti-witchcraft incantation, where the *kaššāptu* is addressed as the evil agent who has forced the figure of her victim to cross the Ḫubur river, in order to send him/her to the realm of the dead, kingdom of Ereškigal.[288]

The cosmic infernal Ḫubur is recorded as a proper god in the Old Babylonian pantheon of Mari,[289] but after this period no further evidence for the Ḫubur as an active agent in ritual performances nor as a divine entity is attested. In contrast, the terrestrial Ḫabur is often recorded accompanied by the divine determinative. This evidence suggests that probably the Ḫabur was not venerated in its cosmic features, but rather in its physical bodily presence of a mass of flowing waters. Mentions of ^{d}ḪABUR are found in the Ur III documentation, while this river recurs as a theophorous element in Assyrian personal names.[290] The Old Assyrian *Šu-Ḫaburā*, "Hand-of-Ḫabur", and the Neo-Assyrian *Ḫabur-šēzibanni*, "Ḫabur-rescue-me!" and *Ḫabur-taqqinanni*, "Ḫabur-keep-me-straight",[291] are evidence for the conception and veneration of Ḫabur as a deity. In fact, despite the lack of the divine determinative, the Ḫabur is referred to as a god in the onomastic. It should be noted that an Old Assyrian name displays a dual form, which might hint at the notion of the Ḫabur as a dyad or as a dual entity, which could have informed the conception of the Neo-Assyrian divine couple Ḫabur and Ḫaburtu.[292]

The divine pair Ḫabur and Ḫaburtu occurs once in the Neo-Assyrian royal rituals,[293] and it is attested in the *Götteraddressbuch* among the gods of the House of Šarrat-nipḫa.[294] The evidence of male and female rivers leads to different interpretations.[295] In my view, this divine fluvial couple should be understood in the light of the iconographical evidence, where the River deity is often represented as a dyad. Accordingly, this textual reference represents the clearest evidence for the gender duality of the River.[296] Furthermore, this duality might be understood as a reference to the karstic feature of this river, whose trait is both underground and over-ground, in a dialectic between above and below. This geomorphological feature stresses the infernal nature of the Ḫabur, which informed the notion of the cosmic Ḫubur.[297]

---

286 Durand 2008, 291.

287 Horowitz 1998, 356.

288 *CMAwR* 8.3: 54 and *CMAwR* 8.7: 61′, *ana gulgulli ipqidu* [*ana Gilgameš ip*]*qidu ušēbiru ana Ḫubur*, "(the *kaššāptu*) has handed (them) over to a skull, [has han]ded (them) over [to Gilgameš] and thus has made (them) cross the Hubur!" (Abusch/Schwemer 2011, 285 and 345).

289 Sasson 2015, 236–237.

290 Woods 2005, 22–23; Meinhold 2009, 160.

291 Meinhold 2009, 160.

292 See also the dual form attested in the Old Assyrian toponym *Ḫa-bu-ra*^{ki} (Frankena 1954, 124: 88; Woods 2005, 14)

293 SAA 20, 49: 88, ^{d}*Ḫa-bur* ^{d}*Ḫa-bur-tum* (Parpola 2017, 134).

294 *Götteraddressbuch* 88 (Meinhold 2009, 436: 88).

295 See Meinhold 2009, 160; Woods 2005, 21.

296 See above in this chapter § 2.1.

297 Meinhold 2009, 160.

4.4.3 The Ulāya

The Ulai or Ulāya is a river in Elam which is attested in the cuneiform sources from the late 2nd millennium onward, and corresponds to the Biblical ʾÛlāy, the Greek Eulaios and Latin Eulaeus. This river has been associated by scholars with different watercourses –such as the Kārūn, Karḫe, and the Šā'ūr rivers.[298]

In the literary texts, the river Ulāya is mentioned as a holy river and as a personal agent called upon in order to act specifically on behalf of the invoker. In the Gilgameš Epic, at Enkidu's death Gilgameš calls upon every creature in order to mourn his beloved friend. In this litany within the epic, the sacred river Ulāya (*Ulāya qadištu*) is invoked with the river Euphrates by the mourning hero:

libkīku Ulāya qadištu ša šamḫiš nitallakku aḫīša	"May the sacred River Ulāya mourn you, along whose banks we would walk so proudly!
libkīku elletu Purattu	May the holy Euphrates mourn you,
[*ša nit*]*taqqû mê* [*nād*]*āti*	which [we used] to pour in libation (as) water from skins!"[299]

As previously seen, the river Ulāya is called upon in the *Lipšur Litanies*, where it is addressed as a flowing goddess "who brings her plenty to the sea" (*ana tiāmtim ubbalu ḫiṣibša*). Indeed, in the incantations, the Ulāya is referred to as a creating and nurturing being. In an Old Babylonian incantation against a reptile, we read that while the Tigris gave birth to the reptile, the river Ulāya raised it (*Ulāya urabbišu*).[300] In a 1st-millennium anti-witchcraft incantation, the river Ulāya is mentioned as the original place where a purifying wood found its birth. In this text, the patient affected by witchcraft identifies himself with the 'wood-of-release', which is called "the pure herb that emerged from the River Ulāya" (*ellu šammu ša ina Ulāya aṣû*). The spell follows, saying: "the River Ulāya created m[e, the ea]rth bore me, [*Enlil and Ninlil brought me down*] to the land" (*Ulāya ibnânni erṣetu ūlidanni* [*Enlil u Ninlil ušēridūni*(?)] *ana māti*).[301]

The Ulāya was considered a crossing point for dispelling demons, a feature that shows the connection of the river Ulāya with the netherworld. In an incantation against the Lamaštu, the great demoness of the Mesopotamian world is dispelled over the Ulāya river. Here the Ulāya is addressed as the "ocean, the wide sea", probably referring to the waters

298 Frame 2014, 302–303; Potts 1999, 236. The most up-to-date identification associates the Ulāya river with the "ancient course of the Karḫe river, which had its source in the Zagros Mountains and then flowed south, passing to the west of Susa, and then, according to recent palaeo-environmental and archaeol. research, splitting into two main branches about 15 km south of Susa. The course of the northern branch was identical to part of the modern Šā'ūr and joined the ancient Āb-e Dez in the Šā'ūr anticline about 55 km north of Ahvāz" (Frame 2014, 302).

299 *Gilg.* VIII 18–19 (George 2003, 650–651: 18).

300 Sb 12630: 1–2, [*I*]*diglat ūlissu Ulāya urabbīšu*, "The river Tigris bore it, the river Ulāya raised it" (Cavignaux 2003, 61–62: 1–2).

301 *CMAwR* 7.8.4: 69'–77' (Abusch/Schwemer 2011, 190: 69'–77'). See Chapter IV, § 3.

of death.[302] According to a Babylonian tradition, the Ulāya was a river leading to the realm of the dead: this belief locates the threshold of the netherworld in Elam or in the far East, deep in the Zagros. This Eastern tradition has its roots in the Sumerian and Old Babylonian encounter and mingling with their Elamite neighbor. This tradition persists in the 1st millennium, when the river Ulāya is explicitly referred to as the river at "the gate of the netherworld" (*Ulāya ša bāb Irkalli*) in a Neo-Assyrian 'legal transaction of a genie'.[303]

The divine nature ascribed to Ulāya is featured in Assyria from the 2nd millennium onward. The god Ulāya is attested for the first time in the city of Aššur with the nominal form Ilulāya (^d^*I-lu-la-a*).[304] This reference is found in an inscription of the Old Assyrian king Puzur-Sîn, which declares that he has built a wall for the façade of the "gate of the god Ulāya" (*bāb Ilulāya*).[305] This evidence is relevant both for the clear conception of the Ulāya as a god and for its characterization as protector of gates. The divinity of this river is expressed by the presence of both the divine determinative and of the nominal form *ilu*+god name.[306] In the Neo-Assyrian rituals Ulāya recurs several times, addressed among the gods of the Assyrian pantheon. In all these occurrences the name Ulāya is accompanied by the determinative for gods, evidence that speaks to the fully divine status of this river in these ritual contexts. A stone is placed to represent the divine Ulāya in a royal ritual,[307] while the divine Ulāya is listed among the gods of the House of Bēl-labria,[308] and, together with Ebiḫ, among the gods of the House of Anu and Adad of the Inner City.[309] Moreover, in a text which records all the gods, shrines and holy places of Aššur, the divine Ulāya is referred to as the *maṣṣar ālišu*, "guardian of its city".[310]

This evidence leads us to understand the god Ulāya as a protective and apotropaic deity in charge of guarding the city gates. This fluvial god should thus be understood as a guardian and a healer, who was venerated within the city of Aššur. It is probable that a channel named Ulāya also flowed within the city perimeter, encircling the city as the cosmic *marratu* was believed to encompass the earth.[311] Furthermore, the connection of custodian of the thresholds ascribed to the river Ulāya might also refer to its infernal nature: as seen in the *Song of Bazi*, the gates of the netherworld were guarded by dead gods.[312]

302 Incantation VII 46, *ušebberki Ulâ ayabba tâmata rapašta*, "I will make you sail over the Ulāya river, the ocean, the wide sea" (Farber 2014, 169: 46). The cosmic ocean, ^id^*marratu*, was, in fact, conceived of as a wide sea encircling the earth (see Horowitz 1998, 332–333).

303 SAA 6, 288: 16 (Kwasman/Parpola 1991, 232: 16).

304 Meinhold 2009, 105–106.

305 RIMA 1, 78: 31, KÁ ^d^*I-lu-la-a* (Grayson 1987, 78).

306 For this nominal formation see also Schwemer 2001, 32.

307 SAA 20, 7 rev. iii 20, [1 NA_4] ^d^*Ú-la-a* (Parpola 2017, 17).

308 SAA 20, 38 ii 30, ^d^*Ú-la-a* (Parpola 2017, 105).

309 SAA 20, 40 ii 10, ^d^*Ú-la-a* (Parpola 2017, 112).

310 SAA 20, 49: 134, ^d^*Ú-la-a ma-ṣar* URU-*šú* (Parpola 2017, 135). See also the *Götteraddressbuch* (Text 15) 21, ^d^*Ú-la-a-a* (Meinhold 2009, 431: 21).

311 Meinhold 2009, 105–106.

312 The thresholds between the human and divine world and the gates of access between worlds are often said to be guarded by different types of gods and *Mischwesen*, which are also liminal personalities (e.g *Song of Bazi*, *Adapa*, and the famous case of the Scorpion-men guarding the passage through Mt. Māšu in the Gilgameš Epic).

5 Rivers as borders, ritual settings and communication channels

In their topographical aspect, rivers are natural borders, and in the Mesopotamian view, the courses of the Tigris and of the Euphrates represented the main boundaries between civilization and wilderness. A clear example is offered by an anti-witchcraft incantation, where the Tigris and Euphrates are addressed as the boundaries that the *kaššāptu* is forbidden to cross.[313] If the *kaššāptu* crossed the river, she would break a taboo, capturing the attention of the river and its inhabitants.[314]
Due to their pure waters being capable of carrying away any defilement, sin and disease, rivers were considered the ideal place for rituals, especially purifying ones –such as *Maqlû*, *Šurpu*, *Bīt rimki*, *Bīt šalā' mê* and *Mīs pî*– which took place on the river bank or had some parts of the cultic performance on its banks. During the ritual *Mīs pî*, before the wooden statue of the god was brought to the river bank, offerings of *maṣḫatu*-flour and *miḫḫu*-beer were poured into the river.[315] While presenting the offerings to the river, the *āšipu* recited three times each in front of it the incantations "Apsû-temple, to determine fates ..." (é n é š - A b z u n a m t a r - t a r - [e - d è . .]), "Quay of the Apsû, pure quay (...)" ([é n k] a r A b z u k a r k u g - g] a - à m) and "Shining quay, quay of En[ki])" ([é n k] a r z a - g ì n - n a k a r ^{d}E n - [k i]).[316] This evidence speaks to the notion that the river bank is considered the quay of the Apsû, while the flowing waters of the river are the Apsû itself, comprising a continuous dialectic between the topographical aspect of the river and the physicality of the fluvial deity.

The tides of the river and the opposition upstream/downstream constitute performative and symbolic meanings, with the river comprising also a time and place for magical practices. In *Maqlû,* the *kaššāptu* is told to perform her evil craft both when the river was at its fullest (*ina mīli nāri*) and at its lowest (*ina mīṭi nāri*).[317] During the performing of the ritual *Maqlû*, the *āšipu* called for any witchcraft to be carried away by the waters flowing downstream, while the person being healed of witchcraft was considered to go upstream.[318]

The river was also considered an ideal place for contacting the gods (normally Enki/Ea). The custom of drinking water from the river, probably mixed with other substances, was possibly utilized in Old Babylonian Mari as a divinatory and prophetic means.[319] The practice of sleeping by the river and/or presenting offerings and prayers to the river as a way to contact the gods is well attested in the Flood Story. In its Old Babylonian, Neo-Assyrian and Neo-Babylonian manuscripts this incubation ritual is recorded. While the Neo-Assyrian version tells that Atra-ḫasīs is in contact with his god, Ea, and places his bed on the river bank, the Babylonian accounts offer more details of this

313 *Maqlû* V 125, *Idiqlat u Puratta lā tēbiranni*, "You shall not cross over the Tigris and the Euphrates to me" (Abusch 2015, 252: 125).

314 See above for the whole incantation, § 2.3.

315 *Mīs pî*, Niniveh Ritual Tablet 18, [*ana*] *nāri tallakma maṣḫata ana nāri tanaddi mih*[*ḫa tanaqqi*], "You go [to] the river and throw *maṣḫātu*-flour into the river. [You libate *miḫ*]*ḫu*-beer" (Walker/Dick 2001, 54).

316 *Mīs pî*, Niniveh Ritual Tablet 19–22 (Walker/Dick 2001, 54).

317 *Maqlû* III 117–118 (Abusch 2015, 309: 117–118).

318 *Maqlû* VIII 22'–23' (Abusch 2015, 359: 22'–23')

319 Nissinen 2003, 42–43; Nissinen 2014, 39–42; Sasson 2015, 282.

nocturnal fluvial setting.[320] Atra-ḫasīs is said to pass his days weeping and bringing offerings of incense along the river. At night, when the stream was calm, the wise man presents incense to the river, while praying that the watercourse would carry his prayers in its waters and bring them to Ea, who would respond with a dream. After having sent his message to the stream, Atra-ḫasīs weeps sitting beside the river. Meanwhile, the flow has reached the Apsû and delivered his message to Ea. The god did not hesitate to respond, as he sends his sea-monsters, the Laḫmu, through a dream.[321] Despite such an incubation rite being attested only in the Atra-ḫasīs story, it is presumable that it was a widespread practice. The conception of rivers as channels of communication between the human and divine worlds seems, in fact, deeply rooted among the Mesopotamians.[322]

320 Lambert/Millard 1999, 76–79 and 116–117; Ermidoro 2017, 128–129.
321 Lambert/Millard 1999, 76–79; Hecker 2015, 142; Ermidoro 2017, 96–97 and 146–148.
322 For Mesopotamian incubation see Zgoll 2006, 309–351. Cf. Hittite incubation practices (Mouton 2007).

Chapter IV

Sacred Trees and Plant Persons

"You will find something more in woods than in books.
Trees and stones will teach you that which you can
never learn from masters." (Bernard of Clairvaux)

1 Trees as sacred animate beings worldwide and in ancient Mesopotamia

The conception of trees as powerful sentient beings, often partaking of the divine, is found in many cultures past and present. Trees play a central role in many civilizations: they provide oxygen, timber, leaves, fruits, resins, and shade, all essential elements for breathing, building, fueling, eating, healing and scenting. Being the center upon which human life is based, trees engage in the religious life of each human community past and present, comprising several attributes and symbolic meanings.[1] Trees are regarded as conscious, wise, animate beings, often considered kin to humans, as furnished with a spiritual potency and a mysterious nature, and as cosmic and sacred entities, pillar of the world, often partaking of the divine realm.[2]

Several world mythologies portray a cosmic tree or Tree of Life, which is conceived of as the vital source of all existence. From the Mesoamerican myths to Yggdrasil, the sacred ash tree of Scandinavian mythology, to the cottonwood of the Sioux nation, all these religious traditions speak of the cosmic and life-bringing nature of the tree.[3] With its branches, the tree stretches into the sky and with its roots it reaches the depths of the subterranean earth. Indeed, the tree is not only the cosmic pillar of the world, but it is the main mediator between worlds. Moreover, with its cycle of growth-death-rebirth, the tree

1 "Trees worldwide have played a great variety of roles in the religious life of human beings; they engage a diversity of meanings and have been used for a multitude of religious purposes (Haberman 2013, 32). See also Rival 1998; Hall 2011.

2 See, e.g., Eliade 1958, 265–330; Brosse 1989; Rival 1998; Bloch 1998; Cusack 2011; Hall 2011; Hall 2013; Haberman 2013.

3 Haberman 2013, 32.

embodies the energy of life and its ever-renewing power. According to Eliade, the cosmic tree that stands as *axis mundi* in a wide range of religious mythologies represents "the living cosmos, endlessly renewing itself".[4] Traditionally, the tree has also been understood as the abode or the body of a divinity, representing its physical embodiment. Furthermore, the arboreal nature has been somehow connected to the human one, and felt as kin. As pointed out by Haberman, "many people throughout history have felt powerful kinship with trees, whom they consider fellow sentient beings, and have established mutually beneficial relationships with them".[5]

All these shared conceptions about trees speak to the notion of individual trees as sacred animated beings. Certain trees in specific cultures, depending on the environment where a human community dwelled, have been worshipped as sacred trees and as "other-than-human" persons, comprising a multifaceted personality. In their divine, ever-renewing and mediating role, individual trees have been approached with respect and gratitude and worshipped in the quest for fertility, growth, good health, companionship, protection, long life, and material abundance.[6]

In Europe, the Greeks, Celts and Germans considered the oak as the most sacred of all trees and as an embodied form of divinity, whereas in Africa, the most greatly venerated trees have been the sycamore and the fig tree. As for Asia, the Chewong people in Malaysia view trees as conscious beings capable of thoughts and feelings, and they are approached with great reverence, while in India three trees appear particularly venerated as sacred tree-persons: the pipal, neem, and banyan trees.[7] Moreover, the Bodhi is the tree under whose shade the Buddha reached illumination, and consequently it is conceived of as a living presence of the Buddha.

In North America, cedar trees, redwoods, cottonwood, and white oak have been regarded as sacred trees by the different native peoples. As noted by the anthropologist Mauze: "Trees, especially cedar trees, were considered to be animate beings imbued with both material and spiritual value. They were believed to possess a spirit or a living force that humans should respect when interacting with trees. Conversely, this living force or vital energy could be communicated to humans, and help them throughout their lives".[8]

Turning to the Middle East, in his classical anthropological work on the religion of the Semites, Robertson Smith points out that in the Semitic cultures trees were worshipped as divine beings, and were treated as real persons, since they are "animate, have perceptions, passions and a reasonable soul".[9] Consequently, prayers were addressed to the sacred tree to help in sickness and to aid fertility, and trees were also identified as sources of oracles, divination, and divine revelation.[10] Robertson Smith points out that tree worship continued to be practiced into the nineteenth century, in particular the worship of solitary trees, which "survived the fall of the great gods of Semitic heathenism".[11] This "survival" of the ancient

4 Eliade 1958, 267 ff.; Haberman 2013, 33.

5 Haberman 2013, 33.

6 Haberman 2013, 41.

7 Haberman 2013, 36–37. For the specific case of Northern India, see Haberman 2013, *passim*.

8 Mauze 1998, 240.

9 Haberman 2013, 36; Robertson Smith 1972, 132 (cited in Haberman 2013, 36).

10 Haberman 2013, 36.

11 Robertson Smith 1972, 186–187 (cited in Haberman 2013, 36).

practice of tree worship can be spotted in contemporary Israel, where people turn to "wishing trees" when seeking health, children, good marriages and long life.[12] The work of Robertson Smith, with his evolutionistic approach, does not include the ancient Mesopotamian cultures. Thus, the conceptions of trees and plants within Mesopotamian religious life remain unexplored, besides the countless studies concerning the Assyrian Tree.[13]

Trees engaged in a multitude of ways with the human life of the ancient Mesopotamians, creating a profusion of entangled meanings. The portrayal of a cosmic tree, whose roots go deep into the Apsû and whose branches stretch up to heaven, is a recurrent image in Mesopotamian mythology and iconography throughout the three millennia of Sumerian and Akkadian cultures. Moreover, the tree is referred to as the bone and body of the divinity: in its becoming the physical body of the gods, it is imbued with and partakes of the divine. Trees and plants are also described and referred to as persons, actively participating in both the mythical and ritual contexts. An eloquent example is found in the myth *Lugale*, where the demon Asag, arch enemy of Ninurta, has established his sovereignty over the mountains. Asag was able to capture the allegiance of the mountain's inhabitants: the plants recognize him as their king and the stones have become his valiant warriors against the cities.[14]

Trees are not only considered as persons, but also as relatives of human beings and gods. In the Sumerian myth the *Marriage of Martu*, a kinship between trees and gods is declared. The beginning of this myth describes a primeval world, where some things were already formed and others had yet to come into existence. In this still forming world, the god Martu presents himself as a relative of trees:

⸢ad⸣-da-ab-ba ^{ĝiš}eren kug-ga-me-en bíl-ga ⸢^{ĝiš}⸣mès-me-en	"I am the grandfather of the holy cedar, I am the ancestor of the *mēsu*-tree,

12 See Dafni 2002. Dafni argues that, "in spite of a monotheistic ban against these ancient pagan manners of tree veneration, trees are still actively worshipped in Israel by Moslem, Druze, and Jewish people" (Dafni 2002, 325; cited in Haberman 2013, 36)

13 See Parpola 1993, 161–208; Giovino 2007. See *passim* in this chapter.

14 *Lugale* 35–38, téš-ba mu bí-íb-sa$_4$ [$^{\text{na4}}$]ú lugal-bi-šè murub$_4$-ba am gal-gin$_7$ á ba-ni-ib-íl-íl-i $^{\text{na4}}$šu-u $^{\text{na4}}$saĝ-kal $^{\text{na4}}$esi $^{\text{na4}}$ú-si-um $^{\text{na4}}$ka-gen$_6$-na ur-saĝ $^{\text{na4}}$nu$_{11}$ gàr-ra-du-um-bi iri^{ki} im-ma-ab-laḫ$_4$, "The plants have unanimously named it king over them; like a great wild bull, it tosses its horns amongst them. The *šu*, the *saĝkal*, the *esi* (diorite), the *usium*, the *kagena* (haematite), and the heroic *nu* stones, its warriors, constantly come raiding the cities" (ETCSL 1.6.2: 35–38; van Dijk 1983, 37–39: 35–38; Seminara 2001, 56: 35–38). Besides the plants, the stones are regarded as animated beings in this myth: they are, in fact, referred to as the warriors who rebel against the authority of the gods of Sumer. Thus Ninurta wars against this rocky army, where every single stone has a proper name, role and status. The end of the war sees Ninurta's victory with the cataloging of the different stones as objects: it is notable as a process from animate into inanimate. The personalistic and divine features of stones and metals should also be studied in depth, but this subject is beyond the scope of this book.

ama ad ^{ĝiš}eren babbar-ra-me-en su ḫa-šu-úr-ra-me-en	I am the mother and father of the white cedar, I am the relative of the *ḫašurru*-tree".[15]

By stating that the god is the grandfather of the cedar and of the *mēsu*-tree, mother and father of the white cedar and relative of the *ḫašurru*-tree, a powerful kinship between gods and trees is established, and the divine nature of trees is affirmed.

The following paragraphs present the most relevant evidence of cosmic trees, of plants and trees conceived of as animated beings and as holy entities in the rich repertoire of incantations, rituals and myths. Since trees and plants are copious in the literature, only those evidences where these natural elements are referred to as holy and divine beings, mediators between worlds, as acting specifically on behalf of humans and related to a mythical narrative, are taken into account.

2 Cosmic trees, sacred trees and tree-persons

2.1 The cosmic tree, the flesh of the gods, and the tree of life

The portrayal of a cosmic tree or Tree of Life is a recurrent image in Mesopotamian literary and iconographical sources. Sumerian and Akkadian mythology abounds with descriptions of trees, whose roots sink deep into the Apsû and whose branches stretch up to the top of the sky. Generally, individual trees are referred to with this cosmic description, but a generic cosmic tree also occurs in the literature. This figure refers to the tree as a cosmic foundation, a pillar between the depths of earth and the loftiness of heaven. The cosmic tree thus constitutes a medium and means of contact between the deities inhabiting the different cosmic and divine realms, as we can read in the myth of Erra: "Aloft its crown leans against the heaven of Anum" (*qimmassu ina elâti emdetu šamê ša Anim*).[16] The cosmic tree does not only symbolize a connection between divine worlds, but also participates in the divine cosmos. It is indeed considered a pure, holy and sacred entity, which features several symbolic meanings: its tangible and present physicality is transcended by its infinite and intangible features. The tree, with its yearly cycles, represents the wholeness of life in its ever-renewing nature. A tree is simultaneously physical and symbolic, immanent and transcendent, alive and dead, finite and infinite, earthly and heavenly.

The tree is also referred to as the bone of the gods (*eṣemtu ilūti*). From its trunk, in fact, the wooden body of the gods was carved. The pure wood from the pure tree coming from the pure places is addressed in the ritual *Mīs pî*, which was performed daily before the wooden divine effigy. The invocation "As you come out, as you come out in greatness from the forest" addresses any tree which might become the one chosen for the body of the god.[17] It might come from any pure place, such as the forest, the mountain, the orchard, the

15 *The Marriage of Martu* 7–8 (ETCSL 1.7.1: 7–8; Kramer 1990, 14–15; Klein 1997a, 110–111).

16 *Myth of Erra* 153 (Cagni 1977, 74).

17 *Mīs pî*, Incantation Tablet 1/2 (STT 199) 13–40 (Walker/Dick 2001, 118–121: 13–40). See also Chapter II, § 2.2.

high plain, the river bank, the sea, the flood, the swamp, and can be one of these trees: *hašurru*, cedar, cypress, fig-tree, *taskarinnu*, mulberry-tree, *ušû*-tree, and nettle-trees. The wood is addressed as bright and pure, due to deriving from a sacred tree, whose description refers to the cosmic tree:

ĝiš-šuba idim-íd-an-kug-ga-ta ù-tu-ud-da ki-sikil-la dagal-⸢la⸣ pa-zu an-⸢šè⸣ x dim$_4$-mà ki-ta ⸢ri$_8$⸣-zu a-kug-ga ^{d}En-ki nag-⸢nag⸣ a-ra-zu alam ĝis-tuk-tuk	"Bright tree, born from the source of the river of the pure sky, spreading over the pure earth, Your branches (reach?) to the sky, Enki makes your roots drink the pure water from the earth/netherworld. Your prayer for the statue is heard".[18]

The tree is said to hear the prayer, and this circumstance gives an insight into the conception of trees not as mere activated *materia magica*, but as living and animated beings, which partake of the purity and holiness typically ascribed to the gods. The relationship between trees and gods finds its best expression in the divine wooden statue of the gods: in this ritual and symbolic context, the physical tree is clearly referred to as a divine entity, while, conversely, the god becomes an earthly and corporeal entity, whose body is the tree trunk itself. The tree is not only the god's abode, but it is the incarnated deity itself.[19]

Cosmic and mythical trees belonging to the realms of the gods recur in the literature and they are sometimes described as made of precious stones. A forest or orchard with trees of precious stones is described in the Epic of Gilgameš. After having wandered through deserts and steppes, and entered the realm of the gods through the dark path of Mt. Māšu, the desperate hero in search of immortality finds himself among the "trees of the gods" (*iṣṣī ša ilī*) growing at the sea-shore:

[...*itt*]*aṣi lām Šamši*	[... he] came out before the Sun.
x [...*n*]*amirtu šaknat*	[...] there was brilliance:
a-x[*xx*]*xx-hi iṣṣī ša ilī ina amāri īšir*	upon seeing ..., the trees of the gods, he went straight (up to them)
sāmtu našât inibša	A carnelian (tree) was in fruit,
isḫunnatum ullulat ana dagāla ḫīpat	Hung with bunches of grapes, bright to gaze on.
uqnû naši ḫasḫalta	A lapis lazuli (tree) bore foliage,
inba našīma ana amāri ṣayyah	carried fruit and amusing to gaze on.[20]

Besides the trees of carnelian and lapis lazuli, other trees appear in this marvelous garden: a cypress, a cedar with leaf-stems of precious stones, a carob-tree made of *abašmu*-stone, *šubû*-stone and haematite. The portrayal of trees made of stones or bearing stone-

18 *Mīs pi*, Incantation Tablet 1/2 (STT 199) 30–32 (Walker/Dick 2001, 118–121: 30–32) .
19 See further in this chapter § 2.2 and § 2.3.
20 *Gilg.* IX 170 –176 (George 2003, 672–673: 170–176).

fruits might be a reference to the cosmic skies of the gods, which were believed to be made of stones, especially of lapis lazuli. But it can also be a hint at some type of tree-worship, which would include the dressing or decorating of the trees, or it might allude to representations of trees in precious metals within the temple. Another hint of the connection of trees with metals and precious stones is the royal inscription of Šu-ilišu, which proclaims the fashioning of a divine standard. This standard is referred to as a wondrous tree adorned with gold, silver and lapis lazuli.[21]

2.2 The Sumerian *mēsu*-, *ḫuluppu*-, and eagle-trees

A tree closely connected with divinity and kingship is the *mēsu*-tree, which is a tree with a long history in Mesopotamian literature. Its identification is still uncertain, but it can be assumed that the *mēsu*-tree was a tall tree, with white bark, whose roots and branches were considered to extend below into the netherworld and above to the sky.[22] In Sumerian mythology the *mēsu*-tree is portrayed as a white tree, which bears fruit and provides protection and shade thanks to its branches extending widely.[23]

The *mēsu*-tree is considered a sacred tree, growing out of the Apsû, and it is often compared to a mountain.[24] Conversely, the cosmic mountain is compared to this particular tree. In *Enmerkar and the Lord of Aratta*, the mountain range of Aratta is described as a *mēsu*-tree "grown high in the sky: its roots form a net, and its branches are a snare. The claws of ... (are) those of the eagle Anzû" (hur-saĝ gal ^{ĝiš}mèš an-da mú-a úr-bi-šè sa-par$_4$-àm pa-bi ĝiš-búr-àm ⸢x (x)⸣ umbin-bi Anzud^{mušen} hu-rí-in-na).[25] The symbolism of the mountain mingles not only with that of the tree, but also with that of the bird. Mountains, trees and birds are all entities which connect the wide sky with the earthly domain.

The *mēsu*-tree recurs as a sacred tree strictly connected with divinity. Gods are, in fact, compared to a *mēsu*-tree, with their epithets involving this sacred arboreal entity. Ninurta is called the "great mēs-tree in a watered field" (mès maḫ gán-e a),[26] while Enki is

21 Šu-Ilišu 15–20, ^{d}šu-nir-gal ĝiš buru$_{14}$-a tum$_4$-ma u$_6$-di-dè hé-du$_7$ kù-GI kù za-gin-na gùn-a mí-ul-lá, "A great divine standard, a tree fit for a (rich) harvest, evoking wonder, with gold, silver and shining lapis lazuli coloured" (Frayne 1990, 17).

22 See van de Mieroop 1992, 159; Powell 1987, 149. Powell suggests the identification with the European nettle tree, or lote-tree (*Celtis australis*).

23 See *Enmerkar and the Lord of Aratta* 27, šà-bi ^{ĝiš}mès babbar-gin$_7$ gurun si$_{12}$-ga-àm "its interior flourishes bearing fruits like a white mēs-tree" (ETCSL 1.8.2.3 27; Mittermayer 2009, 114–115); Praise Poem of Ur-Namma (*Ur-Namma* I) 3, lugal mèš babbár urim$_5$^{ki}-ma ki dùg-ge mú-a, "King, white mēs-tree growing in a pleasant place in Ur" (ETCSL 2.4.1.a: 3).

24 *Gudea Cylinder* A col. xxv 18–19, kur-šár-da mes-kù-Abzu-a gùrun íl-la-àm, " the sacred mēs-tree of the Apsû, standing among innumerable mountains, and bearing fruit" (Edzard 1997, 85).

25 *Enmerkar and the Lord of Aratta* 243–245 (Mittermayer 2009, 128–129: 243–245; ETCSL 1.8.2.3: 243–245).

26 *Lugale* 310 (ETCSL 1.6.2: 310; van Dijk 1983, 95: 310).

referred to as the "mēs-tree planted in the Apsû" (mès Abzu-a dù-a).[27] The most intriguing case of the deep engagement among the *mēsu*-tree, Enki, the Apsû and Eridu is found in the myth *Enki and the World Order*. Here the *mēsu*-tree is called the wild goat of the Apsû, and is referred to as the sacred punting pole, which was decorated in the Apsû and which received supreme powers in Eridu:

urin gal Abzu-ta sig$_9$-	Great emblem established on the Apsû,
ga an-dùl-e-eš ak-e	offering protection,
ĝissu-bi ki-šár-ra lá-a ùĝ-	Whose protecting shade hangs on all
e ní te-en-ten	the lands and refreshes people,
ús-saĝ dimgul ambar[muš]	The cosmic bond and pole erected in
-a dù-a kur-kur-ta íl-la	the marsh ..., raising over the
	mountains,
en énsi gal Abzu-ke$_4$	Lord, great ensi of the Apsû,
taraḫ-Abzu-ka á ša-mu-un-	Instructed the wild goat of the Apsû,
áĝ-e	
mès Abzu-ta še-er-ka-an	The mēs-tree being ornament from
dug$_4$-ga	the Apsû,
Eridug^{ki} ki kug ki kal-kal-	which received the supreme powers of
la-aš me maḫ šu ti-a	Eridu, the holy place, the most
	esteemed place,
nu-bànda maḫ kur-ra	The great overseer of the land, son of
dumu ^{d}En-líl-lá-ke$_4$	Enlil,
gi-muš kug-ga šu im-mi-	holds in his hands the sacred punting
in-du$_8$	pole.[28]

Enki is here described as the great ruler of the Apsû and its emblem, being the provider of shade and protection. This portrayal generally characterizes the *mēsu*-tree. In this context, it is hard to distinguish when the narrative refers to the god and when to the tree. Perhaps this narrative aims exactly at interweaving these entities, both emerging from the Apsû. In fact, the *mēsu*-tree is referred to as the tree sprouting from the Apsû, Enki's abode. It is in this pure and powerful subterranean cosmic water that the tree has been charged with the magical powers of Enki, powers that permeate his earthly cult place, the city of Eridu. Accordingly, the *mēsu*-tree appears as a magical tree, from which pure punting poles were produced, having been charged with the wondrous powers of Enki, and as a sacred tree of Eridu.

Sacredness, divinity and kingship are all traits peculiar to the *mēsu*-tree which continue further in the first millennium. In the Akkadian *Myth of Erra*, the *mēsu*-tree is considered divine, being called the flesh of gods, and is referred to as a young man apt for kingship:

---

27 *Enki and the World Order* 4 (ETCSL 1.1.3: 4). See also Kramer/Maier 1989; Vanstiphout 1997, 117–134; Mittermayer 2012, 243–258;

28 ETCSL 1.1.3: 166–174.

ali mēsu šīr ilāni simāt šar gim[ri]	Where (is) the *mēsu*-tree, the flesh of the gods, befitting the king of totality,
iṣṣu ellu eṭlu šīru ša šūluku ana belūti	The pure tree, fierce young man who is fitting for lordship,
ša ina tâmtim rapaštim mê 1 me *bēru išissu ikšudu šupul aral[lê]*	whose foundation reached one hundred double hours through the vast sea of water, the depth of the underworld.[29]

Once more, the purity and holiness ascribed to this tree, whose massive dimensions and roots sink deep into the inner profundity of the underground world, and whose "flesh" was used for the statues of the gods, is evident. All these features point to the representation and conception of the cosmic tree. Furthermore, its royal personality and kinship with the king is here established.

A tree sacred to Inana is the *ḫaluppu*-tree (Sum. ḫ a l u b ; Akk. *ḫuluppu*), which is the protagonist of the beginning of the myth of *Gilgameš, Enkidu and the Netherworld*, and the cause itself of the adventures of the two heroes. In primeval times, a storm shipwrecked Enki's sailing boat, and it also uprooted the *ḫaluppu*-tree which was growing on the banks of the Euphrates:

u d - b i - a ĝ i š 1 - à m ^{ĝiš}ḫ a - l u - ú b 1 - à m ĝ i š 1 - à m	At that time, there was a single tree, a single ḫ a l u b -tree, a single tree,
g ú ^{íd}B u r a n u n - n a k u g - g a - k a d ù - a - b i	Growing on the bank of the pure Euphrates,
^{íd}B u r a n u n - n a a n a$_8$ - n a$_8$ - d a - b i	Being watered by the Euphrates.
á u$_{18}$ - l u ú r - b a m u - n i - i n - b u r$_{12}$ p a - b a m u - n i - i n - s u ḫ	The force of the South wind uprooted it and stripped its branches,
^{íd}B u r a n u n - n a a i m - m a - n i - i b - r a	And the Euphrates picked it up and carried it away.[30]

A woman, who turns out to be Inana, brings the tree to her luxuriant garden (k i r i$_6$ g i - r i n) in Uruk. Inana does not plant the *ḫaluppu*-tree with her hands, but with her feet, and waters it with the hope that the tree would thrive again, and she would use its timber for furniture. However, the tree becomes the dwelling place of malevolent creatures –an Anzû-bird, a snake and the ghost of a prematurely dead maiden:

m u 5 - à m m u 1 0 - à m b a - e - z a l - l a r e	Five years, ten years had gone by,
m u b a - g u r$_4$ [k u š] - ⌜b i⌝ n u - m u - u n - d a - d a r	The tree had grown massive; its bark, however, did not split.
ú r - b i - [a m u š t u$_6$] n u - z u -	At its roots, a snake immune to

29 *Myth of Erra* 150–152 (Cagni 1969, 74; Cunningham 1997, 28).

30 *Gilgameš, Enkidu and the Netherworld* 27–31 (ETCSL 1.8.1.4: 27–31; Gadotti 2014, 154 and 162).

e gùd im-ma-ni-ib-ús	incantations made itself a nest.
pa-bi-a mušen Anzu^{mušen}	In its branches, the Anzû-bird
amar im-ma-ni-ib-ĝar	settled its young.
šab-ba-[bi]-a [ki]-sikil líl-	In its trunk, the ghost-maid built
lá-ke$_4$ é im-ma-ni-in-ús	herself a dwelling,
ki-sikil ⸢zú⸣[li$_9$]li$_9$ šag$_4$	The maid who laughs with a joyful
ḫúl-ḫúl	heart.[31]

Thus, Inana turns to her brother, Šamaš, for help, but at his refusal, she turns to Gilgameš. The king of Uruk is able to dispel the infesting creatures from the tree, and subsequently reduces it to timber. With the wood of the *ḫaluppu*-tree, Gilgameš produces two objects for play (i.e. the ellag and the ekidma), which, by falling down into the underworld during the game, represent the reason for the heroes' enterprises into the netherworld. A possible visual representation of the scene portraying the disinfesting of the *ḫaluppu*-tree by Gilgameš is found in the glyptic, where Gilgameš pulls down a tree in front of the goddess Inana (Illustration 10).[32] However, the scene represented on the seal portrays a smaller god that emerges from the trunk of the tree: his identity is mysterious and this character does not match the mythical narration.

Illustration 10: Seal possibly representing the *ḫaluppu*-tree with the goddess Inana and Gilgameš while disinfesting the tree.

This tree recurs in the Sumerian literature as a tree sacred to the goddess Inana, together with the boxwood (Sum. taskarin, Akk. *taškarinnu*), and closely associated with the city of Uruk.[33] Moreover, the Sumerian literary tradition describes the *ḫaluppu*-

31 *Gilgameš, Enkidu and the Netherworld* 83–88 (ETCSL 1.8.1.4: 83–88; Gadotti 2014, 155 and 163).
32 Collon 1987, 178.
33 Gadotti 2014, 27–49.

tree as the dwelling place of the Anzû-bird, along with snakes and ghosts.[34] The latter tradition might explain the paucity of attestations of the *ḫuluppu*-tree in both Sumerian and Akkadian literary sources.[35] Indeed, in the omen series *Šumma Ālu*, the *ḫuluppu*-tree is attested three times and in all instances its presence is a sign of doom for both the city and the individual.[36]

The *ḫaluppu*-tree has been identified variously as the willow,[37] the carob-tree,[38] the oak,[39] the Turanga poplar,[40] another word for date palm,[41] and, more recently, as a mulberry tree, specifically the maḫlab cherry.[42] What emerges clearly from the epigraphic evidence is that this arboreal entity was non-native to Sumer, and it was originally from the South-East. It could be found in the wilderness and along the roads (*ḫalub ḫarrān*), as well as planted in orchards and along watercourses, thus implying human and/or divine intervention. It was a hardwood tree, which produced seed or fruits, and it was utilized for its curative properties and in magical rituals.[43]

The eastern origin and characterization of the *ḫuluppu*-tree is transmitted also in the literature. In the Sumerian myth *Inana and the King,* the *ḫuluppu*-tree is mentioned in a passage dealing with a play of oppositions in order to comprehend the entirety of the world. The *ḫuluppu* is here paired with the cedar: according to the traditional association of cedar with the west, the *ḫuluppu* should be considered here the symbol of the east.[44]

Another tree which was considered the abode of the Anzû in Sumerian mythology is the so called "eagle-tree" (^{ĝiš}ḫu-rí-in) of Enki. This tree's representation features all the elements for the prototype of the cosmic tree:

ud-ba giri$_{17}$-zal ^{ĝiš}ḫu-rí-in ^{d}En-ki-ke$_{4}$	Now the splendid 'eagle'-tree of Enki,
ḫur-saĝ ^{na4}gug igi gùn ^{d}Inana-ka	On Inana's mountain of multicolored carnelian
ugu-ba u$_{18}$-ru-gin$_{7}$ ki ḫé-ús-sa-ba	Its pastures impose on the earth like a tower,
a-ru-gin$_{7}$ siki lá-lá-a-ba	Hanging shaggy like an *aru*(?).

34 Gadotti 2014, 36–42.

35 In the Akkadian corpus, this tree occurs in letters and ritual texts among trees for ritual purposes, and in the omen series *Šumma Ālu*.

36 Gadotti 2014, 44–46.

37 Kramer 1938; Campbell Thompson 1949; Klein 2002; Keetman 2007 (see Gadotti 2014, 27).

38 Lambert 1959 (see Gadotti 2014, 27).

39 Van de Mieroop 1992; Veldhuis 1997; Glassner 2000 (see Gadotti 2014, 27).

40 Diakonoff 1995 (see Gadotti 2014, 27).

41 Stuckey 2001 (see Gadotti 2014, 27).

42 Gadotti 2014, 27.

43 Gadotti 2014, 27–28 and 41.

44 CT 42, ii 13–17, ^{d}Utu-è-ta ^{d}Utu-šú-šè ^{im}ù-lu-ta $^{tum10-mu-ul-lu-ta}$ ^{im}mir-ra-a-šè $^{tum10-mu-AN-mi-ra}$ a-ab-ba-igi-nim-ta a-ab-ba-sig-šè ^{ĝiš}ḫa-lu-úb-ta ^{ĝiš}eren-na-ta ki-en-gi-[ki]-uri-a šíbir šibir sum-mu-na-ab$^{!}$,"From Sunrise to Sunset, from the northwind to the southwind, from the Upper Sea to the Lower Sea, from the *ḫuluppu*-tree, from the cedar, in Sumer and Akkad, give him the scepter and the staff" (Horowitz 1998, 333). See below § 2.4 on the cedar.

kur-ra ĝissu-bi ki maḫ-ba	The shade of the mountain is majestic,
túg-gin$_7$ i-im-dul gada-gin$_7$ i-im-búr	Covering like a cloak, spreading like a vest.
^{ĝiš}i-ri$_9$-na-bi muš-saĝ-kal-gin$_7$ íd ka 7 ^{d}Utu-ka šag$_4$-ba mu-un-še$_{21}$-še$_{21}$	Its roots lie down like *saĝkal*-snakes in the midst of Utu's river of the seven mouths.[45]

The cosmic "eagle-tree" is a tree sacred to Enki, as its roots lie deep in the netherworld. The tree emerges from the waters of the River of the Seven Mouths, the cosmic and netherworld river of the Sumerian mythology, which comprises the course of the Sun-god during the night and which was conceived of as pouring out of the eastern mountains.[46] The tree stands like a tower on the mountain of carnelian sacred to Inana, enshrouding it with its shade and magnificence. This picture recalls the description of the Anzû, its famous inhabitant, which is said to cover the mountain with its *melammu* in the Akkadian myth. All the elements describing the "eagle-tree" point to the clearest representation of the Sumerian cosmic tree, which is inhabited by the Anzû and sacred to the deities Enki and Inana. Once more, the tree merges with the mountain showing a synergy and a special entanglement between deities, *Mischwesen* and cosmic realities.

2.3 The Tamarisk and the Date Palm

The most recurrent trees in Mesopotamian literature are trees typical of Southern Iraq, the tamarisk and the date palm. These two trees are recorded together in the *Dialogue between a tamarisk and a palm tree*, where a dispute between them is described. This dialogue is attested both in the Sumerian and in the Akkadian literary traditions. What should be highlighted about this quarrel between trees is that both the tamarisk and the date palm are conceptualized as tree-persons, being described with human attributes: they have a mouth and they speak, sharing with humans the feelings of envy, jealousy and anger. Moreover, in the Akkadian narrative, the two trees are referred to, and refer to one another, as brothers.[47] Their kinship is declared by the tamarisk, which addresses itself as the same flesh/body of the date palm.[48]

Relevant and diverse details concerning the personalities of the two trees can be inferred from both versions of this fable. In the Sumerian dispute, the tamarisk is said to be the body of the gods in their shrines, and thus subject to devotion. People are said to build daises and adorn them for the tamarisk, which receives the dates that the date palm bore as offerings. Moreover, its wood is used to produce measuring vessels.[49] In the Akkadian

45 *Lugalbanda and the Anzud-bird*, 28–35 (ETCSL 1.8.2.2: 28–35; Wilcke 2015, 255: 28–35).

46 This mythical location might be a reference to the Sumerian *pī nārāti*, see Chapter II, § 3.5 and Chapter III, § 3.

47 Wilcke 1989, 161–190; Streck 2004, 250–290.

48 *Date Palm and Tamarisk* 22 (Wilcke 1989, 173 and 180; Streck 2004, 256).

49 Sumerian *Dialogue between a tamarisk and a date palm* 1–19 (ETCSL 5.3.7: 1–19).

debate, this tree proclaims himself proudly as the "*mašmaššu* of the gods": *mašmaššākuma bīt ilim uddaš/ullal*, "I am the *mašmaššu*-priest and I renew/purify the temple of the god".[50] This testimony stresses the tamarisk's main role as purifier of the temples and of the gods themselves, but the Akkadian version lacks the tree's typical attribute of flesh or bone of the gods. Instead, its flesh/bones are said to be the same as those of the date palm, thus stating the close kinship between the two arboreal beings, which partake of the same nature.

On its part, the date palm argues against its brother the tamarisk, addressing it negatively as a useless tree, because of its not bearing any fruit.[51] Conversely, as part of the dispute, the tamarisk addresses the date palm as a slave, because of it being obliged to give away its most precious and dear things, its sweet fruits.[52] The date palm is, in fact, identified by its main attribute of bearing fruits, a characteristic that leads to the symbolic meanings of abundance, fertility and motherhood traditionally ascribed to this tree.[53] This feature recurs in both narratives, but the Old Babylonian version from Emar is the most eloquent about the diverse features of the date palm. The date palm proclaims itself as the tree of royalty: it is a constant dweller in the palace orchard, being the favorite tree of the royal family and its fruits are always present at the king's table.[54] The royal attribute of the date palm is attested widely in the iconographical evidence. Palm trees are always represented in the garden of the Neo-Assyrian kings, together with the vine and another recurrent arboreal entity, whose features resemble those of a cypress (Illustration 11). The date palm shows its prominent role in the ritual performances, since it is said that no offerings to the gods (i.e. Sîn) can be held without its presence (probably through its dates), and some rites are said to be performed in honor of the tree itself. The Akkadian manuscript refers to hand-washing rites honoring the palm tree, and of unspecified date palm festivals, where its fronds are heaped on the ground.[55]

50 *Date Palm and Tamarisk* 36 (Wilcke 1989, 174 and 180–181; Cunningham, 1997, 28; Streck 2004, 256).

51 *Date Palm and Tamarisk* 15–16 (Wilcke 1989, 172 and 179; Streck 2004, 256).

52 *Date Palm and Tamarisk* 23–24 (Wilcke 1989, 173 and 180; Streck 2004, 256).

53 See below in this section.

54 *Date Palm and Tamarisk* 17–20 (Wilcke 1989, 172–173 and 179–180; Streck 2004, 256).

55 *Date Palm and Tamarisk* 38–40 (Wilcke 1989, 175 and 181; Streck 2004, 256–257). For festivals and processions involving the ritual usage of palm fronds see Çağirgan/Lambert 1991–1993, 89–106; George 2000, 259–299.

Illustration 11: The "Garden Scene" displays a banquet scene, showing the king Assurbanipal and his wife surrounded by a luxuriant variety of botanical species in the royal garden.

The date palm and the tamarisk constitute a synergic and evergreen couple throughout Mesopotamian culture. These trees appear intertwined in a double and opposite thread, since they are linked both because of their opposite nature and because of their similarities.[56] Their opposition lies in the urban and familiar presence of the date palm in the royal and temple orchards, located within the city borders, which points to its social and familiar character. In contrast, the tamarisk is the tree growing in the harsh environments of the desert and of the steppe, a feature that speaks of its being a symbol of wilderness, strength and solitude.[57] Conversely, the two trees share relevant similarities: they partake of the same arboreal nature, they are both a source of shade and protection, and they play major roles in the rituals.[58] In the ritual context the date palm and the tamarisk assume the main roles of purifiers, always recurring together as a very powerful duo, often alongside the *maštakal*-soapwort.[59]

The identification of the Akk. *bīnum* and the Sum. ^{ĝiš}š i n i g with the tamarisk is based on the etymological relationship with Aramaic and Syriac *bīnā*, "tamarisk". The reference to its trunk, from which the statue is made, indicates that, at least in this context, the *Tamarix aphylla* is meant, being the only species with a proper tree-like shape.[60] The tamarisk is the most important and common tree growing in the steppes, the deserts and in saline environments, which makes it a natural presence in Mesopotamia. The most striking features of the tamarisk are its particularly long roots, a trait that played a role in the Mesopotamian association with the Apsû and consequently with its purification properties widely attested in rituals and incantations.[61]

56 Streck 2004, 254–255.
57 This traditional portrayal of the tamarisk does not fully reflect its materiality: the tamarisk was also cultivated since early times as attested in the administrative and economic texts from the Ur III period (see, e.g. Heimpel 2011).
58 Streck 2004, 254–255.
59 See below in the present chapter, § 3.
60 For a comprehensive discussion of the identification of the tamarisk, see Streck 2004, 251–254.
61 Krebernik 1984, 226f.

In the ritual *Mīs pî*, all the fundamental features of the tamarisk are expressed. The tamarisk is called upon as a pure tree, originating in a pure place, as the favorite tree for becoming the wooden body of the deities, and as the purifier of the gods:

én ĝiš-šinig ĝiš-kug-ga ki-sikil-ta mú-a	Incantation: "Tamarisk, pure tree, growing up from a clean place,
ki-kug-ga-ta mu-un-è-a	Coming out from a pure place,
pa$_5$ hé-nun-na a mu-un-nag-nag	Drinking water in abundance from the irrigation-channel:
šà-bi-ta dingir-re-e-ne mu-un-dím-e-ne	From its interiors deities are made,
pa-bi-ta dingir-re-e-ne mu-un-sikil-e-ne	With its branches gods are cleansed.
^{d}Igi-sig$_7$-sig$_7$ nu-kiri$_6$-gal-An-na-ke$_4$	Igisigsig, the chief gardener of Anu
pa-bi im-ma-an-kud šu im-ma-an-ti	Cut off its branches and took them".[62]

The tamarisk is explicitly referred to as the "bone of the divinity" (*eṣemtu ilūti*) and as a consecrated (*quddušī*) tree in a ritual aimed at producing protective wooden figurines that would be placed in someone's house to defend against epidemic diseases:

eṣemtu ilūti bīnu quddušī	"The bone of divinity, the consecrated tamarisk,
eṣ ellu ana bunnanê ṣalmāti	the holy wood for the image of the statues
ša ina bīt ananni mār ananni ana sakāp lemnūtu izzuzzu	that will stand in the house of NN son of NN to throw back the evil ones".[63]

The tree is subjected to a ritual before being cut in order to become a protective figurine. The performer should go to the woods at sunrise, bringing with him a golden axe and a silver saw, and consecrate the tamarisk with a censer, a torch and holy water. Facing the sun, he should sweep the ground in front of the tamarisk, and there sprinkle clear water and set up an offering table, where he will sacrifice a sheep and present offerings of dates and cakes. A libation of beer and a fumigation of juniper wood in the censer and the sprinkling of holy water is also included in the purification rite for the tamarisk, in front of which the performer kneels down and proffers the abovementioned incantation.[64]

This ritual is a peculiar example of tree-worship in Mesopotamian lore. The ritual acts do not aim merely at purifying the tree destined to become the wooden divine body, but they show an attitude of respect and thanksgiving, which is generally found toward the deities. The presenting of offerings and libations, together with the act of kneeling down, all

62 Incantation Tablet 1/2: 1–7 (Walker/Dick 2001, 97 and 100–101: 1–7).
63 Wiggermann 1992, 8– 9: 81–83.
64 Wiggermann 1992, 8–9: 67–78.

point to this understanding. The divine and sacred nature of the tamarisk is here evident. It is impossible to know whether its divinity derives from its being the favorite tree for making the statues of the deities, or, conversely, whether the reason for its trunk being utilized for the earthly body of the gods derived from its being conceived of as a tree imbued with divinity.[65]

The tamarisk is not only considered the body of the gods, but its own body is connected to deities in the Sumerian tradition. In a pre-Sargonic incantation the roots of the tamarisk are referred to as Enki and Ninki, and Enlil is its neck.[66] In another incantation, we read:

^{ĝiš}šinig ĝiš-gi ĝiš-An	"Tamarisk, firm tree, tree of Anu;
úr-bí ki-šè	Its roots towards the underworld
^{d}En-ki ^{d}Nin-ki	(are) Enki and Ninki;
pa-bí-ta	From its branches
An-gudu$_4$-nun	(it is) Anu, the princely gudu-priest".[67]

The tamarisk is here clearly addressed as the tree of Anu, and its bodily parts are linked to the specific deities of the cosmic parts of the world: its roots, which go deep into the netherworld, are Enki and Ninki, the lord and the lady of the Apsû, while its branches, stretching to the sky, are An, the king of heaven. This passage not only expresses the full divinity of the tree but also portrays it as a medium between heaven and earth, a typical trait of the cosmic tree. The fullest description of the tamarisk in its cosmic features and with its entanglements with the great gods is found in an Old Babylonian incantation, which calls upon the tamarisk in order to purify and release from any defilement:

šinig [ĝiš zi]	"O tamarisk, [upright tree],
ĝiš an ĝiš [An$^{?}$]/Enki	Tree of heaven, tree of Anu/Enki![68]
úr-zu eren [duru$_5$]	Your roots are [sappy] cedar,
pa-zu ḫa-šu-úr-ra [àm]	Your branches [are] (a canopy of) *ḫašur*-tree!
úr-zu-ta$^{!}$ En-ki-ke$_4$ a im-ta-dé$^{!}$-dé$^{!}$	At your roots Enki pours out water,
⸢pa-zu-ta⸣ Utu [nam]-tar in-kud$^{!}$-dè	In your branches Utu determines destinies.
pa-⸢zu⸣-ta A-nun-na dingir gal-gal-e-ne	With your branches the great Anunna-gods
an-ta sikil-e-dè-eš	Become pure in the sky.

---

65 According to Berlejung, "the statue was never solely a religious picture, but was an image imbued with a god, and as such possessed the character of both earthly reality and divine presence" (Berlejung 1997, 51).

66 Krebernik 1984, 102f. B 20 i 4–ii 2, ^{ĝiš}šinig úr-be ^{d}En-ki ^{d}Nin-ki ^{ĝiš}šinig gú-da ^{d}En-líl, " Tamarisk, its roots are Enki and Ninki. Tamarisk, from its neck it is Enlil".

67 Cunningham 1997, 27, text 30.

68 See George 2016, 68–69, in particular note 16 on George's restoration of the text.

šinig ĝiš[!] sikil ḫé-em-kug-ge	May tamarisk, the pure tree, make holy,
⸢ḫé⸣-em-sikil-e ḫé-em-dadag-ge	Make pure, make clean".[69]

The tamarisk here encompasses the cosmic dimensions of heaven and of the Apsû. Its constitutive parts are referred to as other trees, the cedar and the *hašurru*, which are the literature's evergreen and mythological trees.[70] The god of spring water, Enki, is said to pour water at its roots, which stretch into the underground dimension of the Apsû, whereas the sun god, Utu, fixes the destinies of the world and mankind while roosting on its branches. This depiction is a clear allusion to the cosmic tree, which are generally the cedar and the *ḫašurru*-tree, and the symbolism of the cosmic mountain in the east, over which the sun rises every morning. Dawn is the time of the day when destinies are decreed by Utu after their gestation overnight.[71] Finally, the Anunnaki are said to use its branches to clean themselves in the sky. This notion is further evidence for the belief that this tree possessed a powerful cleansing power.

All this evidence expresses the deep connection between this tree, with its cosmic nature, and the anthropomorphic gods, while they highlight the tamarisk's main role in the ritual context with its mythical background. As seen, the tamarisk is one of the most powerful purifying entities in the rituals. Its purity and holiness derive from its cosmic nature, since its roots grow in the mist of the Apsû, and its branches stretch into the sky. In the purification rites the tamarisk's branches with their leaves were plunged into the basin of holy water, generally together with the palm tree's shoots and the *maštakal*-soapwort.[72]

In the incantations against demons, the tamarisk appears as a lonely tree far away from civilization, i.e. in the steppe and desert. Thus, it becomes an appropriate entity and place suitable for dispelling malevolent creatures, such as the demoness Lamaštu. The demoness is said to be bound to a lonely tamarisk in the middle of the sea (*itti bīni aḫî u kušāri ēdi šēpēki arakkas*) in an incantation aiming at dispelling this malevolent creature beyond the borders of the Mesopotamian cosmos.[73]

---

69 CUSAS 32, II.A.9, col. vi 15–25 (George 2016, 68–69). See also the Ur III incantations as forerunners of the Old Babylonian incantation (George 2016, 68–69).

70 George 2016, 68–69; Woods 2009, 183–239. See below in the present chapter, § 2.4.

71 Woods 2009, 183–239. See Chapter II.

72 See Streck 2004, 272–273, for a botanical explanation regarding tamarisk as a fixed ingredient in the water, where he suggests that the branches of the tamarisk were pounded to produce the "water of tamarisk". See below in the present chapter, § 3, on this trio of magical purifying entities.

73 *Lamaštu* II 41–49, *atlakī ana šadî ša tarammī ṣabtī ajjalī u turāḫī ummāt la'î kalīšina ṣabtī eppušakki makurra šaḫḫūta ušellēki ina libbi ušelle ittiki erbēt kalbī šinā peṣûti šinā ṣalmūti ušebberki Ulāya ajabba tâmata rapašta itti bīni aḫî u kušāri ēdi šēpēki arakkas zisurrâ alammīki tummâti lū tamâti utammīki I/ita abulla M/mīšara u ribīta*, "Be gone to the mountain which you love, take deer and ibexes, take all the mothers of (their) young! I will make for you a canvas boat, will let you board it. I will let four dogs, two white (and) two black get on board with you. I will make you sail over the Ulāya river, the ocean, the wide sea. I will bind your feet to a free-standing tamarisk and a lone reed stalk. I will surround you with a magic circle of flour. You are conjured! May you be bound by the spell! I have conjured you by ordeal river, city gate, justice and main square"(Farber 2014, 168–169: 41–49). See also another incantation against Lamaštu (Lamaštu II 143–146): *ammīni ša nibnû nuḫallaq u ša nušabšû*

The date palm (Sum. ĝišimmar, suḫḫuš, Akk. *gišimmaru*), bearing its sweet dates, is the traditional tree of Iraq. The date palm occurs in the literature and in the ritual texts, often associated with the tamarisk as a main purifying agent. As we have seen in the *Debate between a Palm Tree and a Tamarisk*, it is generally referred to as a symbol of fertility, multitude and motherhood, but also of kingship.[74] The aetiology of the date palm is reported in the myth *Inana and Šukaletuda*, as the result of a task assigned by Enki to the raven. The origin of this tree is both magical and accidental: the raven, following the god's instructions, gathers and chops kohl for the *āšipu* of Eridu and mixes it with oil and water found in a lapis lazuli bowl. This mixture is planted in a trench for leeks, but, instead of leeks, a new tree grows. This tree is described as having scaly leaves surrounding its inner trunk and with gleaming shoots, and each of its parts is mentioned for its usage: its dried fronds will be used as weaving material, its branches are used for cleaning the king's palace, while its dates are destined to be the offerings of the great gods.[75]

All the main characteristics typically attributed to the personality of the palm tree are expressed in a bilingual Middle Assyrian incantation which aims at treating a sick person afflicted by the *Utukkū Lemnūtu*, the Evil Spirits:[76]

én suḫḫuš kug-ga pú kiri$_6$-ta gar-ra *gišimmari ellu šūpû ša ina ṣippāti šaknu*	Incantation: "O date palm, pure and resplendent, planted in the orchards,
su-dadag-ga me-te ^{ĝiš}banšur-ke$_4$ *mullil zumri simat paššūri*	Purifier of the body, appropriate to the table,
bala níg-kéš-da me-te nam-lugal-la-ke$_4$ *markas palê simat šarrūti*	Bond of the reign, symbol of kingship.
^{ĝiš}ĝišimmar níg-kala-ga á nam-ur-sag-gá-ke$_4$ *gišimmaru dannu idān qardāti*	The mighty date palm, with the arms of heroism,
pa$_5$-šitá-na ki-kug-ga mu-un-gub-ba *ina rāṭi ašri elli izzâz*	Stands on the water-channel of the pure place,
ussu-a-ni-ta an-na uš-sa	Its might leans on heaven."[77]

ubbal šaru leqēšima ana tâmti ṣupur šadî itti bīni 1 aḫî u kušāri ēdi rukussima, "Why should we destroy what we have created, and why should the wind carry away what we have produced? Indeed, take her to the sea, (or) to the (highest) outcrop of the mountain! Indeed, bind her to a free-standing tamarisk or a lone reed stalk!" (Farber 2014, 176–177: 143–146). See also Chapter III, § 4.4.3, on the river Ulāya.

74 See e.g. the ritual *SpTU* 5, 248 33–40, where a woman with difficulties in pregnancy asks for the help of a palm tree, calling upon it in order to dispel barrenness from her womb. The palm tree is involved in the ritual among other entities (i.e. an oven, a sheep and a donkey) typically connected with fertility and motherhood. The date palm is obviously one of them, because of the multitude of its dates.

75 *Inana and Šukaletuda* 49–84 (Volk 1995, 126–127: 49–84).

76 Geller 1980, 28–29 and 35: 51'–70'. See also the 1st-millennium canonical *Utukkū Lemnūtu* incantation, Tablet XIII 122–145 (Geller 2007, 171–172).

emūqāšu šamû enda

Its purity and shining qualities are praised together with its might, whereas its urban setting, being planted in the orchard, and its being a constant presence at the dining table express its convivial and familiar features. The date palm is clearly addressed as a purifier of the body, probably referring to both the human and divine bodies, and as a symbol of royalty. Moreover, the notions of its standing on a source of water, in a pure place and with its height imposing on the sky well express its cosmic nature. Its cosmic and sacred nature, partaking of divinity, is featured in the last part of the incantation, where we read that the great gardener of Anu, Igisigsig, collects the date palm fronds with his pure hands, and then the incantation-priest of Eridu recites the healing spell. Contextually, the date palm is referred to as a sacred tree of the divine garden in Eridu.

The date palm, with its palm shoots (*suḫuššu*), recurs in the rituals and incantations as a purifying agent, often together with other purifying entities, such as the tamarisk and the *maštakal*-soapwort.[78] In the anti-witchcraft incantations, this powerful purifying trio is called upon and said to have released the steppe,[79] while its palm shoots are invoked together with the *maštakal*-soapwort in order to undo the witchcraft affecting the sick person.[80]

In the Sumerian literature, a son's letter to his mother brings a curious description of his parent. Lu-diĝira portrays his mother to the messenger comparing her to anything good, sweet and scented in his world, including a "palm tree with the sweetest fragrance" in his fifth description.[81] Besides the allegoric description of the human mother to anything good belonging to the son's world, it is worth emphasizing that once more the palm tree is clearly connected to motherhood.

Furthermore, the palm tree is addressed as a family member, featuring a kinship with humans. In the *Babylonian Theodicy*, the palm tree is referred to as a precious brother:

[giš]immaru iṣ [ma]šrê aḫi aqru	Palm, tree of wealth, my precious brother,
gimil nagab nēmeqi illūk li[qti]	Endowed with the whole wisdom, jewel of g[old].[82]

The palm tree is here referred to with its typical epithet of "tree of wealth", but it also appears described as a person. Being addressed as a brother, the tree is considered a person, with a moral connotation. It is, in fact, not only a precious brother but a wise one, equipped with the immense wisdom pouring out from the Apsû. The personhood of the palm tree

77 Geller 1980, 28–29 and 35: 51'–62'.

78 See below § 3.

79 *CMAwR* 7.8.4: 3', *iptašrū bīnu maštakal u ĝišimmaru ṣēram*, "Tamarisk, *maštakal*-soapwort and palm tree have released the steppe" (Abusch/Schwemer 2011, 188–189).

80 *CMAwR* 8.5: 96', *maštakal* (*u*) *suḫuššu lipašširū kišpīya*, "May the *maštakal*-soapwort and the date palm undo the sorcery against me"(Abusch/Schwemer 2011, 326).

81 *The message of Lu-diĝira to his mother* 48, a m a - ĝ u $_{10}$ ^{ĝiš}ĝ i š i m m a r i r - s i - i m d ù g - d ù g - g a , "My mother is a palm-tree, with the sweetest fragrance" (ETCSL 5.5.1: 48).

82 *The Babylonian Theodicy*, VI 56–57 (Lambert 1960, 74–75).

stands alongside its divinity, since such wisdom is mainly attributed to the anthropomorphic gods. Once more, a tree comprises a multi-layered combination of meanings: it is considered kin to humans, and as an "other-than-human" person, while also being closely related to divinity, and the perfect medium between the worlds, human and divine, below and above, earthly and heavenly.

The intimate relationship between humans and the palm tree is also evident in the iconography. An Akkadian seal displays Inana in her warlike aspect, equipped with wings and weapons, and rising from a mountain slope, under which a mysterious deity is represented (Illustration 12). Behind her, a mountainous terrain is portrayed in the typically 3rd-millennium drill pattern. At the center of the scene a palm tree stands, while two gods stand at its left. One of them might be identified with Enki because of its characteristic overflowing vase. Both gods seem to be in an attitude of blessing toward the palm tree.[83] This scene has been also interpreted as a visual representation of the birth of the palm tree as narrated in the myth *Inana and Šukaletuda*. Another composition featuring a palm tree at its center is on display in another Akkadian seal, where two women are represented standing at the sides of a palm tree. A third woman is present in the scene and she receives a date from the female figure standing close to the tree. The scene takes place within a garden or an orchard, where other smaller trees stand, and the palm tree is portrayed in a naturalistic way.[84] Whether this scene aims at merely representing the collecting of sweet dates from the palm tree, or whether it refers to a less probable ritual performed for the tree, this composition comprises one of the earliest examples of a garden or orchard scene, or even one of the earliest iconographical representations of arboriculture.

Illustration 12: Seal displaying Inana standing on a mountainous terrain, under which a smaller deity is portrayed, while a palm tree is worshipped by two gods.

83 Orthmann 1985, 236, fig. 135i.
84 Orthmann 1985, 237, fig. 137h.

This iconographical evidence supports the existence of special devotion to and intimate relationship with trees in ancient Mesopotamia. The most eloquent case is the Neo-Assyrian motif of the sacred tree, whose actual identity remains mysterious: either the sacred tree derives from an extreme stylization of a palm tree, or rather it comprises a combination of naturalistic and symbolic features of the sacred and ideal tree.[85] The famous Neo-Assyrian Tree (or Tree of Life) motif is a stylized tree, which is normally displayed at the center of a composition while some cultic performers and *Mischwesen*s approach it with reverential behavior and ritual gestures. In most reliefs, the cultic performers (dressed as the sage *Apkallū*s of the Apsû) and other mythical creatures associated with purification rites are portrayed in the act of sprinkling and/or anointing the tree. Such acts would speak for some type of rite performed for the tree person. It should be emphasized that upon or beside the tree, an effigy of the king often accompanies the stylized tree. This evidence suggests once more the close interrelation between trees and the royal person that we encountered in the written sources. The several variations of the Neo-Assyrian sacred tree have been the subject of numerous studies and speculations over its cultic and symbolic meanings.[86] As far as the present research is concerned, the Assyrian Tree attests both the sacredness ascribed to trees, and the powerful kinship between the arboreal person and the human person of the king.

2.4 The Cedar and the *ḫašurru*-tree

The cedar (Sum. ĝišeren, Akk. *erēnu*) is the coniferous tree *par excellence* in the eyes of the Mesopotamians, that has populated the slopes of the mountain ranges along the Mediterranean for millennia.[87] The Lebanon, Anti-Lebanon and Taurus ranges were inhabited by cedar forests until a few centuries ago, while today only few exemplars have survived.

The cedar has an intriguing and long tradition of belonging to the cosmic and mythical realm, and as a purifying agent in Mesopotamian literature and religion. Its fame is closely connected to the forest of Ḫuwawa, the guardian of the cedars themselves. In the 1st-millennium account of the Gilgameš Epic, the mountain of cedars appears in front of the eyes of Gilgameš and Enkidu with a wondrous view, filled with life and joy, and referred to as the abode of the gods. The forest and the mountain are described as a living organism. Here the cedar is described as a tree of abundance and plenty, a joyful and sweet entity, whose scent fills the air, and under whose shade a thriving undergrowth intertwines with its trunk.[88] The cedar, the forest, the mountain and their custodian are all deeply entangled in a

85 The art of the Neo-Assyrian empire is the peak of naturalistic and stylized arboreal representations in ancient Mesopotamia. For a specific focus on the flora portrayed on the Neo-Assyrian reliefs, see Bleibtreu 1980.

86 Black/Green 1992, pp. 170–171; Parpola 1993; Porter 1993, 129–139; Winter 1999, 67; Seidl/Sallaberger 2005–2006, 54–74. For a comprehensive discussion of the history of studies of the Neo-Assyrian tree, see Giovino 2007.

87 Klein/Abraham 1999, 66.

88 *Gilg.*V 1–10 (George 2003, 602–603: 1–10). The full passage is given in Chapter II, § 3.4.

synergic way, so that when Ḫuwawa is slain by Gilgameš and Enkidu, the forest with its living trees is violated and killed as well.

A tragic scene is presented, where Gilgameš commits sacrilegious acts, by trampling through the forest, discovering a secret and sacred territory belonging to the divine, the abode of the Anunaki (*mūšab Enunaki*).[89] The felling of the cedars displays the transformation from animate to inanimate. The majestic living trees are, in fact, reduced to timber, a mere lifeless object to be utilized by humans without any respect. A moment of conscience hits Enkidu, who realizes that they committed an act against the gods' will, since the cedars partake of the divine sphere. With the words "My friend, we have cut down a lofty cedar, whose top abutted the heavens" (*ibrī nittakis erēna šīḫu ša muḫḫašu šamê nakpi*),[90] Enkidu acknowledges the animate and cosmic nature of the cedar, and its being a mediator between heaven and earth.

The cedar is also referred to as a purifying agent, called upon in order to cleanse from any defilement and evil creature.[91] Its purifying power can be ascribed to its connection with the Apsû and its god, Enki/Ea. In the Sumerian myth *Lugale*, the god Enki is symbolically conceptualized as a "cedar, grown forth out of the Apsû, a crown with a wide shade" (^{ĝiš}eren Abzu-a mú-a aga-ĝissu-daĝal-la).[92] An interrelation between anthropomorphic deity and tree is established in virtue of their original pure place and due to their protective attributes. In the ritual *Šurpu* an incantation addressing the cedar in its essential cosmic and cleansing attributes is preserved:

én ^{ĝiš}eren-gal kur-gal-ta mú-a	Incantation: "Tall cedar, growing in the high mountain!
kur ki-sikil-la-ta nam-tar-ra	Whose fate was determined in the mountain, the pure place,
kur ^{ĝiš}Ḫa-šur-ra-ta an ús-sa	Which from the Ḫašur-mountain reaches toward heaven,
ir-si-im-bi a-šà-ga diri-ga	Whose fragrance drifts over the fields,
u$_4$-ge$_6$-ba u$_4$-zalág u$_4$-dùg-ga a sud-a du-a kur-ta DU-a	Which constantly day and night makes pure the water, coming from the mountain,
ka lú-u$_x$-lu mu-un-sikil mu-un-dadag	You cleanse, you purify the mouth of the humans,
eme-ḫul-gál bar-šè ḫè-im-ta-gub	May the evil tongue stand aside!"[93]

In this incantation, the cedar is addressed as a powerful purifying entity, whose scent spreads in the air. The purity of the tree is affirmed by its mountainous origin, where its fate is decreed. In this text, the high mountains where the cedar grows are referred to as the

89 *Gilg.* OB Iščali 37'b–40' (George 2003, 264–265). See Chapter II, § 3.4 for the full passage.

90 *Gilg.* V 293–294 (George 2003, 612–613).

91 See below in the present chapter, § 3.

92 *Lugale* 189 (ETCSL 1.6.2: 189; van Dijk 1983, 79: 189; Seminara 2001, 104–105).

93 *Šurpu* IX 42–48 (Reiner 1970, 46: 42–48).

Ḫašur mountains, which we encountered as one of the cosmic mountains on the eastern horizon.[94] The cosmic feature of the cedar as mediator between heaven and earth, its role as purifier of mankind and as belonging to the cosmic mountain are all displayed here. However, the reference to the Ḫašur mountain raises a question, since the cedar is generally regarded as a tree belonging to the western horizon.[95]

The association of the e r e n -tree with the eastern mountains is not new in the ancient literature. The Sumerian traditions of the Gilgameš Epic point to the understanding that the heroes travelled eastward in order to reach the Cedar Forest.[96] As pointed out by the scholars, this evidence might indicate that the term e r e n underwent a significant change over time. According to Bottéro, the term ĝiše r e n was originally a generic term for any resinous or coniferous tree, and only from the Old Babylonian period onward did its identification with the cedar stabilize.[97] The understanding of the term e r e n as a broad designation for any coniferous tree matches botanical observations.[98] Indeed, cedars do not grow on the central and southern Zagros, whose coniferous species are the tall juniper (*Juniperus excelsa*) and the Indian juniper (*Juniperus polycarpos*).[99] Among those species, the Indian juniper is the best candidate for identification with the *ḫašurru*-tree, which is referred to as a coniferous tree growing on the eastern Mountain of Sunrise in both Sumerian and Akkadian literature.[100] Its name is intrinsically entangled with the mountain where it grows, with its setting being both geographically and symbolically specific.

The association of the cedar with the *ḫašurru*-tree and Mt. Ḫašur is a recurrent feature in Sumerian and Akkadian literature. Both trees are referred to as mythical and cosmic arboreal entities, whose traits often mingle when connected to the Mountain of Sunrise, but they also comprise opposite symbolic meanings. Cedar and *ḫašurru*-tree are paired together in Sumerian hymns,[101] and in the previously seen Old Babylonian incantation addressing the tamarisk.[102] According to this evidence, both trees should be considered entangled with the Mountain of Sunrise, when they are referred to in their cosmic and purifying features. This evidence supports the early understanding of e r e n as a more general term referring to coniferous trees, whereas the *ḫašurru*-tree is specifically bound to its mountain, Mt. Ḫasur.

94 See Chapter II, § 2.1 and § 3.5.

95 As seen in the Sumerian literary composition *Inana and the King*, while the ḫ a l u b -tree represents the east, the e r e n -tree stands for the west (CT 42, ii 13–17). See Horowitz 1998, 333.

96 See the *Sumerian Flood Story* (ETCSL 1.7.4; Lambert/Millard 1969, 1138–145).

97 Bottéro 1992, 28; Klein/Abraham 1999, 66; Woods 2009, 190–191.

98 Two major types of forest featured in the Ancient Near East: the Zagrosian forest, whose main arboreal species are oaks, pistachio trees, almond trees, maples and small junipers, and the Mediterranean forest, whose dominant conifers are pine, firs, tall junipers, cypresses and cedars. Moreover, tall junipers and pines grow on the western slopes of the northern Zagros and in the anti-Taurus (Zohary 1963, 30 ff.; Guest 1966; Klein/Abraham 1999, 65).

99 Zohary 1963, 30 ff.; Guest 1966; Klein/Abraham 1999, 65.

100 Woods 2009, 190. See Chapter 2 for the literary references to the *ḫašurru*-tree, Mt. Ḫašur and the Sun.

101 UET 6, 105: 4–5 (Charpin 1986, 287–288); CUSAS 32, II.A.9 col. vi 15–25 (George 2016, 68–69). See also the Sumerian *Hymn to Utu* 10, g u d ĝiše r e n d u r u₅ n a ĝ - a ḫ a - [š u] - ú r - [r a p e š] - a , "(Utu) bull who drinks among the dewy e r e n -trees, which grow on Mt. Ḫašur" (ETCSL 4.32.2: 10). For further reference see Chapter II.

102 CUSAS 32, II.A.9 col. vi 15–25 (George 2016, 69–69). See above in the present chapter, § 2.3.

Conversely, the couple of cedar and *ḫašurru*-tree can also comprise the polar opposition of West and East.

In the religious discourse, it is relevant that both trees are referred to as cosmic trees growing on the cosmic mountain, whose entanglement with the purity of the mountain and the rays of the sun made them powerful cleansing trees and mediators between the worlds. Noteworthy are also the continuous allusions to the sensual dimension of smell. References to the sweet fragrance bursting out from the cedar are copious throughout the literature, and they connect the tree to the ritual performance, which would comprise a fully sensorial experience.

2.5 The *kiškanû*-tree

A mysterious holy tree strictly connected with Enki/Ea's domains and with the cosmic *pī nārāti*, is the *kiškanû*-tree (Sum. ^{ĝiš}kín).[103] This sacred tree is attested in a few incantations, whose provenance and dating range widely. The *kiškanû*-tree is mentioned in an Old Akkadian incantation from Susa, in a Middle Assyrian incantation that is part of the *Utukkū Lemnūtu* series, and as part of the canonical 1st-millennium *Utukkū Lemnūtu*. The Old Akkadian incantation from Susa represents the basis for the later developments into the bilingual incantations, but it is far from being considered a precise duplicate.[104] This incantation aims at comparing the figure of Enki, the king of the Apsû, to that of the *kiškanû*-tree.[105] The god's traits are intertwined with those of this pure and sacred tree: the god is said to have been created in a pure place and to share with the tree the appearance of lapis lazuli and the giving of shade. This merging of representations of a god with a tree, and of a tree as a god, are remarkable in the network of religious meanings concerning the arboreal entity.[106]

The focus of the later bilingual incantations is the *kiškanû*-tree, which is referred to as a black tree that is sacred in Eridu: the Middle Assyrian[107] and Neo-Assyrian recensions are

---

103 Geller 1980, 23–51; Geller 2007, 169–170. See also Haas 1994, 145; Horowitz 1998, 342; Woods 2009, 221.

104 MDP 14, 91 obv. 1–13, én ⸢é⸣-nu-ru [lugal] ^{ĝiš}kín-gin$_7$ ki-sikil mú-a ^{d}En-ki ^{ĝiš}kín- gin$_7$ ki-sikil mú-a kur-ku-rá-a-ni kur ḫé-gál sù ki-DU-DU-ni gissu-bi múš(!) za-gìn-na-gin$_7$ ab-šà-ga là-a lugal ^{ĝiš}kín-gin$_7$ ki-sikil-e íb-mú-a gin$_7$ ^{d}En-ki ^{ĝiš}kín- gin$_7$ ki-sikil-e íb-mú-a gin$_7$, "Enuru-incantation: The king, like the *kiškanû*-tree, is created in a pure place; Enki, like the *kiškanû*-tree, is created in a pure place. His flood fills the earth with abundance. His 'place of walking' is his shade, which like 'the appearance' of lapis lazuli stretches over the sea. Like the king, which a pure place has created like the *kiškanû*-tree! Like Enki, which a pure place has created like the *kiškanû*-tree!" (Geller 1980, 24–25).

105 Geller 1980, 25.

106 See also Eliade 1958, 271–273.

107 Middle Assyrian *Utukkū Lemnūtu* XII 2'–20', èn nun^{ki} ^{ĝiš}gín ki-sikil-la mú-a : *ina Eridu kiškanû ina ašri ellim ibbani* múš-bi ^{na4}za-gín-duru$_5$ Abzu-ta lá-a : *zīmūšú uqnî ellu ina Apsî tarṣu* ^{d}En-ki-ke$_4$ ki-DU.DU ḫé-gàl BU-ta-àm : *ša Ea* ki.DU.DU *ḫengalli malât* ki-tuš-a-na ki-ganzer-àm : *mūšabšu ašar erṣetimma* ki-ná-a-na itima^{ma} : *ina kiṣṣi mayyālišu* é-ge$_6$-ge$_6$-ga-a-ni-šè tir gissu dù-a lú nu-mu-un-ku$_4$-ku$_4$-da : *ina bītim ellim ina qišti ša ṣillaša tarṣu mamman la irru* šà

similar but they display some interesting differences. In both the Middle Assyrian and the Neo-Assyrian incantations, there is no further comparison of the tree with Enki as in the Old Akkadian spell. The *kiškanû*-tree is entangled in a complex network of cosmic regions, real cities and gods, as we can read in the Neo-Assyrian recension:

én Eridu^{ki} ĝiš-gín-ge$_{6}$-e ki-sikil-ta mú-a *ina Eridu kiškanû ṣalmu irbi ina ašri ellu ibbani*	Incantation: In Eridu a black *kiškanû*-tree grew, created in a pure place,
múš-bi ^{na4}za-gìn-duru$_{5}$ Abzu-ta lál-a *zīmūšu uqnû ebbi ša ana Apsî tarṣu*	Its appearance is pure lapis lazuli, which extends into the Apsû.
^{d}En-ki-ke$_{4}$ ki-DU-DU-a-ta Eridu^{ki}-ga ḫé-gál si-ga-àm *ša Ea tallaktašu ina Eridu ḫegalla malâti*	Ea's activities in Eridu are full of abundance,
ki-tuš-a-na ki-ganzir-àm *šubassu ašar erṣetimma*	His dwelling is the place of the netherworld,
ki-nú itima ^{d}Namma-ke$_{4}$ *kiṣṣušu mayyālu ša Nammu*	And his sanctuary is Nammu's bed.
é kug-ga-a-ni-ta ^{ĝiš}tir gissu là-e šà-bi lú nu-mu-un-du-ku$_{4}$-ku$_{4}$-dè *ina bītim ellu ša kīma qištu ša ṣillašu tarṣa ana libbišu manma la irrubu*	In a pure temple, which is like a forest with its stretching shadows, (where) no one shall enter its midst,
šà ^{d}Utu Ama-ušumgal-an-na-ke$_{4}$ *ina qerbišu Šamaš u Dumuzi*	(There) are Šamaš and Tammuz.
dal-ba-an-na íd ka-min-na-ta ^{d}Ka-ḫé-gál ^{d}Igi-ḫé-gál ^{d}Laḫ-mu-Abzu Eridu^{ki}-ga-ke$_{4}$ *ina bīrīt pī nārāti kilallān Kaḫegal Igiḫegal Laḫmu Apsî ša Eridu*	Between the mouth of the two rivers – Kahegal and Igihegal– the Lahmu-of-the-Apsû of Eridu,
ĝiš-kín-bi šu im-ma-an-ti	Took that *kiškanu*-tree, cast the spell of

^{d}Utu Ama-ušumgala-na-ke$_{4}$: *ina qerbi ša Šamaš u Dumuzi* dal-ba-na íd-da ka-min-kám-ma ^{d}Ka-ḫé(!)-gal ^{d}Igi-ḫé-gal ^{d}La-ḫa-ma Nun^{ki}-gal-ke$_{4}$: *ina bīrīt nārāti kilallān Kaḫegal Igiḫegal Laḫama ša Eridu* mu$_{7}$-mu$_{7}$ Abzu a-ra-an-šè sag-lú-u$_{x}$-lu pap-ḫal-la-kám ba-an-gar-re-eš : *šipat Apsî iddû ina qaqqadi amēli muttalliki iškunū*, "Incantation. In Eridu a *kiškanû*-tree was created in a pure place; Its appearance of pure lapis lazuli stretches forth into the Apsû. The way of Enki/Ea is full of abundance, and his dwelling is the place of the underworld. In the shrine of his bed, in a holy temple in the forest, whose shade stretches (where) no one can proceed, in the midst of Šamaš and Dumuzi, between (the mouths of) the two rivers –Kaḫegal and Igiḫegal–, and Laḫmu of Eridu, recited the incantation of the Apsû, and placed it on the head of the restless man." (Geller 1980, 23–51: 2'–20').

tu$_6$ Abzu ba-an-sì sag lú-u$_{18}$-lu pap-ḫal-la-ke$_4$ ba-ni-in-gar-re-eš *kiškanû šuātu ilqû šipat Apsî iddû ina rēš amēli muttalliki iškunū*	the Apsû, and placed it on the distraught patient's head.[108]

The *kiškanû*-tree is said to be a tree with a black bark, created in a pure place and having the appearance of pure lapis lazuli, which stretches into the Apsû. It is addressed as a tree sprouting from the Apsû, whose abode is the netherworld, and whose shrine is Nammu's bed.[109] These features indicate a nocturnal setting enshrouded in darkness. Darkness is also expressed by the reference to the shade of the tree, which is here equated to the shade cast by the shrine, but also to the darkness which abides in the midst of both the shrine and the forest. The sensorial allusion to non-visibility should be understood as a double reference to the fact that human eyes were unable to see the innermost interior of the temple, much as they were unable to see the midst of the forest on the cosmic mountain. In the Middle Assyrian version, the passage concerning the original place where the tree grows alludes explicitly to the existence of a holy temple or shrine within a forest, whose shade stretches where no one can proceed. This characterization of secrecy refers directly to the forest located on the slopes of the Mountain of Sunrise.[110]

In the midst of the dark forest, the gods Šamaš and Dumuzi stand. This notion is a further reference to the netherworld setting of the *kiškanû*-tree, but it also affirms the entanglement with the eastern mountains. The mentions of the place "in between the two rivers" in the Middle Assyrian manuscripts and of the place "in the midst of the mouth of the two rivers" in the Neo-Assyrian sources, clearly speak to the association of the sacred tree of Eridu with the cosmic tree growing on the slopes of the Mountain of Sunrise, where the source of the two rivers lies. In these texts, the names of the mouths of the two rivers are here made explicit: Kaḫegal, "Mouth-of-Plenty", and Igiḫegal, "Eye-of-Plenty".[111] The water which nurtures the roots of the tree is thus the water flowing from the cosmic spring, whose water comes directly from the Apsû. The connecting figures between the Apsû, through the *pī nārāti*, to the city of Eridu, are Enki/Ea's water monsters, the fifty Laḫmu.[112]

What is on display here is a dense network of allusions and a play of correspondences and oppositions between darkness and light, and between the urban sanctuary of the Apsû in Eridu and the mythical background and origin of the tree on the cosmic mountain of the rising sun, where it was nurtured by the pure waters of the Apsû. The place of darkness and of mystery, where the roots of the tree grow, ensures the pristine purity of the *kiškanû*-tree. The allusion to the *pī nārāti* and to the Mountain of Sunrise counterbalance the sense of

108 *Utukkū Lemnūtu* XIII 95–103 (Geller 2007, 245: 95–103; Geller 2016, 460–463: 95–103). See especially Geller 2016 for the partitur of the different versions. Here a comprehensive but simplified transcription of the bilingual incantation is offered.

109 For the Apsû and the netherworld see Horowitz 1998, 342.

110 MA *Utukkū Lemnūtu* XII 2'–20' (Geller 1980, 23–51: 12'–13'). See Chapter II, § 2.1.

111 Haas 1994, 145. See the Mari shell for a possible iconographical representation of the Two Mouths of the Rivers, Kaḫegal and Igiḫegal (see Chapter III, § 2.1).

112 For a brief overview of the Laḫmu see Wiggermann 1992, 164–166.

darkness and mystery which envelops this sacred tree, while stressing once more the cleansing and healing properties of the arboreal being.

The incantation of the *kiškanû*-tree, which is also referred to as the *Incantation of Eridu* or the *Incantation of the Apsû*, is included in the rituals for dispelling the evil demons of Mesopotamian lore. The text continues by calling upon all the benevolent entities that can counteract the evil demons' power. This spell was chanted during the healing rite, while a piece of *kiškanû*-wood was placed on the head of the patient. The tree acts as a repository of favorable energies and of divine protections. The therapeutic properties ascribed to the tree were reinforced by the cosmic and divine powers embodied in it. Through the physical presence of the tree, the gods and benevolent spirits associated with it are also gathered around the sick person during the rite.

It can be inferred from this incantation that the *kiškanû*-tree was a sacred tree of Ea, and it was probably planted within his sanctuary in the city of Eridu. The close connection of this tree with the religious and temple setting is attested also in the Sumerian hymn of Rīm-Sîn, where the *kiškanû*-tree is said to be guarding the gates of the interior of the temple, which is addressed as the Apsû itself.[113] This hymn refers to the Apsû as a physical part of the temple, as the foundation of the ziggurat, and describes the constitutive parts of it, which are all intertwined in a dense network of symbolic allusions between the temple and the mountain, and between the trees guarding its gates with those growing on the cosmic mountain. The mysterious identity of the *kiškanû*-tree has been subject to different interpretations. It has been identified as a reed stalk or a date palm or even a cedar, and a correspondence with the iconography of the Neo-Assyrian Tree has been established.[114] Since there is no clear evidence for establishing the identity of this tree, every interpretation remains purely speculative.

2.6 The Juniper, the Boxwood and the Cypress

Another purifying and cleansing tree with a cosmic characterization is the juniper (Sum. ^{ĝiš}šim-li, ^{ĝiš}li, Akk. *burāšu*). In one Sumerian incantation, the juniper is called upon as a great purifier of a vessel (i.e. the censer), of earth and heaven, which makes the land shining with its ascending.[115] The purifying parts of the juniper are the leaves, which were burnt in censers, and whose smoke purified the passage between the earth and the sky. The smoke's ascension affirms the role of the juniper as a mediator between realms. The cosmic

113 UET 6, 105: 1–13 (Charpin 1986, 287–289).

114 Giovino 2007, 12–13. As argued by Giovino, "various texts, as well as clues from the archaeological record, lead us to suppose that the *kiškanû*-tree was (a) an actual tree connected to temples, (b) an artificial tree connected to temples, (c) part of a sacred grove, and (d) used in a cultic role similar to that of a standard." (Giovino 2007, 197).

115 YOS 11, 47: 9–15, ^{šim}li an-na [dim]-gal-bi-im dug mu-un-sikil im mu-un-sikil an mu-un-sikil ki mu-un-dadag-ge ^{šim}li-an-na im mu-un-sikil ki mu-un-sikil dug mu-un-sikil-la-gim ki mu-un-sikil ki-mu-un-dadag-ge, " Juniper, great pillar of heaven, you purified the vessel, you purified earth, you purified heaven, you make the earth brilliant. Ascending juniper, you purified earth, you purified heaven, you purified the vessel, you purify the earth, you make the earth brilliant. (Conti 1997, 254: 9–15).

features of juniper as mediator between worlds is clear in the same incantation, in a passage where the tree is referred to as the "great pillar of the sky" (an-na dim-gal-bi-im), while in another Sumerian incantation this tree is considered not only the pillar of heaven, but also of the temple of Eanna, and it is conceptualized as the standard of the netherworld:

^{š}[^{im}li t]ir-ra [mú-a]	"Ju[niper, who grows] in the forest
^{š}[^{im}li an-na] dim-[bi]	Ju[niper,] pillar [of the sky]
^{š}[^{im}li é-an-na-ka] dim-[bi]	Ju[niper,] pillar [of Eanna]
[ki-a ùri-gal-bi]	[great standard of the netherworld]".[116]

Together with the cedar and the juniper, the boxwood (Sum. ^{ĝiš}tamkarin, Akk. *taškarinnu*) and the cypress (Sum. ^{ĝiš}šur-min, Akk. *šurmēnu*) are often mentioned as purifying entities, too. However, they do not appear to be referred to as proper animate agents or cosmic trees. Only one attestation from the Gilgameš Epic reports these two trees, together with the cedar, as animated arboreal agents. In this ritual context within the myth, they are called upon in order to participate in the mourning for Enkidu's death: "May [boxwood], cypress and cedar mourn you, through whose midst we crept in our fury!" (*[libkīkā taškarinnu] šurmēnu erēnu libkīkā [ša ina bīrišunu ni]ḫtallupu ina uzzini*).[117]

2.7 The *e'ru*-wood

Another tree that features a complex network of ritual and symbolic meanings is the *e'ru* (Sum. ^{ĝiš}ma-nu, Akk. *e'ru*). The identification of this tree is still a matter of debate: it is either translated as cornel[118] or a type of willow.[119] This wood is generally utilized for carving small wooden objects and its twigs were used for binding. This evidence indicates a tough and elastic wood, features that rather match those of the willow.

The cosmic notion of this tree and its connection with the divine and the great gods is reflected in its epithet "august weapon of Anu", as attested in a Middle Babylonian incantation against the *Utukkū Lemnūtu*.[120] A further reference to its cosmic nature is found in Sumerian literature, where the *e'ru* -wood is called the "great pillar of heaven" and "great pillar of the gods".[121]

Another Sumerian incantation addresses this wood in its cosmic features and as an entity with precise apotropaic and healing attributes:

---

116 Conti 1997, 254: 1–4.

117 *Gilg.* VIII 14–15 (George 2003, 650–651).

118 Wiggermann 1992, 60–65.

119 Steinkeller 1987a, 91–92. See also Heimpel 2011.

120 ^{ĝiš}ma-nu ^{ĝiš}tukul-maḫ An-na-ke$_4$ sag-gá-na ba-ni-in-gar, *e'ra kakka ṣīra ša Anim ina rēšišu iškunma*, "He placed on his head *e'ru*-wood, the august weapon of Anu." (Geller 1980, 34–35: 75'–76').

121 ^{ĝiš}ma-nu idim-gal-an-na-ke$_4$ ^{ĝiš}ma-nu idim-gal-dingir-re-e-ne, "*e'ru*-wood, great pillar of heaven, *e'ru*-wood, great pillar of the gods." (Conti 1997, 266: 4–5).

^{ĝiš}ma-nu dim-an-na ^{ĝiš}ma-nu [dim-È]-an-na	The *e'ru* -wood, the pillar of the sky, the *e'ru* -wood, the pillar of Eanna;
úr-bi gi_6 na-nam pa-bi ^{ĝiš}banšur-an-na	Its roots are in the darkness, its branch is the table of heaven;
an gakkul-àm ugu ĝiš i-íb-šú	Above, it is like a gakkul-vessel, the top is covered with wood;
ki e-sír-ra-àm gìr ĝiš ba-ni-in-si	Below, it is like a shoe, the soles are lined with wood.
kaskal ì-ḫaš izi ba-an-lá	It diverts the road, clears it with fire.
^{d}Geštin-an-na sila-si-ig-ga-ra ḫé-im-ma-da-dib-bé	With Geštinanna of the silent streets it shall go around,
^{d}Dumu-zi úr ĝešdan-ra-àm ḫé-im-ma-da-dib-bé	and with Dumuzi entering the lap of the beloved one it shall go everywhere.
sag-tab-mu ḫé-a ḫu-mu-un-ta-ab-ri	May it be my helper, may it lead me,
sag-kal ^{d}Nin-urta ḫu-mu-un-ta-ab-ri	And may strong Ninurta lead me!
lú-ḫul-gál sil_6-lá igi-mu-ta	Evil one, be gone from in front of me!
ka-inim-ma-^{ĝiš}ma-nu-kam	Incantation-formula for the *e'ru* -wood".[122]

The incantation features the different attributes of the tree: its symbolic and ritualistic aspects are mentioned, together with its material uses in daily life. The traditional cosmic features of the tree are here expressed: it is called the link with heaven and the link with the abode of An, while its roots sink deep into darkness. The incantation then probably mentions two of the uses of the *e'ru*-wood by comparing it to a vessel and to a shoe. The wood is then described as an entity able to open a road and cleanse it with fire. These actions probably allude to its purifying and evil-dispelling abilities. The nocturnal apotropaic setting is further expressed by the mentioning of two deities connected with the night and the netherworld: the *e'ru*-wood is said to escort Geštinanna and Dumuzi. In both cases, the wood is here envisioned after being fashioned into a magical stick. This wood was, in fact, principally utilized for manufacturing sticks and wooden figurines, which were believed to have wondrous abilities. The reference to Dumuzi might also be a hint at another ritual utilization of this wood in the incantations to restore male potency: the *e'ru*-wood is often mentioned and called upon due to its being strong and hard, qualities which the man affected by impotence is trying to regain.[123]

Its apotropaic and life-giving attributes are expressed in the incantation whose incipit is "Evil Spirits of the Broad Steppe", where the *e'ru*-wood is called the "mace that hits evil" (^{ĝiš}ḫul-dùb-ba) and "wood of life" (ĝiš nam-til-la).[124] The notion of the *e'ru*-wood conceived of as a mighty purifying and evil-dispelling power is stressed by the

122 VAS 17, 18: 1–11 (Wiggermann 1992, 82–83).
123 See Biggs 1967; Biggs 2002.
124 Wiggermann 1992, 65.

fact that it was used to fashion the statuettes embodying the *ūmu-apkallū*, the "leading sages", which were stationed in different parts of the house of the sick person in order to protect and heal. Moreover, the rites which were performed in honor of the tree before it was cut and used to fashion the protective wooden sculptures of the *ūmu-apkallū* speak to the conception of this tree as a sacred and animated entity which was approached by the cultic performer with an attitude of respect, similar to that shown toward the tamarisk.[125] The ritual that preceded and involved the cutting of the tree should thus be understood as a rite of thanksgiving: the performer should enter the wood at sunrise, taking with him a golden axe and a silver saw, and consecrating (*qadāšu*) the *e'ru*-tree with a censer, a torch and holy water. A *kusāpu*-loaf shall be placed in front of the tree, while, facing toward the sunrise, the performer is to sprinkle clear water and set up an offering table. On it, a sacrifice of a sheep shall be made and offerings of dates and a cake made of ghee and butter shall be presented. The performer will then purify the tree with a censer of juniper (*nignakku burāši*) and offer a libation of first-class beer. To conclude, the performer shall "kneel down and then stand up in front of the *e'ru*-tree, reciting the incantation 'Evil [spirit] in the broad steppe' (*tuškên ina maḫar e'ri izzâzma šiptu utukku lemnu ṣēri rapšim tamannu*)".[126] As noted regarding the tamarisk, these ritual actions display grateful and respectful behavior, implying an animistic attitude toward the arboreal person.

3 The animate and relational universe of plants, wood and trees in the anti-witchcraft incantations and healing rituals

The world of healing magic offers a multifaceted portrait of animated entities, which are called upon in order to dispel evil creatures and diseases, and to purify and protect the affected person. Plants and trees occur as animated agents and benign persons capable of specific actions against diseases, demons, and other evil entities.

An Old Babylonian incantation against the *kaššāptu* addresses several *materia magica* used for the ritual proper.[127] The ritual should be performed on a day without moon and comprises several elements: a torch, barley, the sulphur of a *maštakal*-plant (*kibrīt ammaštakal*), the 'magic-stick'-plant (*iṣi pišrim*), the *šalālum*-reed (*qan šalālum*), a tamarisk (*bīnum*) and a young date palm (*suḫuššum*). These purifying entities are addressed as the "pure ones" (*ellūtum*), who are called upon in order to release the house of the man (*ana bīt awīlim puššurim*), probably from witchcraft. To my understanding, these magical entities should not be considered only mere *Kultmittelbeschwörungen*, which are activated as a function of the ritual performance. The magical worldview implies an analogical and relational perception of reality, according to which every entity, human and non-human, is immersed in a thick network of connections, and has its own power, function and purpose, in a word, agency.[128] All the elements of the world, in which humans are immersed and of which they are part, partake of the life of humans. A Middle Babylonian incantation against

125 See § 2.3 in the present chapter.
126 Wiggermann 1992, 6–7: 28–40.
127 UET 6/2, 193: 1'–17'.
128 See further in Chapter V, particularly § 2.

Lamaštu addresses plants, stones, earth, heaven, and the reed of the alfalfa-grass, which are all invoked to play their role in expelling the demoness to the mountains:

liktallûki šammū ša mitḫāriš a[ṣû]	"The plants [growing] everywhere may restrain you!
erṣetu u šamû liktallûki	The earth and heaven may restrain you!
abnāt šadîm liktammāki	The stones on the mountains may capture you!
šikkurrāt elpeti lisaḫḫilā šēpēki	The reed of the alfalfa-grass may pierce your feet!
elīma ana šadî erīši ṭābī	Rise to the mountains of sweet scents!"[129]

Natural elements not only act by protecting human life and dispelling evil forces, but also appear to be emotionally involved. In an incantation for treating sheep affected by the *sikkatum*-disease, the god Sumuqan (i.e. Šakkan), the herb and the path, are praised and rejoice at the recovery of the sheep.[130]

In the rich repertoire of the anti-witchcraft incantations and rituals, several plants and trees are recorded as benign beings, considered to have specific roles and effective actions against the evil crafts of the *kaššāptu*. In the first tablet of the great anti-witchcraft ritual *Maqlû*, the tamarisk, the date palm and the *maštakal*-soapwort are called upon on behalf of the *kaššāptu*'s victim:

bīnu lillilanni ša qimmatu šarû	"May the tamarisk that is copious of crown clear me,
gišimmaru lipšuranni māḫirat kalû šārī	May the date palm that withstands all winds release me,
maštakal libbibanni ša erṣeta malâta	May the soapwort that fills the earth cleanse me,
terinnatu lipšuranni ša še'a malâta	May the cone that is full of seeds release me".[131]

The tamarisk (*bīnu*) and the date palm (*gišimmaru*) recur often in these rituals because they are considered purifying trees. The tamarisk is said to release (*pašāru*) and to purify (*elēlu*), and the date palm with its shoots (*suḫuššu*) to release and to undo witchcraft (*pašāru kišpī*). Another tree often mentioned in connection with rites of purifications is the cedar (*erēnu*), which is reported to cleanse (*ebēbu*),[132] while in this passage it is the cone

129 BM 120022 (*MC* 17, 443 ff.) rev. 13–17 (Farber 2014, 120–125). See also Zomer 2018, 425–429.

130 YOS 11, 7: 1–17, *liḫdu Sumuqan liḫdu šammum lirīš šulûm*, "May Sumuqan rejoice! May the herb rejoice! May the path be happy!" (van Dijk 1985, 21).

131 *Maqlû* I 21–24 (Abusch 2014, 229).

132 *CMAwR* 7.8.4: 3'–4', *iptašrū bīnu maštakal u ĝišimmaru* EDIN … […] *yâši lipšurū'inni*, "Tamarisk, *maštakal*-soapwort and date palm have released *the steppe* … […]. May they release me!" (Abusch/Schwemer 2011, 188–189); *CMAwR* 8.6: 95'–96', *bīnu lillilanni erēnu libbibanni maštakal* (*u*) *suḫuššu lipašširū kišpīya*, "May the tamarisk purify me, may the cedar cleanse me, may *maštakal*-

(*terinnatu*) that is called upon in order to release. The *terinnatu* was probably a pinecone, whose seeds (or nuts) were a symbol of plenty, and which should be compared with the iconographic motif of the cone that was utilized for purification rituals in the Neo-Assyrian reliefs.

The tamarisk and the palm tree often recur associated with the *maštakal*-plant.[133] This trio appears to be particularly powerful, as we can read in the *Lipšur Litanies*: "May the tamarisk purify him, may the *maštakal*-plant absolve [him], may the date palm heart release his sin, may Nisaba, the queen, take his sin off him, may the incantation-formula of Ea and Asalluhi keep away his sin".[134] In this prayer, the tamarisk, the palm tree and the *maštakal*-plant are invoked together with the goddess Nisaba in an incantation formula of the gods Ea and Asalluḫi, showing a peculiar interaction and engagement between powerful vegetable elements and the anthropomorphic gods. Moreover, these purifying entities are equated to the great gods in a ritual commentary: *bīnu* with Anum, *libbi gišimmari* with Dumuzi, *maštakal* with Ea and *qan šalāli* with Ninurta.[135]

The *maštakal*-plant (Sum. innuš) is widely attested as a powerful herb with purifying properties. It is referred to as a medicinal plant and is generally considered a type of soapwort.[136] In a Sumerian incantation the *maštakal*-plant is addressed as a cosmic entity, whose therapeutic properties derive from the pristine purity of its dwelling and growing place, and from its connection with the Apsû and the ancestral gods. The incantation opens by addressing the cosmic features of the plant, with references to its pristine origin and its intrinsic purity due to its roots sinking deep into the Apsû and growing in a holy place with Enki, and its branches reaching the sky.[137] The *maštakal*-plant is then said to have been created and nurtured with all the gods traditionally associated with the pristine purity of the ancestral time and with the purity of the underground and river waters:

^{d}En-ki ^{d}Nin-ki	"Enki and Ninki,
^{d}En-ul ^{d}Nin-ul	Enul and Ninul,
^{d}A-nun-na du$_6$-kug-ga-ke$_4$-e-ene	The Anunna-gods of the Holy Mound,
La-ḫa-ma Abzu Eridu^{ki}-ga	The Laḫmu-of-the-Apsû of Eridu,
⸢Ḫal⸣-ḫal-la ama ḫur-sag-gá-ke$_4$ šu dadag-ga-mi mí um-ma-ni-in-dug$_4$	(and) the Ḫalḫalla, the mother of the mountains, nurtured it (with) her clean hands".[138]

soapwort and palm shoots undo the witchcraft affecting me" (Abusch/Schwemer 2011, 331). See above in the present chapter, § 2.3 and § 2.4.

133 See above in the present chapter, § 2.3.

134 Reiner 1956, 137: 74 –76, *bīnu līlilšu maštakal lipšur[šu] libbi gišimmari aranšu lipṭur Nisaba šarratum šēressu lit[bal] šiptu ša Ea u Asalluḫi ennintašu linassi.*

135 Livingstone 1986, 176f.

136 See CAD M, 391 s.v. *maštakal*; Abusch/Schwemer 2011.

137 CUSAS 32, II.A.4 (Nr. 5i) col. v 7'–16' (George 2016, 60).

138 CUSAS 32, II.A.4 (Nr. 5i) col. v 17'–23' (George 2016, 60).

In this passage, the Holy Mound and the river Ḫalḫalla mark the cosmic dimension of the plant, together with its particular connection with the deities of the watery realm of the Apsû and its lord, Enki/Ea. Enki's earthly abode is the city of Eridu, where his fifty sea-creatures, the Laḫmu, are in charge of protecting the god's domain and act as messengers between humans and the god through the river.[139] Its mighty purifying power is stressed throughout the rest of the incantation, which was chanted during healing rituals while cleansing the patient with the *maštakal*-plant.[140] This soapwort was particularly used in rituals against witchcraft, where it is called upon in order to release from witchcraft (*pašāru*), to undo spells (*pašār kišpī*) and to crush witchcraft (*eli kišpīki maštakal limqut*).[141] The latter reference is found in an incantation which involves specific natural elements counteracting the *qumqummatu*- and *naršindatu*-witches:

ÉN *ēpištu qumqummatu kaššāptu naršindatu*	"The sorceress is a *qumqummatu*-witch, the witch is a *naršindatu*-witch,
ša imlû ṭīdâya ina nāri	Who have filled clay from the river (to make figurines) of me!
mīna tubbalī napištī ana malkī	Why do you want to carry my soul to the (netherworld) *malkū*-deities?
anāku ana puššur kišpīki maštakal našâku	As for me, in order to undo your witchcraft I hold up *maštakal*-soapwort,
imḫur-līm lā māḫir kišpīki	'Heals-a-thousand'-plant that is immune to your witchcraft,
iṣ pišri ša nadâti terinnatu ša qašdāti	The 'wood-of-release' of the *nadītu*-priestesses, the cone of the *qadištu*-votaries!
upīšī linē' šadâ eli kišpīki maštakal limqut	May the mountain drive back the sorcerous devices, may the *maštakal*-soapwort fall upon your witchcraft!
u imḫur-līm limḫaṣ lētki iṣ pišri lipaššira amâtīki	And, may the 'heals-a-thousand' plant strike your cheek, may the 'wood-of-release' undo your words!
gamal siparri lipaṭṭer [qibīt?] kiṣir	May the bronze curved staff release

139 Black/Green 1992, 114. George 2016, 60–61. On the Laḫmu, see also the incantation for the *kiskanû*-tree (above § 2.5) and Atra-ḫasīs (Chapter III, § 5).

140 CUSAS 32, II.A.4 (Nr. 5i) col. v 24'–36', ᵘin-uš an im-ta an im-sikil ki im-tag ki im-dadag an im-tag an im-sikil-la ki im-tag ki im-dadag ᵈEn-ki lugal Abzu-ke$_4$ lú-ùlu dumu dingir-ra-a-ni ki-gub-ba-bi mi-ni-in-dadag in[im h]ul-gál bar-šè [ḫé]-em-ta-gub ka-inim-ma ᵘin-uš a-tu$_5$-[kam], "The soapwort touched the sky, it purified the sky. It touched the earth, it cleansed the earth. (With the plant that) touched the sky, that purified the sky, (that) touched the earth, that cleansed the earth, Enki, lord of the Abzu, (will now) purify and cleanse the place where stands a man, son of his god. May evil speech stand aside! Incantation formula for washing with soapwort" (George 2016, 60).

141 *CMAwR* 7.8.4: 3'–4' (Abusch/Schwemer 2011, 188–189); *CMAwR* 8.6: 95'–96' (Abusch/Schwemer 2011, 331); *CMAwR* 8.7: 105'''–112''' (Abusch/Schwemer 2011, 347).

kuppud libbik	(the command of?) the knot devised in your heart!
ina qibīt Ea Šamaš bēl ilī tê šip[*ti*]	At the command of Ea (and) Šamaš, the lord of the gods!" Incant[ation] formula.[142]

In this incantation, together with the *maštakal*-plant, other natural elements are invoked: the 'heals-a-thousand'-plant (*imḫur-līm*), which is immune to witchcraft (*lā māḫir kišpī*), the wood-of-release (*iṣ pišri*) of the *nadītu*-priestesses, and the cone of the *qadištu*-votaries. Some of these entities are not only specified as effective against witchcraft, but they are explicitly called upon to act against the *kaššāptu*: the 'heals-a-thousand'-plant is summoned to strike her cheek (*imḫur-līm limḫaṣ lēt*) and the 'wood-of-release' to undo her words (*iṣ pišri lipaššira amâti*). In addition, the mountain is also called upon to "drive back the sorcerous devices" (*upīšī linē᾿ šadâ eli kišpī*).[143]

The 'heals-a-thousand'-plant (*imḫur-līm*) is a powerful herb against witchcraft and other diseases and demons. As shown, it is considered immune to any evil craft, being capable of undoing everything and of physically striking the *kaššāptu*, who is afraid of its power. The portentous actions of the 'heals-a-thousand'-plant are praised in an incantation directly calling upon it, where both the mythological framework and the ritual roles of the plant are expressed.[144] The incantation opens with the mythical and symbolic setting of the plant, which is said to have emerged in former times (*šammu ša ina maḫri aṣû*). The herb is described as having a crown reaching the sky and its roots filling the ground below (*elēnu qimmassu* [*šamê šann*]*at šaplānu šuršūšu qaqq*[*ar*]*a malû*). This description corresponds to the traditional symbolism of trees and plants as the medium and connection between the earth and the sky, which stresses its cosmic features. Moreover, the plant is believed to have a great efficacy against several evil crafts: it is referred to as the plant which "undoes anything" (*mupašširu kalāma*), which "breaks the evil bond" (*ša teḫeppe riksa lemna*), and that does not allow any witchcraft to approach the person who applies it to his body. The details of this incantation offer a glimpse into the symbolic and ritual roles of certain elements in the ancient Mesopotamian material religion. The mythical and symbolic references, together with the actions ascribed to the plant, constitute evidence that speaks of the fact that ancient Mesopotamians considered plants not only as merely activated *materia magica*, but as partaking of their complex and multilayered relational cosmos.

142 *CMAwR* 8.7: 106‴–115‴ (Abusch/Schwemer 2011, 347).

143 See Chapter II, § 2.3.

144 *CMAwR* 7.8.3: 17'–30', ÉN *attā imḫur-līm šammu ša ina maḫri aṣû mupašširu kalāma elēnu qimmassu* [*šamê šann*]*at šaplānu šuršūšu qaqq*[*ar*]*a malû īmurkama kaššāptu īruqū pānūša u ša*[…]*ša*(?) … *iṣlimā šaptāša* [*ša kaššāpti*(?) …] … …*ša teḫeppe riksa lemna* [*attā*] *imḫur-līm ša ana šākinīšu ipša* [*bārtu*] [*amāt lemut*]*ti zīra dibalâ ziku*[*rudâ*] [*kadabbedâ*] *dimmakurrâ la uqa*[*rrabu*], "Incantation: "You, 'heals-a-thousand'-plant, are the herb that emerged in former times, that undoes anything, whose top above [reach]es [the sky], whose roots below fill the ground. The witch beheld you and her face turned pale, and her … *became* … , her lips grew dark. [You …] the … [*of the witch*], you break the evil bond, [you are] the 'heals-a-thousand'-plant that does not allow sortilege, [rebellion], [evi]l [word(s)], hate-magic, 'distortion-of-justice'-magic, 'cutting-of-the-[throat'-magic], ['seizing-of-the-mouth'-magic] (and) confusion to co[me near] the person who applies it" (Abusch/Schwemer 2011, 187).

The 'wood-of-release' (Sum. g a n - u₅, Akk. *iṣ pišri*) has specific anti-witchcraft actions and properties. As seen in the incantation against the *qumqummatu-* and *naršindatu-*witches, this wood is capable of undoing the *kaššāptu*'s words and is said to belong to the *nadītu*-priestesses, viz. cultic performers connected to the entourage of Ištar. In another spell the 'wood-of-release' is said to "undo witchcraft" (*iṣ pišri ša upaššaru kišpī*).[145] The 'wood-of-release' is explicitly referred to as a pure and holy herb, which emerged from the river Ulāya:

ÉN *anāku iṣ pišri ellu šam*[*mu ša ina Ul*]*āya aṣû*	Incantation: "I am the 'wood-of-release', the pure he[rb that] emerged from River Ulāya.
Ulāya ibnânn[*i er*]*ṣetu ulidanni*	River Ulāya created m[e, the ea]rth bore me,
[*Ellil u Ninlil ušēridūni*(?)] *ana māti*	[Enlil and Ninlil brought me down] to the land.
[*m*]*ala qaqqadiya šamû qašdū*	[As] much as my head, heaven is holy;
[*mala šēpīya erṣetu*] *qašdat*	[as much as my feet, earth] is holy".[146]

The origin of the 'wood-of-release' is attributed to the waters of the Ulāya and to the earth. The magical properties and holiness of this wood derive from the pristine purity of its original place. The body of the plant is holy and pure, being born from the womb of the earth and generated by the watercourse pouring from the Apsû itself. The river Ulāya is a sacred river in the East, probably flowing in Elam, with cosmic and infernal features.[147] The gods Enlil and Ninlil are said to bring this portentous herb from the East to the urban population. The participation of the gods in the life of a plant is intriguing. In this context, the gods are not involved with the creation of the 'wood-of-release', but they are said to bring it to civilization. The association of this wood with the river Ulāya and its foreign provenance, are hints that suggest its eastern origin and provenance.

Another plant emerging from the water and connected to the anthropomorphic deities is the *ašqulālu*-plant. This plant features a saline context, since it is said to emerge from the midst of the sea. The *ašqulālu*-plant is carefully guarded by the gods: Anu guards its top, Nudimmud its roots, and Ningišzida its entirety. Thanks to the divine guards, the *ašqulālu*-plant is a powerful herb, which is capable of withstanding extreme weather conditions – such as raging waves, cold, frost and ice– and of healing several diseases and attacks by demons.[148] This protection of a plant by the great gods is intriguing, and speaks to a deep

145 *CMAwR* 7.8.1: 23' (Abusch/Schwemer 2011, 185).
146 *CMAwR* 7.8.4: 69'–73' (Abusch/Schwemer 2011, 190).
147 See Chapter III, § 4.4.3.
148 *CMAwR* 7.8.6: 14′–24′, [ÉN *an*]*āku ašqulālu šammu ša ina qereb tâmti aṣû elēnu qimmatī* [*Anu*(?)] *inaṣṣar* [*šap*]*lānu šuršiya inaṣṣara Nudimmud ina muḫḫiya Ninĝišzida iškun maṣṣarta* [*li*]*mtaḫḫar agê ezzūti ša tâmāti rapšāti* [*limt*]*aḫḫar kuṣṣa ḫalpâ šurīpa kīma attūʾa šipta elīšu iqbû ina zumrīš*[*u*(?) …] [*u ziq*]*īqū*(?) *ša šāri lā … pān zumr*[*īšu*] [*ana annanna mār ann*]*anna šākiniya murṣu diʾu šuruppû kišpū ruḫû* [*rusû*] [*upšāš*]*û lemnūtu ša amēlūti ay iṭḫûšu ay iq*[*ribūšū*] [*ay isniq*]*ūšu ina qibīt Ea Šamaš u Marduk*, "[Incantation: "I] am the *ašqulālu*-plant, the plant that emerged from the midst of the sea. Above, [*Anu*] guards my top, [be]low, Nudimmud guards my roots. Ninĝišzida

and multifaceted connection between the anthropomorphic deities and the vegetable entities, that features purity, sacredness and divine protection.

Another active agent against the *kaššāptu* is the *anḫullû*-plant. This plant is immune to witchcraft (*anḫullû lā māḫir kišpī*),[149] constitutes the witch's adversary in court (*bēl dabābī*),[150] and is called upon to turn the *kaššāptu*'s words back to her mouth, to scatter the clouds and to summon a storm (*tēr amāssa ana pîša suppiḫ urpātu pite ūma*).[151]

The universe of plants actively counteracting witchcraft is lively and densely populated: the 'heals-twenty'-plant (*imḫur-ašrā*) is invoked in order to not allow magic to come near the (human) body (*imḫur-ašrā ša lā uqarrabu ruḫê ana zumru*),[152] the AD.SAG-plant is addressed as the "witch's persecutor" (ᵘAD.SAG *bēl dīnīkunu*),[153] and the *tiskur*-plant is called upon on behalf of the victim because of its ability to undo the witch's words (*tiskur šammu mupašširu ša amâ[tīkunu]*),[154] and to block the witch's mouth and/or change her words (*tiskur musakkiru ša pîkina* (var. *munakkira ša amâtīkina*)).[155]

Another plant believed to have an effective agency against the *kaššāptu* is the *kukru*-plant. This plant was widely utilized against witchcraft thanks to its purifying and espunging agency. The *kukru* is a pure and purifying agent, offspring of the mountains (*takur šadî*).[156] The purity of this plant derives from the pure place where it has its birth and subsequently grows: the mountains are explicitly referred to as the "pure holy mountains" (*ina šadânī ellūti quddūti*).[157] The *kukru*-plant is called upon in order to break up the *kaššāptu*'s bond (*kukru ša šadî liḫteppâ*(?) *rikiski*).[158]

The animated universe of plants is fully expressed and evident in an incantation where the plants and woods are invoked as persons (i.e. as children) and benign agents on behalf of the patient:[159]

ašapparakkimma mārī inbiya u dādiya	"I have sent against you the children of my fruitfulness and my plenty:
[*anḫullâ*] *iṣ pišri elikulla amēlānu ēdu* ᵘKA.BAD ᵘAD.SAG	[*anḫullû*-plant, G]AN.U_5-wood, *elikulla*-plant, *amēlānu*-plant, KA.BAD-plant, AD.SAG-plant,

established a guard over me (saying): ['Let it] always withstand the raging waves of the wide seas, [let it al]ways withstand cold, frost (and) ice!' When he spoke my incantation over him, [...] *from h*[*is*] *body*, [*and the gh*]*ostly gusts* of the wind shall not ... in front of [his] bod[y]. [To N.N., son of N.]N., who equipped himself with me: let illness, *diḫu*-disease, shivers, witchcraft, magic, [sorcery], (and) the evil [machi]nations of men not approach him, not come [near him], [not rea]ch him –at the command of Ea, Šamaš and Marduk!" [Incantation formula]. (Abusch/Schwemer 2011, 192).

149 *CMAwR* 7.8.1: 22' (Abusch/Schwemer 2011, 185).

150 *CMAwR* 7.8.6: 28' (Abusch/Schwemer 2011, 193).

151 *CMAwR* 7.8.6: 30' (Abusch/Schwemer 2011, 193).

152 *CMAwR* 7.8.1: 24' (Abusch/Schwemer 2011, 185).

153 *CMAwR* 7.8.6: 28' (Abusch/Schwemer 2011, 193).

154 *CMAwR* 7.8.6: 29' (Abusch/Schwemer 2011, 193).

155 *CMAwR* 7.8.1: 21' (Abusch/Schwemer 2011, 185).

156 *Maqlû* V 49 (Abusch 2015, 250). See Chapter III, § 2.2.

157 *Maqlû* VI 25 // 35 (Abusch 2015, 255–256).

158 *Maqlû* VI 67 (Abusch 2015, 256).

159 *CMAwR* 7.8.3: 35′–41′ (Abusch/Schwemer 2011, 188).

[$^{\acute{u}}$MA.GIL *t*]*iskur* [*qa*]*ran ayyali u nikiptu*	[MA.GIL-plant, *t*]*iskur*-plant, [ho]rn of a stag and *nikiptu*-plant,
šammī ša šadî u māti ša qāt apkal ilī Marduk	The plants from the mountain(s) and from the low land at the disposal of the sage of the gods, Marduk.
ikaššadūki ina ḫarrānimma imaḫḫaṣū lētki utarrū amātki ana pîk[*i*]	They will catch you in the road and strike your cheek. They will return your word to you[r] mouth.
kaššāptī surqīnīki ša kala šatti tusarriqī ušabbalū TU$_6$ ÉN	My witch, they will have (the wind) carry off your strewn offerings that you have strewn during the whole year!" Incantation formula.

This incantation presents interesting features concerning the animate and relational world of magic. The plants are considered the invoker's children, who are called upon in order to act against the *kaššāptu* by catching her, striking her cheek, returning her word to her mouth, and carrying off her strewn offerings. The combination of the conception of the plants as persons and the actions ascribed to them supports the suggestion of a lively animate and relational universe, which finds its fullest expression in the magical and ritual performance.

In another spell, the entire gathering of the plant-persons, represented by the plants of the mountains and of the lowland, is considered to be at the disposal of Marduk. The god is here referred to as the healer and magician god, who is expert in the secrets of the world's floral inhabitants. This passage highlights the intrinsic and complex connection between plants and the anthropomorphic deities. This engagement is notable in another ritual, where we read: "*ḫašû*-plant, *nuḫurtu*-plant, cypre[ss], the (plants) of good health from the temple of Marduk. You cast the incantation into (it, and) he drinks (it)" (*ḫašû nuḫurtu šurm*[*ēnu*] *ša napišti ša bīt Marduk šipta ana libbi tanaddi išattī*[*ma*]).[160] This passage introduces also the matter of the existence of orchards in the temples of the great gods.

160 *CMAwR* 7.8.8: 12′–14′ (Abusch/Schwemer 2011, 194).

Chapter V

Nature, Divinity and Personhood in Ancient Mesopotamian Religion

1 How animism can contribute to assess some emic notions of nature, divinity and personhood

The concepts of nature, divinity, and personhood are all involved in the anthropological concept of new animism. Within the realm of Mesopotamian religion, myths and incantations offer several glimpses into the ways in which the ancient Mesopotamians conceived of and related to their surroundings.[1] This book has explored a precise group of natural elements (i.e. mountains, rivers and trees), with their associated entities (i.e. anthropomorphic gods, *Mischwesen*, animals and threatening agents). Mountains, rivers and trees have been chosen because they display a synergic relationship, which could however be extended to stones and minerals, and to specific animals and *Mischwesen*. In order to offer a comprehensive concluding picture while tackling further aspects, I wish to highlight some major insights on how the discussion promoted by the new animism can shed new light upon the ancient cuneiform cultures.

Animism is an anthropological category and conceptual tool which enables a great variety of questions about the relationship between humans and nature, and which can contribute to shed light upon various aspects of Mesopotamian conceptions and practices involving religion, magic and nature. Through this anthropological category, the modern Western dichotomies such as immanent/transcendent, natural/cultural, natural/supernatural, are called into question within the ancient Mesopotamian polytheisms.

The Mesopotamian religious framework features a complex and fluid picture in its notion of what lies beneath the category of "god": alongside the gods with their anthropomorphic features, natural elements are considered living beings, often defined through the category of d i n g i r /*ilu*, thus partaking of the divine community and acting as

1 However, it has to be stressed that myths and rituals can offer only one of several and possible perspectives into the ancient Mesopotamian *Sitz im Leben*. Rochberg argues that "myth, that is to say, myths, were indeed one of the ways in which what we call the natural was framed in the cuneiform textual record. It was not, however, the only way" (Rochberg 2016, 46 ff.).

persons within the animate cosmos of ancient Mesopotamians. The same anthropomorphic gods comprise diverse representations (animal, natural element, and abstract forms, together with the physical one embodied in the statues). As we have seen throughout this study, mountains and rivers are often, but not always, conceived of as proper deities, and when they are not so considered, they are called upon in the performance of magic as active agents with specific roles. Mountains and rivers in particular are not only categorized with the determinative for deity, but are also treated, referred to and approached with an attitude which is traditionally ascribed to deities. Like mountains and rivers, trees and plants are also considered to partake of the living community with specific agencies, and they are sometimes clearly referred to as partaking of divinity.

Mountains, rivers, trees and plants all partake of the divine cosmos as conceptualized by the ancient Mesopotamians. As pointed out by Frankfort, "the gods were in the nature".[2] This observation, deprived of its evolutionistic connotations, can still be maintained. Accordingly, the realm of nature and the realm of gods were not distinguished in a civilization which did not have the same notion of nature as the modern Western world.[3] In reassessing Frankfort's arguments, Rochberg considers Sahlins' question of whether "the determination of nature as pure materiality –absent gods, incarnate spirits, or any such non human persons– is a unique Western invention",[4] and discusses his interpretation that sees the origin of a material nature in the Biblical text. However, such a concept of a fully material and inanimate nature was unknown also in the western European context until after the Middle Ages and the Renaissance.[5] As a consequence, the professed nature/culture dichotomy should be regarded as a "'highly abstract and rather eighteenth-century' piece of Western intellectualism" alien to non-Western cultures, including the ancient Near Eastern ones. As pointed out by Rochberg,

> In ancient Mesopotamia, as in any number of premodern and non-Western cultures, engagement with the world did not give rise to a term for nature, nor to a conception of nature as an alleged objective reality. But this peculiar conception of the objective reality of nature was a comparatively late development in the West. For the ancient Near East, then, it is not a matter of reconstructing a notional counterpart to nature, so to speak before the beginnings of the conceptual history of nature, but of defining the various ways in which phenomena that we think of as belonging to nature were of interest in cuneiform texts.[6]

It is not within the scope of this study to establish a broader discussion of nature in Mesopotamia within the history of science, but rather to specify some issues and offer one

2 Frankfort *et alii* 1949, 19 (quoted in Rochberg 2016, 40).

3 Frankfort argues that "the ancients saw man as always part of society, and society as imbedded in nature and dependent upon cosmic forces. For them nature and man did not stand in opposition and did not, therefore, have to be apprehended by different modes of cognition" (Frankfort *et alii* 1977, 4; Rochberg 2016, 44).

4 Sahlins 2000, 564 (quoted in Rochberg 2016, 40).

5 Tambiah 1990, 52–53; Descola 2013a, 83.

6 Rochberg 2016, 54. On the question of nature/culture, see also Latour 1993; Descola 1996; Descola 2013a; Harvey 2013a; Harvey 2013b.

perspective on the diverse possible ways in which the ancient Mesopotamians related to, engaged with, and conceptualized their natural surroundings in their religious life as attested by the written and iconographical sources. The emerging polyvalent conception of divinity suggests that dichotomies such as natural/supernatural, immanent/transcendent, natural/cultural do not appear to be emic in ancient Mesopotamian worldviews.[7]

As argued by Abram regarding indigenous communities in contemporary Asia, the landscape is a sensuous reality inhabited by different forces, including the gods:

> The sensuous world itself remains the dwelling place of the gods, of the numinous powers that can either sustain or extinguish human life. It is not by sending his awareness out beyond the natural world that the shaman makes contact with the purveyors of life and death, nor by journeying into his personal psyche; rather, it is by propelling his awareness laterally, outward into the depths of a landscape at once both sensuous and psychological.[8]

This acknowledgment refers to a proper animist and shamanic worldview, but it represents good "food for thought" for exploring the different ways in which the ancient Mesopotamians perceived and conceptualized their world. In the case of the ancient Mesopotamian polytheisms, some animistic features, or at least some matters which are closely associated with the anthropological and ethnographical evidence concerning animist notions, are traceable. Indeed, the notion of a sensuous and animate world, densely inhabited by entities such as gods, stars, demons, animals, mountains, trees, rivers, and humans, calls into question one of the most striking features of the Mesopotamian mythical and ritualistic frameworks, and it brings us to the matter of personhood.[9]

The Mesopotamian cosmos was inhabited by several entities, which were interconnected and related to one another, and that partook of the divine. As argued by Cassirer, the perception of nature in myths is that of a "a dramatic world –a world of actions, of forces, of conflicting powers, where 'things' are not dead, or indifferent stuff. All objects are benign or malign, friendly or inimical, familiar or uncanny, alluring and fascinating or repellent and threatening", that means personal.[10] As pointed out by Rochberg while discussing Frankfort's arguments, the ancient Near Eastern world is not to be understood as "animistic or that natural phenomena were personified", but rather it was "simply and thoroughly animate, that is, 'personal'":[11]

> The world appears to primitive man neither inanimate nor empty but redundant with life; and life has individuality, in man and beast and plant, and in every phenomenon which confronts man –the thunderclap, the sudden shadow, the eerie and unknown clearing in the wood, the stone which suddenly hurts him when he stumbles while on a

7 Rochberg 2016, 38–58.
8 Abram 1996, 10.
9 See Zgoll 2012 for another new approach to personhood. Specifically pertaining to the human personhood, Zgoll argues for the concept of humans as multi-personal beings themselves (Zgoll 2012, 83–106).
10 Cassirer 1944, 78 (quoted in Rochberg 2016, 51).
11 Rochberg 2016, 52.

> hunting trip. Any phenomenon may at any time face him, not as "It", but as "Thou". In this confrontation, "Thou" reveals its individuality, its qualities, its will. "Thou" is not contemplated with intellectual detachment; it is experienced as life confronting life, involving every faculty of man in a reciprocal relationship. Thoughts, no less than acts and feelings, are subordinated to this experience.[12]

Deprived of its evolutionistic background, Frankfort's arguments comprise a fertile shoot by paving the way to readdress the notion of personhood in the ancient Mesopotamian religion. As seen in Chapter I, the concept of personhood has been subjected to a comprehensive reassessment by Hallowell's pioneering study on the Ojibwa worldview (1960), with the introduction of the notion of the "other-than-human" person. This notion partakes of a broader philosophical and ontological debate which is still ongoing, and which involves disciplines as varied as cognitive sciences, ethology, philosophy and biology. According to the new notion of 'other-than-human' person, the salient trait for defining a person is not physical appearance, but behavioral and relational features. Thus, the matter of personhood cannot be reduced to mere anthropomorphism or anthropocentrism. As pointed out by Hallowell, anthropomorphism is not a marker of what distinguishes a person from a non-person. What characterizes a person is behavior and relationality: according to Hallowell, "animate persons" are "relational beings, actors in a participatory world".[13] Within the Ojibwa myths, Thunderbirds are conceived of as acting like human beings. Other indicators of the animate nature of relational beings are movement, gift-giving and conversation.[14] Thus, "all beings communicate intentionally and act toward each other relationally: this makes them 'persons'".[15] In his definition of what a person is, Harvey argues that

> Persons are those with whom other persons interact with varying degrees of reciprocity. Persons may be spoken with. Objects, by contrast, are usually spoken about. Persons are volitional, relational, cultural and social beings. They demonstrate agency and autonomy with varying degrees of autonomy and freedom.[16]

In mythology and magic, the notions of personhood and relationality are fully expressed and, together with the concept of anthropomorphism, call into question the ways in which the ancient Mesopotamians engaged with and conceptualized their cosmos. Mountains, rivers and trees are all to be considered "other-than-human" persons, not only because of their external representation, but also because of their intentional acting within the community of different agents, and because they evince some moral and social features.

12 Frankfort 1977, 6.

13 Harvey 2013b, 125.

14 Harvey 2013b, 124. As Harvey further argues, commenting on Hallowell, "persons are known to be persons when they relate to other persons in particular ways. They might act more or less intimately, willingly, reciprocally or respectfully. Since enmity is also a relationship, they might act aggressively" (Harvey 2013b, 124). See also Chapter I, § 1.2.1 and § 1.2.5.

15 Harvey 2013b, 125. See also Levy-Bruhl's "law of participation" (1985), and Buber's I-You relational ontology and the "mystery of reciprocity" (1970) (Rochberg 2016, 52).

16 Harvey 2005, preface xvii; Hall 2011, 105. See also Chapter I, § 1.2.5.

Their physical representation displays an alternation, or rather a coexistence, of natural features and human-like features. The clearest evidence of this alternation is offered by the literary description of Ebiḫ, alternately portrayed as a bearded man with a divine status, and as a luxuriant mountain rich in lakes, trees and animals.[17] This coexistence of features finds its correspondence in the visual representations of mountain and river deities throughout the centuries. Indeed, mountains and rivers in their divine garb are portrayed with half-anthropomorphic and half-mountain/river bodies.[18] Trees are also described acting and interacting like humans: for instance, in the dialogue between the tamarisk and the date palm, the two trees are said to open their mouths in order to speak.[19] This evidence might refer to a rhetorical feature typical of literary metaphorical narration, but the actions and roles which are later ascribed to the trees speak for their more comprehensive personhood in Mesopotamian eyes.[20] Rivers, mountains, and trees are all conceptualized as actual rivers or mountains or trees, but they can also be described with human-like features.[21]

In the written evidence, these natural and topographical entities feature behavioral and moral specificities. Mountains are called upon on behalf of humans for their protecting and helping attributes, as much as for their mighty strength. Ebiḫ is not only addressed as a bearded man, tall and beautiful, but also due to his goodness, purity, divinity and rebellious spirit.[22] Rivers feature a motherly and nurturing personality, but they are also conceptualized as impartial judges, showing an ethical rigor which aims at keeping the cosmic order.[23] Trees show the most personalistic portrayals, being conceived of as sentient beings, with social features. Each species displays a peculiar personality: the palm tree is a wise and motherly arboreal person, whose social behavior is antithetic to the solitary tamarisk.[24]

Specific trees feature kinship with humans. Emblematic is the case of the palm tree, that is referred to as a wise brother to humans, and it is closely associated with the royal person. A totemic association of the king with the palm tree might be suggested if we assume the definition of totem argued by Descola, according to which a totemic relation comprises a set of shared physical and moral attributes that crosses the boundaries of

17 See Chapter II, § 3.2.
18 See Chapters II and III.
19 See Chapter IV, § 2.3.
20 The dialogical format presents several non-personal entities (e.g. the debate between gold and copper, or that of sheep and grain) acting as persons. But is also possible that only entities regarded as persons (or with personalistic traits) could be integrated into this mode of narration (Zgoll's personal communication).
21 For anthropomorphic and non-anthropomorphic gods, see Porter *et alii* 2009. On the matter of anthropomorphism, see Guthrie 1993. According to Guthrie, "religion essentially is anthropomorphism", and he bases his assumptions onto the "continuity between the human and nonhuman worlds in many cultures that do not draw sharp lines of distinctions between plants, animals, and humans –a view that is increasingly confirmed by the contemporary biological sciences" (quoted in Haberman 2013, 22). Moreover, for him "both animism and anthropomorphism are effective and universal perceptual strategies that are not only at the root of all religion, but are fundamental to all forms of human perception" (quoted in Haberman 2013, 23).
22 See Chapter II, and below § 2.2.1.
23 See Chapter III, and below § 2.2.2.
24 See Chapter IV, and below § 2.2.3.

species,[25] but should be further explored within Mesopotamian cosmology, ontology and epistemology.

Trees were widely utilized in ritual performances and were transformed into divine statues of the gods, or into protective statuettes with magical purposes. The transformation of the arboreal or plant person into a man-made cultic object should not be understood as a mere objectification nor as a loss of its intrinsic personhood. As noted by Harvey about artifacts made with wood,

> … the transformation of living persons from trees to 'artifacts' is not experienced as a destruction of life and personhood, nor their consequent transformation into artificiality. Human artifacts not only enrich the encounter between persons, but are often themselves experienced as autonomous agents.[26]

The bodies of those trees which were utilized for manufacturing the statues of the gods are addressed as the flesh or bones of the god. The god is incarnate in the wooden body of the tree, which, simultaneously, partakes of the divinity with its status of autonomous living being, in an intriguing network of symbolic and ritualistic aspects.[27]

Consequently, mountains, rivers and trees should be considered fully "other-than-human" persons, often partaking of the divinity within a sacred and relational cosmos. Following Harvey, we can argue that they are "superhuman but not supernatural. They are cosmic in a communal cosmos. They are powerful in relation to other beings, but remain kindred".[28]

2 From myths to magic: animism, analogism and the community of living beings

Further animistic attitudes are notable throughout the literature, the most eloquent case is offered by the description of the social habits of the Thunderbird in the Sumerian myth of *Lugalbanda and the Anzû-bird*. In this mythical account, the Anzû is portrayed with god-like features and human-like behavior. The Thunderbird is here equated to a god in its abode, manners and social habits. In its nest, its offspring is also described with human-like features and cultural attitudes: the bird's eyes are painted with kohl, and sprigs of white cedar adorn its head.[29] This evidence speaks for a proper animistic mode of identification between humans and nature, as argued by Descola. His notion of animism insists upon the fact that natural beings share dispositions and social attributes with humans, but have different external biological traits.[30] Furthermore, the fully divine nature and cosmic personhood ascribed to the Anzû is expressed with its self-proclamation as the one

25 Descola 2013a, 82. See Chapter I, § 2.2.3.
26 Harvey 2005, 56.
27 See Chapter IV, and below § 2.2.3.
28 Harvey 2013b, 103.
29 Wilcke 1969, 100–101: 93–95; ETCSL 1.8.2.2: 93–95.
30 Descola 1996, 87–88. See Chapter I, § 1.2.3.

appointed by Enlil as the prince who established the destinies of the rivers, and the custodian of access to the mountains:

íd Ḫal-ḫal-la nun nam tar-re-bi-me-en	"I am the prince who establishes the destiny of the "Rolling River",
zid-du šag$_4$ kúš-ù ^{d}En-líl-la-ka ^{ĝiš}igi-tab-bi-me-en	I watch over the righteous who takes counsel with Enlil.
a-a-ĝu$_{10}$ ^{d}En-líl-le mu-un-de$_6$-en	My father Enlil brought me here;
kur-ra ^{ĝiš}ig gal-gin$_7$ igi-ba bí-in-tab-en	He made me guard the entrance of the mountain like a great door.
nam ù-mu-tar a-ba-a šu mi-ni-ib-bal-e	If I decree a destiny, who shall change it?
inim ù-bí-dug$_4$ a-ba-a íb-ta-bal-e	If I say a word, who shall transgress it?
lú gùd-ĝá ne-en ba-e-a-ak-a	Whoever has done this to my nest:
diĝir ḫé-me-en inim ga-mu-ra-ab-dug$_4$	If you are a god, I will speak with you,
gu$_5$-li-ĝá nam-ba-e-ni-kur$_9$-re-en	Indeed, I will let you become my friend.
lú-ùlu ḫé-me-en nam ga-mu-ri-ib-tar	If you are a human, I will establish your destiny,
kur-re gaba-šu-ĝar nam-mu-ri-in-tuku-un	I will not let you have any rival in the mountains".[31]

From being the custodian of the mountains and of the rivers, and the establisher of destinies in accordance with the cosmic order appointed by Enlil, Anzû becomes the one who steals the Tablet of the Destinies in primeval times in the Akkadian mythical account. Here a completely different, contrasting consideration of the Anzû is on display, where the *Mischwesen* plays the role of a wicked Trickster, and is closely intertwined with his mountain, Šaššar. Bird and mountain will be both killed by the god Ninurta.[32] This evidence points to historical changes and developments between the Sumerian and Akkadian mythical and religious frameworks. However, the personality of this legendary character, which was connected with the sacred mountain and with the destinies of the world, engendered a profound legacy down the centuries.

Contrasting visions about the natural elements and their associated dwellers are notable not only between historically different and culturally distant literary compositions, but also within the same narrative. This evidence indicates that different and contrasting visions of the world and the divine can coexist within the same cultural and religious framework, and do not necessarily speak to different chronological stages nor cultures (i.e. Sumerian vs. Akkadian tradition). In the Sumerian myth *Inana and Ebiḫ*, Inana's will to destroy and tame Ebiḫ is contrasted with Anu's advice not to touch such a majestic and

31 Wilcke 1969, 100–103: 99–109; ETCSL 1.8.2.2: 99–109.

32 See Chapter III, § 3.3.

divine mountain, which is said to tower over the urban plain of Sumer with its temples. Thus, Inana's capricious will becomes a sacrilegious act toward a divine entity, which was protected by the same gods and partook of their divinity.[33] Also within Akkadian literature, contrasting theologies or cosmologies are notable, the most eloquent example being found in the Gilgameš Epic. The mission of Gilgameš and Enkidu against the Cedar Forest and its guardian Ḫuwawa shows two radically different worldviews. Ḫuwawa protects the forest with its cedar trees, and the mountain is addressed as partaking of the divine realm, being the abode of gods and goddesses. The synergy between the mountain, its custodian, and the trees speak to the envisioning of this sacred mountain as a holistic and animate organism permeated by sacredness. The notion of secrecy and mystery which enshrouds the Cedar Forest further affirms its belonging to the cosmic and divine realm.[34]

The killing of Ḫuwawa is followed by the felling of the cedar trees, which is described as a doubly sacrilegious act performed by the two heroes. Enkidu's remark to Gilgameš offers a further hint of the animate and sacred nature of the trees: he wonders why his royal companion should have destroyed the entire forest after killing its guardian. The cedar trees are referred to as living beings, which have been killed by the two daring heroes and transformed into mere timber, revealing a process of transformation from animate into inanimate.[35] The case of the Cedar Mountain and of Ḫuwawa might represent the clearest example of an "ecological" theology within the Mesopotamian religious framework. This theology or worldview sees nature partaking of the realm of the gods, who, as we have seen, do not merely inhabit the world, but also relate to and protect it. Indeed, the heroes' conscience knows that they are acting against the will of the gods and against the cosmic order, thus breaking a taboo. They are, in fact, hurrying in fear of the anger of the great gods, especially of Enlil, while leaving a wasteland behind.[36]

The notion of taboo is probably expressed by the Sumerian n í ĝ - g e $_{17}$ (g) and the Akkadian *ikkibu*, which both refer to something interdicted and forbidden.[37] Both terms denote something reserved for the gods, but do not involve any further concept of abomination which is on display, for instance, in the Biblical world.[38] Another Akkadian term which can be understood as somehow related to the modern notion of taboo is *māmītu*. This term is hardly understood, and is translated alternatively as "oath" or "curse" in English. Apparently, every entity partaking of the Mesopotamian cosmos possessed a *māmītu*: mountains, the Euphrates and trees are attested as having their own *māmītu*, which is a commonly shared feature of most entities in the Mesopotamian world. In the Sumerian milieu, every entity possessed a m e : for instance, Aratta is addressed to as the "mountain of the shining m e".[39] Its broad semantic utilization renders proper understanding, and, subsequently, translation, into a contemporary language, very hard.[40] At the present state of

33 See Chapter II, § 3.2.
34 See Chapter II, § 3.4.
35 See Chapter II, § 3.4.
36 See Chapter II, § 3.4.
37 See CAD I, 55–57, s.v. *ikkibu*: 1. "interdicted, forbidden thing, place or action"; 2. "sacred, reserved thing, place or action". Geller proposes the translations of "affront" or "offense" toward the deities.
38 Geller 1990, 105–117; Geller 2011/2013, 394–395.
39 See Chapter II, § 3.2.
40 It has been translated as "göttliche Kräfte" in German, "divine ordinances" in English and "fonctions

the scholarly discourse, it can be assumed that the m e refers to the conception of an immanent divine and to the intrinsically animate Sumerian cosmos. As a further support for this suggestion, it should be noted that m e is etymologically related to the verb m e , "to be", and it should be understood as the status of being, existing in the world.[41] All these terms should be considered together in a comprehensive attempt to explore their utilization in the different genres, in order to reach a general reassessment of Mesopotamian worldviews through their emic terminology and categories.[42]

What is notable in myths and incantations is a constant tension between a more "ecological" worldview, which tends to behave with a respectful and protective attitude toward the natural entities and to the cosmic order, and one which aims at objectifying and taming the natural world. Interestingly, these two worldviews appear both to belong to the same realm, presided over by the great anthropomorphic gods. Throughout literature, some transfers of genres and changes in religious beliefs and symbolic meanings are also traceable. Mountains and their mythical dwellers are defeated by the anthropomorphic gods, but they later reappear as divine entities worshipped in the temple (Ebiḫ) and called upon in the ritual performances as deities, or become tutelary animals of the gods (Anzû) during the 1st-millennium rituals.[43] Rivers are conceived of as flowing deities, which operate in the world as nurturing mothers, healers and judges, in cooperation with the great gods, but their traits are mingled with the god of water, Ea, and his cosmic divine dwelling, the Apsû, in a dense network of symbolic and ritualistic relations.[44] All this evidence should be further studied in greater detail according to the geographical and historical contexts, in order to shed light onto the peculiarities, differences and developments of the various traditions.

Anthropomorphic deities, non-anthropomorphic River- and Mountain-deities, sacred trees– all partake of a fluid religious framework within the ancient Mesopotamian panthea. Accordingly, the ancient Mesopotamians understood and related to a cosmos all of whose entities were connected and in relationship with each other, in a continuous exchange. This notion is fully expressed in the realm of magic, with its rituals and incantations.[45] According to Heeßel,

---

divines" in French (Farber 1987/1990, 610). See also Cavigneaux 1978, 177–185.

41 Farber 1987/1990, 610–613. See also Klein, who understands m e as a physical entity, such as an emblem or a standard of the deity, institution or office that it belonged to and which it represented (Klein 1997b).

42 See also the discussion of the different terms *šiknu* and *šīmtu* in Rochberg 2016, 90–92, pertinent to the appearance, property and nature of the plants used in the healing crafts. Notably, every being was also considered as having its own "destiny, fate" or even "nature"(?) (Sum. n a m , Akk. *šimtu*), which is decreed by the Sun on the cosmic Mountain of Sunrise at every daybreak.

43 See Chapter II. See also Gabbay 2018, 1–47, for his discussion on ancestral deities defeated by younger gods.

44 See Chapter III.

45 The term magic is still valid and should be maintained as should that of animism. Both terms are to be deprived of their evolutionistic and Cartesian legacy, since they represent still fertile categories which enhance the exploring of the ways in which non-western and ancient societies were engaging with their surroundings. See Schwemer 2011; Rochberg 2016, 149–163; Heeßel 2005,16–17.

Babylonian scholars have conceived all the things of nature as an (invisible) web woven from sympathies and antipathies and were interconnected. All things, be they stones, plants, wood, clay, metals or human constructions such as temples and streets thus have certain characteristics, qualities that attract or repel other things".[46]

These correlations and correspondences among the particular and individual entities of the world indicate an analogical type of correlation.[47] As pointed out by Descola, analogism refers to "the idea that all the entities in the world are fragmented into a multiplicity of essences, forms and substances separated by minute intervals, often ordered along a graded scale, such as in the Great Chain of Being that served as the main cosmological model during the Middle Ages and the Renaissance".[48] As seen, peculiar to analogism is the fusion of the contrasts of the different entities into a "dense network of analogies linking the intrinsic properties of each autonomous entity in the world".[49] Accordingly, in such systems any resemblance between entities constitutes a method of deduction and explanation of the life events, especially in the prevention and treatment of illness and adversity.[50] In this sense, "analogy plays an important part in both the literary and the scientific imagination as it did in the scholarly imagination of the scribes" of the cuneiform world.[51]

However, the evidence that has emerged throughout the present study points to a more complex understanding of what is generally defined as *materia magica*, with more nuanced boundaries between the analogical and the animistic modes of interaction between humans and natural entities. The network of correspondences is constituted by the different agents, or rather by the many "other-than-human" persons, which populated the Mesopotamian cosmos. Deities, demons, *Mischwesen*s, witches and spirits all existed and partook of the world, as much as mountains, rivers, trees and plants, to whom were ascribed the notions of personhood and, to a varying degree, of divinity.[52]

The explicit status as deities of mountains and, especially, of rivers, manifests their being conceived of as "other-than-human" persons, who would partake in and affect the life of humans according to their ascribed roles and agencies. Trees feature the clearest status of arboreal persons in Mesopotamian literature, with a complex and multifaceted relationship with humans and deities. Together with trees, plants and herbs are also attested as animate entities, especially in the magical realm of healing. Trees and plants are considered entities sacred to specific deities, while being autonomous cosmic beings, not created by the gods, but nurtured by them, in an intimate connection of botanical beings and anthropomorphic deities.[53] The so-called *Kutlmittelbeschwörungen*, which address plants, wood and trees, in

46 Heeßel 2005,16–17 (quoted and translated by Rochberg 2016, 154).

47 Rochberg 2016, 154.

48 Descola 2013a, 83. See Chapter I, § 2.2.3.

49 Descola 2013a, 83.

50 As pointed out by Rochberg, "connections were made between many ominous signs and their anticipated events where the connective tissue between them could be based on orthographies, homophony, or analogy between key words in the protasis and apodosis" (Rochberg 2016, 157).

51 Rochberg 2016, 156.

52 Schwemer 2011, 420.

53 See below § 2.2.3.

rituals are not to be considered merely as a tool to activate an inanimate *materia magica*, rather they offer a glimpse into their agencies in the healing crafts, and into their mythical, symbolic and cosmic place within the animate cosmos of ancient Mesopotamians.

Consequently, the definition of "embedded holistic elements within the theistic domain",[54] with its evolutionistic legacies and dichotomous vision, should be dismissed to leave space for a much more lively and dynamic cosmos, which displays, in my view, a blended coexistence of analogical and animist modes of interaction between humans and natural entities. The borders between these two modes of interaction should be understood as more nuanced and as often converging in the notion of personhood. In the therapeutic domain, the magical reality is fully permeated and inhabited by different kinds of forces and entities, which are connected to each other according to the associative system of analogism. These different entities are to be understood as "other-than-human" persons, which inhabited the Mesopotamian cosmos. The system of omens is another eloquent indicator for such a relational cosmos, where the gods could send signs and communicate with humans through the other dwellers of the world.[55] In such a relational cosmos, the notions of natural and supernatural,[56] and of immanent and transcendent, dissolve, leaving the ancient written sources to speak for different ontologies and epistemologies, where the concept of personhood plays a key role, together with its essential aspect of communication.[57]

The best definition for such a relational cosmos is offered by the relational aspect of the new animism. Differently from its metaphysical counterpart of Tylorian memory, the new understanding of animism should be considered not as "a deluded belief that everything is alive", but rather as a "sophisticated way of both being in the world and of knowing the world", thus being "a relational epistemology and a relational ontology".[58] The animistic universe is permeated by personalities, forces and spirits, which are interconnected and related to one another. According to Harvey, animist people "recognize that the world is full of persons, only some of whom are human, and that life is always lived in relationship with others".[59] As argued by Abram about modern indigenous magicians or healers in rural Asia:

> For the magician's intelligence is not encompassed within the society; its place is at the edge of the community, mediating between the human community and the larger community of beings upon which the village depends on its nourishment and

54 van Binsbergen/Wiggermann 1999, 3–34.

55 Rochberg 2016, 103–109. Rochberg further argues that "the Babylonian scribes's investment in magical ritual and incantations was predicated on the idea of divine communication, to appeal to the divine to effect desired changes in the world" (Rochberg 2016, 161).

56 As pointed out by Descola, commenting on Durkheim, "the supernatural is an invention of naturalism, which casts a complacent glance at its mythical genesis, a sort of imaginary receptacle into which one can dump all the excessive significations produced by minds said to be attentive to the regularities of the physical world but, without the help of the exact sciences, not yet capable of forming an accurate idea of them" (Descola 2013a, 82, quoted in Rochberg 2016, 162).

57 Rochberg 2016, 44; Harvey 2013b, passim.

58 Hall 2011, 105 (commenting on Harvey 2006).

59 Harvey 2006, xi.

> sustenance. This larger community includes, along with the humans, the multiple nonhuman entities that constitute the local landscape, from the diverse plants and the myriad of animals –birds, mammals, fish, reptiles, insects– that inhabit or migrate through the region, to the particular winds and weather patterns that inform the local geography, as well as the various landforms –forests, rivers, caves, mountains– that lend their specific character to the surrounding earth.[60]

Ancient Sumerian, Babylonian and Assyrian myths and incantations reveal the features of a world which is first and foremost a "community of living beings".[61] The best mythical example of this notion is offered by the literary narration of Enkidu's mourning in the Gilgameš Epic, where the entire cosmos is called upon in order to participate in his sorrow. All the "other-than-human" persons that have had an encounter (i.e. a relationship) with Enkidu in his life are invoked and participate in his funeral: the paths of the Cedar Forest, rivers, meadows, mountains, and the same cedar trees that were "killed" by the impious fury of the two young heroes, all share in the grief for the person they had known.[62]

Further animistic behaviors and attitudes are also notable in those scarce testimonies to tree worship in Mesopotamian lore. Within the rituals which were performed for producing protective wooden statuettes, rites of thanksgiving were held in front of two trees, the tamarisk and the *e'ru*-wood, before being cut.[63] These rites imply a respectful attitude toward the sacred arboreal persons, and bring us into the broader community of living beings that the ancient Mesopotamians lived in and engaged with. Offerings to the mountains and to the rivers are also attested in the cuneiform literature as ritual performances in order to communicate with the gods by the mean of dreams.[64] This evidence stresses the aspect of communication among the different beings of the cosmos.

The relational and personalistic features that are notable in myths and incantations should not be considered exclusive. As pointed out by Descola, the different modes of identifications are not mutually exclusive and can be organically present within a single society, or "each human may activate any of them according to circumstances".[65] It can thus be suggested that one of the ways in which reality was experienced, known and conceptualized in ancient Mesopotamian mythology and magic displays animistic, or rather personalistic, features to varying degrees. The notion of personhood which has been readdressed by the school of new animism, especially in its relational aspect, speaks to the ancient Mesopotamian notion of a "pervasively relational cosmos",[66] while shedding light

60 Abram 1996, 6–7.
61 Harvey 2013a, 2. See also Sahlins 2017, 121–123.
62 George 2003, 484–485; Rochberg 2016, 45. As argued by Rochberg, "these passages seem to reflect more of a connection between the human being and the environment than a separation of nature from culture" (Rochberg 2016, 45).
63 See Chapter IV, § 2.3 and § 2.7, and below § 2.2.3.
64 See Chapters III and IV.
65 Descola 2013a, 85.
66 Harvey 2013b, 102; Hall 2011, 105.

on the actual fluidity and sensuous reality of an ancient religion understood as a daily life experience.[67]

3 Mountains, rivers and trees: an entangled relationship

3.1 Cosmic, sacred and animate landscapes

Every landscape contains a dense network of meanings within the profusion and uniqueness of its topographical, geological and botanical features. Landscape is "the world as it is known by those who dwell therein",[68] and thus comes into existence through the encounter of humans with their surroundings, and becomes a place of imagination, memories and stories.[69] It includes an imaginary and conceptual formation, but also a sensorial one, with its sounds, smells, taste and touch, and its intrinsic dynamism and changing features.[70] According to Hirsch, a landscape contains and comprises "the meaning imputed by local people to their cultural and physical surroundings".[71] Thus, every landscape is also a cultural feature, "a cluster of images with both a local and a chronological extension".[72] A landscape can also be understood as a "heterarchy of related beings", as argued by another anthropologist, Rose, regarding the Aboriginal Australian conception of a sentient and subjective landscape.[73]

Talking about the Anatolian landscape, Harmanşah, argues for a holistic relationship between humans and natural elements which is clearly manifested in landscapes of water and rocks. In his view, "lakes, marshlands, river basins and prominent springs are holistic landscapes of water that are hybrid products of natural and cultural processes".[74] Hence, a landscape should be understood as "an animated ecology of live performances, a landscape of springs, mountains, lakes and rivers which participate in the political configuration of the world and the cultural makeup of what we consider as the Anatolian countryside".[75] A landscape is not made up only by the major political actors, but finds its multifaceted portrayal in the interactions of the local communities, which generate a proliferation of memories and stories.[76] In ancient Mesopotamia, mountains, with their static bulky

67 Harvey 2013b; Faure 2015.

68 Ingold 1993, 156.

69 Schama 1995; Nora 1989, 7–24; Hirsch *et alii* 1995; Black 2002, 41–61.

70 Black 2002, 41–43.

71 Hirsch *et alii* 1995, 1 (quoted in Black 2002, 43).

72 Black 2002, 44.

73 Rose 1999, 178 (quoted in Hall 2011, 107). Talking about Aboriginal Australian landscape, Rose further argues that "subjectivity, in the form of consciousness, agency, morality and law is part of all forms and sites of life, of non-human species of plants and animals, of powerful beings such as Rainbow Snakes, and of creations sites, including trees, hills and waterholes" (Rose 1999, 178).

74 Harmanşah 2015, 55–56.

75 Harmanşah 2015, 55–56.

76 Harmanşah continues his argument, pointing out the relevance of the local communities in the formation of a landscape: "Like elsewhere, in Anatolia intimate cultural engagements of local communities with the mineral world, especially with the geological features such as springs, caves, sinkholes, river gorges and prominent rock outcrops resulted in locally distinct cultural practices and forms of storytelling

presence, and rivers, with their flowing and dynamic corporality, were integral and constitutive parts of the "living sacred geography",[77] which was shared by Sumerians, Babylonians and Assyrians, albeit each with their own peculiar beliefs and conceptions according to their local landscape and chronological framework.[78]

The distant mountains were a crown encompassing the Mesopotamian plain from East to West, and they assumed the traits of cosmic entities, where a state of pristine purity reigned beyond the boundaries of urban civilization. The cosmic mountain is an *axis mundi*, and represents the temple in the wilderness. An intriguing dialectic between mountain and temple is noticeable in the cuneiform cultures: the temple embodies the microcosm, while mirroring the macrocosm (i.e. the mountain).[79] The ziggurat is, indeed, the mirror of the mountain, as attested both in its architectural features, which represent the main topographical elements of a landscape charged with a dense network of symbolic meanings (e.g. the Apsû, and trees as guardians of its gates), and in the actual names given to the temples (e.g. É.KUR, "House-of-the-Mountain").[80] The cosmic mountain, which is referred to in the cuneiform sources as Dukug, the Holy Mound, is also the mountain which gives birth to the cosmic springs, where the pure pristine water pours out from the Apsû and generates the cosmic sacred rivers in the legendary location of the *pī nārāti*.[81]

Rivers are deities of flowing waters, and dynamic cosmic entities of the sacred animate landscape. They feature a kinship with the mountains and a deep entanglement with the path of the Sun: they are envisioned flowing down from the cosmic Mountain of Sunrise, where the Sun emerges every morning on the eastern horizon after its nocturnal trip underground. It is at this precise moment that the destiny of every being is decreed at every daybreak. This close association of the River with the Sun explains the judicial personality of the River god in the garb of the divine River Ordeal.[82] Rivers are also entangled with the western horizon, where the Sun sets after its trip through the sky, thus assuming infernal features. The north-western rivers Ḫubur and Baliḫ, and the eastern Ulāya, are referred to as infernal and chthonic rivers in Mesopotamian cosmology.[83] The netherworld characteristics of these watercourses are ascribed to the believed underground path of the Sun during the night, in the region of darkness which was associated with the netherworld and/or the Apsû. Accordingly, rivers were conceived of as channels of communication between humans and spirits, ancestors and deities.[84]

By virtue of being vertical columns which connect the depths of the earth and the heights of the sky, trees are conceived of as media and as *axis mundi* in Mesopotamian cosmology. In their cosmic garb, trees are often associated with and equated to the mountains in the mythical narrative. Moreover, specific trees became landmarks for those

---

around them. In reaching out to the nature of these specific practices of place-making, one must be cautious not to prioritize imperial visions of local landscapes" (Harmanşah 2015, 56).

77 Haberman 2011, 38.

78 Black 2002; Harmanşah 2015.

79 See Horowitz 1998; Black 2002.

80 See the Sumerian *Hymns for the Temple*, and George 1993.

81 See Chapter III, § 3.

82 See Chapter III, § 2.

83 See Chapter III, § 4.4.

84 See Chapter III.

mountainous lands beyond the urban plain, with its most famous iconographical example being the Stele of Narām-Sîn.[85] This stele comprises one of the earliest representations of a landscape in ancient Near Eastern art, while commemorating the king's victory over enemies living at the borders of the Akkadian empire. The setting, where the narrative of the Akkadian king takes place, is represented both naturalistically and symbolically. The accurate portrayal of the defeated enemies (with their foreign dress and hairstyles), and of the trees on the slopes of the mountain, aims at marking a precise territory, land and frontier.[86] The mountain represents a conquered hostile land, which is inhabited by the Lullubeans and by its trees: the whole composition and association of mountain+trees+foreigners stand for the otherness of the mountainous lands which stood to the northwest, north, northeast and east of Babylonia.[87] Thus, the cosmic and liminal nature ascribed to the mountain in the eyes of the Mesopotamians is affirmed and highlighted.

A particular entanglement between mountains, trees and rivers is on display in the cosmology of the eastern horizon. The literary and iconographical motif of the Twin Peaks Mountain points to the notion of the cosmic landscape on the eastern horizon, conceived of as a holistic landscape inhabited by divine, fluvial and arboreal beings. As seen portrayed on a seal, the slopes of the cosmic mountain were the setting of mythical and cosmic stories which feature as main characters the goddess Inana, the gods Enki and Utu, the Anzû-bird, and the cosmic tree of the eastern horizon, probably to be understood as an e r e n -tree or a ḫ a l u b -tree.[88]

3.2 "Other-than-human" persons and deities

3.2.1 Mountains: rebellious deities, protectors and mighty persons

In the Mesopotamian literary and religious tradition, mountains are conceived of not only as cosmic topographical entities, but also 1) as the abode of the gods, with a close and intriguing relationship with deities; 2) as "other-than-human" persons with protecting, purifying and motherly attributes. 3) Some specific mountains feature divine qualities, especially when entangled with other mythical figures and deities, 4) while fewer are regarded as deities *per se*.

1) Mountains are associated with the anthropomorphic deities, in a complex symbolic and religious network. Ninḫursag, the "Lady-of-the-Mountain" or "Lady-Mountain", is closely intertwined with the same mountain, being its lady and its guardian at the same time.[89] Inana/Ištar displays a more controversial relationship with the mountainous person:

---

85 Winter 1999, 73, fig 1.

86 The trees here have been identified as an indigenous oak (*Quercus aegilops*) of the middle ranges of the mountains in modern Iraqi Kurdistan. Given such accuracy in the botanical knowledge of the arboreal species in a precise territory, the trees are to be understood as acting as topoi in the stele's narrative (Winter 1999, 70–72).

87 Winter 1999, 68. As pointed out by Winter, the Akkadians "were marking their awareness of the distinction us/not us, projected onto the land" (Winter 1999, 72).

88 See Chapter III, § 1.

89 See Chapter II, § 2.1.

the same goddess is alternatively referred to as she who gave birth to the mountain, bathing on the mountain of carnelian, and as one of the deities that aspires to destroy and conquer the mountains.[90] The champion of subduing the mountains is the god Ninurta, whose main attributes of warrior and conqueror over the mountainous wilderness stretch down the millennia, from the Sumerian to the Akkadian traditions. Another god whose traits mingle with those of the mountain is Enlil, who is considered the god inhabiting the lower heaven, located over the horizon, where the mountains' peaks pierce the sky. The notion of this deity being compared to a big mountain is expressed by his main epithet, KUR.GAL, the "Great Mountain", or when it is simply referred to as ^{d}KUR. The gods belonging to the north-western horizon feature a particularly close connection with the mountains. Gods such as Martu/Amurru and Bazi are gods deeply entangled with the mountains: they are the deities of the mountain people, the Amorites, who were associated with mountains and with shepherding also in the Southern Mesopotamian panthea.[91]

Other gods are traditionally associated with the mountains. As we saw in an Old Babylonian incantation, the divine Mountain is called upon together with Adad, Šakkan, Id and Šamaš.[92] These deities are called the holy gods of the mountains, and are invoked for their purifying and healing powers. Adad is the gods of storms and rain in the Mesopotamian pantheon, and his abode is traditionally believed to be on the mountains' peaks. Šakkan is the god of wild animals and of wildlife in general, while being the son of Šamaš, the divine judge of mankind and the supreme healer, too. Id, the divine River embodying the River Ordeal, is closely related to the Mountain, whose name can actually refer to either the mountain or the River Ordeal. As noticed before, in this literary context, the Mountain lacks any determinative which would clearly characterize it as a deity, but its being included in a list of gods speaks to its agency and divinity.[93]

2) In the rituals, mountains are often called upon as "other-than-human" persons, and are sometimes conceptualized as deities. Mountains are invoked for their protecting and healing powers: they are conceptualized as protective beings, and are objects of devotion because of their attributes of power and physical might. The actions typically ascribed to the Mountain-person are: to cover, to hold, to enshroud, to counteract and to fall upon any malevolent agent which dares to oppose and threaten the supplicant who turns to the mighty mountain. Moreover, a recurrent metaphor associated with the mountain is that of a wall, or of a barrier around the country.[94] The mountain embodies and creates a protecting wall against evil forces, which are to be dispelled beyond it. In this understanding, the mountain is envisioned both in its topographical and cosmic garb and as a person, often with divine attributes.

The powerful personality of the mountain is well expressed by the incantations that aim at calming the different natural and cosmic elements –such as mountains, rivers and the sea–, as attested in the ritual *Šurpu*.[95] Interestingly, in another incantation, the patient is

90 See Chapter II, § 3.2.
91 See Chapter II, § 3.3.
92 See Chapter II, § 2.3.
93 See Chapter II.
94 See especially the case of Ebiḫ (Chapter II, § 3.2).
95 See Chapter II, § 2.3.

compared to a mountain that is said to be calmed down by sulphur.[96] This evidence raises the question on the question on the cultic and therapeutic use of sulphur and on its connection with the river and its flowing waters. Might it be a reference to the sensorial experience of water flowing in a mountainous setting, which was re-enacted during the ritual performance? If this is the case, this evidence would project into the sensorial dimension of the ritual performance with its healing and calming effects on the human body.[97]

The therapeutic attributes of the mountain are to be ascribed to the notion of the mountain as the place of pristine purity. In *Maqlû*, the patient wishes to become pure like the River in his own mountain. In this context, both the waters of the River and its mountainous origin allude to the notion of purity which informs both natural entities. Mountains are also portrayed as motherly figures, despite the lack of any direct reference as mothers. Despite their masculine traits, in opposition to the predominantly feminine attributes of rivers, mountains are viewed as giving birth to several entities. Due to their pristine purity, mountains are a recurrent and privileged place of origin of pure entities (water, plants and trees, honey, incense, stones), but also of threatening ones (demons, witches, and foreigners). Mountains also give birth to gods and *Mischwesen*. In an Old Babylonian prayer, the goddess Nisaba is referred to as the offspring of the mountains,[98] featuring an interesting kinship between mountains and deities. Specific mountains gave birth to some mythical characters which have been famous for millennia in the Mesopotamian traditions: the Anzû-bird and Ḫuwawa, the custodian of the Cedar forest.[99]

Conversely, in the Mesopotamian symbolic framework, mountains are brought to the world by the waters of the rivers. The Ḫalḫalla, the legendary river on the eastern mountains, which merged later with the Tigris, is called the "mother of the mountains".[100] This notion not only speaks of the conception of the rivers as life-generating entities of all life, even mineral life, but also the kinship between these two entities. The close connection between the mountain and the river is stressed by the ritual and mythical references to the practice of the River Ordeal.[101]

3) Specific mountains feature divine traits, but without being fully envisioned as deities. The Sumerian Aratta is called the mountain of the shining m e,[102] while mount Šaššar appears as the setting of a dense network of divine characters, while being itself believed as a mountain with numinous and divine traits. The literary Šaššar, whose more prosaic name is Bašār, was entangled with Amurru, the shepherd god of the Amorites, Bazi, the divine ram, Ea, Šakkan, Šamaš and the divine River, Id. Moreover, Šaššar is referred to as the birth place of the Anzû in the Akkadian tradition, where it is said to be born from the very rocks of the mountain, thus partaking of its nature. Mountain and Thunderbird are seen

96 See Chapter III, § 2.1.

97 The psychological and physical aspects involved in the healing performances should also be explored within the Mesopotamian context, especially regarding the sensorial dimension of the rituals and its effects on the distressed body.

98 UET 6/3, 579–584: 51 (Hallo 1970, 123–130; Sullivan 1980, 97–103).

99 See above, § 1.2.

100 See Chapter III, § 4.1.2 for the syncretism of these two rivers from the 2nd millennium onward.

101 See Chapters III and IV.

102 See Chapter II, § 3.2.

as belonging to one another, and Šaššar is explicitly called his mountain, the inaccessible mount.[103]

Šaššar and the Cedar Mountain are specifically said to be killed together with their famous custodians and dwellers.[104] This evidence indicates the notion of those mountains conceptualized as "other-than-human" persons. Enshrouded by a mystical aura, the Mountain of Ḫuwawa offers the best example of a holistic and entangled relationship between the mountain, with its forest, trees, animals and guardian, and the divine realm in Akkadian mythology.[105]

4) Mounts Dipar and Saggar demonstrate an autonomous status of deities in some periods and locations throughout Mesopotamian history. Dipar was envisioned as a divine mountain or Mountain deity *per se* in the Old Akkadian and Old Assyrian periods, while it re-appears recorded in the rituals of the pantheon of Aššur, as a recipient of offerings, together with Ebiḫ, and the rivers Ulāya and Tigris. The equation of Saggar with ^{d}HAR points to the understanding of this mount as the divine mountain range Jebel Sinjar, which is still considered a sacred mountain by the Yazidis to the present day.[106]

In Mesopotamian religious views, there are two mountains which feature a more elaborate conceptualization as deities: Ebiḫ and Aššur. Ebiḫ has a fully divine status, and appears to be envisioned as a half-anthropomorphic and half-topographical deity. Anthropomorphic and naturalistic aspects are entangled in the description of this Mountain deity, as if they are the two complementary and essential natures of the same divine being. In his anthropomorphic representation, Ebiḫ is conceptualized as a bearded man, who features all traits typically ascribed to a deity. Ebiḫ is said to be arrogant and not submissive toward the goddess Inana, and to have spread its fearful splendor, *melammu*, upon the lands overwhelming the land. Its mystical shining aura alludes to the divinity and power of the mountain, whose divine traits are further expressed by its connotations of beauty, elevation, goodness, dignity and even rebellious spirit. It is noteworthy that physical and moral attributes are used in the description of this Mountain god.[107] Ebiḫ's masculinity is further expressed and attested in the personal names which include Ebiḫ as a theophorous element. In the personal devotion to Ebiḫ as mirrored by the onomastic, his major role is to offer protection and support to his devotees. Moreover, Ebiḫ appears connected to shepherding and to wild life. In the ritual setting of the Neo-Assyrian empire, Ebiḫ is called upon as one of the protecting and healing deities, and is mentioned as a recipient of offerings.[108]

Another major mountain who entered the pantheon of the great gods is Aššur. The mysterious identity of this god should be understood as the result of a process which started from the veneration of a hill as a numinous and sacred mound, through the same mountain achieving fully divine status and entering the pantheon of the Assyrian gods, and culminating in becoming the king of the gods and representing the people of Assyria in the 1st millennium B.C.E.[109]

---

103 See Chapter II, § 3.3.
104 See Chapter II, § 3.3.
105 See Chapter II, § 3.4, and above, § 1.2 .
106 See Chapter II, § 3.1.
107 See Chapter II, § 3.2.
108 See Chapter II, § 3.2.
109 See Chapter II, § 3.6.

The cults of Ebiḫ, of Aššur and of the collective mountains in the Neo-Assyrian religious framework attest a lively religious life of the mountains in the Assyrian context. Due to the mountainous topography of the Assyrian landscape, a proper devotion to the mountains, with an organic religious and mythological network of significances, is fully expressed.[110] Offerings to the mountains as a propitiatory way to get an ominous dream are performed by the same Gilgameš on the top of the each mountain constituting the Lebanon mountain range. However, this is the only literary evidence of cultic practices performed on and for the mountains.[111]

3.2.2 Deities of flowing waters

The River is a polyvalent and fluid entity, which comprises multifaceted conceptions and an intrinsic duality. Some major symbolic and religious notions informed the beliefs and cults on the rivers, which feature a widespread divine status within ancient Mesopotamian religious life. Their features of deity and "other-than-human" person along with their topographical and cosmic nature, are often all expressed together and intertwined. The River 1) comprises an intrinsic duality, and is conceived of 2) as the mother of all life, 3) closely related with the great gods and the Apsû, 4) as a great purifier and healer by virtue of its pure water, and 5) as a severe and impartial judge of mankind, simultaneously presiding over and embodying the River Ordeal. 6) Its divinity is further expressed by the attestations of worship of certain rivers throughout the ages and according to the location. Offerings, prohibitions on entering its waters and the personal names of those devoted to the rivers all indicate an intriguing religious and devotional life of these flowing deities. 7) Rivers are also portrayed as guardians and protectors of life and cities, and 8) were understood as communication channels between earthly and cosmic dimensions.

1) The River features an intrinsic and widespread duality, which is reflected in its gender alternation, as attested both in the literary and iconographical sources, and can be ascribed to both physical and symbolic attributes. This duality can refer to the terminal points of a watercourse (i.e. source and delta), to its upper and lower traits, to an alternation of underground and overground traits, between darkness and light, and also to its opposing banks. Moreover, it is a twofold and contradictory entity, which gives life and death at the same time: its waters bring bounty to the land, but can also carry away everything.[112] The attributes of self-renewing and self-regenerating ascribed to the River speak to its intrinsic duality. Accordingly, the River can be seen as a hermaphrodite being, which is able to regenerate itself. This notion can offer a clue regarding its gender alternation, which is a peculiar and widespread phenomenon in ancient Mesopotamia.[113]

2) In its female garb, the River is conceptualized as a goddess, the mother of all beings. The clearest expression of the motherly notion of the River goddess is presented in the River Incantation. In this widely attested text, the River is called upon as the "creatress

110 See Chapter II.
111 See Chapter II, § 3.4.
112 See Chapter III, § 2.
113 See Chapter III, § 2.

of everything".[114] The life-giving and divine attributes of the River are expressed in an incantation preserved in *Šurpu*, where the River is addressed as the "River of the gods, who has borne everything".[115] Through being characterized by life-giving and creating attributes, the River is thus envisioned as a mother with all the meanings involved in motherhood: it is a regenerating and nurturing goddess, who takes care of all life and provides abundance and fertility to every creature, from the pure waters which comprise their body, to plants, trees, to animals, to humans, to mountains, and even to the gods and the cosmic entities.

Specific rivers are clearly addressed as mothers, especially in personal names and in their accompanying epithets. The Tigris and the Euphrates are both conceptualized as mothers, as attested in personal names, and are connected to bounty and abundance in the epithets of the *Lipšur Litanies*. The Tigris in particular features motherly and fully divine attributes. As recorded in the personal names, the Tigris was conceptualized as a nurturing mother and as a merciful and attentive goddess, who listened to the prayers of her devotees, but also demanded proper worship. Moreover, the Tigris was considered the mother of animals (i.e. reptiles) and of the mountains themselves. The mountains were conceived of as having been generated by the flowing waters of the rivers Ḫalḫalla and Tigris. These two rivers display a syncretism which occurred during the 2nd millennium, according to which the Ḫalhalla, the legendary eastern river of the Sumerian cosmological horizon, merged into the Tigris, which assumed the epithet of "mother-of-the-mountains".[116] Other specific rivers which feature motherly attributes are the Duran, which is called the "mother of the rivers" itself, and the Araḫtum.[117] The latter is a main affluent of the Euphrates and is conceptualized as a nurturing mother in personal names, and is referred to as "the one that brings life to Babylon", in a clear allusion to the life-bringing power of the watercourses to the entirety of the human communities and their cities.[118]

3) The River has a multifaceted and profound relationship with the great gods. The River appears as a cosmic generating principle, while being created by the great gods (i.e. Enki, Anu and Enlil). This notion is expressed both in the incantations and in the myths. In the River Incantation, the River is said to be excavated by the great gods, while in the Sumerian and Akkadian traditions the two main rivers are said to be the offspring of some body parts of the gods. The Tigris and the Euphrates are said to be generated by Enki's sperm (male principle) in the Sumerian tradition, while from the dismembered divine body of the ancestral mother, Tiamat (female aquatic principle), in the Akkadian *Enūma Eliš*.[119] Presumably, the conception of the divine River as the primeval mother-goddess merged with the other attributes ascribed to the River, engaging with the realm of the great gods.[120]

It is worth noting a particular dialectic relationship between the River and the Apsû, with its divine dweller, the god Enki/Ea. In its epithet of "mother of the Apsû", the

114 See Chapter III, § 2.
115 See Chapter III, § 2.
116 See Chapter III, § 4.1.2.
117 See Chapter III, § 4.3.
118 See Chapter III, § 4.3.
119 See Chapter III, § 4.1.1.
120 See Chapter III, § 2.

motherly nature of the River is expressed, along with its purifying and healing powers.[121] This epithet aims at establishing and reinforcing the River's dialectic relationship with the Apsû, which is traditionally considered the cosmic and divine place where sweet pristine waters form in the underground, and which is often referred to as the depths of the River.[122] The Apsû is the abode of Enki/Ea, the god of waters and of wisdom, who is also involved in the healing crafts. Moreover, it is through the waters of the rivers and through its watery monsters, the Laḫmu, that humans can get in touch with Ea. This notion further affirms the dialectic of the river as a person, as a deity and as a channel of communication. Another deity closely connected with the river is Namma, Enki's mother, a water deity who controls the cosmic gates whence flow the rivers. This goddess inhabits the river and she was the recipient of offerings, as attested in an Old Babylonian incantation, where she is offered precious metals and stones in return for her water.[123]

4) The powerful healing agency of the River is fully expressed in the realm of incantations and rituals which aim at dispelling any evil, defilement and disease. Both the divine River (Id) and specific rivers are called upon during the purifying rituals, which are often held (partially or entirely) on the river bank.[124] Further insights into the healing and purifying attributes of the rivers are found in the epithets of specific rivers, and in the association with those deities involved in the therapeutic arts. The Tigris is recorded as part of the entourage of Gula, the healing goddess in the Neo-Assyrian royal rituals,[125] while the Me-kalkal is addressed as "healer of (every) living being" in the *Lipšur Litanies*.[126]

5) The divinity of the River derives both from the life-generating power of its waters, and from their purifying and cleansing nature, which constitute the conceptual basis for the practice of the River Ordeal. The River was conceived of as one of the great cleansers of mankind: its waters are believed to be half-life and half-death in the *Song of Bazi*.[127] These attributes informed the notion of the River as an impartial judge, who often accompanied the Sun, the supreme judge of mankind, during the rituals. The deep connection of the River with Utu/Šamaš is fully expressed in the anti-witchcraft rituals and incantations, where the two divine judging and purifying deities are often called upon together.[128] This occurrence speaks to the cosmic and symbolic framework of the conception which sees the Sun emerging from the cosmic mountain in the East where the destinies are established at every daybreak and from which the cosmic river flows, carrying its pure and healing waters.[129]

In the legal practice of the River Ordeal, the River comprises both the role of the divine judge presiding over the establishment of the verdict, and the physical body of the divine River Ordeal itself. In its judicial garb, the River is generally referred to by the name Id and features male traits. The Sumerian river Id-kura is the embodiment of the Ordeal and

121 See Chapter III, § 2 and § 3.
122 See Chapter III, § 3.
123 CUSAS 32, II.A.6 (George 2016, 64–65).
124 See Chapter III.
125 See Chapter III, § 4.1.3.
126 See Chapter III, § 4.3.
127 See Chapter III, § 2.
128 See Chapter III, § 2.
129 See Chapter III, § 2.

of the infernal characterizations ascribed to the River in association with this legal practice. Moreover, its epithet of "Man-Eating-River" (Idlurugu) clearly expresses this essential feature of Mesopotamian rivers.[130] In the Akkadian context, the divine River, Id, should be mainly identified with the Euphrates. This assumption is based on the joint evidence of the actual settings of the River Ordeal and of a proper worship of the divine River. The cult of the divine River, Id, is consistently attested in the cities of Tuttul, Mari, Hit, and Sippar, particularly during the 2nd millennium. The actual legal practice of the River Ordeal was mainly performed along the course of this river, particularly at Hit, a locality famous for its thermal and sulphurous springs.[131]

6) The fully divine status of the River, both referred to as the generic deity Id, and regarding specific rivers, is demonstrated by those attestations of cultic actions and religious conceptions toward the River deity. Along the course of the Euphrates, the divine River, Id, was worshipped from the 3rd to the 2nd millennium. The emblematic cases of the cities of Mari and Sippar speak of a profound devotion toward the fluvial deity. Personal names, offerings and royal letters attest a particular piety and worship, with the River addressed and praised as lord, god, judge and protector. As seen throughout this book, the Euphrates features a marked gender alternation and it is often recorded with a dual or plural form. The Euphrates is referred to as a mother when clearly addressed as *Purattu*, while it appears mainly concetualized as a masculine deity when referred to as Id. This evidence leads to the suggestion, supported by the iconographical representations of the River, that the Euphrates was conceptualized as a dyad.[132]

The gender alternation featured by the Euphrates is not notable in the conceptualizations of the Tigris, which appears generally conceived of as a motherly goddess, skilled in the healing and nurturing crafts. The divine Tigris is attested as a recipient of offerings already in the Ur III period, and is attested in some Old Babylonian and Neo-Assyrian god lists as part of the entourage of the healing gods Ea and Gula. A devotion to the Tigris as a nurturing mother of all creatures and with fully divine status is attested in Assyria from the 2nd millennium onward: its motherly, merciful and healing personality is mentioned in personal names and in royal rituals.

Other rivers display a fully divine status, in various locations and in different periods. The Baliḫ was conceptualized as a god in Abū Salabiḫ and Ebla during the 3rd millennium and in Mari during the Old Babylonian period.[133] The divinity of this north-western river continues until the 1st millennium, when it is recorded as a god in the anti-witchcraft incantations. The Ulāya is attested as a sacred river, as an "other-than-human" person in the rituals, and as a proper deity. This eastern river was conceptualized as a life-generating entity and as a proper god in Assyria from Old Assyrian times onward. This fluvial deity was regarded and worshipped as a protective and apotropaic god, particularly associated with guarding the gates of the city of Aššur.[134] The Ḫabur displays divine attributes in the Ur III documentation and in Neo-Assyrian personal names. Its divinity is expressed

130 See Chapter III, § 4.2.
131 See Chapter III, § 2.
132 See Chapter III.
133 See Chapter III, § 4.4.1.
134 See Chapter III, § 4.4.3.

especially in the form of a divine couple, Ḫabur and Ḫaburtu, in the Neo-Assyrian rituals and god lists.[135]

Daban, an eastern affluent of the Tigris, was the object of devotion as a deity in an area stretching from western Akkad through the Diyala region in the 3rd millennium, and is attested being venerated as a proper god particularly in Tutub.[136] The Diyala was also conceptualized with a divine status in the 3rd millennium until the Old Babylonian period, and re-emerged as a powerful "other-than-human" person in the 1st-millennium purifying rituals. In a Neo-Assyrian ritual, the Diyala occurs together with the Tigris, the Euphrates and the Upper and Lower Zab. The two Zabs are also recorded as deities, being mentioned among the gods of the land of Aššur in the Neo-Assyrian royal rituals.[137]

With its body of flowing water, which is healing and purifying, generating and destroying, the River was considered a proper non-anthropomorphic (or half-anthropomorphic) deity (either female or male according to the context). Its cosmic and life-generating agency merges with the role of impartial judge to mankind, and with its purifying and expunging attributes. These three concepts are deeply rooted and entangled with regard to the River person and deity in the Mesopotamian worldview.

7) Protective features are also ascribed to the rivers. Along with trees, they are considered guardians. The case of the river Ulāya addresses this notion. In its divine garb, the Ulāya was associated with the gates of city of Aššur and clearly conceptualized as the guardian of the city. Thus, the Ulāya should be considered as an apotropaic deity in charge of the city gates, while also being a healer god in virtue of its fluvial nature. The role of guardian of the thresholds (of human communities and of the realm of the dead) is a further hint of the netherworld nature of rivers.[138]

8) Rivers are not only natural borders and landmarks which separate territories and cities, but also communication channels between the diverse dimensions of the Mesopotamian cosmos. These conceptions feature in the netherworld features of the rivers. Ḫubur, Baliḫ and Ulāya all display the characteristics of either encircling the netherworld itself, constituting an obligatory access to the realm of the dead, or leading to it. Their flowing waters not only carry the spirits of the dead into the underworld, but can transport malevolent and benevolent creatures, ancestors and gods, thus comprising a medium between the human communities above ground and the underground dimensions.[139]

Offerings to the river in order to receive dreams, incubation rites and purification rituals are all different ways to engage with the fluvial entity and with the divine realm. Evidence of offerings to the rivers, generally animals or wheat products, further attest to the sacredness and divinity ascribed to these watery presences.[140] Moreover, a reference to a prohibition on immersing in the waters of the Id-sala is attested in the Sumerian myth *Enlil and Ninlil*, where this river is explicitly addressed as holy.[141] This evidence sheds new light into the religious life of certain rivers in Mesopotamian lore.

135 See Chapter III, § 4.4.2.
136 See Chapter III, § 4.3.
137 See Chapter III, § 4.3.
138 See Chapter III, § 4.4.3.
139 See Chapter III, § 4.4 and § 5.
140 See Chapter III, § 5.
141 See Chapter III, § 4.2.

3.2.3 Trees and plants: bones of the gods, healers and brothers

The cases of trees and plants differ from the cases of the major topographical entities, such as mountains and rivers, because of their predominant lack of fully divine attributes. However, trees and plants comprised several entangled meanings in the eyes of the ancient Mesopotamians, and they fully emerge as "other-than-human" persons. They were conceptualized as 1) cosmic entities, pillars of the world and mediums between dimensions and their inhabitants, and as 2) sacred, protecting and healing "other-than-human" persons. The vegetal and arboreal entities 2a) engaged with the anthropomorphic gods, with benevolent and malevolent beings, and with humans in a dense network, 2b) but also feature autonomous agencies, individual personalities and 2c) a powerful kinship with gods and humans. 3) Particular trees are clearly understood to partake of the divine in those cases where they are called flesh or bones of the deities. 4) Their conceptualization as sacred and living beings is further expressed by the scarce evidence of thanksgiving rites.

1) In their cosmic garb, trees and plants are connecting entities between the height of the sky and the depths of the earth. The traditional portrayal envisions trees and plants with their roots deepening into the Apsû, and their branches stretching into the heavens. Accordingly, trees are the abode of certain deities or other beings: Utu/Šamaš and Anu are envisioned as dwelling between the branches of the cosmic tree, while Enki/Ea lives among its roots. The eagle-tree is specifically conceived of as the abode of the Anzû and a tree sacred to Enki, while the cedar trees are protected by and intertwined with the legendary figure of their guardian, Ḫuwawa. Another tree sacred to Enki is the *kiškanû*, which was probably planted within the sanctuary of this god in Eridu. Malevolent beings (i.e. an Anzû-bird, a poisonous snake and the ghost of a prematurely dead maiden) are said to infest the *ḫuluppu*-tree after its being planted by the holy feet of Inana.[142]

2) Trees are not only the abode of deities and other beings: they feature a multifaceted portrayal with a complex network of entangled meanings. Trees and plants are conceptualized as proper "other-than-human" persons, with agencies and specific roles in the cult and within the religious and mythical framework. They are referred to as sacred entities, featuring wisdom and purity, and display particular healing attributes. Hence, they occur consistently in the purifying and healing rituals, where they play major roles together with other entities. Trees –such as the tamarisk, the cedar, the palm tree, the juniper, the *kiškanû*-tree, and the *e'ru*-wood– and plants –such as the *maštakal*-soapwort, the 'heals-a-thousand'-plant, the 'wood-of-release', the *kukru*-plant and all those plants and herbs invoked and utilized during the anti-witchcraft rituals– are widely attested comprising diverse and powerful healing and evil-dispelling attributes and properties.[143]

2a) Their purifying and benevolent agency towards the life of humans is to be understood by virtue of their connections with the different cosmic and earthly realms, and with the deities and spirits inhabiting these realms and the corresponding parts of the arboreal persons. Trees and plants are conceptualized as repositories of gods and benevolent spirits, especially during the ritual performance: through their physical and active presence in the rituals, the associated benign entities were also participating in the

142 See Chapter IV.
143 See Chapter IV.

healing rite. However, they should not be considered as mere activated *materia medica* and *magica*, but rather as animate beings which feature a precise agency and personal traits, partaking of the sacred and relational cosmos of ancient Mesopotamians. The so-called *Kultmittelbeschwörungen*, which accompany several incantations proffered during the ritual procedures, offer insights into the religious and symbolic framework in which trees and plants are immersed.

Some trees and plants were sacred to the gods themselves. This notion is expressed in those literary passages where plants and trees are said to be born in the pristine wilderness, and then to be nurtured by the gods, who brought them from their original places of pristine purity into the urban temple and palace orchards. The divine gardener of the gods is said to take care of these pure and precious entities, that played independent symbolic and cosmic roles within the religious life of the ancient Mesopotamians. They were conceived of as sacred entities, associated with specific deities and entities, and they were probably subject to devotion within the sanctuaries of the anthropomorphic deities to whom they were sacred (e.g. the *ḫuluppu*-tree in the temple of Inana in Uruk, the *mēsu*-tree and *kiškanû*-tree sacred to Enki in Eridu, the tamarisk seems to have a special connection with Anu, and the palm tree in the royal gardens of Assyria). This notion affirms the multilayered and complex relationship between the tree-persons and the great gods.

2b) Trees and plants are certainly sacred entities associated with specific deities and to other purifying and healing beings, but they also feature an autonomous status in the eyes of ancient Mesopotamians. Through their conceptualization as cosmic beings, as offspring of the pure places –such as mountains and rivers– and as being nurtured by the gods, but not created by them, their status of "other-than-human" person is expressed. A further hint into the ancient Mesopotamian notion of trees as persons is the references to diverse personalities ascribed to some trees. The tamarisk is described as a lonely tree, and as the great purifier of the world, including of the gods, while the palm tree displays motherly attributes, with a particular connection to royalty. Some trees were invested with guardian roles. The clearest example is offered by the *kiškanû*-tree, which is said to be the guardian of the gates of the inner part of the Sumerian temple (i.e. the Apsû).

2c) A powerful kinship between trees, gods and humans emerges from the literary sources. In the Sumerian myth the *Marriage of Martu*, the shepherd god declares himself the ancestor of trees: he is the grandfather of the holy cedar, ancestor of the *mēsu*-tree, mother and father of the white cedar, and relative of the *ḫašurru*-tree.[144] The *mēsu*-tree is further referred to as a tree closely connected with the gods and the royal figure: gods and kings are compared and equated to this arboreal person, which can henceforth be considered an emblem of royalty.[145] The special relationship between trees and kings is fully expressed by the royal nature ascribed to the palm tree. This tree appears as a tree particularly connected to royalty: it is said to be a constant presence at the table of the kings and it is addressed as the symbol of kingship itself.[146] This notion is particularly evident in Neo-Assyrian times, where palm trees are also portrayed in the reliefs of the royal palaces, mirroring their actual reassuring presence at every banquet of the king and in the gardens or

144 See Chapter IV, § 2.1.
145 See Chapter IV, § 2.2.
146 See Chapter IV, § 2.3.

orchards of the palaces. This evidence suggests the notion of trees as emblems or totems of the king himself.[147] The palm tree is notably the tree which displays a particular connection with humans. In the Sumerian literature a mother is compared to a palm tree with its fragrance, while in the *Babylonian Theodicy*, the palm tree is addressed as a wise brother. The latter evidence points to the status of "other-than-human" person of the date palm, which is referred to as kin to humans and with a moral connotation, with whom to engage and relate to.[148]

3) Some trees are referred to as fully partaking of divinity. The *mēsu*-tree and the tamarisk are explicitly called flesh or bones of the gods. Those trees were transformed into the earthly and physical body of the gods. Inherent to the wooden statue of the gods, two main aspects of the Mesopotamian concept of divinity are expressed and intertwined: the tree, by being the body itself of the gods, clearly partakes of divinity, while the god becomes a corporal entity. The tree is not only the gods' abode, but it is the incarnated deity. Furthermore, in their role as great purifiers, trees and plants are referred to as the cleansers of the very body of the gods. This is an allusion to the ritual practices of fumigations and burning of their branches in the censers in front of the wooden statues of the gods, but it also points to the divine nature ascribed to certain trees at least. These features suggest an egalitarian relationship between the gods and the arboreal entities, which partake of the divine realm.

4) Explicit attestations for tree worship are scarce in Mesopotamian lore. Within rituals performed in order to produce wooden figurines that would protect a man's house from any disease and evil, evidence for a reverential attitude toward trees is to be found. The tamarisk and the *e'ru*-wood are, in fact, the objects of a rite of thanksgiving which is performed before they are cut. Fumigations, libations, offerings, and sacrifices are performed in front of the trees. These ritual practices speak of a conception of trees as sacred entities, which deserve respect and devotion, and with whom humans relate to and engage in different ways. This notion implies an animistic attitude toward the sacred arboreal persons, and provides a further hint into the diverse ways that ancient Mesopotamians related to and engaged with the other "other-than-humans" persons of their relational cosmos.

147 See above, § 1.2.
148 See Chapter IV, § 2.3, and above, § 1.1.

Conclusions

This book has focused on how mountains, rivers, and trees were conceptualized, related to and worshipped by the ancient inhabitants of Mesopotamia as mirrored by written religious sources. The animated picture of myths and magic, prayers and offerings, is a reflection of a world where gods and humans were part of a much more complex and multi-layered system, where every single part was interconnected in a dense network of symbolic and ritual meanings.

Mountains. In the Mesopotamian literary and religious tradition, mountains are conceived of not only as cosmic topographical entities, but also as the abode of the gods, with a close relationship to deities, and as "other-than-human" persons with protecting, purifying and motherly attributes. Some specific mountains express divine qualities, especially when entangled with other mythical figures and deities, while fewer are regarded as deities *per se* (e.g. Ebiḫ and Aššur). The unspecified or collective mountain appeared with its proper agency and roles predominantly in the ritual context, while some specific mountains have fully divine status, as attested in both myths and rituals. Furthermore, the mountain in its cosmic topographical garb was widely believed to partake of the relational cosmos and of the sacred landscape of ancient Mesopotamia, entangled both with the eastern horizon and with sunrise, and with the western horizon and its infernal features.

Rivers. The River is a polyvalent and fluid entity, comprising multifaceted conceptions and an intrinsic duality. Some major symbolic and religious notions informed the beliefs and cults of the ancient Mesopotamians with respect to the rivers. Their characters of persons and of deities, along with their topographical and cosmic nature, are often all expressed together and intertwined. Rivers and watercourses have fully divine status within ancient Mesopotamian religious life. The River is conceived of as the mother of all life, as a great purifier and healer by virtue of its pure water, and as a severe and impartial judge of mankind, simultaneously presiding over and embodying the River Ordeal. Its divinity is further expressed by the attestations of worship of certain rivers throughout the ages and depending on location. Offerings and the personal names of those devoted to rivers all indicate a vivid religious and devotional life of these flowing deities. Furthermore, in their personalistic connotations, they are portrayed as guardians and protectors of gates and cities.

Trees. The cases of trees and plants differ from the cases of mountains and rivers, due to their predominant lack of fully divine attributes. However, trees and plants comprised several entangled meanings in the eyes of the ancient Mesopotamians. They were conceptualized as cosmic entities, pillars of the world and media between the dimensions and their inhabitants, and as conscious, wise, protective and healing "other-than-human" persons, who engaged with the anthropomorphic gods, with benevolent and malevolent beings, and with humans. Particular trees are clearly referred to as sacred trees, as kin to deities and humans (i.e. the king), and as fully partaking of divinity in those cases when they are called flesh or bones of the deities.

All this evidence speaks for a relational and animate cosmos which was perceived and conceptualized as populated by several non-human persons. Mountains, rivers, trees and plants were regarded as cosmic entities, deeply entangled with the sacred landscape and the cultic topography, as "other-than-human" persons, and sometimes as deities, who were fully part of the local panthea. These natural elements engaged in a multitude of ways with the life of ancient Mesopotamians, being both intimate neighbors of their immediate surroundings and sacred persons dwelling in and partaking of their shared cosmos. This cosmos was conceived of as a sacred, divine and relational one, where no strict distinction between natural and supernatural, immanent and transcendent, natural and cultural, appears to have existed in the minds of the ancients. According to this picture, new insights into ancient Mesopotamian conceptions of divinity, personhood and nature emerge.

The ancient Mesopotamian religious systems are complex polytheisms, which, by their own nature, consist of complex and multilayered frameworks, and feature an inherent fluidity of symbolic and ritualistic meanings. The evidence collected in this study suggests that one of the ways by which reality was experienced, known and conceptualized in ancient Mesopotamian mythology and magic displays animistic, or rather personalistic, features to varying degrees. The notion of personhood, which has been readdressed within the category of animism, especially in its relational aspect, articulates the conception of a "pervasive relational cosmos", while shedding light upon the actual fluidity and sensuous reality of those ancient religions understood as a daily life experience.

Anthropological theories have offered fertile conceptual tools and a lens through which to look at the multifaceted world of the ancient Mesopotamians. Thanks to the richness and multitude of cuneiform sources and genres, such approaches can be utilized for exploring other natural elements (e.g. stones, stars), animals and human-made entities, from objects used in daily life or cultic life, to temples, cities, and architectural and political entities. Indeed, not only do the notions of natural and supernatural as conceived in the Western world appear to be inapplicable to the ancient cuneiform cultures, but the boundaries between natural and cultural also appear to be much more nuanced and often merge.

The collected evidence supports the contemporary debate which aims at calling into question the Western naturalistic dichotomies concerning nature, culture and religion throughout human history, and at moving forward to explore the emic ways in which the ancient Mesopotamians related to and engaged with their sensuous world, by reconsidering the conceptions of divinity, personhood and nature in an ancient civilization. This book aims at constituting one way to advance a more comprehensive study of the different ways in which the ancient Sumerians, Babylonians and Assyrians engaged with their landscape and with the "other-than-human" persons inhabiting it. Accordingly, this book benefits and contributes to:

1. the field of Assyriology, in particular to the history and anthropology of religions of the ancient Near East;

2. the fields of landscape studies and material religion, especially those researches concerning the topography of the sacred and of the divine in natural contexts;

3. the ongoing debate over human-environmental relationships and the notion of personhood in the scholarly fields of ancient history, religious studies and anthropology;

4. the current debate on animism in the anthropological disciplines, especially in the field of anthropology of religion and of nature.

This research wishes to enter into the thriving field of historical and anthropological studies concerning religion, culture and nature, presenting some evidence from the ancient Near Eastern world. Combining ancient sources and modern anthropological understandings can enhance the shedding of light onto the different ways humans understand, relate to and conceptualize the world with its myriad of inhabitants past and present. The understanding of a relational and personal nature in the ancient Mesopotamian religious sources is just one of the intertwining threads generated by the encounter between human cognition and spirituality with its natural surroundings throughout history.

Bibliography

Abram, D. 1996: The Spell of the Sensuous. Perception and Language in a More-Than-Human World, New York.

–. 2013: The invisibles: toward a phenomenology of the spirits, in: G. Harvey (ed.), Handbook of Contemporary Animism, Durham, 124–132.

Abusch, Tz. 1995: Etemmu, in: K. van der Toorn, B. Becking, and P. W. van der Horst (eds.), Dictionary of Deities and Demons in the Bible, Leiden, 588–594.

–. 1998: Ghost and God: Some Observations on a Babylonian Understanding of Human Nature, in: A. Baumgarten/I. Assmann/G. Stroumsa (eds.), Self, Soul and Body in Religious Experience, Leiden.

–. 2002: Mesopotamian Witchcraft. Toward a History and Understanding of Babylonian Witchcraft Beliefs and Literature(MesWi) (AMD 5), Leiden/Boston/Köln.

–. 2006: Lists of Therapeutic Plants: an Observation, in: A. K. Guinan et alii (eds.), If a Man Builds a Joyful House. Assyriological Studies in Honor of Erle Verdun Leichty, Leiden/Boston, 1–3.

–. 2015a: The Magical Ceremony Maqlû. A Critical Edition, Leiden/Boston.

–. 2015b: Divine Judges on Earth and Heaven, in: A. Mermelstein/S. E. Holtz (eds.), The Divine Courtroom in Comparative Perspective, Leiden, 6–24.

Abusch, Tz./Schwemer, D. 2011: Corpus of Mesopotamian Anti-Witchcraft Rituals (CMAwR), vol. 1, Leiden/Boston.

–./–. 2016: Corpus of Mesopotamian Anti-Witchcraft Rituals (CMAwR), vol. 2, Leiden/Boston.

Abusch, Tz./Van der Toorn, K. (eds.) 1999: Mesopotamian Magic. Textual, Historical, and Interpretative Perspectives (AMD 1), Groningen.

Ainsworth, W.F. 1888: A Personal Narrative of the Euphrates Expedition, London.

Albenda, P. 2005: Ornamental Wall Painting in the Art of the Assyrian Empire, Leiden/Boston.

Albright, W.F. 1919: The Mouth of the Rivers, AJSL 35 (1919), 161–195.

Alster, B. 1983: Dilmun, Bahrain, and the alleged Paradise in Sumerian myth and literature, in: D. Potts (ed.), Dilmun: new studies in the archaeology and early history of Bahrain, Berlin, 39–74.

–. 1992: Tigris, in: K. van der Toorn et al. (eds.), Dictionary of Deities and Demons in the Bible, Leiden, 870.

Al-Rawi, F. N H./George, A. R. 2014: Back to the Cedar Forest: the Beginning and End of Tablet V of the Standard Babylonian Epic of Gilgameš, JCS 66, 69–90.

Amiet, P. 1960: Notes sur le repertoire iconographique de Mari à l'Epoque du palais, Syria 37, 215–231.

–. 1976: L'art d'Agadé au Musée du Louvre, Paris.

–. 1979: L'iconographie archaïque de l'Iran. Quelques documents nouveaux, Syria 56, 333–352.

–. 1980: La glyptique mésopotamienne archaïque, 2nd edition, Paris.

Andrae, W. 1931: Kultrelief aus dem Brunnen des Asurtempels zu Assur, Leipzig.

Annus, A. 2001: The Standard Babylonian Epic of Anzu, SAACT 3, Helsinki.

Archi, A. 1993: The God Ea in Anatolia, in: M. J. Mellink/T. Ôzgüç/E. Porada, Aspects of Art and Iconography: Anatolia and its Neighbors: Studies in Honor of Nimet Ôzgüç, Ankara, 27–33.

Aruz, J./Wallenfels, R. 2003: Art of the First Cities. The Third Millennium B.C. from the Mediterranean to the Indus, The Metropolitan Museum of Art, New Haven/London.

–./Benzel, K./Evans, J.M. (eds) 2008: Beyond Babylon: Art, trade, and diplomacy in the second millennium BC: 279–287, New York.

Attinger, P. 1998: Inana et Ebiḫ, ZA 88, 164–195.

–. 2015: Inanna und Ebiḫ, TUAT 8 NF, Gütersloh, 37–45.

–. 2017: Lexique sumérien-français (texts traduits dans Attinger), online resource: http://www.arch.unibe.ch/attinger.

Bagg, A. M. 2006: Identifying Mountains in the Levant according to Neo-Assyrian and Biblical Sources: Some Case Studies, SAAB XV, 183–192.

Bahrani, Z. 1999: The Extraterrestrial Orient: Colonizing Mesopotamia in Space and Time, in: L. Milano/S. de Martino/F. M. Fales/G. B. Lanfranchi (eds.), Landscapes. Territories, Frontiers and Horizons in the Ancient Near East, Papers presented to the XLIV Rencontre Assyriologique Internationale (Venezia, 7-11 July 1997), Padova, 5–10.

Beaulieu, P.-A. 1992/1993: A Note on the River Ordeal in the Literary Text 'Nebuchadnezzar King of Justice', NABU, 58–60.

–. 2002: The God Amurru as Emblem of Ethnic and Cultural Identity, in: W. H. Van Soldt, Ethnicity in Ancient Meopotamia, Leiden, 31–46.

Beck, P. 1977: A Note on a Syrian Cylinder Seal, Tel Aviv 4, 191–193.

Beckman, G. M. 2014: The babilili-Ritual from Hattusa (CTH 718), Winona Lake, Indiana.

Behr von, B. 2007: Water, in: K. von Stuckrad (ed.), The Brill Dictionary of Religion, Leiden/Boston, 1963–1968.

Behrens, H. 1978: Enlil und Ninlil: Ein sumerischer Mythos aus Nippur, Rome.

Biggs, R. D. 1965: A letter from Kassite Nippur, JCS 19, 95–102.

–. 1974: Inscriptions from Tell Abū `alābīkh (OIP 99), Chicago.

–. 1967: ŠÀ.ZI.GA: Ancient Mesopotamian Potency Incantations (TCS 2), Locust Valley, New York.

–. 2002: The Babylonian Sexual Potency Texts, in: S. Parpola/R.M. Whiting (eds.), Sex and Gender in the Ancient Near East. Proceedings of the 47th Rencontre Assyriologique Internationale, Helsinki, July 2-6, 2001, Part I, Helsinki, 71–78.

Bird-David, N. 1999: 'Animism' Revisited: Personhood, Environment, and Relational Epistemology, Current Anthropology, vol. 40, No. S1, 67–91.

–. 2007, Us, Relatives. Scaling and Plural Life in a Forager World, Oakland, California.

–. (forthcoming): Persons or relatives? Animistic scales of practice and imagination in: M. Astor-Aguilera/G. Harvey (eds.), Rethinking Personhood: Animism and Materiality in Dialogue.

–./Naveh, D. 2013: Animism, conservation and immediacy, in: G. Harvey, Handbook of Contemporary Animism, Durham, 27–37.

–./–. 2014, How persons become things: economic and epistemological changes among Nayaka hunter-gatherers, Journal of the Royal Anthropological Institute 20, 74−92.

Black, J. 2002: The Sumerians in their Landscape, in: Tz. Abusch (ed.), Riches Hidden in Secret Places. Ancient Near Eastern Studies in Memory of Thorkild Jacobsen, Winona Lake, 41–61.

Black, J./Green, A. 1992: Gods, Demons and Symbols of Ancient Mesopotamia. An Illustrated Dictionary, London.

Black, J./Cunningham, G./Robson, E./Zólyomi, G. 2004: The Literature of Ancient Sumer, Oxford.

Blain, J. 2013: Consciousness, Wights and Ancestors, in: G. Harvey (ed.), The Handbook of Contemporary Animism, Durham, 423–435.
Blaschke, T. 2018: Euphrat und Tigris im Alten Orient, Wiesbaden.
Bleibtreu, E. 1980: Die Flora der neuassyrischen Reliefs, Wien.
Bloch, Y./Horowitz, W. 2015: URA = ḪUBULLU XXII: The Standard Recension, JCS 67, 71–125.
Boddy, J./Lambek, M. (eds.) 2013: A Companion to the Anthropology of Religion, Chichester.
Boehmer, R.M. 1965: Die Entwicklung der Glyptik während der Akkad-Zeit, Berlin.
Bord, J./Bord, C. 1985: Sacred Waters, London.
Borger, R. 1969: Die erste Tafel der zi-pa$_3$-Beschwörungen (ASKT 11), in: W. von Soden/ M. Dietrich/W. Röllig (eds.), lišan mitḫurti. Festschrift Wolfram Freiherr von Soden vom 19.VI.1968 gewidmet von Schülern und Mitarbeitern (AOAT 1), Neukirchen-Vluyn, 1–22.
Bottéro, J. 1958: Les divinites semitiques anciennes en Mesopotamie, in: S. Moscati (ed.), Le antiche divinità semitiche, Studi Semitici 1, Rome, 17–63.
–. 1981: L'ordalie en Mésopotamie ancienne", ASNSP 11, 1005–1067.
–. 1985: Mythes et rites de Babylone, Genéve/Paris.
–. 2001: Religion in Ancient Mesopotamia, translated by Teresa Lavender Fagan, Chicago.
Bottéro, J./Kramer, S.N. 1989: Lorsque les dieux faisaient l'homme. Mythologie mésopotamienne, Paris.
Bowen, J. R. 2005: Religion in Practice. An Approach to the Anthropology of Religion, Boston.
Böck, B. 2007: Das Handbuch mušš'u "Einreibung": Eine Serie sumerischer und akkadischer Beschwörungen aus dem 1. Jt. v. Chr. (BPOA 3), Madrid.
–. 2014: The Healing Goddess Gula: Towards an Understanding of Ancient Babylonian Medicine, Leiden.
Brosse, J. 1989: Mythologie des Arbres, Paris.
–. 1998: Postface: The Life of Trees ..., in L. Rival (ed.), The Social Life of Trees: Anthropological Perspectives on Tree Symbolism, Oxford, 299–303.
Buber, M. 1970: I and Thou, translated by W. Kaufmann, New York.
Buccellati, G. 1966: The Amorites of the Ur III Period, Naples.
Butzer, K.W. 2001: Nile, in: D. B. Redford (ed.), The Oxford Encyclopedia of Ancient Egypt 2, Oxford, 550.
Cagni, L. 1969: L'epopea di Erra, Studi semitici 34, Rome.
–. 1977: The Poem of Erra, SANE 1/3, Malibu.
Caplice, R. 1971: Namburbi Texts in the British Museum, Orientalia NS 40, 133–183.
Cassirer, E. 1944: An Essay on Man: An Introduction to a Philosophy of Human Culture, New Haven.
Cavigneaux, A. 1978: L'essence divine, JCS 30, 177–185.
–. 1999: A Scholar's Library in Meturan?, in: T. Abusch/K. van der Toorn (eds.), Mesopotamian Magic: Textual, Historical, and interpretative Perspectives (AMD 1), Groningen, 251–273.
–. 2003: Fragments littéraires susiens, in: W. Sallaberger/K. Volk/A. Zgoll (eds.), Literatur, Politik und Recht in Mesopopotamien: Festschrift für Claus Wilcke, Wiesbaden, 53–62.
Charpin, D. 1986: Le clergè d'Ur au siècle d'Hammurabi (XIXe-XVIIe siècles av. J.-C.), Genève.
–. 1987: Une nouvelle attestation du kiškānû?, NABU 1, 1.
Charpin, D./Ziegler, N. 2003: Mari et le Proche-Orient à l'époque amorrite: Essai d'histoire politique, Mémoires de NABU 6, Paris.
Coccia, E. 2016: La vita delle piante. Metafisica della mescolanza, Bologna.

Collon, D. 1982: Catalogue of Western Asiatic Seals in the British Museum: Cylinder Seals II; Akkadian–Post Akkadian–Ur III Periods, London.
–. 1987: First Impressions. Cylinder Seals in the Ancient Near East, London.
–. 1999: Early Landscapes, in: L. Milano/S. de Martino/F. M. Fales/G. B. Lanfranchi (eds.), Landscapes. Territories, Frontiers and Horizons in the Ancient Near East, Papers presented to the XLIV Rencontre Assyriologique Internationale (Venezia, 7-11 July 1997), Padova, 15–22.
Conti, G. 1988: Su una nuova attestazione di i7-zubir, RA 82, 115–130.
–. 1997: Incantation de l'eau bénite et de l'encensoir, Mari Annales de Recherches Interdisciplinaires 8, 253–272.
Cooper, J. 1986: Sumerian and Akkadian Royal Inscriptions I, New Haven.
–. 1996: Magic and M(is)use: Poetic Promiscuity in Mesopotamian Ritual, in: M. E. Vogelzang/H. L. J. Vastinphout (eds.), Mesopotamian Poetic Language: Sumerian and Akkadian, Groningen, 47–55.
Cunningham, G. 1997: 'Deliver Me From Evil': Mesopotamian Incantations 2500-1500 BC, Rome
–. 1999: Religion & Magic. Approaches & Theories, Edinburgh.
Cusack, C. 2011: The Sacred Tree: Ancient and Medieval Manifestations, Cambridge.
–. 2013, Scotland's Sacred Tree: The Fortingall Yew, Sydney Society for Scottish History Journal, Vol. 14, 106–120.
–. 2018a: Special Feature Introduction: The Sacred Tree, Journal for the Study of Religion, Nature and Culture (JSRNC), 257–260.
–. 2018b: The Glastonbury Thorn in Vernacular Christianity and Popular Tradition, Journal for the Study of Religion, Nature and Culture (JSRNC), 307–326.
Çağirgan, G./Lambert, W.G. 1991/1993: The Late Babylonian Kislīmu Ritual for Esagil, JCS 43-45, 89–106.
Dafni, A. 2002: Why Are Rags Tied to the Sacred Trees of the Holy Land?, Economic Botany 56, n. 4, 315–327.
Descola, P. 1992: Societies of Nature and the Nature of Society, in: A. Kuper (ed.), Conceptualizing Society, London, 107–126.
–. 1996: Constructing Natures: Symbolic Ecology and Social Practices, in: P. Descola/G. Pàlsson (eds.), Nature and Society. Anthropological Perspectives, London, 82–102.
–. 2005: Par-delà nature et culture, Paris.
–. 2013a: Beyond Nature and Culture, in: G. Harvey (ed.), The Handbook of Contemporary Animism, Durham, 77–91.
–. 2013b: Presence, Attachment, Origin: Ontologies of 'Incarnates', in: J. Boddy/M. Lambek (eds.), A Companion to the Anthropology of Religion, Malden, 35–49.
Detwiler, F. 2013: Moral Foundations of Tlingit Cosmology, in: G. Harvey (ed.), The Handbook of Contemporary Animism, Durham, 167–180.
Dhorme, P. 1912: Tablettes de Dréhem A Jérusalem, RA 9, 39–63.
Douglas, M. 1966: Purity and Danger: an Analysis of Concepts of Pollution and Taboo, London.
–. 1973, Natural Symbols: Explorations in Cosmology, London.
Hull, D. 1992: How Classification Works: Nelson Goodman among Social Sciences, Edinburgh.
Durand, J.-M. 1987: Noms des dieux sumeriens a Mari, NABU no. 14, 7–8.
–. 1988: Archives Épistolaires de Mari I/1 (ARM), Paris.
–. 2000: Les documents épistolaires du palais de Mari, vol. III (LAPO 18), Paris.

–. 2005: Le culte des pierres et les monuments commémoratifs en Syrie amorrite, Mémoires de NABU 9 (Florilegium marianum 8), Paris.
–. 2008: La religion amorrite en Syrie a l'epoque des archives de Mari, in: G. del Olmo Lete (ed.), Mythologie et religion des Semites occidentaux, 2 vols., Leuven, 161–703.
Durkheim, E. 1915: The Elementary Forms of Religious Life, New York.
Ebeling, E. 1915/19: Keilschrifttexte aus Assur religiösen Inhalts (KAR), vol. I, WVDOG 28, Leipzig.
–. 1920/23: Keilschrifttexte aus Assur religiösen Inhalts (KAR), vol. II, WVDOG 34, Leipzig.
–. 1932: Amurru, *RlA* 1, Berlin and Leipzig, 99–103.
–. 1953: Literarische Keilschrifttrexte aus Assur (LKA), Berlin.
–. 1957/1971: Flußgottheiten, *RlA* 3, 93.
Edzard, D. O. 1984: Hymnen, Beschwörungen und Verwandtes aus dem Archiv L. 2769 (ARET V), Rome.
–. 1993a: 'Gilgameš und Huwawa'. Zwei Versionen der sumerischen Zedernwaldepisode nebst einer Edition von Version B, Sitzungberichte der Bayerischen Akademie der Wissenschaften. Philosophisch-historische Klasse 4, Munich, 1–61.
–.1993b: Gilgamesch und Huwawa, in: O. Kaiser (ed), Mythen und Epen I (TUAT 3), Gütersloh, 540–549.
–. 1997: The Names of the Sumerian Temples, in: I. L. Finkel/M. J. Geller (eds.), Sumerian Gods and their Representations, Groningen, 159–165.
–. 2003/2005: Personifizierung, *RlA* 10, 434–435.
–. 2015$^{(\dagger)}$: Gilgamesch und Chuwawa, in: K. Volk, Erzählungen aus dem Land Sumer, Wiesbaden, 283–295.
Eliade, M. 1958: Patterns in Comparative Religion, London/Sydney.
Erbil, Y./Mouton, A. 2012: Water in Ancient Anatolian Religions: An Archaeological and Philological Inquiry on the Hittite Evidence, JNES 71, 53–74.
Ermidoro, S. 2017: Quando gli dei erano uomini: Atrahasis e la storia babilonese del genere umano, Torino.
Farber, G. 1987: Rituale und Beschwörungen in akkadischer Sprache, in: O. Kaiser (ed.), Rituale und Beschwörungen I (TUAT II/2), Gütersloh, 212–281.
–. 1987/1990: me (ĝarza, parṣu), *RlA* 7, 610–613.
–. 1990: Mannam lušpur ana Enkidu: Some New Thoughts about an Old Motif, JNES 49, 299–321.
–. 2014: Lamaštu. An Edition of the Canonical Series of Lamaštu Incantations and Rituals and Related Texts from the Second and First Millennia B.C., Winona Lake, Indiana.
Faure, B. 2015: Gods of Medieval Japan. Volume 2. The Fluid Pantheon, Honolulu.
Finkel, I. L./Geller, M. J. (eds.) 1997: Sumerian Gods and Their Representations, Groningen.
Forsyth, N. 1981: Huwawa and his trees: a narrative and cultural analysis, Acta Sumerologica 3, 13–29.
Foster, B. R. 2005: Before the Muses. An Anthology of Akkadian Literature, Bethesda.
Frahm, E. 2017: A Companion to Assyria, New Haven.
Frame, G. 1997: The God Aššur in Babylonia, in: S. Parpola/R.M. Whiting (eds.), Assyria 1995. Proceedings of the 10th Anniversary Symposium of the Neo-Assyrian Text Corpus Project. Helsinki, September 7-11 1995, Helsinki, 55–64.
–. 2014: Ulai A, *RlA* 14, 302–303.

Frankena, R. 1954: Takultu. De sacrale maaltijd in het Assyrische ritueel, met een overzicht over de in Assur verrerde goden, Leiden.
Frankfort, H. 1979: The Art and Architecture of the ancient Orient, 4th revised impression, Harmondsworth, Middlesex.
Frankfort, H./Groenewegen, H.A./Wilson, J.A./Jacobsen, T. (eds.) 1946: The Intellectual Adventure of Ancient Man: An Essay of Speculative Thought in the Ancient Near East, Chicago.
–/–/–/–. 1949: Before Philosophy: The Intellectual Adventure of Ancient Man, Baltimore.
–/–/–/–/Irwin, W. A. 1977: The Intellectual Adventure of Ancient Man: An Essay of Speculative Thought in the Ancient Near East, (second revised edition), Chicago/London.
Frayne, D. 1990: Old Babylonian Period (2003-1595 BC) (RIME 4), Toronto/Buffalo/London.
–. 1993: Sargonic and Gutian Periods (2334–2113 BC) (RIME 2), Toronto/Buffalo/London.
Frazer, J. G. [1890] 1922: The Golden Bough, London.
Freydank, H./Saporetti, C. 1979: Nuove Attestazioni dell'Onomastica Medio-Assira, Rome.
Frymer-Kensky, T. 1977: The Judicial Ordeal in the Ancient Near East, PhD dissertation, Yale University, Yale.
Gabbay, U. 2018: Drums, Hearts, Bulls, and Dead Gods: The Theology of the Ancient Mesopotamian Kettledrum, JANER 18, 1–47.
Gadotti, A. 2014: 'Gilgamesh, Enkidu, and the Netherworld' and the Sumerian Gilgamesh Cycle, UAVA 10, Boston/Berlin.
Gehlken, E. 2012: Weather Omens of Enūma Anu Enlil. Thunderstorms, Wind and Rain (Tablets 44-49), Leiden/Boston.
Geller, M. J. 1985: Forerunners to Udug-hul. Sumerian Exorcistic Incantations, Stuttgart.
–. 1990: Taboo in Mesopotamia. A Review Article, JCS 42, 105–117.
–. 1997: The Landscape of the Netherworld, in: L. Milano/S. de Martino/F. M. Fales/G. B. Lanfranchi (eds.), Landscapes. Territories, Frontiers and Horizons in the Ancient Near East, Papers presented to the XLIV Rencontre Assyriologique Internationale (Venezia, 7-11 July 1997), Padova, 41–49.
–. 1998: An Incantation against Curses, in: S. M. Maul (ed.), Festschrift für Rykle Borger zu seinem 65. Geburtstag am 24. Mai 1994: tikip santakki mala bašmu… (CM 10), Groningen, 127–140.
–. 2007: Evil Demons. Canonical Utukkū Lemnūtu Incantations. Introduction, Cuneiform Text, and Transliteration with a Translation and Glossary (SAACT 5), Helsinki.
–. 2010: Ancient Babylonian Medicine. Theory and Practice, Oxford.
–. 2011/2013: Taboo in Mesopotamia, *RlA* 13, 394–395.
–. 2014: Melothesia in Babylonia. Medicine, Magic, and Astrology in the Ancient Near East, Boston/Berlin/Munich.
–. 2016: Healing Magic and Evil Demons. Canonical Udug-hul Incantations, with the Assistance of L. Vacín, Boston/Berlin.
–./Schipper, M. (eds.) 2008: Imagining Creation, Leiden/Boston.
–./Wiggermann, F. A. M. 2008: Duplicating Akkadian Magic, in: R. J. van der Spek (ed.), Studies in Ancient Near Eastern World View and Society, Presented to Marten Stol on the Occasion of His 65th Birtday, 10 November 2005, and His Retirement from the Vrije Universiteit Amsterdam (Fs. Stol), Bethesda, 149–160.
George, A. R. 1992: Babylonian Topographical Texts, Leuven.
–. 1993: House Most High. The Temples of Ancient Mesopotamia, Winona Lake, Indiana.
–. 1999: The Epic of Gilgamesh. The Babylonian Epic Poem and other Texts in Akkadian and Sumerian, London.

–. 2000: Four Temple Rituals from Babylon, in: A. R. George/I. L. Finkel (ed.), Wisdom, Gods and Literature: Studies in Assyriology in Honour of W.G. Lambert (Fs. Lambert), 259–299.
–. 2003: The Babylonian Gilgamesh Epic: Critical Edition and Cuneiform Texts, Oxford.
–. 2006: Babylonian Texts from the Folios of Sidney Smith, Part Three: A commentary on a Ritual of the Month Nisan, in: A. K. Guinan et al. (ed.), If a Man Builds a Joyful House: Assyriological Studies in Honor of Erle Verdun Leichty (CM 31), Leiden/Boston, 173–185.
–. 2008: Akkadian turru ('urru B) "corner angle" and the walls of Babylon, ZA 98, 221–229.
–. 2009: Babylonian Literary Texts in the Schøyen Collection (CUSAS 10), Bethesda.
–. 2011: Cuneiform Royal Inscriptions and Related Texts in the Schøyen Collection (CUSAS 17), Bethesda.
–. 2012: The Mayfly on the River: Individual and Collective Destiny in the Epic of Gilgamesh, KASKAL 9, 227–242.
–. 2013a: The Poem of Erra and Ishum: A Babylonian Poet's View of War, in: H. Kennedy, Warfare and Poetry in the Middle East, London, 39–71.
–. 2013b: Babylonian Divinatory Texts Chiefly in the Schøyen Collection (CUSAS 18), Bethesda.
–. 2016: Mesopotamian Incantations and Related Texts in the Schøyen Collection (CUSAS 32), Bethesda.
Giovino, M. 2007: The Assyrian Sacred Tree. A History of Interpretations (OBO 30), Göttingen.
Goff, B. L.1963: Symbols of Prehistoric Mesopotamia, New Haven.
Goodnick Westenholz, J. 1997: Legends of the Kings of Akkade (MC 7), Winona Lake, Indiana.
Goody, J. 1977: Domestication of the Savage Mind, Cambridge.
Gordon, C. H. 1991: The Ebla Incantations and their Affinities with North-West Semitic Magic, Maarav 7, 117–129.
–. 1992: The Ebla Exorcisms, Eblaitica 3, Winona Lake, Indiana, 127–137.
Grayson, A. K. 1987: Assyrian Rulers of the Third and Second Millennia BC (to 1115 BC) (RIMA 1), Toronto/Buffalo/London.
Green, A. 1997: Myths in Mesopotamian Art, in I. L. Finkel/M. J. Geller (eds.), Sumerian Gods and their Representations, Groningen, 135–158.
Groneberg, B. 1980: Répertoire géographique des textes cunéiformes III. Die Orts- und Gewässernamen der altbabylonischen Zeit, Wiesbaden.
Guest, E. 1966: Flora of Iraq, Baghdad.
Gurney, O. R. 1989: Literary and Miscellaneous Texts in the Ashmolean Museum (OECT 11), Oxford.
Guthrie, S. 1993: Faces in the Clouds: A New Theory of Religion, New York.
–. 2013: Spiritual beings: a Darwinian, cognitive account, in: G. Harvey (ed.), Handbook of Contemporary Animism, Durham, 353–357.
Günbatti, C. 2001: The River Ordeal in Ancient Anatolia, in: W. H. van Soldt (ed.), Veenhof Anniversary Volume: Studies Presented to Klaas R. Veenhof on the Occasion of his Sixty-Fifth Birthday (Fs. Veenhof), Leiden, 151–160.
Hahn, J. (ed.) 2002: Religiöse Landschaften. Veröffentilchungen des Arbeitskreises zur Erforschung der Relgions- und Kulturgeschichte des Antinken Vorderen Orients und des Sonderforschungsbereichts 493, Band 4 (AOAT 301), Münster.
Haas, V. 1982: Hethitische Berggötter und hurritische Steindämonen. Riten, Kulte und Mythen, Mainz-am-Rhein.
–. 1994: Geschichte der Hethitischen Religion (HdO 15), Leiden/New York/Köln.

Haberman, D. L. 2007: River of Love in an Age of Pollution. The Yamuna River of Northern India, Berkeley/Los Angeles/London.
–. 2013: People Trees. Worship of Trees in Northern India, Oxford.
Halbmayer, E. 2012a: Debating animism, perspectivism and the construction of ontologies, INDIANA 29, 9–23.
–. 2012b: Amerindian mereology: Animism, analogy, and the multiverse, INDIANA 29, 103–125.
Hall, M. 2011: Plants as Persons. A Philosophical Botany, New York.
–. 2013: Talk among the Trees: Animist Plant Ontologies and Ethics, in: G. Harvey (ed.), The Handbook of Contemporary Animism, Durham, 385–394.
Hallo, W. 1970: The Cultic Setting of Sumerian Poetry, in: A. Finet (ed.), Actes de la XVIIe Rencontre Assyriologique Internationale: Université libre de Bruxelles 30 juin-4 juillet 1969, Ham-sur-Heure, 117–134.
Hallowell, A. I. 1960: Ojibwa Ontology, Behavior and World View, in: S. Diamond, Culture in History: Essays in Honor of Paul Radin, New York, 19–52.
Hansen, D. P. 2002: Through the Love of Ishtar, in: J. Curtis/H. Martin/A. McMahon (eds), Of Pots and Plans. Papers on the Archaeology and History of Mesopotamia and Syria presented to David Oates in Honour of his 75th Birthday, London, 91–112.
Hansman, J. 1976: Gilgamesh, Humbaba and the Land of Erin-Trees, Iraq 38, 23–35.
Harding, S. 2013: Toward an animistic science of the Earth, in: G. Harvey (ed.), Handbook of Contemporary Animism, Durham, 373–384.
Harmanşah, Ö. 2007: Source of the Tigris: Event, Place and Performance in the Assyrian Landscapes of the Early Iron Age, Archaeological Dialogues 14 (2), 179–204.
–. 2014: Event, Place, Performance: Rock Reliefs and Spring Monuments in Anatolia, in: Ö. Harmanşah (ed.), Of Rocks and Water. Toward an Archaeology of Place, Oxford/Philadelphia, 140–168.
–. (ed.) 2014: Of Rocks and Water. Toward and Archaeology of Place, Oxford/Philadelphia.
–. 2015: Place, Memory, and Healing. An Archaeology of Anatolian Rock Monuments, London/New York.
Harvey, G. 2005: Animism – A Contemporary Perspective, in: B. Taylor (ed.), Encyclopedia of Religion and Nature, London/New York, 81–83.
–. 2006: Animism. Respecting the Living World, New York.
–. (ed.) 2013a: Handbook of Contemporary Animism, Durham.
–. 2013b: Food, Sex & Strangers. Understanding Religion as Everyday Life, Durham.
Hecker, K. 2015: Atra-ḫasīs: Die Spätbabylonische Fassung des Epos, TUAT NF 8, 132–143.
Heeßel, N.P. 2005: Stein, Pflanze, und Holz: Ein neuer Text zur 'medizinischen Astrologie', Orientalia NS 74, 1–22.
–, (forthcoming), Magie in Mesopotamien, 33–52.
Heimpel, W. 1996: The River Ordeal in Hit, RA 90, 7–13.
–. 1987: Das Unter Meer, ZA 77, 22–91.
–. 2011: Twenty-Eight Trees Growing in Sumer, in: D.I. Owen (ed.), Garšana Studies, CUSAS 6, Bethesda, Maryland, 75–152.
–./Salgues, E. 2015: Lugale oder wie Ninurta dem Tigris mehr Wasser schuf, in: K. Volk (ed.), Erzählungen aus dem Land Sumer, Wiesbaden, 33–67.
Helck, W./Otto, E. 1982: Lexikon der Agyptologie 4, Wiesbaden.

Henkelman, W.F.M./Redard, C. (eds.) 2017: Persian Religion in the Achaemenid Period/ La religion perse à l'époque achémenide, Wiesbaden.

Hirsch, E./O'Hanlon, M. (eds.) 1995: The Anthropology of Landscape: Perspectives on Place and Space, Oxford.

Hogan, L. 2013: We call it tradition, in: G. Harvey (ed.), Handbook of Contemporary Animism, Durham, 17–26.

Horowitz, W. 1998: Mesopotamian Cosmic Geography, Winona Lake, Indiana.

–. 2010: Animate, Inanimate, and Primary Elements in Mesopotamian Creation Accounts: Revisited, in: P. Gemeinhardt/A. Zgoll (eds.), Weltkonstruktionen. Religiöse Weltdeutung zwischen Chaos and Kosmos vom Alten Orient bis zum Islam, Morh Siebeck, 29–45.

Howell, S. 2013: Metamorphosis and identity: Chewong animistic ontology, in: G. Harvey (ed.), The Handbook of Contemporary Animism, Durham, 101–112.

Hrouda, B. 1991: Der alte Orient. Geschichte und Kultur des alten Vorderasien, Munich.

Hunt, A. 2016: Reviving Roman Religion. Sacred Trees in the Roman World, Cambridge.

Ingold, T. 1993: The Temporality of the Landscape, World Archaeology 25/2, 152–174.

–. 2013: Being alive in a world without objects, in: G. Harvey (ed.), The Handbook of Contemporary Animism, Durham, 213–225.

Izre'el, S. 2001: Adapa and the South Wind. Language has the Power of Life and Death, Winona Lake.

Jacobsen, T. 1976: The Treasures of Darkness. A History of Mesopotamian Religion, New Haven/London.

–. 1977: Mesopotamia, in: H. Frankfort/H.A. Frankfort/J.A. Wilson/T. Jacobsen/W. Irwin (eds.), The Intellectual Adventure of Ancient Man. An Essay on Speculative Thought in the Ancient Near East, Chicago/London, 123–219.

–. 1987: The Harps that Once…, New Haven/London.

James, E.O. 1966: The Tree of Life, Studies in the History of Religion, Suppl. To Numen XI, Leiden.

Jiménez, E. 2017: The Babylonian Disputation Poems. With Editions of the Series of the Poplar, Palm and Vine, the Series of the Spider, and the Story of the Poor, Forlorn Wren, Leiden.

Jisheng, X. 2001: The Mythology of Tibetan Mountain Gods: An Overview, Oral Tradition 16/1, 343–363.

Katz, D. 2003: The Image of the Netherworld in the Sumerian Sources, Bethesda.

Kippenberg, H.G. 2002: Rediscovering Religious History in the Modern Age, Princeton University Press, Princeton.

Klein, J. 1997a: The God Martu in Sumerian Literature, in: I. L. Finkel/M. J. Geller (eds.), Sumerian Gods and their Representations (CM 7), Groningen, 99–116.

–. 1997b: The Sumerian me as a Concrete Object, Altorientalische Forschungen 24, vol. 2, 211–218.

–./Abraham, K. 1999: Problems of Geography in the Gilgameš Epic: the Journey to the "Cedar Forest", in: L. Milano/S. de Martino/F.M. Fales/G.B. Lanfranchi (eds.), Landscapes. Territories, Frontiers and Horizons in the Ancient Near East, Papers presented to the XLIV Rencontre Assyriologique Internationale (Venezia, 7-11 July 1997), Padova, 63–73.

Knight, C. 1996: Totemism, in: A. Barnard/J. Spencer (eds.), Encyclopedia of Social and Cultural Anthropology, London, 550–551.

Kramer, S. N. 1936: Gilgamesh and the Willow Tree, The Open Court 50, 100–106.

–. 1938: Gilgameš and the Huluppu-Tree: A Reconstructed Sumerian Text, Acta Sumerologica 10, Chicago.

–. 1947: Gilgamesh and the Land of the Living, JCS 1, 3–46.
–. 1985a: BM 86535: A Large Extract of a Diversified Balag-Composition, in: J.-M. Durand/J. R. Kupper (ed.), Miscellanea Babylonica: Mélanges offerts à Maurice Birot, 115–135.
–. 1985b: BM 2363: Bread for Enlil, Sex for Inanna, Orientalia 54, 117–132.
–. 1990: The Marriage of Martu, in: J. Klein/A. Skaist (eds.), Bar-Ilan Studies in Assyriology, Bar-Ilan, Ramat Gan, 11–27.
–./Maier, J. 1989: The Myths of Enki, the Crafty God, New York/Oxford.
Krebernik, M. 1984: Die Beschwörungen aus Fara und Ebla. Untersuchungen zur ältesten keilschriftlichen Beschwörungsliteratur (TSO 2), Hildesheim.
–. 1986: Die Götterlisten aus Fara, ZA 76, 161–204.
–. 1996: Fragment einer Bilingue, ZA 86, 170–176.
–. 2014: Ulai. B., *RlA* 14, 303.
Kwasman, T/Parpola, S. 1991: Legal Transactions of the Royal Court of Nineveh. Part I: Tiglath-Pileser III Through Esarhaddon (SAA 6), Helsinki.
Kunstmann, W.G. 1930: Die babylonische Gebetsbeschwörung, Leipzig.
Kupper, J.-R. 1961: L'iconographie du dieu Amurru dans la glyptique de la 1re dynastie babylonienne, Bruxelles.
Læessøe, J. 1955: Studies on the Assyrian Ritual and Series bît rimki, Copenhagen.
Lambek, M. (ed.) 2002: A Reader in Anthropology of Religion, Malden, Massachusetts.
–. 2013: What is "Religion" for Anthropology? And What Has Anthropology Brought to "Religion"?, in: J. Boddy/M. Lambek (eds.), A Companion to the Anthropology of Religion, Malden, Massachusetts, 1–32.
Lambert, W. G. 1965: Nebuchadnezzar King of Justice, Iraq 27, 1–11.
–. 1966: Gott. B. Nach akkadischen Texten, *RlA* 3, 543–546.
–. 1968: Myth and Ritual as Conceived by the Babylonians, JSS 13, 104–112.
–. 1975: The Historical Development of the Mesopotamian Pantheon: A Study in Sophisticated Polytheism, in: H. Goedicke/J. J. Roberts (eds.), Unity and Diversity, Baltimore and London, 191–199.
–. 1983: The God Aššur, Iraq 45, 82–86.
–. 1985a: The Pantheon of Mari, MARI. Annales de reschers interdisciplinaires 4, 525–529.
–. 1985b: Trees, Snakes and Gods in Ancient Syria and Anatolia, Bulletin of the School of Oriental and African Studies, vol. 48, London, 435–451.
–. 1988: Götterlisten, *RlA* 3, 473–479.
–. 1989: Notes on a Work of the Most Ancient Semitic Literature, JCS 41, 1–33.
–. 1990: Ancient Mesopotamian Gods: Superstition, Philosophy, Theology, Revue de l'Histoire des Religions, vol. 207, n. 2, 115–130.
–. 1996: Babylonian Wisdom Literature, Winona Lake, Indiana.
–. 1997: Sumerian Gods: Combining the Evidence of Texts and Art, in I. L. Finkel/M. J. Geller (eds.), Sumerian Gods and their Representations, Groningen, 1–10.
–. 1998: The Qualifications of Babylonian Diviners, in: S. M. Maul (ed.), Festschrift für Rykle Borger zu seinem 65. Geburtstag am 24. Mai 1994, Groningen, 141–155.
–. 1999: The Apsû, in: L. Milano/S. de Martino/F.M. Fales/G.B. Lanfranchi (eds.), Landscapes. Territories, Frontiers and Horizons in the Ancient Near East, Papers presented to the XLIV Rencontre Assyriologique Internationale (Venezia, 7-11 July 1997), Padova, 75–77.
–. 2013: Babylonian Creation Myths, Winona Lake, Indiana.

–./Millard, A. R. 1969: Atra-ḫasīs. The Babylonian Story of the Flood, Oxford.

Landsberger, B. 1967: The Date Palm and its By-products according to the Cuneiform Sources, AfO Beiheft 17, Graz.

Latour, B. 1993: We Have Never Been Modern, translated by C. Porter, Cambridge, Massachusetts.

Leick, G. 1999: The Erotisation of Landscape in Mesopotamian Literature, in: L. Milano/S. de Martino/F.M. Fales/G.B. Lanfranchi (eds.), Landscapes. Territories, Frontiers and Horizons in the Ancient Near East, Papers presented to the XLIV Rencontre Assyriologique Internationale (Venezia, 7-11 July 1997), Padova, 79–82.

Lenzi, A. 2011: Reading Akkadian Prayers & Hymns. An Introduction, Atlanta.

Lévi-Strauss, C. 1955: The Structural Study of Myth, The Journal of American Folklore, vol. 68, No. 270, Myth: A Symposium (Oct.–Dec., 1955), 428–444.

–. 1962: The Savage Mind, Chicago.

–. 1963: Totemism, Harmondsworth.

–. 1995: Myth & Meaning. Cracking the Code of Culture, New York.

Lévy-Bruhl, L. 1985: How Natives Think, Translated by L.A. Clare, Princeton.

Litke, R.L. 1998: A Reconstruction of the Assyro-Babylonian God-Lists: An=Anum and Anu šá amēli, Bethesda.

Livingstone, A. 1986: Mystical and Mythological Explanatory Works of Assyrian and Babylonian Scholars, Oxford.

–. 1989: Court Poetry and Literary Miscellanea (SAA 3), Helsinki.

–. 1997: New Dimensions in the Study of Assyrian Religion, in: S. Parpola/R.M. Whiting (eds.), Assyria 1995. Proceedings of the 10th Anniversary Symposium of the Neo-Assyrian Corpus Project, Helsinki, September 7-11, 1995, Helsinki, 165–177.

Lombardi, A. 1999: Il culto delle montagne all'epoca di Tudḫaliya IV: continuità e innovazione, in: L. Milano/S. de Martino/F.M. Fales/G.B. Lanfranchi (eds.), Landscapes. Territories, Frontiers and Horizons in the Ancient Near East, Papers presented to the XLIV Rencontre Assyriologique Internationale (Venezia, 7-11 July 1997), Padova, 83–88.

Lönnqvist, M./Lönnqvist, K. 2011: Jebel Bishri in Focus. Remote sensing, archaeological surveying, mapping and GIS studies of Jebel Bishri in central Syria by the Finnish project SYGIS, Oxford.

Mancuso, S./Viola, A. 2013: Verde Brillante. Sensibilità e intelligenza del mondo vegetale, Firenze/Milan.

Mancuso, S. 2018: L'incredibile viaggio delle piante, Bari.

–. 2019: La nazione delle piante, Bari/Rome.

Mander, P. 2008: Les dieux et le culte à Ébla, in: G. Del Olmo Lete (ed.), Mythologie et Religion des Sémites Occidentaux, Leuven/Paris/Dudley, 1–160.

Matthews, D. M. 1992: The Kassite Glyptic from Nippur, Göttingen.

Matthiae, P.1998: Ninive, Milan.

Maul, S. 1994: Zukunftsbewältigung. Eine Untersuchung altorientalischen Denkens anhand der babylonisch-assyrischen Löserituale (Namburbi) (BaF 18), Mainz.

–. 2004: Altorientalische Schöpfungsmythen, in: R. Brandt/S. Schmidt (eds.), Mythos und Mythologie, Berlin, 43–54.

Mauze, M. 1998: Northwest Coast Trees: From Metaphors in Culture to Symbols for Culture, in: L. Rival (ed.), The Social Life of Trees: Anthropological Perspectives on Tree Symbolism, Oxford.

Meek, T. J. 1913: Cuneiform Bilingual Hymns, Prayers and Penitential Psalms, BA 10/I.

Meinhold, W. 2009: Ištar in Aššur. Untersuchungen eines Lokalkultes von ca. 2500 bis 614 v. Chr. (AOAT 367), Münster.
Mellink, M. 1992: River Gods in Anatolian Art?, in: D. J. W. Meijer (ed.), Natural Phenomena: Their Meaning, Depiction and Description, Amsterdam, 193–214.
Menzel, B. 1981: Assyrische Tempel II, Rome.
Michalowski, P. 2003: The mountain and the stars, in: P. Marrassini (ed.), Semitic and Assyriological Studies Presented to Pelio Fronzaroli by Pupils and Colleagues, Wiesbaden, 407–410.
Mithun, M. 1999: The Language of Native North America, Cambridge.
Mittermayer, C. 2009: Enmekara und der Herr von Arata. Ein ungleicher Wettstreit (OBO 239), Freiburg/Göttingen.
–. 2012: Enki und die Weltordnung Z. 250-262, in: C. Mittermayer/S. Eklin, Altorientalische Studien zu Ehren von Pascal Attinger, Göttingen, 243–258.
Moortgat, A. 1967: Die Kunst des Alten Mesopotamien. Die klassiche Kunst Vorderasiens, Köln.
–. 1969: The Art of Ancient Mesopotamia, London/New York.
Morrison, K. M. 2013: Animism and a proposal for a post-Cartesian anthropology, in: G. Harvey (ed.), Handbook of Contemporary Animism, Durham, 38–52.
Mouton, A. 2007: Rêve Hittites. Contribution à une histoire et une anthropologie du rêve en Anatolie ancienne, Leiden/Boston.
–. 2014: Terre divinisée et autres "genies" de l'Anatolie hittite, Semitica et Classica. Revue Internationale d'Études Orientales et Méditerranéennes/International Journal of Oriental and Mediterraenean Studies, vol. VII, 19–29.
–. (forthcoming): Water and the Gods: Ponds and Fountains in the Hittite State Cult, Ash-Sharq 2, No. 1, 112–120.
Nakata, I. 1991: On the Official Pantheon of the Old Babylonian City of Mari ad Reflected in the Records of Issuance of Sacrificial Animals, Acta Sumerologica 13 (1991), 249–258.
Nashef, K. 1986: The deities of Dilmun, in: H. A. Al Khalifa/M. Rice (eds.), Bahrain through the Ages: the archaeology, London, 340–366.
Nissen, H.J. 1986: The occurrence of Dilmun in the oldest texts of Mesopotamia, in: H. A. Al Khalifa/M. Rice (eds.), Bahrain through the Ages: the archaeology, London, 335–339.
Nissinen, M. 2003: Prophets and Prophecy in the Ancient Near East, Atlanta.
–. 2014: Sacred Springs and Liminal Rivers, in: E. Ben Zvi/C. Levin (eds.), Thinking of Water in the Early Second Temple Period, Berlin, 29–48.
Nora, P. 1989: Between Memory and History: Les lieux de memoire, Representations 26, 7–24.
Nougayrol, J. 1966: Les quatre vents, RA 60, 72–74.
Oates, J. 1986, Babylon, London.
Ornan, T. 2009: In the Likeness of Man: Reflections on the Anthropocentric Perception of the Divine in Mesopotamian Art, in: B. N. Porter (ed.), 2009, What Is a God? Anthropomorphic and Non-Anthropomorphic Aspects of Deity in Ancient Mesopotamia, Winona Lake, Indiana, 93–151.
Oppenheim, A. L. 1949: The Golden Garments of the Gods, JNES 8, 172–193.
–. 1965: On Royal Gardens in Mesopotamia, JNES 24, 328–333.
–. 1977: Ancient Mesopotamia: Portrait of a Dead Civilization, Chicago.
–. 1978: Man and Nature in Mesopotamian Civilization, in: C.C. Gillispie (ed.), Dictionary of Scientific Biography 15, Oxford, 634–666.
Orthmann, W. 1985: Der Alte Orient, Berlin.

Parpola, S. (ed.) 1993: The Assyrian Tree of Life: Tracing the Origins of Jewish Monotheism and Greek Philosophy, JNES 52, 161–208.
–. 2017: Assyrian Royal Rituals and Cultic Texts (SAA XX), Helsinki.
Polinger Foster, K. 1999: Volcanic Landscapes in Lugal-e, in: L. Milano/S. de Martino/F.M. Fales/G.B. Lanfranchi (eds.), Landscapes. Territories, Frontiers and Horizons in the Ancient Near East, Papers presented to the XLIV Rencontre Assyriologique Internationale (Venezia, 7-11 July 1997), Padova, 23–39.
Polonsky, J. 1999: ki-^{d}utu-è-a: Where Destiny is Determined, in: L. Milano/S. de Martino/F.M. Fales/G.B. Lanfranchi (eds.), Landscapes. Territories, Frontiers and Horizons in the Ancient Near East, Papers presented to the XLIV Rencontre Assyriologique Internationale (Venezia, 7-11 July 1997), Padova, 89–100.
–. 2006: The Mesopotamian Conceptualization of Birth and the Determination of Destiny at Sunrise, in: A. K. Guinan (ed.), If a Man Builds a Joyful House; Assyriological Studies in Honor of Erle Leichty, Leiden/Boston, 297–311.
Pongratz-Leisten, B. 2015a: Religion and Ideology in Assyria, Boston/Berlin.
–. 2015b: Imperial Allegories: Divine Agency and Monstrous Bodies in Mesopotamia's Body Description Texts, in: B. Pongratz-Leisten/K. Sonik (eds.), The Materiality of Divine Agency, SANER 8, Boston, 119–141.
–./Sonik, K. 2015: The Materiality of Divine Agency, SANER 8, Boston.
Porada, E. 1948: The Collection of the Pierpont Morgan Library, vol. I. The Collection of the Pierpont Morgan Library, Washington.
Porter, A. 2012: Mobile Pastoralism and the Formation of Near Eastern Civilizations: weaving together society, New York.
Porter, B.N. 1993a: Images, Power and Politics. Figurative Aspects of Esarhaddon's Babylonian Policy, Philadelphia.
–. 1993b: Sacred Trees, Date Palms, and the Royal Persona of Ashurnasirpal II, JNES 52, 129–139.
–. 2000: One God or Many? Concepts of Divinity in the Ancient World, Transactions of the Casco Bay Assyriological Institute, vol. 1, Chebeague Island.
–. 2003: Trees, Kings, and Politics: Studies in Assyrian Iconography (OBO 197), Fribourg/Göttingen.
–. 2009: Blessings from a Crown, Offerings to a Drum: Were There Non-Anthropomorphic Deities in Ancient Mesopotamia?, in: B. Porter (ed.), What Is a God? Anthropomorphic and Non-Anthropomorphic Aspects of Deity in Ancient Mesopotamia, Winona Lake, Indiana, 153–194.
–. 2009: What Is a God? Anthropomorphic and Non-Anthropomorphic Aspects of Deity in Ancient Mesopotamia, Winona Lake, Indiana.
Potts, D.T. 1982: The Zagros Frontier and the Problem of Relations between the Iranian Plateau and Southern Mesopotamia in the Third Millennium BC, in: H.-J. Nissen/J. Renger (eds.), Mesopotamien und seine Nachbarn: Politische und kulturelle Wechselbeziehungen im Alten Vorderasien vom 4. Bis 1. Jahrtausend v.Chr, Berlin, 33–55.
–. 1999: The Archaeology of Elam. Formation and Transformation of an Ancient Iranian State, Cambridge.
–. 2004: Exit Aratta: Southeastern Iran and the Land of Marhashi, Nāme-ye Irān-e Bāstān 4/1, 1–11.
Powell, M.A. 1987: The Tree Section of ur$_5$ (HAR)-ra = hubullu, BSA 3, 145–151.
Propp, V. 1968: The Morphology of the Folktale, Austin.
Radner, K. 2012: Šubria, a safe haven in the mountains, Assyrian empire builders, University College London [http://www.ucl.ac.uk/sargon/essentials/countries/ubria/].

Reiner, E. 1956: Lipšur Litanies, JNES 15/3, 129–149.
–. 1958: Šurpu: A Collection of Sumerian and Akkadian Incantations, Graz.
–. 1960: Plague Amulets and House Blessings, JNES 19, 148–155.
–. 1961: The etiological myth of the 'Seven Sages', Orientalia NS 30, 1–11.
–. 1966: La magie babylonienne, in: Le monde du sorcier, Sources orientales 7, Paris, 69–98.
–. 1995: Astral Magic in Babylonia (TAPS 85/4), Philadelphia.
Rendu-Loisel, A.-C. 2013: Noise, Light and Smoke: the Sensory Dimension in Akkadian Rituals. A General Overview, in: C. Ambos/L. Verderame (eds.), Approaching Rituals in Ancient Cultures, Pisa and Rome, 245–259.
–. 2016: Les chants du monde: le paysage sonore de l'ancienne Mésopotamie, Toulouse.
Rival, L. 1998: Trees: From Symbols of Life and Regeneration to Political Artifacts, in: L. Rival (ed.), The Social Life of Trees: Anthropological Perspectives on Tree Symbolism, Oxford, 1–36.
–. 2013: The materiality of life: revisiting the anthropology of nature in Amazonia, in: G. Harvey (ed.), Handbook of Contemporary Animism, Durham, 92–100.
Roaf, M. 1990: Cultural Atlas of Mesopotamia and the Ancient Near East, Oxford.
Roberts, J.J.M. 1972: The Earliest Semitic Pantheon. A Study of the Semitic Deities Attested in Mesopotamia before Ur III, Baltimore/London.
Robertson Smith, R. 1972: The Religion of the Semites: the Fundamental Institutions, New York.
Robson, E. 2008: Mesopotamian Medicine and Religion: Current Debates, New Perspectives, Religion Compass 2/4, 455–483.
Rochberg, F. 2009: 'The Stars their Likenesses': Perspectives on the Relation between Celestial Bodies and Gods in Ancient Mesopotamia, in: B. Porter (ed.), What Is a God? Anthropomorphic and Non-Anthropomorphic Aspects of Deity in Ancient Mesopotamia, Winona Lake, Indiana, 41–91.
–. 2016: Before Nature. Cuneiform Knowledge and the History of Science, Chicago/London.
Rollinger, R. 2010: Berg und Gebirge aus altorientalischer Perspektive, in: W. Kofler et al. (eds.), Gipfel der Zeit: Berge in Texten aus fünf Jahrtausenden Karlheinz Töchterle zum 60. Geburtstag, Freiburg, 11–52.
–. 2013: Alexander und die großen Strömen: Die Flussüberquerungen im Lichte altorientalischer Pioniertechniken, Wiesbaden.
Rose, D. 1999: Indigenous Ecologies and an Ethic of Connection, in: N. Low (ed.), Global Ethics and Environment, London, 175–187.
Roth, M.T. 1997: Law Collections from Mesopotamia and Asia Minor, Atlanta.
Sahlins, M. 2000: Culture in Practice: Selected Essays, New York.
–. 2013: What Kinship Is –and Is Not, Chicago.
–. 2017: The original political society, HAU: Journal of Ethnographic Theory 7 (2), 91–128.
Saler, B. 1993: Conceptualizing Religion: Immanent Anthropologists, Transcendent Natives, and Unboundend Categories, Leiden/New York.
Saporetti, C. 1970: Onomastica medio-assira 1, Studia Pohl 6, Rome, 310–311.
Sasson, J.M. 2015: From the Mari Archives. An Anthology of Old Babylonian Letters, Winona Lake, Indiana.
Schama, S. 1995: Landscape and Memory, New York.
Schramm, W. 2008: Ein Compendium sumerisch-akkadischer Beschwörungen, Göttinger Beiträge zum Alten Orient 2, Göttingen.

Schuster-Brandis, A. 2008: Steine als Schutz- und Heilmittel. Untersuchung zu ihrer Verwendung in der Beschwörungskunst Mesopotamiens im 1. Jt. v. Chr., Münster.

Schwemer, D. 2001: Die Wettergottgestalten Mesopotamiens und Nordsyriens im Zeitalter der Keilschriftliteraturen, Wiesbaden.

–. 2010: Fighting Witchcraft before the Moon and the Sun: a Therapeutic Ritual from Neo-Babylonian Sippar, Orientalia NS 79, 480–504.

–. 2011a: Evil Witches, Apotropaic Plants and the New Moon: Two Anti-Witchcraft Incantations from Babylon (BM 35672 and BM 36584), WdO 41, Göttingen, 177–190.

–. 2011b: Magic Rituals: Conceptualization and Performance, in: K. Radner/E. Robson, The Oxford Handbook of Cuneiform Culture, Oxford, 418–442.

Scott, C. 2013: Ontology and ethics in Cree hunting: animism, totemism and practical knowledge, in: G. Harvey (ed.), Handbook of Contemporary Animism, Durham, 159–166.

Segal, R.A. 2013: Animism for Tylor, in: G. Harvey (ed.), The Handbook of Contemporary Animism, Durham, 53–62.

Selz, G.J. 1997: The holy Drum, the Spear, and the Harp. Toward an understanding of the problems of deification in the third millennium Mesopotamia, in: I. L. Finkel/M. J. Geller (eds.), Sumerian Gods and their Representations, Groningen, 167–213.

–./ Wagensonner, K. (eds.) 2011: The Empirical Dimension of Ancient Near Eastern Studies, Wien.

Seminara, S. 2001: La versione accadica del Lugal-e: La tecnica babilonese della traduzione dal Sumerico e le sue 'regole', Rome.

Shaffer, A. 1983: "Gilgamesh, the Cedar Forest and Mesopotamian History", JAOS 103, 307–313.

Shafer, A.T. 1998: The Carving of an Empire: Neo-Assyrian Monuments on the Periphery, Unpublished PhD dissertation, Harvard University, Cambridge Massachusetts.

Stadhouders, H.A.I. 2011: The Pharmacopeial Handbook šamnu šikinšu – An Edition, Journal des Médecines Cunéiformes, vol. 10, 1–55.

–. 2012, The Pharmacopeial Handbook šamnu šikinšu – A Translation, Journal des Médicines Cunéiformes, vol. 19, 1–21.

Steible, H. 2015: Enlil und Ninlil. Der Mythos von der Zeugung des Mondgottes, in: K. Volk (ed.), Erzählungen aus dem Land Sumer, Wiesbaden, 21–31.

Stiehler, G./Delgado, A. 1996: Die Kassitische Glyptik, München/Wien.

Steiner, G. 1996: Huwawa und sein "Bergland" in der sumerischen Tradition, Acta Sumerologica 18, 187–215.

Steinert, U. 2013: Fluids, rivers, and vessels: metaphors and body concepts in Mesopotamian gynaecological texts, Journal des Médecines Cunéiformes 22, 1–23.

Steinkeller, P. 1987a: The Foresters of Umma: Toward a Definition of Ur III Labor, in: M.A. Powell (ed.), Labor in the Ancient Near East (AOS 68), New Haven, 73–115.

–. 1987b: On Sand Dunes, Mountain Ranges, and Mountain Peaks, in: M. T. Roth/W. Farber/M. W. Stolper/P. von Bechtolsheim (eds.), Studies Presented to Robert D. Biggs, June 4, 2004, From the Workshop of the Chicago Assyrian Dictionary, vol. 2, Chicago, 219–232.

–. 2003: An Ur III Manuscript of the Sumerian King List, in: W. Sallaberger/K. Volk/A. Zgoll (eds.), Literatur, Politik und Recht in Mesopotamien: Festschrift für Claus Wilcke, Wiesbaden, 267–292.

Steitler, Ch. W. 2019: "Sacred Springs, Spring Sanctuaries and Spring Deities in Hittite Religion", in: B. Engels/S. Huy/Ch. W. Steitler (eds.), Natur und Kult in Anatolien. Akten des 4.

wissenchaftlichen Netzwerks der Abteilung Istanbul des Deutschen Archäologischen Instituts (2014-2016). Byzas 24, Istanbul: Ege Yayınları, 1–29.
Stol, M. 1979: On Trees, Mountains, and Millstones in the Ancient Near East, Leiden.
–. 2000: Birth in Babylonia and in the Bible: Its Mediterranean Setting, Groningen.
Streck, M.P. 2000: Das amurritische Onomastikon der altbabylonischen Zeit (AOAT 271/1), Münster.
–. 2004: Dattelpalme und Tamariske in Mesopotamien nach dem akkadischen Streitgespräch, ZA 94, 250–290.
–. 2005: Pî-nārātim, *RlA* 10, 566–567.
–. 2012: Tamariske, *RlA* 13, 428–431.
–. 2017a: Zeder. A. In Mesopotamien, *RlA* 15, 3/4. Lieferung, 236–239.
–. 2017b: Zypresse, *RlA* 15, 5/6. Lieferung, 371–37.
Stringer, M.D. 2013: Building of belief: defining animism in Tylor and contemporary society, in: G. Harvey (ed.), The Handbook of Contemporary Animism, Durham, 63–76.
Stuckey, P. 2013: The Animal versus the Social: Rethinking Individual and Community in Western Cosmology, in: G. Harvey (ed.), The Handbook of Contemporary Animism, Durham, 191–208.
Sullivan, B.B. 1980: Sumerian and Akkadian Sentence Structure in Old Babylonian literary bilingual Texts, University Microfilms.
Tallqvist, K.L. 1932: Der assyrische Gott, Studia Orientalia 4/3, Helsinki.
Tambiah, S.J. 1968: The Magical Power of Words, Man, New Series, vol. 3, 175–208.
–. 1990: Magic, Science, Religion and the Scope of Rationality, Cambridge.
Tsouparopoulou, C. 2014: Progress Report: An Online Database for the Documentation of Seals, Sealings, and Seal Impressions in the Ancient Near East, Studia Orientalia Electronica, vol. 2, 37–68.
Tylor, E.B. 1871: Primitive Culture: Researches into the Development of Mythology, Philosophy, Religion, Art and Custom, 2 vols., New York.
Vallat, F. 1987: KUN / zibbatu: embouchure, NABU 3–4, no. 7.
Van Binsbergen, W./Wiggermann, F. 1999: Magic in History. A theoretical perspective, and its application to ancient Mesopotamia, in: Tz. Abusch/K. van der Toorn (eds.), Mesopotamian Magic. Textual, Historical, and Interpretative Perspectives (AMD 1), Groningen, 3–34.
Van de Mieroop, M. 1992: Society and enterprise in Old Babylonian Ur, Berlin.
Van der Toorn, K. 1985: Sin and Sanction in Israel and Mesopotamia, Assen.
–./Becking, B./Van der Horst, P.W. (eds.) 1995: Dictionary of Deities and Demons in the Bible, Leiden/New York/Köln.
–. 1995: Euphrates, in: K. van der Toorn/B. Becking/P. W. van der Horst (eds.), Dictionary of Deities and Demons in the Bible, Leiden/New York/Köln, 594–599.
van Dijk, J.J.A. 1983: LUGAL UD ME-LÁM-bi NIR-ĜÁL. Le récit épique et didactique des Travaux de Ninurta, du Déluge et de la Nouvelle Création, 2 vols., Leiden.
–./Goetze, A./Hussey, M. I. 1985: Early Mesopotamian Incantations and Rituals (YOS 11), New Haven.
Van Soldt, W. H. 2003: Ordal. A. Mesopotamien, *RlA* 10, 124–129.
Vanstiphout, H. L. J. 1997: Why did Enki organize the world?, in: I. L. Finkel/M. J. Geller (eds.), Sumerian Gods and their Representations, Groningen, 117–134.
Veldhuis, N. 1990: The Heart Grass and Related Matters, OLP 21, 27–44.
–. 2004: Religion, Literature, and Scholarship. The Sumerian Composition of Nanše and the Birds, with a Catalogue of Sumerian Bird Names (CM 22), Leiden/Boston.

Verderame, L. 2013: Their Divinity is Different, their Nature is Distinct! Origin and Features of Demons in Akkadian Literature, Archiv für Religionsgeschichte, vol. 14, Issue 1, 117–127.
Viveiros de Castro, E. 1992: From the Enemies' Point of View: Humanity and Divinity in an Amazonian Society, Chicago.
–. 1998: Cosmological Deixis and Amerindian Perspectivism, Journal of the Royal Anthropological Institute 4, 469–488.
Vogelzang, M. A. 1988: BIN ŠAR DADMĒ. Edition and Analysis of the Akkadian Anzu Poem, Groningen.
Volk, K. 1995: Inanna und Šukaletuda. Zur historisch-politischen Deutung eines sumerischen Literaturwerkes, Wiesbaden.
–. (ed.) 2015: Erzählungen aus dem Land Sumer, Wiesbaden.
Walker, C./Dick, M. B. 1999: The Induction of the Cult Image in Ancient Mesopotamia: the Mesopotamian mīs pî Ritual, in: M.B. Dick (ed.), Born in Heaven. Made on Earth. The Making of the Cult Image in the Ancient Near East, Winona Lake, Indiana, 55–121.
–./–. 2001: The Induction of the Cult Image in Ancient Mesopotamia. The Mesopotamian Mīs Pî Ritual. Transliteration, Translation, and Commentary (SAALT 1), Helsinki.
Waschow, H. 1936: Babylonische Briefe aus der Kassitenzeit (MAOG 10/1), Leipzig.
Wasserman, N. 2003: Style and Form in Old-Babylonian Literary Texts (CM 27), Leiden/Boston.
–. 2008: On Leeches, Dogs and Gods in Old Babylonian Medical Incantations, RAI 102, 71–88.
–. 2015: Piercing the Eyes: An Old Babylonian Love Incantation and the Preparation of Khol, BiOr 72, 601–612.
Wiggermann, F. A. M. 1992a: Mesopotamian Protective Spirits. The Ritual Texts (CM 1), Groningen.
–. 1992b: Mythological Foundations of Nature, in: D. J .W. Meijer (ed.), Natural Phenomena: Their Meaning, Depiction and Description, Amsterdam, 279–306.
–. 1993: Mischwesen. A. Philologisch. Mesopotamien, *RlA* 8, 222–246.
–. 1997: Transgridian Snake Gods, in: I. L. Finkel/M. J. Geller (eds.), Sumerian Gods and their Representations, Groningen, 33–55.
–. 2000: Lamaštu, Daughter of Anu. A Profile, in: M. Stol, Birth in Babylonia and the Bible: Its Mediterranean setting (CM 14), Groningen, 217–252.
–. 2013: Die symbolische Landschaft Mesopotamiens, in: A. Zgoll/R. G. Kratz (eds.), Arbeit am Mythos. Leistung und Grenze des Mythos in Antike und Gegenwart, Frankfurt am Main, 109–132.
Wilcke, C. 1975: Ḫuwawa/Ḫumbaba, *RlA* 4, 530–535.
–. 1989: Die Emar-Version von 'Dattelpalme und Tamariske', ZA 79, 161–190.
–. 2015: Vom klugen Lugalbanda, in: K. Volk (ed.), Erzählungen aus dem Land Sumer, Wiesbaden, 203–272.
Wilson, E. J. 1994: "Holiness" and "Purity" in Mesopotamia, AOAT 237, Kevelaer, Neukirchen-Vluyn.
Winter, I. J. 1987: Legitimation of Authority through Image and Legend: Seals Belonging to Officials in the Administrative Bureaucracy of the Ur III State, in: M. Gibson/R.D. Biggs (eds.), The Organization of Power: Aspects of Bureaucracy in the Ancient Near East, Chicago, 69–106.
–. 1992: 'Idols of the King': Royal Images as Recipients of Ritual Action in Ancient Mesopotamia, Journal of Ritual Studies 6, 13–42.
–. 1999: Tree(s) on the Mountain. Landscape and Territory on the Victory Stele of Naram-Sîn of Agade, in: L. Milano/S. de Martino/F. M. Fales/G. B. Lanfranchi (eds.), Landscapes. Territories,

Frontiers and Horizons in the Ancient Near East, Papers presented to the XLIV Rencontre Assyriologique Internationale Venezia, 7-11 July 1997, Padova, 63–72.

–. 2010a: On Art in the Ancient Near East. Volume I. Of the First Millennium B.C.E., Leiden/Boston.

–. 2010b: On Art in the Ancient Near East. Volume II. From the Third Millennium B.C.E., Leiden/Boston.

Wohlleben, P. 2015: Das Geheime Leben der Bäume. Was sie fühlen, wie sie kommunizieren – die Entdeckung einer verborgenen Welt, München.

–. 2017: Bäume verstehen: Was uns Bäume erzählen, wie wir sie naturgemäß pflegen, Darmstadt.

Woods, C. 2005: On the Euphrates, ZA 95, 7–45.

–. 2009: At the Edge of the World: Cosmological Conceptions of the Eastern Horizon in Mesopotamia, JANER 9.2, Leiden, 183–239.

Yamada, S. 2000: The Construction of the Assyrian Empire. A Historical Study of the Inscriptions of Shalmaneser III (859-824 BC) Relating to His Campaigns to the West, CHANE 3, Leiden/Boston/Köln.

Zernecke, E. 2008: Warum sitzt der Skorpion unter dem Bett? Überlegungen zur Deutung eines altorientalischen Fruchtbarkeitssymbols, ZDPV 124, 107–127.

Zgoll, A. 2006: Traum und Welterleben im antiken Mesopotamien. Traumtheorie und Traumpraxis im 3.-1. Jahrtausend v. Chr. als Horizont einer Kulturgeschichte des Träumens, AOAT 333, Münster.

–. 2000: Ebeḫ und andere Gebirge in der politischen Landschaft der Akkadezeit, in: L. Milano/S. de Martino/F. M. Fales/G. B. Lanfranchi (eds.), Landscapes. Territories, Frontiers and Horizons in the Ancient Near East, Papers presented to the XLIV Rencontre Assyriologique Internationale (Venezia, 7-11 July 1997), Padova, 83–90.

–. 2011: Der Mythos Enlil und Ninlil: Vom Schrecken des Kanalbaus durch Stadt und Unterwelt, in: L. Vacín (ed.), Ancient Near Eastern Studies in Memory of Blahoslav Hruška, Dresden, 287–299.

–. 2012: Der oikomorphe Mensch. Wesen im Menschen und das Wesen des Menschen in sumerisch-akkadischer Perspektive, in: B. Janowski (ed.), Der ganze Mensch. Zur Anthropologie der Antike und ihrer europäischen Nachgeschichte, Berlin, 83–106 + 320.

–. 2013: Fundamente des Lebens. Vom Potential altorientalischer Mythen, in: A. Zgoll/R. G. Kratz (eds.), Arbeit am Mythos. Leistung und Grenze des Mythos in Antike und Gegenwart, Frankfurt am Main, 79–107.

–. 2015: Der akkadische Bazi-Mythos und seine Performanz im Ritual. Wie der Gott Bazi Königtum und Tempel erlangt, in: B. Janowski/D. Schwemer (eds.), Texte aus der Umwelt des Alten Testaments, Neue Folge, Band 8, Weisheitstexte, Mythen und Epen, Munich, 68–73.

Zohary, M. 1963: On the Geobotanical Structure of Iran, Bullettin of the Research Council of Israel, Section D. Botany, Supplement, vol. 11, Jerusalem.

Zomer, E. 2018: Corpus of Middle Babylonian and Middle Assyrian Incantations, Wiesbaden.

Index